WHAT'S LUCK GOT TO DO WITH IT?

EDWARD D. KLEINBARD

WHAT'S LUCK GOT TO DO WITH IT?

HOW SMARTER GOVERNMENT CAN RESCUE THE AMERICAN DREAM

OXFORD
UNIVERSITY PRESS

Oxford University Press is a department of the University of Oxford. It furthers
the University's objective of excellence in research, scholarship, and education
by publishing worldwide. Oxford is a registered trade mark of Oxford University
Press in the UK and certain other countries.

Published in the United States of America by Oxford University Press
198 Madison Avenue, New York, NY 10016, United States of America.

Library of Congress Cataloging-in-Publication Data
Names: Kleinbard, Edward D., author.
Title: What's Luck Got To Do With It?: How Smarter Government Can Rescue the American
Dream / Edward D. Kleinbard.
Description: New York, NY : Oxford University Press, [2021]
Identifiers: LCCN 2020024092 (print) | LCCN 2020024093 (ebook) |
ISBN 9780190943578 (hardback) | ISBN 9780190943592 (epub)
Subjects: LCSH: Equality—United States. | Social mobility—United States. |
Income distribution—United States. | Human capital—United States. |
Insurance—United States. | United States—Economic policy. | United States—Social policy.
Classification: LCC HN90.S6 K574 2021 (print) | LCC HN90.S6 (ebook) |
DDC 305.50973—dc23
LC record available at https://lccn.loc.gov/2020024092
LC ebook record available at https://lccn.loc.gov/2020024093

9 8 7 6 5 4 3 2 1

Printed by LSC Communications, United States of America

"Waiting for God to reveal himself, I believe that his prime minister, Chance, governs this sad world just as well."

—STENDHAL*

The Wheel of Fortune, Hortus Deliciarum, Herrad of Landsburg (1130–1195), Hohenburg Abbey, Alsace.

* As quoted in Julian Barnes, *Nothing to Be Frightened Of* (New York: Alfred A. Knopf, 2008), 72.

CONTENTS

List of Figures and Tables ix

Introduction: Bad Luck Changes Everything *xi*

PART I. AN OVERVIEW OF MY ARGUMENT

CHAPTER 1 Buffeted by the Winds of Fortune *3*

CHAPTER 2 The Denial of Luck *27*

PART II. EQUALITY OF OPPORTUNITY BETRAYED

CHAPTER 3 Born on Third Base—Or Out on the Street? *45*

CHAPTER 4 It's Better to Be Lucky Than Smart *67*

CHAPTER 5 Education Is the Engine of Opportunity *81*

PART III. INSURANCE TO THE RESCUE

CHAPTER 6 Insurance as Product *123*

CHAPTER 7 Insurance as Metaphor *155*

CHAPTER 8 The Social Mortgage *177*

PART IV. OPPORTUNITY RESTORED

CHAPTER 9 From Insurance Theory to Political Reality   207

CHAPTER 10 Healthcare and Medicare for All   241

CHAPTER 11 Epilogue: Progressive Policies, Progressive Paradigms   257

Notes   265

Index   295

LIST OF FIGURES AND TABLES

FIGURES

1.1 Stylized Representation of Distributional Lifetime Earnings vs Birth Circumstances 5

1.2 Results of Flipping 8 Coins as a Group 1000 Times 6

3.1 Poverty Rate, Selected Developed Economies (2017) 47

3.2 Real GDP Per Capital, Median Household Incomes, and Male Full-time Wages (1984–2018) 49

3.3 Percent of Children Earning More Than Their Parents, by Year of Birth 52

3.4 Percent of Children Earning More Than Their Parents, by Parent Income Percentile 53

3.5 Cumulative Growth in Income After Transfers and Taxes, by Income Group (1979–2016) 56

3.6 Income Inequality as Measured by the Gini Coefficient (1979–2016) 59

3.7 Income Inequality, USA, by Pre-Tax National Income (1954–2014) 60

3.8 Wealth Inequality, USA by Net Personal Wealth (1966 to 2014) 61

4.1 Relative Mobility, Percent of Adults in Each Income Quintile by Birth Income Quintile 72

4.2 Intergenerational Earnings Elasticity, Selected Countries 73

4.3 The Great Gatsby Curve: Inequality vs. Mobility 77

5.1 Median Annual Earnings of Full-Time Workers 25 Years Old and Over, by Educational Attainment (2016) 84

5.2   Relative Earnings by Educational Attainment, Selected Countries (2016)   *85*

5.3   Enrollment Rate in Preprimary Formal Education Programs, Selected Countries (2016)   *95*

5.4   Average Achievement Gains following Participation in Two UPK Programs   *98*

5.5   Spending on Pre-Primary Education as a Percentage of GDP, Selected Countries (2015, 2010, 2005)   *102*

5.6   First-Time College Entry Rates Below the Age of 25, by Gender, Selected Countries (2005, 2016)   *109*

5.7   University Degrees and Family Businesses, Wealthy vs. Others   *110*

5.8   Average Annual Public College Tuition for Full-Time National Students, by Education Level, Selected Countries   *112*

5.9   Estimated Education Debt Burden by Race   *116*

5.10   Higher Returns to Education Associated with Lower Intergenerational Mobility   *118*

5.11   Enrichment Expenditures per Child (1972–2005), Top and Bottom Income Quintiles   *119*

6.1   Public Social Spending on Families, % GDP   *147*

8.1   Poverty Rate, Selected Developed Economies (2017)   *193*

8.2   Public Social Spending as a Percentage of GDP, Selected Developed Economies (2018)   *194*

9.1   Market vs. Disposable Income Inequality, Selected Developed Economies (2014)   *217*

9.2   Tax Revenue as a Percentage of GDP, Selected Developed Economies (2018)   *218*

TABLES

6.1   US Federal Mandatory Spending Programs (2019)   *144*

8.1   Principal Targeted Federal Anti-Poverty Programs (2019)   *191*

INTRODUCTION: BAD LUCK
CHANGES EVERYTHING

This book asks you to think a bit more deeply about bad luck. Like gravity, brute luck is a universal force that cannot by itself be turned off. We like to think that we control our destinies through the decisions we make, but in fact our careers and our happiness are shaped to a large extent by the consequences of luck, favorable or unfavorable, that are not only out of our control, but often are unobserved by us. Many successful people expend enormous energy denying this fact, but a franker acknowledgment of the importance of luck as a driver of people's outcomes leads to all sorts of salutary policy responses.

In particular, the accidents of where, when, and to whom you are born casts a long shadow over your ability to develop fully your native skills and interests in order to lead a productive and fulfilling life. None of us has the luxury of choosing our parents, but all of us are affected throughout our lifetimes by the circumstances of our birth more than we might like to admit.

Choosing your parents unwisely is a form of "brute" bad luck, which means bad luck that does not come from any gamble you consciously undertook. A cancer diagnosis or a car accident (at least if you were sober) also is an example of brute bad luck. Brute luck is randomness by another name, not poor life choices or unwise investments.

One of Americans' central credos is that ours is a country that espouses equality of opportunity. Instantiating equality of opportunity, however, requires more than a collection of facially neutral statutes, or even the best of intentions. There is an irreconcilable conflict in American society today between our collective aspiration to live in a country that fully embraces equality of opportunity, on the one hand, and our failure to grapple seriously with the inescapable role of the brute luck of where, when, and to whom we are born in determining our material outcomes.

A shopworn American trope maintains that feeding a man a fish keeps his belly full for a day, but teaching him how to fish keeps him fed for a lifetime. In practice, this is used to justify withholding "handouts" from the poor. Although we invoke it frequently, we do not take this trope seriously. If we did, we would teach a man to fish by sending him to a university for a graduate degree in fisheries management. Specifically, if we were serious about equality of opportunity, we would offer all Americans of comparable ability comparable investments in their human capital—in particular, through education—knowing that the different economic returns achieved by individuals in our modern post-industrial and globalized world are linked closely to the amount of education they are able to ingest.

The United States today assures unequal distributions of human capital not attributable to differences in ability, and a resulting national shortage in total income-producing capacity, because we require that family resources play too large a role in the investments made in the human capital of individuals. Private investor markets do not and cannot adequately fill the gap, because one person cannot own the output of another. This market failure in turn erodes authentic equality of opportunity. We can, however, modulate the destructive impact of our excessive reliance on personal and family resources to fund adequate investments in a person's human capital by invoking the intermediation of government.

Money, not systematic differences in virtue, thrift, intelligence, or diligence, explains the differences that are observed between the scions of the affluent and kids born to straitened circumstances. As one quick example, it is much easier for a mediocre student from a rich household to get into a top-tier college than it is for a talented student from a poor one.[1] When we allow private funding to have an outsized role in access to education, we dishonor authentic equality of opportunity with respect to millions of our fellow citizens.

In our modern post-industrial world, education—lots and lots of it—is the principal driver of lifetime earnings and many forms of lifetime satisfactions. Education is thus the engine of absolute material sufficiency, and access to education is the key to a society imbued with equality of opportunity. But this virtuous cycle breaks down when education is a market product, because to that extent access to education becomes available only to those who start life with the resources to buy top-tier education, to sign up for every conceivable enrichment program, and to complete graduate or professional school debt-free, and with a nest egg to boot.

The explosion of student loan debt is a symptom of the problem, not an instance of free markets providing a workable and equitable solution. It is a symptom of human capital investment *demand*, for which the supply mechanism we have fashioned leaves millions of Americans overburdened and unable to pursue the lives that fairness would dictate.

Bad brute luck in where, when, and to whom we are born thus limits opportunity, by choking off investment in the human capital of those facing the headwinds of these existential forces. The most pressing question that this book asks is: What policy responses might usefully follow from recognizing the heavy hand that bad luck places on the unlucky-at-birth among us? My answer is not simply to offer up a potpourri of big-ticket government programs for consideration, but rather to frame the problem and the solutions along the lines of the discipline of insurance, in both a commercial and a metaphorical sense.

Insurance is an effective tool whose entire purpose is to mitigate the financial consequences of bad luck. It is a subtle financial instrument, honed over the last 700 years, from the time of medieval Italian merchants forward to today. If equality of opportunity is the great organizing principle of American economic life, and bad brute luck the unresolved universal force that knocks too many people off course in their pursuit of their economic dreams, then the application of insurance principles is the response that can be used to make equality of opportunity more than a hollow phrase.

I have no interest in simply cutting the rich down to size. I am, however, vitally concerned to offer every young person the tools she requires to fish, or to code, or to practice medicine or law. The only way to do this in the real world is to invoke the principles of insurance to figure out what kinds of bad brute luck call out for government to step into the shoes of an insurer, and then to apply those same principles in designing programs that respond most efficiently to the harms of these instances of bad luck.

You probably drive an automobile. Once in a blue moon, you might have an accident. If the harm of the accident is only to your car, the remedy is simple: you call up your insurance company and arrange for the damage to be repaired at the insurer's expense.

When you are confronted by a diagnosis of cancer, you also turn—if you are lucky—to your insurance to absorb the overwhelming financial costs of healthcare as it is practiced in America today. If you are over 65 you probably have insurance through Medicare, which is just a very large insurance company run by the federal government, for which you paid in part by premiums collected during your working career. About 150 million Americans are covered by private health insurers, with premiums collected beneath the surface in the form of lower salaries, and with a very large hidden federal subsidy to boot.[2]

Alternatively, you might be one of the millions of working-age Americans without health insurance because, for example, you do not have the good luck to work for an employer that provides health care as a benefit. You are indistinguishable from those who are covered, save for your bad luck in living in a state that has not expanded its Medicaid coverage, or otherwise being able to buy insurance at a remotely affordable cost.

You probably do not have a personal insurance policy to cover the financial consequences of every other calamity that might befall you. If you are more careful than most and you live in California, you might for example have (very expensive) earthquake insurance. That covers the cost of rebuilding your home, but even so you do not have insurance to cover the disappearance of your job or the many other crushing blows that the "big one" would bring.

When an earthquake, hurricane, tsunami, wildfire, or other natural disaster hits an area, we respond as a nation with disaster relief. We do so out of an understanding that all Americans are part of one organic community, and that bad luck writ large can devastate lives and communities for a generation or more. In these circumstances, we turn to our own government to function in effect as the insurer of last resort.

Our reaction is not tantamount to asking for handouts, but rather an implicit invocation of standard principles of insurance as applied on a national scale. In the language of insurance, when it comes to mitigating the financial consequences of large-scale natural disasters, all Americans are in the same "risk pool." The national commitment to mitigate financial loss following a disaster is one of many fundamental unstated understandings that in the aggregate define us as a country and motivate our construction of what a government is good for.

But now think about the still deeper kind of bad luck with which I began—the bad luck of not being able to choose your parents wisely. In the United States today, if you find yourself born into a family that is struggling financially, your own *expected* lifetime income and life satisfaction will suffer. No one's future is foretold at birth by wizards, warlocks, or crones, and bad-luck deniers are always quick to point to the occasional poor-kid-makes-good story as proof that birth circumstances are not very important in life—and to insinuate that other poor kids who do not make good must be victims of their own character flaws. But this overlooks the power of the word "expected."

At the instant of their births, all infants embark on the adventure of life with different mixes of native but undeveloped talents. Under no circumstances, however, do poor kids start life from the moment of their births with systematically inferior raw abilities or characters to those possessed by infants born into more comfortable circumstances.

And yet, when examined as a group, kids growing up in financially straitened circumstances will systematically earn less as adults than will kids from more affluent circumstances. Moreover, when viewed from a national perspective, this systematic underperformance by adults who came from less advantaged backgrounds means that the economy will grow more slowly, and that growth will be shared more unequally, than if we grappled with the underlying dilemma that these instances of bad luck pose.

When we drill down to individual circumstances, there will be a range of outcomes, including outliers in every direction, but the central tendency of the future adult earnings profiles of poor kids will be a materially lower income level than the same central tendency among kids from wealthier backgrounds once they also grow up. The word "expected" captures this difference in central tendencies in outcomes. Putting it another way, the relative income level of one's parents in the national distribution of incomes tells far more than it should about the income level that you are likely to achieve as an adult.

As the first few chapters of the book develop—and as many of you probably also accept—the United States today is a bit of an economic enigma. The country grows richer from decade to decade, but Americans in the middle class or further down the economic ladder feel more and more squeezed; they grow angrier by the day over the unfairness they perceive at the root of the economic system. At the same time, even those at the top of the ladder acknowledge that the US economy is growing more slowly than they would like; they argue that if only growth were magically accelerated, the rising tide would lift all boats equally.

The middle-class anger is justified, and a faster incoming tide would not be shared equally. Ironically, the structural economic problem that we face is the mirror image of the traditional "supply-side" narrative that regularly pops up in the editorial pages of the *Wall Street Journal*—the fetishistic belief that all problems in American economic life stem from an undersupply of investment capital (money that businesses can use to buy the equipment or raw material they need to make stuff). In the United States today, this claim is preposterous on its face, as we have seen from the hundreds of billions of dollars of potential investment capital that US firms have used in the last couple of years, not to reinvest, but rather to return to their owners through share repurchases or dividends. Investment supply-side cheerleaders today are trying to change our growth path by pushing on a string.

The real supply-side crisis that we face is that we are systematically underinvesting in *human* capital, which in practice equates to education (and to early life childcare). Almost two-thirds of our national income is attributable to labor (meaning the contributions of individuals, regardless of whether actual sweat is produced). In turn, the greater the investment in a person's education, through college or post-graduate degrees, the higher that person's lifetime income, and presumably her lifetime satisfactions as well. But because we do not make available sufficient public funds adequately to fund the development of all Americans' human capital, we allow the accident of where, when, and to whom we are born to constrain that supply, and in doing so leave the unlucky among us without the tools necessary to lead a life of their own choosing that yields sufficient income and dignity for those individuals to flourish. As a result, our national income is that much the lower, and our growth that much the slower.

Our systematic underinvestment in human capital chokes our economic output as individuals and as a country. That underinvestment in turn is driven by two factors: our refusal to acknowledge the pervasive presence of brute bad luck in our lives, and our great discomfort at relying on solutions to mitigate that bad luck that come from outside our "free" private markets. The result is to undercut one of the basic principles around which the American national identity is built.

In this book, I endeavor first, to remind readers of the importance to us all of the credo of equality of opportunity; second, to bring front and center as a policy concern the importance of brute luck in our lives—in particular, bad luck in where, when, and to whom we are born—and third, to articulate policy solutions that respond to this fact of nature, organized around actual or metaphorical forms of insurance. My presentation acknowledges how contingent our lives really are—that is, how we swim in a sea of luck, even when we are unaware of its forces. It then uses insurance as a product and metaphor to define where and how government is able to respond to bad luck in ways that enhance the lives of citizens and bind ourselves more closely to one another. Finally, it employs the insurance metaphor to design and explain the importance of the progressive income tax as the means by which these social responses are feasible. In every case, the reason for these interventions is to breathe life into our commitment to provide equality of opportunity to all Americans.

* * *

In writing this book, I have tried my best to restrain my usual pedagogical zeal, which was fully on display in my prior book, *We Are Better Than This: How Government Should Spend Our Money*.[3] This book stands on its own, but if you wish to pursue further some of the economic and social issues touched on here—for example, the different ways of measuring income inequality, or more extensive cross-country report cards—*We Are Better Than This* might be just the ticket. The endnotes here try to help by occasionally making explicit reference to it.

PART I

AN OVERVIEW OF MY ARGUMENT

CHAPTER 1

BUFFETED BY THE WINDS OF FORTUNE

FORTUNE'S WHEEL

I cycle regularly and have a standard fifteen-mile route that I follow a few times a week. On ordinary days my time around the course does not vary by more than a minute or two. On some occasions, however, there is a strong headwind blowing down from the mountains. On those days, I push myself as hard as I can against the wind in my face, but despite my best efforts I finish the route far behind my usual time. There are some fortunate days, though, when I feel that I am barely touching the pedals, and yet I fly through the route and finish at or near a personal record. Like every other cyclist, I've suffered through many tough headwinds, but don't ever recall feeling a tailwind.[1]

Our economic lives are the same. Brute luck—luck that follows from impersonal forces whose consequences we have not invited (as in a gamble)—is an important determinant of our material outcomes, clearly visible in the economic data. When that luck is consistently bad, most of those affected never achieve their full potentials. When our luck is unusually good, we behave like cyclists enjoying the wind at their backs: we believe that we can be distinguished from others entirely through our claims to superior talents, virtue, or dedication, not the good fortune of a tailwind to which we are insensible.

Brute luck is an inescapable condition of the universe, like gravity. Fortune turns her Wheel,[2] wholly indifferent to our prayers, and without more care raises some up while casting others down. But as this book shows, we have available to us strategies to modulate the impact of bad brute luck through the mediation of government. By seizing those opportunities, we not only do right by our fellow citizens, but also set the country on the path to greater national income, more broadly shared.

The pervasive impact of brute luck directly challenges our most cherished national economic myth: that every American enjoys economic opportunities for success at the career of her choice equal to the opportunities available to all others. We particularly dishonor the meaning of equality of opportunity by ignoring the importance to our material prospects of suffering bad economic luck at birth. By this I mean the negative financial consequences that are attributable to "choosing" the circumstances of our birth unwisely—to being born into poverty, or into a geographic area with limited public support for personal development, or at a time that means that we come of age in the midst of a recession. To this I add bad luck in health, both because many instances of bad luck in health in fact have genetic components, and because our existing private health insurance markets are so conspicuously dysfunctional that a health crisis can often completely derail the financial prospects of an affected family.

Chapters 3, 4, and 5 demonstrate that the consequences of bad luck at birth are evident in the data describing the economic life of affected individuals, as if they had been condemned to cycle into a perpetual headwind. This does not mean, however, that every child born into poverty is necessarily predestined to a life of economic failure.

When Fortune turns her Wheel and randomly distributes bad luck in economic circumstances at birth, she leaves in her wake different *expected values* for the lifetime incomes, social mobility, and life satisfactions of the members of each group with similar quanta of good or bad birth luck. She does not, however, control every contingency in our lives, nor does she determine the personalities and characteristics with which we address these uncontrollable forces. This means that the *actual* outcomes of individuals with a similar allocation of existential luck will cluster around the expected value for that group, in what you might remember from high school math as the normal distribution (or one close to it), with most outcomes close to the expected value, but a few far to the left or the right of that. When luck deniers point to a rags-to-riches story to justify our current indifference to our fellow citizens (and to our collective economic future), they mistake the outlier for the central tendency.

Figure 1.1 might help to clarify my point:

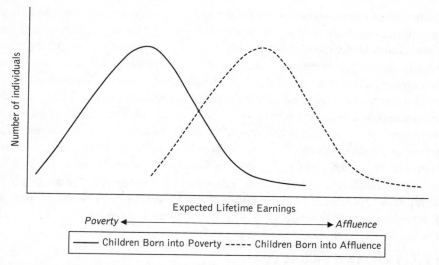

FIGURE 1.1 Stylized Representation of Distributional Lifetime Earnings vs. Birth Circumstances

Technically, this distribution is not strictly normal, but rather skewed to the right. This reflects the fact that zero is a hard lower bound on lifetime earnings, while the sky's the limit on the upside. In a case like this, the mean (average) of the distribution will be to the right of the median (middle of the pack) figure.

What the figure conveys is that actual lifetime earnings vary widely, but that the data are clear that the central tendency in outcomes of the unlucky-at-birth falls at a much lower point along the lifetime earnings continuum than that of those born into affluent circumstances. This is what I mean when I suggest that the economic milieu into which we are born is a strong predictor of our own expected economic outcomes. Birth and health luck set some of us on an easy economic path, and others on a difficult one. Chapters 3 through 5 explore the relevant research, but the key takeaway is that the data compel the conclusion that these instances of luck are an important determinant of the material outcomes that each of us achieves.

These differences in outcomes in turn are driven by a handful of unassailable facts. First, in our complex modern world, our investments in our own human capital, particularly education and health maintenance, are the principal drivers of lifetime earnings. ("Education" here is shorthand for policies that from birth encourage the flourishing of the child, including adequate parental leave and early childhood childcare in stimulating surroundings.) Second, the United States is unique among developed countries in relying so heavily on private resources—which is to say, oneself and one's family—to fund those investments in human capital. One of the great failures of our political discourse today is our insensitivity to the harms done by our excessive cheerleading for private enterprise and individual initiative against this background of differential access to human capital investment.

The conflict between today's relatively laissez-faire approach to bad economic luck at birth and in health, on the one hand, and the myth of equality of opportunity, on the other, is the core problem with which this book wrestles. It is true that someone somewhere can always overcome any obstacle, but that is not the right question. The right question is: Why do we offer some of our fellow citizens a downhill trot to prosperity, while others are asked to run the same distance uphill, with a sack of potatoes tied to their waists? From this follows all the philosophical, economic, and policy conundrums with which the book wrestles.

DRILLING DOWN ON BRUTE LUCK

It is not easy to convince some people of the importance of brute luck in their lives, precisely because Fortune's Wheel turns for us all, and Her outcomes are often invisible. It's like trying to convince a child that our atmosphere presses down on us at 14.7 pounds per square inch, even though none of us feels the weight.

This little exercise I did with my students might help. The class took eight coins and flipped the coins as a group 1,000 times. (We didn't waste class time by actually wearing out our thumbs, because we relied on one of many online coin flipper simulations.)[3] Then we toted up how many Heads were represented in each toss of the eight coins. Our results looked like this (see Figure 1.2).

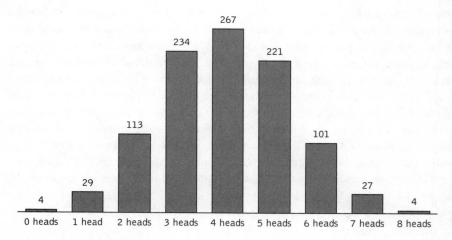

FIGURE 1.2 Results of Flipping Eight Coins as a Group 1,000 Times

In other words, in 267 out of our 1,000 trials, the result of flipping eight coins at once was that we obtained four Heads. This is the central tendency of this simple game, but there are a few outliers who managed to flip no Heads, and another handful who flipped eight Heads out of all eight coins they tossed.

Now imagine that we attach some financial consequences to this game. I assigned each trial of flipping eight coins at once to one (imaginary) individual, and I awarded (again imaginary) payouts to those individuals based on the number of Heads they tossed. Those individuals who flipped eight coins and got zero Heads (four unlucky souls) received nothing. If you were one of the 29 participants whose flip turned up one Head, I awarded you $10. I kept increasing the payout by a factor of 10 for each Head you tossed, which means that the group of 113 players who tossed two Heads got $100 each, the 234 players who tossed three Heads got $1,000 each, and so on, all the way up to those individuals who somehow managed to toss eight coins and have them all turn up Heads (four individuals), who received $10 million each.

My opening question for class discussion was this: Did any of the four players who won $10 million in this game *not* write a book titled *The Secrets of My Success*?

The larger point is that even if you have forgotten all the statistics you ever studied, you can see at a glance the central tendency of the outcomes from this coin-flipping game. You can also see how preposterous it is to hold up the four individuals now $10 million to the richer as proof that "anybody" can achieve great financial success in the lottery of life, if only they apply themselves. Every game of chance has outliers.

You might object to this simple little game as unrepresentative of life as it is lived, because individuals' wealth inside the game was determined solely by chance. But researchers have created more sophisticated simulations, in which random events of good and bad luck are thrown at virtual industrious individuals. One important recent paper along these lines, by Alessandro Pluchino and colleagues,[4] begins by stating the following central dilemma in economics. Intelligence, talent, and other characteristics that are valued in the marketplace are randomly distributed around a normal distribution (one that looks more or less like my coin toss results). Many individuals are close to the center of the talent, brains, or beauty distribution, and a few are outliers on the upside. But the wealth distribution that we observe does not follow this pattern: it follows a "power law" (like my awarding of 10 times more wealth for every coin that comes up Heads), which means that outliers on the upside outstrip the middle of the pack by many orders of magnitude.

The Pluchino paper first reviews some of the large literature in which one or another random factor has clear statistical value in explaining professional success. (As one famous example not cited by Pluchino, Gregory Mankiw and Matthew Weinzierl have written a well-known paper that first demonstrates a positive correlation between a person's height and his income, and proposes a tax on height as a (possibly tongue in cheek?) response.)[5] The Pluchino paper then proposes a conceptually simple model that has substantial explanatory power in relating the normal distribution of talent to the orders of magnitude more skewed distribution of wealth.

The Pluchino model begins with all individuals having the same starting wealth, but different amounts of talent. They all set to work and accumulate wealth in proportion to their talents. Every six months over the forty-year professional life of the individuals inside the model, a snapshot is taken: basically, either nothing happens, a good luck event occurs, or a bad luck event is recorded. Bad luck cuts the player's capital at that moment in half. Good luck doubles a player's capital, but with a probability determined by her talent: only the most talented get to enjoy a full doubling of their capital at that time. This is designed to reflect the intuition that it takes talent to fully harness the effects of good luck. The authors then run the model over and over and observe what happens to the virtual individuals in the model.

The authors' conclusions are important along two margins. First, their model confirms what moral philosophers, novelists, and fair-minded readers already know: luck has a lot to do with outcomes. Second, the unusually lucky fellow with no great talent will outperform a highly talented counterpart who does not enjoy as much good luck:

> The model shows that, actually, randomness plays a fundamental role in selecting the most successful individuals. It is true that, as one could expect, talented people are more likely to become rich, famous or important during their life with respect to poorly equipped ones. But—and this is a less intuitive rationale—ordinary people with an average level of talent are statistically destined to be successful (i.e. to be placed along the tail of some power law distribution of success) much more than the most talented ones, provided that they are more blessed by fortune along their life.[6]

As one more example, economist Hal Varian (later the chief economist at Google) concluded in an influential paper on the intersection of luck, tax policy, and government spending that individual incomes in fact contain a large random component—an element that cannot be attributed to family background, cognitive skill, educational attainment, or occupation. In fact, the element of randomness seems to dominate all other explanatory factors for why one person achieves great affluence and another similarly endowed person does not.[7]

The Pluchino model may not fully satisfy you, because after all it is just a model, not a study of reality. Chapter 2, previewed immediately below, explores possible reasons drawn from social psychology research for our resistance to the idea that our successes, and that of all other persons, are significantly determined by the turning of Fortune's Wheel. Having, I hope, broken down resistance to the idea that we swim in a sea of luck, subject to its currents and tides, Chapters 3 through 5 make the affirmative case for the long shadow that the circumstances of our birth, in particular, cast on our economic futures. The data speak for themselves: the circumstances in which we are born have clearly measurable consequences for the material lives we lead as adults. Moreover, the gap between the normal distribution of talent and the "power law" multiplicative distribution of wealth needs to be explained, and old-fashioned luck—the kind that means that someone somewhere will toss six, or eight, or fourteen Heads in a row—fills the bill. It may be that we live in a "winner takes all" economy, but the important question is: What determines who is the winner?

THE DENIAL OF LUCK

Most of us are remarkably bad at distinguishing who we are from the impact of luck in our lives. Because luck affects our material success and personal happiness so pervasively, it is difficult for us to untangle our construction of ourselves from it, and thereby examine the importance of luck objectively. If we were able to do so, the inescapable randomness of the forces that influence life's outcomes would probably terrify us.

Here I may lose some readers who have enjoyed favorable material outcomes, because the suggestion that your success has not been attributable solely to your own hard work and inner merit will rankle you. Many affluent individuals fall victim to this powerful unconscious mechanism that attributes all their success to their inner virtue.

It might be small comfort to such persons, but it is worth stressing that I do not propose to undo the entire impact of all the elements of brute luck (including here the birth talents that we did nothing to earn) that explain so much of where we end up in economic terms. That is, I am not a strict "luck egalitarian." I do, however, insist that our commitment to equality of opportunity as a defining credo means that we must address head-on the sorts of bad luck that motivate this book.

We all lead our lives swimming in a sea of luck, with tides and currents pushing us one way or another, yet the most successful among us usually are the first to deny that Fortune's whims played any role in their accumulation of wealth. Why do they—indeed, most of us—go through mental gymnastics to deny that luck plays a large role in our material outcomes? Why is it likely that the four imaginary $10 million winners in my little coin-flipping game would, were they flesh and blood, even now be holding seminars to sell the secrets of their thumb-strengthening exercises?

One possible answer is that we live in a world populated with immature narcissists, some of whom happen to luck into great wealth. We certainly have more than our share of such underbaked parodies of mature adults running loose in America. But something more is going on. Look, for example, at the long letter published by billionaire Leon Cooperman in 2019, responding to what he saw as Senator Elizabeth Warren's unfair attacks on the billionaire class.[8] The tone is not one of obnoxious self-satisfaction, or demeaning of others, but rather one of overwhelming defensiveness. Cooperman wants to be understood, to be respected, and even to be admired for his charitable giving. In the letter he is insensitive to the situations of others, insufficiently grateful for his great success, and arrogant in his implied claim that he can spend his money in charitable endeavors more effectively than could the democratic process allocate the same amount of spending. As a result, his case for his entitlement to his great wealth is completely unconvincing. Nonetheless, he is just a run-of-the-mill smart guy with a lot of money, not a pathological figure oozing disdain for others. Something more fundamental by way of a psychological operation must be afoot to explain the angry rejection of the suggestion that they have received the slightest help from Fortune's Wheel.

Chapter 2 explores possible reasons drawn from social psychology research for our resistance to the idea that our successes, and that of all other persons, are significantly determined by the turning of Fortune's Wheel. Social psychologists call this phenomenon the "Belief in a Just World." The idea is encapsulated in the mental construct that *people get what they deserve and deserve what they get.* That is, individuals frame their understanding of the universe and their role in it from the premise that the universe is completely fair and just, as are the institutions that we have constructed that regulate our economic lives. In that case, affluence must reflect a universal cognizance of inner merit, and poverty must reflect a cosmic condemnation of someone who suffers from some great personal failing, like laziness.

Social psychologists have conducted many experiments that show that the hypothesis explains all sorts of personal behaviors. This internal ordering mechanism also fits neatly into contemporary policy discourse, in which cutting taxes is actually a virtuous act, because it recognizes the greater inner merit of those with large incomes.

The systematic denial of luck by those who have had enjoyed good fortune is profoundly unhealthy in its implications for the public policy choices we make, in particular our government taxing and spending policies. No book can overcome decades of ingrained patterns of thought, but Chapter 2 at least presents the evidence here, to suggest to open-minded readers another way of conceptualizing their relationships with others and with the universe.

As individuals, we are not quite cosmic flotsam and jetsam, completely unable to steer the ship of our own identities. But by the same token when Fortune turns her Wheel, we are knocked about by random forces that lead to all sorts of unexpected outcomes. By brooding on the pervasive importance of brute luck to the material lives we end up experiencing, we can, perhaps, tame our egos and establish a stronger sense of connection to all our fellow citizens, not just to those whose bank accounts are overflowing. This introspection brings with it humility and a stronger sense of community—for example, the realization that perhaps we are too quick to confuse bad luck with moral defects.

WHAT KINDS OF LUCK ARE WE TALKING ABOUT?

Economics, moral philosophy, and even theology all address from their different perspectives what kinds of bad luck should trouble us, and why. In general, policy advice today is infected far too thoroughly with the findings of economics papers alone. This is true in particular when we try to think constructively about how seriously we as a society should respond to the brute bad luck endured by others. Here, economics offers one perspective on how we are doing, but moral philosophy and religious ethics also have contributions to make in fashioning our responses.

For example, philosophers also have invested a great deal of energy under the heading of "moral luck" in inquiring when a person can fairly be held responsible for her actions, or whether instead circumstances beyond her control (whether at birth or otherwise) absolve her of accountability. Their arguments sometimes have the quality of aggressive dancing on top of a pin, but some of the categories of luck that they have defined are helpful in distilling where we might draw the line between just plain bad luck and luck for which some sort of government mitigation might be appropriate. Chapter 7 summarizes some of these arguments in a high-level sort of way that will not satisfy moral philosophers, but that by the same token, I hope, will not deter most readers. The same can be said of developments in religious social thought; Chapter 8 touches on one important example of this.

I am not a philosopher, and you are unlikely to be interested in a discussion of sufficientarianism vs. prioritarianism. Let's keep things at a more palatable level, then, by beginning with the observation that every life is full of serendipitous events of no great importance to the rest of us. If you see your high school sweetheart at a reunion twenty years later, pick up where you left off, and live happily ever after—well, mazel tov. I would say the same, or express my regret, if you run into an old friend who knows of a job opening that suits your talents, or if your car breaks down on the first day of work. In each case, lives are affected, but not a lot of national policy implications follow. Government is not in the business of taxing all forms of good luck or compensating every instance of bad luck.

I also have no interest here in circumstantial bad luck, by which I mean losses suffered through random events (not the consequences of choices you have made) that arise in everyone's life and that generally are not life-altering. Stated differently, one can go out and buy private insurance against most forms of circumstantial bad luck, like automobile accidents.

The intersection between the credo of equality of opportunity and the turning of Fortune's Wheel snaps into focus only when we abstract from the micro-targeted or circumstantial luck that Fortune deals us every day to examine more systematically consequential phenomena. Of these, the most important are the good and bad luck that as a result of birth or health set some of us on an easy economic path, and others on a difficult one.

One strand of modern moral philosophy generally argues that we do not really own the unfettered exploitation rights to the accidents of our birth that establish the personal attributes that we see as the bedrock of our identities. To a "luck egalitarian" philosopher, these also are just instances of brute luck, because unless you adopt a strict reincarnation model of your existence, you did nothing to earn those birth talents. Instead, they were bestowed on you, somehow, by Fortune or whatever other agent you wish to name. If I had been given the choice, for example, I would have opted to be 10 percent less smart, and 10 percent better looking—but life does not offer us a prenatal checklist from which to choose our fundamental characteristics.

These sorts of personal attributes (height, intelligence, beauty, ability to hit a curveball or play the flute) bear directly on the ease with which we navigate through economic life. While they might be said to define who we are in a conventional sense, many moral philosophers argue that it does not follow that the world should be set up to reward every use of those talents exclusively through private market pricing. Ronald Dworkin, for example, believed that all instances of birth luck, good or bad, should be neutralized, so that the supremely talented could not in fact coast effortlessly through a life of both wealth and ease.[9]

Because I do not pretend to be a philosopher, I reject this.

Instead, in a move destined to have me excluded from Philosophy Department workshops for the rest of my life, I take people as they are.[10] "Taking people as they are" means radically separating the attributes with which people are born from the money invested in their human capital, in health insurance, or in other areas susceptible to policy responses measured in monetary terms.[11] Tall people in general earn more than short people, which is terribly unfair, but by taking people as they are, I allow this unfairness to continue.

My approach thus honors the philosophically naïve understanding of ourselves that most of us share. We think that there is some there, there—some fixed and inalienable core to our being that is the essence of us. (No matter what the future may hold, I'll always be a tall fellow, and no one else has my memories.) We also think that we rightly own the fruits of exploiting those essential characteristics that define ourselves. Philosophers, Buddhists, and scientists of the mind and brain might disagree, but national fiscal policy is a democratic exercise whose premises must reflect commonsense understandings of points as fundamental as this.

Because I accept people as they are, I simply ask whether our society offers pathways for individuals to develop the tools necessary to achieve their ambitions in light of whatever their native talents might be—recognizing that many will not fully succeed, notwithstanding the investments we have made in them, and that others will by virtue of their bountiful birth endowments enjoy an easier time of life than will others. In short, do we offer everyone a fair opportunity to develop whatever talents she might have, and the opportunity in turn to exploit those mature talents in the manner most congenial to her? Many moral philosophers will throw up their hands at my reducing the egalitarian enterprise to what they would call a "mere starting gate" theory, but ask yourself, how many moral philosophers have gotten themselves elected to Congress?

My emphasis on equality of *opportunity* is consistent with this commonplace intuition, because it means that my focus is forward-looking from birth. Without more, bad luck at birth might be thought to incorporate expressions of our DNA that we might think to be suboptimal—not being born smart enough, or beautiful enough, or tall enough to have an easy time of it in life. But again, this is not what I mean. I distinguish all the characteristics of who we are at the moment of our birth—all the potential we contain—from external factors that threaten that potential. Being born unable to hit the curveball is just who you are: being born into a poor household where you cannot obtain the investment in your human capital needed to allow your native brilliance to flourish is an instance of bad luck to which policies can respond.

In sum, I distinguish between different forms of bad luck by adopting a premise that most of us should find satisfying, even if philosophers might call it illusory. We legitimately own our personal attributes and whatever use we can put them to, but we cannot be held responsible for a lack of external financing for our development, an immediate physical environment that is starved of stimulation or prospects, ill health, or similar instances of bad luck that are exogenous to our construction of who we are, as opposed to what we want to do. Our responses to these forms of bad luck drive equality of opportunity as a lived truth. Since government does have access to financial capital, but not to height-leveling technologies, this is an intuitively sensible place to end up.

My distinction between personal attributes and deficiencies in external resources is also important because it preserves the critical role of *agency*. Personal freedom to act and responsibility for the consequences are the hallmarks of what is meant by agency. As Richard Reeves has written, "Every American should have the space and resources to construct, independently, his or her own path through life."[12] In our modern post-industrial society, agency is inextricably bound up with resources, and when we starve the children of the poor of the resources necessary to permit their flourishing, we simultaneously dishonor our commitment to their personal agency.

If we think deeply enough, we may convince ourselves that we are nothing but motes of cosmic dust whose every move was programmed eons ago by the interactions of random forces in the universe. But bridges don't get built or new apps created without people having at least the illusion that they are in control of themselves, which really is what the concept of agency is all about. People wish to live (or believe they live) in a society in which they are free to choose what actions they take and are prepared to take responsibility for most consequences that follow. This stands in complete opposition to the conclusions of the most radical philosophers, but it does seem necessary to help us get out of bed in the morning. Neoclassical microeconomics, with its central metaphor of the rational agent choosing to increase her utility (her satisfactions) through her conscious choices, is the apotheosis of agency as an ordering principle.

Throughout the book, I therefore look for instances of brute bad luck that befall some Americans that are not the result of explicit risks undertaken by them ("option bad luck," in the terminology of Ronald Dworkin), *and that are external to who those Americans are in this straightforward sense.* In turn, the kinds of bad brute luck that interest me most are those that have important consequences for the economic lives that our fellow citizens lead, are ones for which private markets do not and cannot have remedies, and that can be addressed through the application of money.

Of these predictable instances of brute luck, the most susceptible to thoughtful government intervention are those I have already identified as the consequences of bad economic luck at birth and bad luck in health. Our private markets cannot resolve the first and have conspicuously failed at the second. Bad luck along these two margins impairs an individual's ability to invest in her own human capital, and thereby diminishes her prospects for fully capturing the economic rewards that her native talents and ambitions might predict. And as we will see, these forms of bad luck can be mitigated through the application of money, in amounts that will not break the collective bank.

In my nerdiest moments I call these kinds of bad luck *existential adverse fortuities*, by which I mean the negative financial consequences that can follow from where we are born, to whom we are born, and when we are born, as well as health crises. The most important example is the inability of those born into straitened circumstances to obtain the private resources necessary fully to build out their human capital through education.

The term "existential adverse fortuity" is a bit daunting, which is why I regularly substitute "bad luck at birth" or "existential bad luck," but it is intended to play off the doctrine of insurance law that liability insurance covers only *adverse fortuities*—unpredictable events not in the control of the insured that lead to clearly measurable financial loss. My use of "adverse fortuity" thus reminds the reader that I not only take people as they are, but also look for harms that are random in their distribution and that can be mitigated by reasonable sums of money.

In turn, my use of the word "existential" here is not meant to trigger images of Kierkegaard or Sartre. I use it in the same sense as we regularly talk about "existential threats"—as something that imperils the core of our existence or our potential for human flourishing.

So existential adverse fortuities are those circumstances at birth outside the characteristics we ordinarily employ to define the core of a person's individuality that expose that person to more challenging economic opportunities (particularly through worse access to investment in her human capital) than those born to more favorable circumstances, together with health crises. This book focuses on existential adverse fortuities (including health) because they can be separated from our construction of ourselves, are consequential to our individual flourishing and shared prosperity, and are susceptible to analysis and policy solutions centered around the actual or metaphorical collection of premiums and payment of indemnities.

Existential bad luck goes to the essence of whether this country takes seriously the credo of equality of opportunity. As introduced a few pages ago, the core reason is that the United States relies much more on private resources—which is to say, family resources—than do most other developed economies to make investments in human capital through education. In turn, family income and wealth are very unequally divided. And to make matters more dramatic, nearly half of the wealth in this country is inherited, which enables the perpetuation of economic inequality through the expenditure of accumulated family capital to invest in the next generation.

If talented poor kids get educations of comparable quality to those of rich kids (including placement counselors who can help overcome the knowledge and fear gap that keeps many poor kids from pursuing top-flight colleges), many more poor kids will find their way to college. The kids thereby benefited will enjoy greater productivity and (presumably) satisfaction in life, which redounds to the overall productivity of the country, to economic mobility, and to our collective welfare.[13] Here is an instance where existential bad luck (being born poor) has clear and important negative implications for the affected group, and where government (and government alone) can respond on the scale required.

More provocatively, if it can be demonstrated—as unfortunately it can—that being born black has profoundly negative implications for your future financial success, well again that should be a topic that shapes national debates and policies. Please do not misunderstand: being born black is not a misfortune. Being born black in a white-dominated society with large reservoirs of unexamined racial prejudice, on the other hand, means a life facing headwinds, while others enjoy the tailwinds of their dominant skin color. Is being black in this society nonetheless a personal attribute, or is it an existential adverse fortuity in the sense that I employ the term? This is a fraught topic that I defer until Chapter 7.

Our health also fits within my construction of existential brute luck. A surprising number of us, including (as I was surprised recently to learn) me, are born with genetic defects of one kind or another. Some are visible from a child's earliest years to the casual eye, other defects impair cognitive development, and still others, like my defect, are largely invisible until they manifest themselves years later in one disease or another. These instances of congenital health issues are a direct extension of the existential adverse fortuities I just listed.

In addition, all of us discover that our health has an element of randomness throughout our lives, no matter how productive we have been and how careful we are to follow the latest medical guidelines. Genetic predisposition to cancer or heart disease are risks we all run, not the invariable result of a moral failing or bad habit. Just as we fail to invest in the supply of human capital, because we rely too heavily on family resources to make those investments, so too we fail to maintain that human capital, by virtue of our fragmented and obscenely expensive healthcare system, the delivery of which also depends to some extent on brute luck (such as whether you work for an employer that provides comprehensive healthcare insurance).

One way of conceptualizing healthcare in this context, consistent with the intuitions of many of us, is that *who* we are is different from *how well* we are. We do not define ourselves through our illnesses. My visitation from the cancer fairy was as random as the circumstances of my birth, and at least as far as I am concerned was an attack on me, not an aspect of who I am.

Your bad luck in health, whether congenital or otherwise, can drive your family to bankruptcy. To an economist, you are a "factor of production"—a unit of productivity who creates income not only for yourself, but for society as a whole. To anyone with even the most rudimentary moral compass, you are a fellow citizen, deserving of an equal opportunity to enjoy a life of dignity according to your inclinations and talents. From either point of view, the economic destruction worked by any serious health crisis destroys value. Here, national policies, in the form of fostering orderly and universal healthcare insurance, can mitigate the financial consequences at least. For the reasons I will develop later, healthcare insurance necessarily requires an active role for government: private markets by themselves fail miserably here, as we can see amply demonstrated in America today.

Government cannot make every disadvantage disappear. Existential adverse fortuities (including health crises), however, have particular claims to our attention for both moral and economic reasons. They affect millions, they are problems solved by capital allocation and straightforward policy design, and we have available well-understood government policy instruments, such as greater investment in public education, that do mitigate their impact and lead to greater national prosperity. These are the sorts of issues on which we should focus.

EQUALITY OF OPPORTUNITY

"To the famous question posed by Nobel laureate Amartya Sen, 'equality of what?,'" writes Brookings Institution fellow Richard Reeves, "America has always had an answer ready: equality of opportunity."[14]

To call equality of opportunity a myth is not to deny its power or its kernel of truth. Every country has its core foundational myths and national credos. These serve to inspire citizens and to call them to account when society drifts too far from these essential national beliefs. In the United States, one of our central national tenets is that we are a country of equal opportunity—one in which any child can grow up to be President, or founder of a corporate unicorn. We have instantiated that principle through laws that are facially neutral and through enforcement of prohibitions on many forms of extralegal discrimination.

But have we in fact fashioned a society imbued with authentically equal opportunities, as our frequent invocations of that credo would imply? My argument is that we have not, because we have not seriously addressed how a kid born into poverty nonetheless can attract the investment in her human capital necessary to equip her to develop and pursue her native talents and interests. Nor do we have an answer for the tens of millions of Americans who either have no health insurance or are woefully underinsured, and who thereby suffer needlessly from health crises that hold back their economic progress and life satisfactions.

"Equality of opportunity" has many different connotations. As one starting point, the great philosopher John Rawls articulated what he called "fair equality of opportunity," which he defined in his most famous work as, "Those who are at the same level of talent and ability, and have the same willingness to use them, should have the same prospects of success regardless of their initial place in the social system, that is, irrespective of the income class into which they are born."[15]

Rawls's fair equality of opportunity does not by itself guarantee equal outcomes, or anything close to that. Rather, it looks to those skills valued in the marketplace, and demands that all citizens have the same "prospects of success." In my thinking, this requires focusing both on opportunities to *develop* the requisite skills, and on opportunities to *exploit* them in the marketplace.

In the same vein, the philosopher T. M. Scanlon has written what is probably the most recent serious inquiry into the meaning of equality of opportunity.[16] He divides the credo into Procedural Fairness and Substantive Opportunity. Scanlon develops a very complete account of Procedural Fairness that goes beyond facially neutral rules or barriers to their underlying motive or purpose. Rawls and Scanlon agree that Procedural Fairness by itself is a necessary but terribly insufficient articulation of equality of opportunity. The really important contribution of Rawls and Scanlon here is their emphasis on Substantive Opportunity; the difference between them is simply that for rhetorical reasons Scanlon separately treats these two aspects of equality of opportunity, while Rawls rolls them both into his "fair equality of opportunity."

Substantive Opportunity is really what this book is all about. That is, in developing my arguments I assume that procedural discrimination has been addressed about as well as can be expected of any ordinary society still riddled with unexamined racism and other prejudices. I know this to be untrue, but I do not have anything useful to add along this margin to the work of thousands of dedicated public-interest lawyers, academics, and policymakers.

My story begins with the substantive question of whether children and young adults of comparable talents but different economic backgrounds are able to develop and exploit those talents to the same extent, or whether instead systematic differences in investments in human capital made in respect of children from different economic backgrounds mean that children of the affluent are much more likely to develop whatever talents they have than are children of the poor. Once the facts are investigated, the answer becomes brutally obvious, but then the issue becomes how to respond. The idea motivating this book is to encourage readers to reframe their thinking by emphasizing that luck, not deservingness, drives these differences, and that a broad understanding of insurance can help us to construct responses to existential bad luck in particular.

In other words, if we think about equality of opportunity solely as an inquiry into Procedural Fairness, then even as ordinary citizens and not philosophers we have failed to take equality of opportunity seriously. Our current failure to honor Substantive Opportunity is a scandal, and one that can be mitigated to a large extent by the application of money, in the form of investments in the human capital of children whose parents cannot afford to make those investments on their own. We should do so because these differences in human capital investment are driven largely by luck, and because we can metaphorically insure against this bad luck just as we literally insure our homes against fire damage.

We do not need to spend any more time neck-deep in philosophy to make progress here. We all intuitively know equality of opportunity when we see it—that's why for most of us it is understood as a credo and not a term plucked from political theory tracts. Nonetheless, it is useful to articulate explicitly and in practical terms a few overarching themes to which we all should agree.

Equality of opportunity is different from equality of outcomes. A great deal follows from this seemingly self-evident proposition. It means that, contrary to the suspicions of some of my plutocrat friends, by emphasizing equality of opportunity as the flag around which policymakers and citizens should rally, I am not quite as much of a communist as my friends would like to believe. I accept that life outcomes will range all over the map, both through the turning of Fortune's Wheel and through the attributes with which we are born. It is intolerable, though, not to offer every individual the tools necessary to enable them to flourish according to their own lights, and the cost of those tools in turn must come from public resources.

Policies that emphasize fair equality of opportunity (Substantive Opportunity, in Scanlon's terminology) cost money, and that money will come from progressive tax structures, but the rationale of the entire process is not redistribution for its own sake. I take no pleasure in cutting people down to my size, and neither do most Americans. I do, however, find it unacceptable not to use available policy instruments to mitigate the most important headwinds that follow from the accident of being born poor—or, increasingly, being born middle class.

Equality of opportunity in practice further comprises at least two related themes. The first is captured by every Frank Capra movie in which America is described as a "land of opportunity." This use signifies that each of us has available a rich smorgasbord of interesting and satisfying possible career paths that answer to our predilections and talents. These paths include those that take as their first priority the satisfaction of material desires, but also those involving national service or commitments to family, charities, or religious organizations. We are not precluded from any of these by virtue of our race, skin color, religion, national origin, or other invidious distinction.

At an individual level, the prospect of a job with dignity is much more important to our respect for ourselves and to our life satisfactions than can possibly be captured by national income statistics. Indeed, I believe that much of the national distress that marks the present day is a response not simply to a lack of financial resources, but also to the loss of self-respect inherent in so many contemporary jobs. We are not a nation of café habitués who pass the day sipping espresso and debating post-deconstructionism. In America, we are what we work.

I thus fully endorse the principle that equality of opportunity implies the availability of a range of meaningful career paths from which we reasonably can expect to derive a satisfying life imbued with self-respect. For example, public investment in infrastructure offers the prospect of greater national income (through the substantial economic returns on those investments, net of the cost of financing those projects through taxes), which income in turn is more broadly shared through new well-paying jobs that bring with them a sense of personal dignity. Public infrastructure projects thus expand the set of available work opportunities.[17]

The second meaning of "opportunity" in the phrase "equality of opportunity"—and the one on which this book focuses—signals that we should all have available to us the tools required to develop and exploit our individual predilections and talents in pursuit of the career path of our choice. Equality of opportunity in this second sense means a great deal more than the absence of legal barriers to particular schools or occupations. Its underlying motivation is *fairness*—that we each run a roughly similar racecourse with others chasing the same goals, despite differences in family wealth. This, I think, is what Rawls meant by *fair* equality of opportunity, and this is what motivates this book.

That is, America as a land of opportunity asks whether there are interesting and satisfying life opportunities arrayed in front of us. This second use asks: Can we in fact follow the path of our dreams and ambitions? In particular, in our complex and largely post-industrial society, do we all enjoy comparable investments in our education and healthcare? No government can make things perfectly equal for rich and poor, white and black, rural and urban—but we can do a great deal more than we do right now to breathe some life into this second meaning of "opportunity."

Here you see the difference between the Belief in a Just World and similar modes of thought (developed in Chapter 2), on the one hand, and fairness as the motivation for instantiating opportunity, on the other. The former habits of mind operationalize the intuition that we deserve what we get, and get what we deserve—that is, our material outcomes reflect our *deservingness*. Fairness as the underlying principle of opportunity, on the other hand, does not draw any moral inferences from material circumstances. It asks only that every person have available to her the material resources sufficient to develop her human capital, in light of her talents, inclinations, and ambitions.

Traditional economic analysis done well is not the enemy of a more vigorous government that embodies deeper commitments to alleviate the financial adversities that follow from existential bad luck. The basic reason is simple: somewhere between three-fifths and two-thirds of our national income (as measured by GDP) is derived from the efforts of people—from labor, as economists say, rather than from returns to capital. What we see in the United States today is a systematic underinvestment in people—in ourselves—because we rely on private markets to address what private markets cannot possibly reach.

From the Reagan era to the recent Trump tax bill, it has been fashionable to talk about "supply-side" economics, which is a fancy way of saying that government should cut taxes on income from investments (capital), so that more capital would be supplied to businesses, and those businesses thereby would grow faster.

But the United States today is awash in financial capital.[18] The long-term crisis from which working- and middle-class Americans suffer is a *deficit in the supply of human capital.*

We do not remedy that shortfall through cutting taxes on the highest incomes, whether derived from labor or capital. We remedy the human capital supply-side deficit instead by making investments in people who do not have the family resources to make those investments themselves, thereby making them smarter, more intellectually nimble, and more resilient to ever-accelerating technological changes. We make those investments principally through high-quality free child care, public education, and healthcare. Once we see human beings as in part income-generating dynamos who are largely responsible for our national income, we inevitably should ask: Why don't we comprehensively invest in all those dynamos, as opposed to our current practice of relying primarily on family resources? And why don't we take care of those machines through proper maintenance (that is, through healthcare)? Every worker who dies young because she didn't receive cancer screening represents a human tragedy, but in this small context also is like an engine that blows up because we let its oil run dry.

RESPONDING TO EXISTENTIAL BAD LUCK

The poor will be with us, always, and equality of opportunity has always operated as an aspiration rather than a fact. So what's new here? In fact, things have changed when compared with a generation or two ago, along four related margins.

First, as a general matter, to succeed today you must invest much more by way of money and time in yourself before you even enter the workplace than was true in the past, principally in the form of education. (Family connections, social networks, and familiarity with the mores of different business social environments also help to grease the wheels of success; these are difficult to buy in an open market but come easily when growing up in an affluent household.)

Second, the United States is unique among large peer economies in relying heavily on private resources (family) to finance these critical investments in what economists call "human capital"—the training and expertise we obtain in the first instance from education that command large returns in the marketplace, in the form of higher wages than we could capture without those investments.

Third, economic inequality has soared at the top end: the top 1 percent today hold vastly more wealth relative to that of middle-income Americans than was the case fifty years ago. This allows a small minority of Americans to fund these critical investments in their offspring's human capital and in healthcare without much sensitivity to the cost. By doing so, the affluent turn today's top-heavy wealth distributions into a hereditable gene, by overendowing the children of the affluent with unlimited human capital investment. That is, even if inheritances were taxed at 100 percent, wealth (in the form of anticipatable future income) would already have been passed from one generation to the next through a parent's fulsome investment in her offspring's human capital. Fourth, inheritances are not in fact taxed at 100 percent. To the contrary, nearly half of the wealth in America today was inherited, not earned. Here again, luck—in this case, the good luck of "choosing" one's parents wisely—leads to very unequal prospects in life, not just in how many toys we can buy from the outset, but also in how easily we can amass the human capital required to be productive members of our complex society.

In short, the modern world demands that each of us embody much greater explicit investment in our human capital than used to be the case. These investments are expensive both in terms of out-of-pocket costs, and also in terms of the time in which a student is not earning a significant income as she holds herself back from the full-time job market to concentrate on building her human capital. As the human machine becomes more specialized, and in need of more dollars of investment (and more time held back from the labor market) to bring to full productivity, the head start afforded to some lucky souls by investments funded from family resources becomes more and more difficult for ordinary Americans to equalize.

The underlying policy problems here are neither technical nor insoluble, but rather ideological. Unlike most other developed economies, the United States today leaves to the private sector fundamental responsibilities for human development that the private sector cannot honor, or at best can uphold only very inefficiently. We further expressly tolerate intergenerational transfers of almost inconceivably large pools of wealth with little friction in the form of taxation.[19] This is the shadow that market triumphalism casts over the instantiation of equality of opportunity.

Private markets do not work well to channel investments into the human capital of those without family resources, for the obvious reason that private investors would have no enforceable mechanism to capture their share of the returns generated by investments in other human beings. (Yes, creditors can dun you to repay your student loan, but they cannot compel you to pursue a degree in engineering rather than medieval literature, and they further cannot compel you to work at all.) And as we all know from our personal experiences, private markets are an expensive and inefficient way to pay for maintaining the human machines that generate most of our national income—which is to say, healthcare.

The United States thus is unique among rich countries: our fixation on the virtues of private enterprise means that we extend those imagined virtues into arenas for which they are ill-suited, and in doing so beggar our fellow citizens' futures. The modern trend to sharply increasing payoffs for more and more specialized education compounds the problem.

We can mitigate some of the financial harms that follow from existential bad luck, and by doing so reinvigorate the meaning of equality of opportunity, if we collectively respond through the mediation of government. But why, when, and how much should we respond?

This book invokes the principles of insurance to answer these questions. Government spending and taxing policies oriented around the principles of insurance, understood as both a literal product and as metaphor, can efficiently address the sorts of existential bad luck that are uninsurable in traditional insurance markets but that have a large impact on our material outcomes. Public insurance understood in this broad sense thus can ameliorate the troika of bad decisions that dominate our economic lives—our unusual insistence that private enterprise should dominate in arenas outside its natural scope, our diffidence toward income and wealth inequality, and our insensitivity to the large role played by serendipitous luck in the form of inheritances in the wealth distribution.

Despite the profusion of geckos, ducks, and emus flooding television advertising, insurance is a sophisticated and subtle financial product. For the last 700 years it has played a salutary role in mitigating the financial harm of random bad events—an adverse fortuity, in the specialized language of insurers—in both our business and our personal lives. But it can do so only when the conditions are ripe for its principles to operate.

Insurance of any kind mitigates the financial consequences of some form of bad luck—for example, the financial burden of your house burning to the ground. The essence of insurance begins with a pool of individuals who are exposed to similar possibilities of some form of random bad luck that brings with it *financial* loss. Broken hearts are serious business for those so afflicted, but insurance cannot mend them. Randomness is important here; no company can write insurance, in the proper sense of the word, against the risk of a meteor hitting the earth and destroying all life as we know it. The firm that did offer this protection would be betting, not insuring, and of course could not possibly (were it around) pay off all those bets. Those exposed to the risk agree to pay a small sum into the pool (the insurance premium) so that those who actually suffer the loss can receive financial compensation from the pool. When you buy insurance you substitute a small but certain loss (the premium) for the possibility of a much larger but uncertain loss (your house burning down).

The reach of insurance in turn is limited by several factors. The first is that the adverse fortuity covered by the insurance must be at least fairly uncommon in occurrence, so that premiums are not unreasonably large relative to indemnity payments. Second, insurance is vulnerable to the problem of *adverse selection*. This is the business risk that when insurance is offered, those who know they need it the most will be the first in line to buy it. Finally, insurance also is vulnerable to *moral hazard*—to the concern that people with insurance will behave more recklessly in some instances than they would if they were uninsured. Chapter 6 expands on these points. All of these serve to constrain the scope of public as well as private insurance.

An old joke among policy wonks describes the US federal government as an insurance company with its own standing army. Like all good jokes, it reveals a fundamental insight about its subject. In 2018, healthcare (Medicare, Medicaid, exchange subsidies, etc.), Social Security, and other so-called mandatory payments (e.g., government employee pension plans, unemployment insurance, and food stamps) accounted for two-thirds of government spending, excluding interest payments.[20] If you follow through on the joke and add in military spending, you find that you have accounted for five-sixths of all federal government non-interest spending.

But what if we were to take the joke seriously? That is, what if we were to examine critically the range of insurance products the government provides today? What if we were to ask what kinds of insurance *should* government offer? When is government the best provider of insurance? And how much government insurance can we afford? And finally, what happens if we extend the principles of insurance beyond their literal application to ask the following question: Had we the choice, how much insurance against existential adverse fortuities would we have wanted to buy in the moment before our birth? And how would we have proposed to pay for it? These are the sorts of questions to which this book is addressed.

The theme of public insurance, as a literal product and as a metaphor, responds directly to my central concerns over existential bad luck, such as the inability of those born into straitened circumstances to obtain the private resources necessary fully to build out their human capital through education. Insurance is the mental framework through which we identify these forms of bad luck, design actual or metaphorical premium payments to create funds from which we can mitigate their economic harms, create the right conditions for our metaphorical insurance to operate efficiently, and fashion metaphorical indemnities when the bad luck happens.

Insurance in a metaphorical as well as literal sense therefore serves as my central organizing principle for addressing the kinds of bad luck that fairly fall within the purview of our citizens' commitments to each other. Thinking by reference to insurance principles helps to define *why* we should use the mechanism of government to intervene in response to some kinds of bad luck, and thereby advance the goal of equality of opportunity. Moreover, it informs *when* government should intervene, and *how much* intervention is appropriate.

I will argue that our government should implement more programs that implement or are inspired by the theme of insurance than we offer today, but mine is not a call to creeping socialism. Instead, my recommendations are designed to complement private enterprise in places that private markets cannot effectively reach. Public policies that accord with the principles of insurance encourage risk-taking, rather than deadening individuals to ambition. Every private business relies on insurance to mitigate the risks of fire, accidents, the death of a key employee, or a myriad of other adverse fortuities. By doing so, private enterprises can take on the risks that they are best suited to absorb in the pursuit of their success. The same is true for the relationship between well-designed public insurance and the opportunities we wish to pursue in our lives.

Public insurance thus is not a "safety net." When you make an auto insurance claim, you do not say to your spouse, "Thank goodness I have a safety net to protect me." "Safety net" is a derogatory phrase whose purpose it is to imply a non-economic cocooning of people from the consequences of their laziness or poor planning. Businesses buy insurance, not safety nets, and so do countries—which is to say, all of us, working together.

The book's inquiry ultimately leads beyond recommendations to tweak this or that program, to a fundamental rethinking of how citizens engage with each other through the intermediation of government. Said simply, in the United States today we dramatically underinsure ourselves—we do not use government to its full capabilities of enhancing our society.

More government insurance of the right type leads to *higher* economic growth, not slow strangulation from the creeping vines of socialism. Our naïve understanding of government as the enemy of freedom means that the lucky declare themselves to be smart and keep their marketplace winnings as their due, while the unlucky systematically are relegated to lives of lower satisfaction and productivity than otherwise would be the case. Insurance as metaphor addresses the systematic underinvestment in the human capital of millions of citizens that follows when the ravages of existential bad luck are left unaddressed. To achieve faster growth, and in turn to share that growth more broadly, is a true "double dividend," in the words of the Organisation of Economic Co-operation and Development.

At the same time, government insurance is the mechanism by which we declare solidarity with all our fellow citizens. In the end, government is all about making commitments to people you do not know, and, if you did know, might not like. But those strangers have in common with you and me that we all are citizens of one country, with all the ethical implications that follow. Government insurance programs are how we breathe life into the moral dimension of a shared destiny as one country. When we ignore these economic opportunities and ethical commitments, we spite our fellow citizens, depriving them of fair opportunities to pursue their own happiness, and simultaneously impede economic growth.

When insurance as a product is extended to the realm of metaphor, we need to think carefully about what kinds of bad luck should be swept into our collective obligations to each other as citizens, how we can extend the metaphor to backwards-looking bad luck like existential bad luck, how we will collect the metaphorical premiums, and how we will collectively deliver payouts to those who fall afoul of the bad luck in question. These questions fundamentally distinguish government insurance of the sort that motivates this book from traditional private insurance—or, for that matter, social insurance programs like Social Security.[21]

Once understood, though, public insurance, whether as fact or as metaphor, can help us determine why, when, and how much insurance the public sector should undertake. What is more, the insurance metaphor ties tax policies to spending policies. The progressive income tax can be seen, not as a soak-the-rich scheme, but rather as a rational approach to designing real-world insurance premiums to pay for the social insurance programs that respond to the crisis of our healthcare system and to the heavy hand of existential bad luck.

By marrying a more honest acknowledgment of the critical importance of luck in our lives to its implications for the cherished national credo that America is a place of equal opportunity, we can begin to confront how invidiously important forms of bad brute luck work to strip millions of their fair chance. We also can develop a little bit of humility about ourselves and our individual accomplishments, and a stronger identification with other Americans. Perhaps, if we take the exercise seriously enough, we might even get to the point where we understand that great material success is not simply a sign of unique inner merit, and material disappointments not simply evidence of moral failure.

CHAPTER 2

THE DENIAL OF LUCK

"I do not know why it is that, as soon as one's lot improves, his relaxed mind begins to grow puffed up and that under the influence of prosperity he becomes oblivious to his real condition. Not without cause is it said and used among our countrymen as a proverb that it is a difficult task to endure prosperity."

—PETRARCH, *Remedies for Fortune Fair and Foul (1366)*[1]

A FUNDAMENTAL DELUSION

Why is it so difficult for many of us to accept that Fortune and her Wheel constantly nudge the directions that our lives take? Why do those of us who have enjoyed material success resist the idea that we have anything for which to be grateful, and instead persist in believing that by force of our wills alone we have controlled every aspect of our destinies? And most perniciously, why do we unconsciously deprecate the characters of those who have not succeeded as well as we have in the economic game of life?

In Chapter 1 I outlined a coin toss experiment, in which 1,000 virtual players each flipped eight coins at one time. Four out of the 1,000 players managed to toss 8 Heads at once and thereby claim a $10 million payout. My little joke at the time was to ask: How many of these four did *not* write a book titled, *The Secrets of My Success?*

The very unfunny extension of that small joke is that many of us would buy this book. We would do so, not because we are fools, but because at a deep instinctive level we reject luck as an explanation for what happens to people. Instead, we organize our engagement with the world around the fundamental principle that *people get what they deserve*. Hard work, good deeds, patience, or great talent all lead to visible rewards, because our world at its core is just and will treat us fairly.

Further, through the application of a transitive principle, we believe that *people deserve what they get*. No one just wins $10 million because she is lucky; the existence of this bountiful reward must signify some inner merit. We buy the book because someone this rich must have useful insights to share with us—perhaps eye/wrist coordination drills, or useful incantations to utter, or a spiritual journey that yields a psychic connection with the coins.

In the words of Melvin J. Lerner, a social psychologist and the leading researcher in this field, all this is "a fundamental delusion."[2]

Lerner coined the phrase "Belief in a Just World" to describe this delusion. We believe that our world *must* be fair in ways that are comprehensible to us, and that the universal moral force animating that principle of fairness is *deservingness*. As first Lerner and now a small army of fellow social psychologists have demonstrated over the last several decades, we impose on random events a belief system in which, in some way or other, here and now, or in the future, or in the afterlife, people get what they deserve, and deserve what they get. In other words, we overlay random events with arbitrary moral content. We do so to hold at bay the demons of chaos, uncertainty, or randomness—whichever name you choose to give to blind Fortune spinning her Wheel.

The deep-seated belief that people get what they deserve attenuates the terror that would come from soberly facing the prospect of unpredictable and uncontrollable events that could send our lives careening first in one direction, and then another. It also can foster long-term planning; without this delusion, it takes a great deal of courage to make long-term plans while acknowledging the certainty that life is highly uncertain. And for many people the Belief in a Just World suppresses the fear of death through reinforcing the belief in an afterlife.[3] As a result, we can get up in the morning, make plans for tomorrow, and face the world (or at least the world as we have chosen to construe it). The social psychologists call this psychic Xanax the "adaptive" side of the Belief in a Just World.

In many other regards, however, the Belief in a Just World is deeply maladaptive, as when the transitive principle, that people deserve what they get, leads to the intuition that great material success must imply some sort of ineffable talent, or that poor people must deserve their lowly state. Through dozens of published experiments, social psychologists have demonstrated that the transitive principle of a Belief in a Just World colors our impressions of the character and deservingness of those who experience otherwise inexplicable twists of good or bad fortune.

Melvin Lerner summarized much of his work in this field in his 1980 classic, *The Belief in a Just World: A Fundamental Delusion*,[4] and in a 2011 book with Susan Clayton, *Justice and Self-Interest: Two Fundamental Motives*.[5] Lerner and Clayton set out to demonstrate that individuals have a fundamental commitment to justice, whose origins arise early in childhood. In their view, this commitment to justice is separate from self-interest or behaviors learned through social interactions. Further, the justice motive has equal priority to self-interest in mental processes, and often conflicts with it. They thus sought to rescue "the justice motive" from the clutches of the economists, who see everything as motivated by self-interest.[6]

As part of their ordinary development, very young children learn to forgo immediate pleasures for larger future rewards. Lerner's theory is that they do so through an unconscious inner dialog, in which they negotiate a "personal contract" with themselves to evidence their commitment to this trade-off. But this contract rests on a "need to believe in a just world," because that is the state of the world in which the terms of the personal contract will be honored.

All parents are familiar with the power that the personal contract has over a small child, when, for example, the cookie that had been promised for good behavior is not promptly delivered. The child's wails that the situation is unfair are not born simply from greediness for chocolate chips, but rather that the entire apparatus of the personal contract has been gravely threatened.

As the individual grows and matures, the terms of the personal contract get more complex, and reality often intrudes. The maturing individual eventually abandons a narrow construction of her personal contract and replaces it with a more general commitment to live by the principle that one deserves what one gets and gets what one deserves. This is what Lerner and others mean by "the justice motive"; to a greater or lesser extent, it is shared by most individuals.[7]

But this understanding of justice is a specialized one, because its core principle, going all the way back to the personal contract, is deservingness. That is, it is by weighing the deservingness of individuals (through their goodness or good actions) that we judge whether their outcomes are just. Conversely, through the transitive principle we infer that those in good or bad situations must deserve them, through some moral virtue (or defect), or good (or bad) deed.

For Rawlsians, my joke here is that this is *Fairness as Justice*. Instead of Rawls's principle of Justice as Fairness, in which the moral philosopher explores the meaning of justice and concludes that its motivating principle is a commitment to fairness, the justice motive begins with the imperative that the world must be understood to be fair, as measured by deservingness, and then finds that this interpretation of the world instantiates justice.

In Lerner's view, "For most people, most of the time, the personal contract forms the basis of their goal-seeking and psychological stability. . . . The commitment to his personal contract creates the basis for the person's motivation to see that others get what they deserve." Yet evidence of injustice—of people getting less than they deserve—is all around us. These are perceived unconsciously as threats to the justice motive belief system. For those in comfortable circumstances, the convenient way to resolve these threats is to "maintain [one's] separation from the world of victims by various devices." Fortunately for the psychological stability of the comfortable and willingly deluded, their world and the world of victims "are often separated geographically and by social cues. The world of victims is located in the hospital, behind bars, 'across the tracks,' or on the assembly line—or distinguished by a different skin color or kind of nose."[8]

The justice motive (this fundamental commitment to justice as deservingness) is broader than and encompasses the Belief in a Just World, which is just one means by which the justice motive finds expression.[9] For example, the justice motive can operate as a morally praiseworthy instinct to right wrongs, because the agent believes that the world is or should be just, he perceives an injustice (a victim does not *deserve* the situation in which he finds himself), and the agent has the actual or imagined capacity to restore order. When a GoFundMe project is opened for a cyclist killed or badly injured in a car crash, I often contribute. As a cyclist myself, I identify with the victim and believe that I can help mitigate the pain. No doubt I also engage in some unconscious magical thinking concerning the prophylactic effect of my kindness on my own future safety on the road. This sort of magical thinking is another mental operation from earliest childhood that we all carry into our adult lives, and which in some cases overlaps with the Belief in a Just World.

Underlying the Belief in a Just World is the same commitment to deservingness as a universal moral force, just as gravity is a universal physical force, that motivates the larger justice motive. But the Belief in a Just World puts this commitment to work to resolve the cognitive dissonance that results when this putative universal force is confounded by actual injustice, random events, or thoughts of uncertain futures; the mind does so by inventing a soothing narrative of cause and effect, in which visible outcomes stem from latent causes of moral virtues or vices. We operationalize all this in ordinary speech in various forms of karma kitsch, as in the saying that "whatever goes around comes around."

The adaptive side of the Belief in a Just World allows an individual to make long-term plans and is associated with less neuroticism. An individual who is a strong adherent of the Belief in a Just World, and as a result comfortable in his own life situation, thus scores well on various psychological health indices, but the internal narrative required to support this psychic ease strikes me as no different from the state of mind of those who ask to be reattached to the Matrix.

Of course, the world is not fair. Bad things happen to good people, scoundrels become presidents, and disagreeable neighbors win the lottery. The maladaptive side of the Belief in a Just World comes into full force in these circumstances, by reassigning moral shortcomings to the unlucky, or ineffable talents to the fortunate. It imposes order on randomness, but that order is entirely fictitious. It relies on the principle of deservingness and false transitive reasoning to work back from observable circumstances to infer immanent character. In doing so, the belief system fundamentally distorts how we perceive our fellow citizens and what actions we should collectively undertake through the intermediation of government.

To be clear, individuals differ in their adherence to the Belief in a Just World, just as they differ in the strength of their attachments to any other belief system. Moreover, individuals often differentiate between their attitudes toward their own luck or deservingness and the deservingness of others.[10] Further, some individuals may be asymmetric in their internal attitudes toward luck—being quick to blame luck when things go badly for them, while finding that their own good luck is due to some subtle deservingness.[11] Women may use the Belief in a Just World as an internal organizing principle in ways that differ from men. And so on.

Ultimately, however, what is important for this chapter is whether the Belief in a Just World is real, whether it informs adherents' judgments about other people's inner characters (their deservingness) through the observation of their circumstances, and whether those judgments color how we relate to each other in the real world through social and political institutions. My focus, then, is on the utility of the transitive form of the Belief in a Just World to explain how people evaluate the moral standing of strangers. Here the evidence is overwhelming that the Belief in a Just World carries enormous explanatory weight.

One of the advantages that social psychologists hold over moral philosophers is that the psychologists get to perform real-world experiments and surveys, not just thought experiments. To that end, social psychologists have tested the Belief in a Just World theory through dozens—perhaps hundreds—of experiments. The literature is so vast that it is difficult to keep up with even the review literature—the summaries of experiments designed to shape consensus conclusions and point to future research directions.[12] I will highlight only a few experiments, but the key takeaway is that, notwithstanding the rigors of roughly fifty years of testing, the theory is robust and a powerful explanation for what otherwise would be logically inexplicable behaviors.

Social psychologists have developed many competing surveys to measure an individual's Belief in a Just World. Those surveys show strong positive correlations between adherence to the Belief in a Just World and acceptance of authoritarianism, religiosity, and political conservatism. I do not think it useful, however, to dwell on these correlations: the Belief in a Just World is not the exclusive domain of one mode of religious expression or one political party, and to focus on these overlaps in preferences ignores the primal power of the Belief in a Just World and related motivations like magical thinking. It is better to take on those primal instincts more directly.

As one early example of the experimental literature, many decades ago Melvin Lerner conducted an experiment in which two students apparently were set to work on a common task; one of the two was to receive a cash prize at the end through a pure lottery. An audience of fellow students were the subjects; they could hear but not see the two student workers. "Tom" (a former professional radio announcer) was described by the student audience as "tall, dark, and handsome," and "Bill" as "thin, with glasses." Regardless of who won the prize, the student audience felt drawn to Tom over Bill. The audience nonetheless convinced themselves that whoever won the pure lottery must have "deserved" to do so through having worked harder on the assigned task (which factually was untrue). Further, when Tom won the after-task lottery, all was right in the world, and his performance was particularly highly rated. When Bill won, the audience deprecated the efforts of both workers.[13]

Or consider this. The year is 1971. The war in Vietnam is raging. For the first time in a generation, the Selective Service Draft has been reinstated, with those young men whose birthdays fall on a date picked early in the lottery likely to serve in the war. If you were a nineteen-year-old male in 1971 and received a late number in the draft, so that you were unlikely to be called up, would that change how you feel about yourself? Would the numbers that other men received in the draft change what you thought of them? In both cases the outcome of the lottery should have had no effect, because its results were driven wholly by chance. And yet the self-esteem of those who received high numbers rose, and those with low numbers fell. More interestingly, while in most cases the young men felt empathy for those with low draft numbers, within one group the effect was precisely the opposite: those men who scored highly on a test for their Belief in a Just World were likely to deprecate their counterparts with low numbers, as if the cosmos somehow had decided that these young men were more expendable than most.[14]

More troubling, strong adherents to the Belief in a Just World were quick to derogate a "victim" in a controlled experiment as deserving her fate, even when the "facts" were established that the victim was innocent of any responsibility for that fate. In other words, the participants overlaid onto the "victim" a moral failure of their own construction to explain why an innocent victim was suffering, where none existed within the reality of the experiment.

This victim derogation has been replicated countless times, in ever more carefully controlled experiments; it is now seen as one of the classic examples of the maladaptive mental constructs to which those with a strong Belief in a Just World are subject. In one famous setup, the purported victim was a young woman receiving (fake) electric shocks; when audiences were offered the opportunity to vote to compensate her for her suffering, they felt more at ease, because they had restored justice. When the audience was not offered this opportunity, however, those with a strong Belief in a Just World responded in an extraordinary way that reveals the heart of the maladaptive side of this phenomenon: they blamed the victim for her situation. This derogation of the victim was even more pronounced when the audience was told that she had volunteered for the assignment. (Fortunately for the fate of humanity, not all audience members responded in this way; some thought the entire enterprise to be pointless and cruel.)[15] Other experiments have replicated this result by presenting to an audience a young woman who was said to have contracted an STD in different circumstances.

In other experiments, "corpses" of pretty young women "killed" in staged accidents elicited greater emotional responses than did corpses of plain ones, and physically attractive (and alive) people were judged to "deserve" better outcomes than less attractive ones, because if one is attractive, then surely that happy outcome must be the outward sign of inner virtue.[16] So too, if under the facts of an experiment a "bad" person were to be in an automobile accident, where the victim's prior behavior had no connection to the accident, participants in the experiment nonetheless were more likely to conclude that the "bad" person deserved his fate.[17]

Magical thinking and a Belief in a Just World often overlap. In one experiment, students were contacted on one of two dates, either four weeks before midterms or two days before midterms, and were asked to volunteer to read to a blind student. Those students with low Beliefs in a Just World were unaffected by the timing of the request. Students with strong Beliefs in a Just World volunteered at about the same rate as did their low-belief counterparts when contacted four weeks before midterms. When students were contacted two days before midterms, however, the strong-belief students volunteered much more than did their low-belief counterparts. The apparent reason is that since people get what they deserve, by doing virtuous acts two days before midterms (instead of studying more, it should be noted), the high-belief students were increasing their deservingness, and therefore setting themselves up for the cosmic reward of better midterm grades.[18]

In sum, the experimental literature is convincing that the Belief in a Just World is not some simple cultural meme that good things happen to good people, stemming from the consumption of too many Disney movies. We are susceptible to a short in our hard wiring, through which we confuse character with outcomes. This is what I mean by the moralization of randomness: we overlay inferences about the nature of people from the circumstances in which we observe them.

As already intimated, the maladaptive side of the Belief in a Just World has pro-found implications for our relationships as citizens to one another, because its false logic provides a means to derogate the character or equality claims of others who are simply in bad circumstances. As one tragic example, many wellsprings feed anti-Semitism, but there is suggestive evidence that the Belief in a Just World has played a part in the derogation of Jews, whether in the case of ordinary Germans under the Nazi regime, or in the United States during the same time frame, where anti-Semitism among Americans increased along with the Nazi atrocities.[19] To the same effect, the Belief in a Just World can easily combine with underexamined racist or sexist instincts to confirm that persons of color, or women, somehow de-serve any economic hardships they might face.

The more general point is that the Belief in a Just World enables people to conveniently deny the existence of bad brute luck in others' lives—and to rest in psychic comfort with respect to every material advantage that life has thrown their way. At every turn, a high-belief individual infers pathways of causation that ex-plain other individuals' circumstances, which causes in turn all relate back to the putative character of the individuals being observed. In the same way, the good fortune of a high-belief individual carries no moral awkwardness, because that good fortune must relate to the believer's own deservingness. Randomness is pushed out of the picture, and thus insurance also loses any purpose. Cancer no longer is something that happens to people, but rather something that happens to people who deserve to contract cancer. The same extends to poverty or other diffi-cult circumstances.

For example, in 1985 Kevin Smith published a paper analyzing the attitudes of Americans to those in different socioeconomic circumstances.[20] He proposed and then tested six hypotheses applicable to individuals who were strong adherents to the Belief in a Just World: first, that they would perceive less inequality in America than would others; second, that they would find those inequalities that do exist as fair; third, that they would derogate the poor; fourth, that they would praise the wealthy; fifth, that they would stress "individualistic" explanations of wealth and poverty over structural ones; and sixth, that they would see inequalities as rela-tively inevitable. Smith's results supported all six hypotheses, although admittedly some more strongly than others.

More recently, Lauren Appelbaum and colleagues designed a complex and in-teresting study around "Lisa," a fictitious character struggling to escape poverty. Participants were presented with different scenarios and asked whether Lisa was deserving of government assistance. Participants who were strong adherents of the Belief in a Just World were willing to recommend government assistance when Lisa was doing little to better herself. Extraordinarily, however, when adherents of the Belief in a Just World were presented with a scenario in which Lisa struggled mightily, but remained mired in poverty, those participants found their Belief in a Just World threatened by Lisa's failure, and as a result found her to be *less* deserving of aid than when Lisa did not make any significant effort.[21] These findings of a correlation between the Belief in a Just World and the derogation of the poor and admiration for the rich fits directly into the experimental results of Lerner and others mentioned earlier, in which students would effectively turn on one of their own by concluding that her miserable circumstances (e.g., being subjected to electric shocks) implied that she must in some way have deserved her fate.

The Belief in a Just World theory provides an explanation for the etiology and power of this preconscious mode of thought. As such, it helps in the interpretation of academic work by specialists working in other disciplines. For example, the sociologist Jonathan Mijs attracted attention in 2019 with a paper demonstrating that individuals in unequal societies (like the United States) are more accepting of inequality than are citizens of more egalitarian countries. The reason, he found, is that the more unequal a society, the more likely are its citizens to believe that those inequalities are attributable to differences in merit:

> [W]hat explains citizens' consent to inequality is their conviction that poverty and wealth are the outcomes of a fair meritocratic process. Citizens' meritocracy beliefs are solidified by the fact that people are unable to see the full extent of inequality in their society, nor develop an awareness of the structural processes shaping unequal life outcomes. The reason for people's inability to see what separates them from their fellow citizens is that the lives of the rich and poor are increasingly divided between separate institutions: people live in neighborhoods, go to schools and pick romantic partners and friends that fit their education and income level. . . .
>
> While countries have grown more unequal since the 1980s, nowhere have citizens lost faith in meritocracy. In fact, the empirical record suggests that belief in meritocracy in the Western world has never been as strong as it is today.[22]

The factors that Mijs lists are relevant, at least in the United States, but they do not by themselves seem sufficient to explain the steadily increasing *belief* in meritocracy. The Belief in a Just World offers that explanation. Moreover, since it is a device for resolving cognitive dissonance, the Belief in a Just World becomes more entrenched as its premises are threatened—just as Mijs found.

The economist Matthew Weinzierl has also recently explored Americans' surprisingly accepting attitudes toward inequality.[23] Simplifying, Weinzierl constructed a survey that posed a hypothetical fact pattern involving two individuals, imaginatively named A and B. A coin is flipped; A wins, and receives $60,000; B receives $30,000. But there is a catch: A and B must collectively pay $18,000 as the cost of the game. The question for survey recipients was: What was the fairest way for them, as observers rather than participants, to allocate this burden between A and B?

To complicate things further, a survey participant could direct one party to pay more than $18,000, in which case the "excess" would go to the other party.

Weinzierl in effect had set up a question of tax policy, where the $18,000 is the tax due from all players on their winnings, and any excess payments reflect the "redistribution" of the remaining lucky profits from one to the other. If survey participants were smart enough to understand the question, and if they had fully internalized that the initial distribution of $60,000 to A and $30,000 to B was entirely a matter of brute luck, then they might be expected to reach the "economic" answer that A should pay $24,000. That would cover the $18,000 tax bill, and leave another $6,000 to go to B, raising B's "after-tax" winnings to $36,000, and leaving A as well with $36,000. In other words, since the initial distribution of winnings ($60,000/$30,000) was driven entirely by brute luck, and since the facts did not admit of any way to distinguish A from B, survey participants might logically have chosen not to give any weight to the initial distribution, and instead considered only the final "after-tax" allocation.

But, of course, that is not what the survey participants did. The great majority of participants did not fully offset the initial distribution through the "tax" allocations that the survey participants controlled. In effect, they imbued the initial distributions as having moral significance—as something to which A in particular was entitled—when the only fact that supported this belief was that A "won" the game of chance. Weinzierl relates this preference among survey participants to a belief in "classical benefits-based taxation"—that taxes should follow from how much someone benefits from the economic system, where pretax income carries weight as the indicator of that benefit.

Perhaps. For some individuals, pretax lucky winnings might hold the same moral status as pretax earnings due to effort or talent, either for no considered reason, or because the game was fairly played and the consequences must then be accorded weight, or *faut de mieux*. After all, no one suggests confiscating the wealth of a Mega Millions lottery winner—but perhaps the reason we do not is that confiscation would mean that no one would play the next time around.

To my mind, however, the explanation for the attitude of many participants probably lies farther from the domain of economics. Looking past the possibility that some participants were simply unable to solve the calculations required fully to equalize A and B, Weinzierl might have stumbled onto a perfect illustration of the Belief in a Just World. Survey participants could not help but unconsciously inject deservingness into A's "pretax" winnings, simply because A won them. This is consistent as well with another recent paper, cited by Weinzierl, that found that Americans were more tolerant than were Norwegians of differences in pretax incomes attributable to differences in luck as well as in ability as having moral valence, just as Mijs also found.[24]

THE AGE OF CHASTISEMENT

The Belief in a Just World literature nicely complements the work of Yascha Mounk in his important book, *The Age of Responsibility*.[25] Mounk's central point is that our public policies have been reshaped over the last several decades to focus on a poor person's deservingness, rather than her needs. Society has been reconceived to have no duties (no responsibility) to the poor in general, and income-support programs have become exercises in probing the putative character of the unfortunate (her willingness to accept personal responsibility for her predicament).

In Mounk's view, the word "responsibility" thus has been turned on its head. Those of us who have done well have no responsibility to others—why should we, given that we got what we deserved?—while those who struggle financially have not yet internalized that they bear responsibility for their economic failures, through some shortcoming in their characters—which is why they've gotten what they deserved as well.

Mounk argues that politicians over the last several decades increasingly have sought to design incentives for the poor based on their "taking responsibility" for their predicaments, without much regard for actual circumstances or available resources. At every turn, the poor are classified as deserving or undeserving, based on this perceived duty to take responsibility. Mounk writes, "Far from being a realm in which citizens are guaranteed a basic social minimum irrespective of their ability to succeed on the market, the welfare state has, in central respects, come to mirror the market's responsibility-tracking attributes."[26]

What's wrong with asking people to take responsibility for themselves? Of course, that is a desirable state of self-regulation, but institutionalizing deservingness as the key that unlocks public assistance leads to pernicious outcomes, because it requires "fine-grained distinctions between those who have supposedly acted 'responsibly' and those who have supposedly acted 'irresponsibly.' Responsibility-tracking institutions thus routinely force welfare applicants to go through a humiliating application process, in the course of which they are forced to divulge potentially embarrassing information about their private lives."[27]

Politicians on the left who resist calls to cut income-support programs have been reduced to arguing that such programs are required to address outcomes traceable to a low-income person's brute luck rather than to his option luck (the outcomes of choices consciously made). But this requires the same sort of fine-grained cross-examination to determine which sort of luck explains the predicament of each individual in poverty.

In our zeal to root out the lazy and to offer minimal benefits only to the most deserving of the poor, we have set ourselves up as a sort of secular Inquisition into the morals, motivations, and effort of our own fellow citizens. In so doing we have thrown away any sense of actual connection to them—any sense that we are all fully cooperating members of a society of free and equal citizens. Like any Inquisition, our methods are cruel—perhaps made crueler in practice by the wide-spread misperception that the poor are Others, too easily distinguished in many cases by the color of their skins.

These inquisitorial methods are ethically corrosive and are doomed to practical failure, because just as in theology, inquiries into First Causes (in this case, the ultimate causes of a person's situation) are always inconclusive. But the methods employed are profoundly demeaning, and by being so assert the oppression of some citizens over other putatively equal ones.

The Belief in a Just World and Mounk's arguments come together in showing how eager we are to infer a person's character through the false logic of an imagined chain of causation. Our construction of a causal pathway begins with current circumstances and works backward to past personal moral or character defects that must have determined these current circumstances. Both modes of thought de-mean the individual who finds herself in difficult circumstances, and both aggres-sively deny the existence of just plain bad luck in explaining those circumstances. By denying luck its due, these beliefs *moralize randomness*, to our collective shame.

The Belief in a Just World and the new age of individual responsibility assume away the fact that our own social institutions themselves deserve the lion's share of the blame for many deeply unequal circumstances, in ways that cannot be laid at the feet of Fortune and her Wheel. If we wish to embark on a systematic inquiry into responsibility, or into whether we really get what we deserve, we should begin by considering the responsibilities we collectively bear for the social institutions that we have chosen to adopt.

By considering only real or imagined individualistic factors, the Belief in a Just World and our topsy-turvy interpretation of responsibility ignore the power of highly imperfect social institutions colored by racism, sexism, and other institu-tional biases as explanatory factors. And finally, both modes of thought comfort the comfortable, because again finding oneself in congenial material circumstances must evidence the strong moral backbone of an individual who has taken respon-sibility for himself, and so is entitled to reap the rewards of his strong character. Because they operate through similar mechanisms, the two modes of thought lead to overdetermined belief systems, which is to say beliefs that are very difficult for believers to outgrow and replace with more nuanced understandings of the causes of differences in our respective material outcomes.

VERY RICH, NO THANKS TO LUCK

It is not original on my part to note that narcissism stalks great wealth like a shadow on a sunny day. On the occasion of any paper that I write, I am provided with a fresh example. Like manna from heaven, these narcissistic expressions appear, as if for my convenience, in the form of a confessional by some rich man (they are always men) explaining why he is aggrieved that he is insufficiently admired.

One well-publicized recent example is the angry missive penned by Leon Cooperman, a billionaire, to Senator Elizabeth Warren in October 2019.[28] (I introduced this letter in Chapter 1.) This followed the same general pattern as a letter that he wrote to President Obama several years earlier, and even repeated a couple of paragraphs of his sanitized autobiography.[29] I'll skip over the faults in Cooperman's economic arguments in favor of the psychological side of things.

In his letter to Senator Warren, Cooperman acknowledged in passing that luck had been on his side, but he emphasized his modest family background and his hard work as by themselves explaining his great wealth—along with the great wealth of some other "self-made billionaires" he listed. Oddly, in summarizing his brilliant career, Cooperman skipped over his invoking the Fifth Amendment in 2016 to avoid testifying in connection with criminal charges alleging that he had engaged in insider stock trading.[30] Cooperman's firm ultimately paid a multimillion-dollar fine to settle this case.

Throughout, Cooperman's argument in his letter was that self-made billionaires provide useful goods and services—an almost self-evident point (how else would they be billionaires?) that answers nothing about how tax policy should address these great concentrations of wealth—and therefore are to be admired for their contributions to society. Cooperman did not consider that others of equal intelligence and industriousness have had to make do with a great deal less than his $3 billion or so.

More important, Cooperman offered no theory as to the size of the ethical obligations—what Chapter 8 calls the social mortgage—that attaches to truly great wealth, whether inherited or "self-made." His position though was plain— billionaires should pay taxes, but not too much, and only of the sort he authorized.

Ordinary mortals engage in internal dialogues through which they negotiate with death; billionaires like Cooperman, by contrast, believe that they can negotiate with the United States as equal parties in interest to set the terms under which they will agree to be taxed. The fact that we conduct tax policy in just this manner, by polling the wealthiest individuals or the most profitable corporations to inquire as to what sort of taxation they might be willing to accept, is testament to the sorry state of our political processes, not an endorsement of this as a norm.

At one point in his letter, Cooperman suggested that he would accept a 50 percent income tax rate. My skeptical response to this empty talk is to say that I would love to see him present at the signing ceremony when that is enacted into law.

Like other billionaires, Cooperman believes that he is a better steward of largesse than is the U.S. government, and he therefore presumptively should be kept with more assets that he can control and disburse in favored charitable endeavors. (As it happens, as best I can determine, Cooperman's "named" gifts in recent years amount to much less than $100 million—more than I give, but not a great sum in relation to $3 billion of assets.)[31] This is a common form of narcissism, often expressed by billionaires in words to the effect that they would be willing to pay more in tax, if only the government were not so bloated, inefficient, and corrupt. At every turn, there is contempt for the democratic political process in favor of the position that the very rich can be trusted to do right by way of their charities—as if one were a meaningful trade-off for the other.

Whether billionaires who write these sorts of letters are motivated by a supercharged Belief in a Just World, in which their great rewards prove their incomparable ineffable talents, or whether instead these billionaires simply are narcissists, is not really very important. What is important is their intense attachment to their wealth as a signifier of their value, and a simultaneous frustration that not enough people honor them for this. When they invite Senator Warren and others to negotiate with them, it is a trap—one designed to subvert the democratic process in favor of uncontentious bonhomie, affirmation of the billionaire set's egos, and modest tax burdens.

Cooperman and his fellow billionaires of course find support as well as criticism from academics. My favorite in this regard is Gerard J. Tellis, who cohabits my university with me (albeit in different schools). In a long opinion piece published in *The Hill*, Tellis explained that there cannot be such a thing as luck, because people whom he admired and who succeeded in capturing great wealth were obviously intelligent and industrious.[32] Would he have felt further vindicated were I to report that all four of the winners in my coin toss game exercised vigorously, followed a draconian fruitarian diet, and scored highly on IQ tests?

Tellis rightly noted that success is skewed far to the right-hand side of the income distribution (i.e., only a few people are "superstars" who capture great wealth), but that simply tells us who was successful, and says nothing about why. Tellis proclaimed that "success flows from unusual talent, extreme effort, extraordinary risks and relentless persistence against failure." All these admirable qualities are easy to spot in retrospect, but this observation is uninformative about whether the self-made individuals he lists were alone in possessing these virtues at the outset of their careers. Superstars have superior talents, but that tells us nothing about the entire population of people with superior talents.

Like Cooperman, Tellis explained that highly successful people employ many ordinary folk, which is reason enough to say thank you to these rich souls, and that many successful entrepreneurs are immigrants, as if that had any relevance other than as some sort of political distraction. Tellis listed the many accomplishments of Thomas Edison, apparently because if it were not for him and him alone,

I would be showering in the dark. And of course Tellis employed the same sort of throwaway leaps of illogic as did Cooperman, to the effect that the Soviet Union didn't work out so well, so we should keep a respectful distance from taxing those who today measure their net worth in the billions.

Tellis's infatuation with Thomas Edison is particularly ironic, given the obvious comparison of Edison to his great competitor, Nikola Tesla. Tesla was a scientific genius, not simply an inventor, and it was Tesla's alternating current system of electricity distribution that ultimately prevailed over Edison's—notwithstanding Edison's borderline business ethics. But Tesla did not die rich, in part because of completely unrelated financial bad luck (the panic of 1890) that put pressure on Tesla's champion, Westinghouse, and indirectly on Tesla, and in part because Tesla spent all his money pursuing new ideas, in particular the transmission of electric power wirelessly.

Contrary to Tellis, superstars do not prove the nonexistence of luck in our lives. To the contrary, the evidence presented in Chapters 3 and 4 clearly points to an in-escapable core of brute luck that now propels us along, and now holds us back. Nor does great success mean that fortunate individuals should be entitled to opt out of serious tax burdens, as the warning shots of Tellis and Cooperman are designed to imply. We all understand that at some point crushing taxation is counterpro-ductive, but all the evidence points to the fact that we are a very long way from that point. The effective tax burdens of superstars are at most in the low 20s as a percentage of their economic incomes, and in some cases far lower than that. People like Cooperman and Tellis wish to blanket policy debates with a dense fog of admiration for the rich, from inside which taxing them at more reasonable rates becomes misperceived as class warfare.

The most interesting side of things—the willingness of ordinary people to ad-mire the rich because their wealth must signify some sort of great inner merit—fits directly into justice motive theory. The phenomenon has been studied at least since Adam Smith wrote his first great book, *The Theory of Moral Sentiments*, about 250 years ago. In that treatise, Smith wrote:

> This disposition to admire, and almost to worship, the rich and the powerful, and to despise, or, at least, to neglect persons of poor and mean condition, . . . is the great and most universal cause of the corruption of our moral sentiments. That wealth and greatness are often regarded with the respect and admiration which are due only to wisdom and virtue; and that the contempt . . . is often most unjustly bestowed upon poverty and weakness, has been the complaint of moralists in all ages. . . .
>
> We frequently see the respectful attentions of the world more strongly directed towards the rich and the great, than towards the wise and the virtuous. . . . The great mob of mankind are the admirers and the worshippers, and, what may seem more

extraordinary, most frequently the disinterested admirers and worshippers, of wealth and greatness.[33]

For all his brilliance, Smith did not have a very good explanation for this phenomenon, but Smith was working only with history and intuition as his analytical instruments. Nonetheless, Smith was pointing in the right direction: we admire the rich simply because they are rich, and we derogate the poor precisely for their poverty. The Belief in a Just World provides a satisfying explanation for this otherwise odd behavior: we believe that people get what they deserve, and deserve what they get.

The remarkable fact in all this is how much mental effort we expend to deny the existence of luck, even though its universal presence is as plain as the nose on your face. Instead we have locked ourselves into prisons of our own fashioning, in which the bars are made from a fundamental delusion. We rely on that delusion to ward off the terror of a more direct understanding of reality and to evade the painful search for more courageous principles around which to fashion our lives and make long-term plans. We undertake this enormous mental effort even when it requires that we imbue the rich with some indescribably great ability whose only physical evidence is the existence of the wealth we observe.

Life is not like *The Matrix*, and I have no red pills to distribute to readers. I do hope, however, that as you work through the remainder of this book you have occasion to reflect on the power of the fundamental delusion this chapter has described, in the hope that the solutions I offer might not seem quite so crackpot after all.

PART II

EQUALITY OF OPPORTUNITY BETRAYED

CHAPTER 3

BORN ON THIRD BASE—OR OUT ON THE STREET?

INEQUALITY OF INCOMES YIELDS INEQUALITY IN OPPORTUNITIES

What's so bad about economic inequality? Economists like to observe that inequalities in income or wealth are the fuel that makes private markets function (because if you have more than do I, I will work that much harder to catch up), and up to a point that is true. The reason we should care about extreme economic inequality of the sort visible in the United States today is threefold: First, the United States is unique among rich countries in how much private wealth it requires of its citizens to fund investments in their own or their children's human capital (principally through education and healthcare).[1] Second, economic inequality by definition means that some families will find these investments much easier to make than do families with modest financial resources. Third, these differences are imposed on children by virtue of their family circumstances, not by reason of who they are.

So long as we rely so heavily on private sources to fund investment in human capital and healthcare, where will most Americans find those resources, and thereby live prosperous and satisfying lives according to their own lights? That is, can we honor the national credo of equality of opportunity when the resources available to millions of young people to invest in themselves are insufficient to the task? Research and our own engagement with the world both demonstrate that while some are able to escape the handicaps of poverty or racial discrimination, many cannot—and no one deserves to be required to run an obstacle course when others are offered a smooth and straight track.

My interest is the plight of ordinary Americans. The importance of income and wealth inequality to this book is that it systematically vitiates our ability to breathe life into authentic equality of opportunity, given that our society allocates investments in human capital and healthcare largely on the basis of private family resources. Further, top-end inequality is relevant to the design of tax policy instruments, in particular the progressive income tax and functioning gift and estate taxes (Chapter 9). Beyond that, I do not have an agenda to level the rich down to size; I am not engaged in an exercise in envy.

Another way of saying this is that my focus is on leveling up, not down. I wish to improve the prospects for most Americans to develop and pursue the best lives they can in light of their own talents and ambitions, which, as I argue throughout, requires a reorientation in our attitudes to appreciate the heavy hand of adverse birth luck on lifetime prospects, and a concomitant commitment to public resources to respond to it. I completely appreciate that there are vitally important additional social issues surrounding top-end inequality relating to the power of great wealth to bend the levers of government to its own ends, but that really is the subject of a different book.[2]

Many readers will approach this chapter's discussion of the runaway growth over the last few decades in the incomes and wealth of top earners with a predisposition to believe that this narrative is true. The good news here is that this intuition is basically borne out by the research, so if you wish to skim this material, no great harm will be done to my narrative. From the other direction, there is a sort of mini-industry within the economics profession and the commentariat carping that the most visible academic proponents of the accelerating top-end inequality story overstate their case. The difference in claims, however, relates primarily to the rate of *acceleration* in top-end inequality growth, not to the basic idea that the *velocity* of this growth continues to separate further the most affluent citizens from the rest of us.

This chapter does not emphasize another phenomenon unique to the United States that is directly relevant to my agenda: the shocking number of Americans who continue to live in dire poverty. I defer this depressing topic until Chapter 8. Nonetheless, it is worth laying down a marker here.

When we look to our peer countries in the Organisation for Economic Co-operation and Development (the OECD), we find that we do less to mitigate poverty, and that we inevitably are left with much higher poverty rates, than is true of any of our peers, given that we start with such high levels of income inequality. The OECD is a sort of trade association and information clearinghouse for the world's largest economies (other than the BRICs—Brazil, Russia, India, and China), along with some hangers-on, like Turkey, the Slovak Republic, and Lithuania. It is funded by the member countries and is scrupulously data-driven in its research, given the disparate policy agendas of its members. It collects data from its thirty-four member countries (and in some cases from others) and presents the information in a consistent fashion.

The data in Figure 3.1, from the OECD, tell the story.[3] The poverty level used here, in keeping with the OECD's definitions, is set at one-half the national median income. (This is a different definition from that used by US domestic government agencies.) The data are after-tax, after-government transfer numbers.

Here again we see equality of opportunity smothered in its crib.

No other developed economy has anywhere close to the US level of poverty. In France, the poverty rate is just over 8 percent of the population; in the United States, applying the OECD's metrics, the rate is almost 18 percent. Top-end incomes and wealth can help to fund the public interventions necessary to fund public investment in human capital, because those public interventions are the only way that adverse birth luck can be addressed and meaning restored to our credo of equality of opportunity.

Following the publication of Thomas Piketty's magisterial *Capital in the 21st Century*,[4] dozens of books and academic papers have appeared on the topic of income and wealth inequality, expounding, elaborating, criticizing, or denying Piketty's fundamental themes: first, that income and wealth inequality in the United States in particular have increased dramatically in recent decades; second, inequality has grown from the very top (as opposed to the bottom falling out at the other end of the income/wealth distribution); and, third, that in the absence

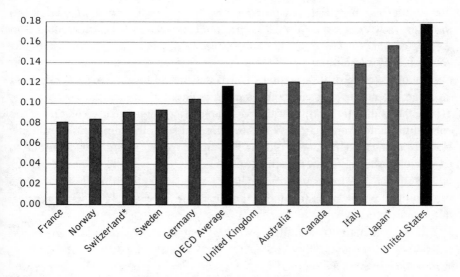

FIGURE 3.1 Poverty Rate, Selected Developed Economies (2017)

Source: OECD Income Distribution Database, September 10, 2019.

of government intervention, income and wealth concentration will continue to increase, because the return on capital (investments) over time exceeds the rate of growth of the economy as a whole.[5]

This is not still another book dissecting the minutiae of these claims. My overarching focus in this chapter is on the grossly disproportionate resources that families can devote to their offspring. In the next chapter I show how we can see the effects of those disproportionate resources on life outcomes. All of this takes place against the background of a country that by design requires more by way of private resources to fund investment in human capital and healthcare than do most of our peer countries.

The social sciences do not progress in the linear fashion that we outsiders imagine that the physical sciences do: economists, for example, do not discover a new element or phenomenon and then simply build on it to the next discovery. Instead, like a swarm of angry bees, economists greet every new thesis with alternative explanations, differing assumptions, or confounding conclusions drawn from different data sets. Only gradually, over time, and from a distance can the swarm of bees be seen to move in a coherent direction. This has been particularly true for Piketty's work, because its enormous success precipitated an inevitable blizzard of carping, nitpicking, and alternative measurements. That is how the social sciences proceed, but it is not a particularly enjoyable process for outsiders to watch. How many readers, for example, wish to weigh in on whether we should measure economic progress by reference to "households," "families," or "tax units"? Or whether we should measure "wage income" or "total income"?[6]

Nonetheless, the public imagination and the consensus view of economists converge on some straightforward propositions: income and wealth inequality in the United States is very high, and top-end inequality has increased substantially in the last few decades.

The next section of this chapter, "Failed Policies and Public Anger," advances my larger agenda by discussing the economic plight of the median worker—the man or woman in the middle of the pack. Scholarly and popular focus on the top 1 percent and their toys has diverted our attention from the hundreds of millions in the middle to a handful of millions (the top 1 percent amounts by definition to 3.3 million) or fewer fellow citizens.

The section titled "Income Inequality in a Nutshell" then briefly reviews the current state of inquiry on income inequality at the top end, relying wherever possible on the most anodyne of sources.

Following this, the section titled "Wealth Inequality" focuses on a more important point for this book, which is the surprising amount of wealth in America that is inherited, rather than earned from scratch. (For convenience, I treat lifetime gifts as falling within the scope of bequests or inheritances—the important point is not when the gratuitous transfer is made, but rather that much wealth depends on one's parents or grandparents taking a liking to one, rather than the sweat of one's brow.) And critically, these gratuitous transfers do not all come in the form of new polo mallets for Christmas. When affluent parents stuff their children with education, those acts also are gratuitous transfers, and ones that have happy implications for a child's lifetime earnings.

Inherited wealth changes everything—from standard economic income tax theory to equality of opportunity, to the consequences of bad luck more generally.

In the long run, the inequality that matters is wealth inequality, and in particular inherited wealth. But income inequality begets wealth inequality, because income not spent this year becomes an addition to next year's stockpile of wealth. For this reason, and because income inequality is a bit more susceptible to quantification than is wealth inequality, the place to start is by summarizing trends in income inequality.

FAILED POLICIES AND PUBLIC ANGER

Would you like to see our fractious politics and our public policy failings explained in just a couple of figures? First, take a look at Figure 3.2:

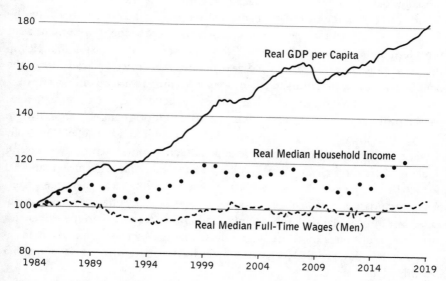

FIGURE 3.2 Real GDP Per Capita, Median Household Incomes, and Male Full-Time Wages (1984–2018)

Source: US Bureau of Economic Analysis, Federal Reserve Bank of St. Louis.

What this figure reveals is that, in real (that is, inflation-adjusted) terms, our national income has grown pretty steadily. Adjusted for the growth in population, our inflation-adjusted Gross Domestic Product (GDP) was 81 percent higher at the beginning of 2019 than it was in 1984; that's a compounded real growth rate of about 1.75 percent per year. (Don't confuse this with the usual nominal growth rate data that you read, which includes inflation as part of the growth rate and which does not adjust for the growth in our population.)

On average, then, each of us might reasonably expect to have roughly 80 percent higher real incomes than we did thirty-five years ago. Sounds like we're doing great!

But then look at real median household incomes. This curve shows how the median household (whichever household was smack in the middle of incomes for each year) has done from 1984 to the beginning of 2017 (the last available date as of the time of this writing). There we see a much more disappointing state of affairs: real median household incomes over that period went up only 21.5 percent, not the 76 percent that real GDP per capita recorded to that date. Measures of household income are affected by lots of statistical exotica, including the definition of how we assign individuals to households, and household sizes have changed over the last few decades, but however adjusted, the trend remains obvious.

Finally, look at how the median (again, the middle of the pack) male full-time worker has been doing in inflation-adjusted terms. The answer is shocking: the median working man took home only 4.5 percent more at the beginning of 2019 in real terms than did his father thirty-five years earlier—and most of that pickup came in a single year (2018). In the year ending May 2019, and despite all the hoopla, average real (inflation-adjusted) weekly earnings were up only 1 percent.[7]

Median household income has done somewhat better over time than the wages received by the median male worker, but the reasons for this largely come down to the entry into the workforce of the second-to-earn adult in a household (typically a wife), and the narrowing of the wage gap between incomes earned by male and female workers for the same work. (A large and inexcusable gap still remains, of course.) In many cases this no doubt represents the liberation of women from socially ordained careers inside the household, but in many other cases it is attributable, not to personal preferences, but to a family's responses to the exigencies required to make ends meet. In other words, whether increases in household income translate directly into increasing household welfare (life satisfactions) is a very difficult question.

Over the course of 2018 and 2019, unemployment fell to record-low levels. But this figure measures only the quantity of jobs held by Americans looking for work and overlooks several troubling undercurrents. One is that the labor participation rate—the percentage of working-age Americans who are employed—has trended down for decades; unemployment figures exclude individuals who have given up on finding a job or who otherwise are detached from the workforce. A deeper and less appreciated problem is that too many newly created jobs are low-quality ones, when measured in terms of their wages, their prospects for advancement, and their working conditions. These low-wage jobs also typically bring with them fewer available hours of work per week, putting further pressure on take-home pay. According to a major study by the Brookings Institution on this phenomenon, 53 million Americans age 18–64 (44 percent of the workforce) hold such low-quality jobs.[8] Cornell University researchers have moved to bring more clarity to bear on the quality of job formation, not just the quantity, in a newly developed index, the US Private Sector Job Quality Index.[9] Their retrospective analysis shows that that job quality has steadily declined since 1990, meaning that over time a higher percentage of Americans who work full time have done so at jobs with lower pay and lower hours than the national median.

One objection frequently offered to my reliance on household incomes is that it understates the true economic gains captured by middle-class households, because certain kinds of income are invisible in these data. In particular, about 160 million Americans obtain health insurance from their employers. For technical reasons not relevant here, employer contributions to these plans do not show up in the data I have just summarized (or in employees' taxable incomes). If one adds in the cost of these employer contributions, on the theory that they are substitutes for cash wages that otherwise would be paid, the economic path of the middle class over time does not look quite so dire.

I discussed this canard at length in *We Are Better Than This*, but very quickly, the flaw in the argument is that it presupposes that health insurance premiums represent fair value.[10] In fact, as Chapter 10 summarizes, our health insurance markets are dominated by what economists call "rent-seeking" behavior, and which the rest of us call getting ripped off. Insurers, hospitals, drug makers, and medical practices all abuse monopoly power or access to government regulation to increase their profits, not deliver more value to the average citizen. There is, after all, a reason why we spend 18 percent of our GDP on healthcare yet have worse outcomes than do other countries that spend half as much. (For the record, Switzerland right now is Number 2 in the profligacy of its healthcare spending, at 12 percent of its GDP. If we spent at the same rate as does Switzerland, we would put about $1.3 *trillion*/year into the hands of citizens.) And as Chapter 10 reminds us, 28 million Americans today have no health coverage, and another 40 million are underinsured, in the sense that co-pays, deductibles, and other out-of-pocket expenses make it impossible for those citizens actually to avail themselves of their skinny coverage. Finally, the Congressional Budget Office data presented later in this chapter does include the value of employer contributions to employee health-care in its calculations, and yet the CBO reaches similar conclusions.[11]

Figure 3.3 below adds another depressing perspective on economic progress in America; the comparisons in this second figure also are adjusted for inflation. The chart comes from an important paper by economist Raj Chetty and a large team of colleagues analyzing trends in intergenerational earnings growth.[12] The Chetty team's work has been a triumph in the application of really big data (tens of millions of observations, combining several data sets that previously had resided in their own silos) to important social policy questions. It is the kind of analysis that could not have been undertaken even a couple of decades earlier.

The old joke is that a rising tide lifts all boats, and so too do good economic times make everyone feel richer. The Chetty team asked whether the rising tide of steadily increasing national income over a period of many decades lifted our in-dividual boats higher than those of our parents' crafts from a generation earlier? That is, how many Americans born in a given year emerged as adults earning more than their parents had done a generation earlier? Chetty and colleagues refer to this as "absolute" income mobility—a comparison in absolute inflation-adjusted dollars between what parents and children earned in their peak income years.

Is it not straightforward to see from Figures 3.2 and 3.3 the fundamental sources of anger that animate so much of our political discourse?

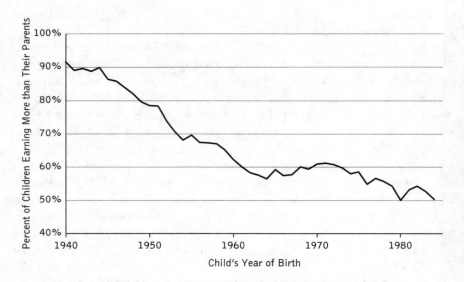

FIGURE 3.3 Percent of Children Earning More Than Their Parents, by Year of Birth

Source: Raj Chetty et al., "The Fading American Dream: Trends in Absolute Income Mobility since 1940," *Science*, issue 6336 (April 2017): 398–406.

You might expect that a child of an extremely successful parent at, say, the 99.9th income percentile would not invariably earn quite so much as her parent, and from the other direction you might also anticipate that the child of parents living in poverty has a good chance of doing better for himself than what his parents were able to learn. But what is particularly troubling about the Chetty research is that across virtually all parent income levels over four decades, kids have performed worse and worse at matching their parents' incomes (see Figure 3.4).

These charts would make intuitive sense if the US economy had limped along for the last several decades. If per capita national income in inflation-adjusted terms had made no progress, we would expect the median male worker not to have seen his wages grow by much, and we would further find it unsurprising that today's young adults would have difficulty exceeding their parents' incomes.

But the opposite is true. The real national per capita GDP of the United States (that is, adjusted for both population growth and inflation) grew more than 400 percent from 1947 through 2018 (from about $14,000 to $57,000 per capita, in constant 2012 dollars).[13]

The underlying message to which these charts point is that, while the country overall has gotten much richer over the last several decades, the middle-of-the-pack male worker has not, and the median household has done better largely by

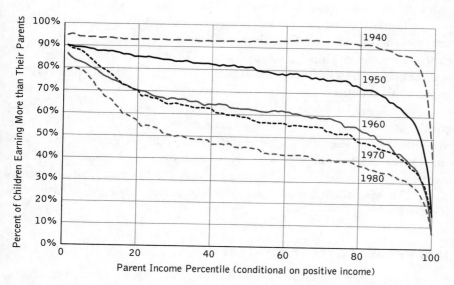

FIGURE 3.4 Percent of Children Earning More Than Their Parents, by Parent Income Percentile

Source: Raj Chetty et al., "The Fading American Dream: Trends in Absolute Income Mobility since 1940," *Science*, issue 6336 (April 2017): 398–406.

working more aggregate hours in the marketplace. At the same time, about one-half of Americans born in 1980 cannot match their parents' incomes.

How is it possible that against the backdrop of a steady increase in the amount of national income attributable to the average person, male median wages have been stuck for over three decades, and fewer and fewer children (in percentage terms) have grown up to earn more than their parents—from about 90 percent of children born in 1940 to about 50 percent of children born in 1984?[14]

More simply: where the hell did the money go? Money does not simply disappear without a trace—so who are the lucky devils who have walked away with a disproportionate share of this steady climb in per capita national income?

Chetty and his co-authors asked themselves this very question. They hypothesized that either or both of two long-term macroeconomic trends might explain the phenomenon. First, growth in real terms since, say, 1980 has been positive, but not as fast as growth in earlier decades. Second, economic inequality has increased. They crunched the numbers and demonstrated that increasing inequality over time was the big driver of their depressing findings.

In fairness, some modest part of the answer lies at the bottom quarter of the income distribution, where Medicare/Medicaid, "means-tested" transfer programs like the Earned Income Tax Credit (the "EITC"), and similar programs have made life more bearable in absolute but not relative terms.[15] (Very simply, the EITC is a very successful program designed to "make work pay." It subsidizes low-wage workers, particularly those with families. It does so in part because it is actually expensive to take the first step onto the wage-earning ladder—transportation, meal, and uniform costs are examples. The benefits of the EITC are aggressively clawed back as an employee's income starts to go up.) These are not extravagant gestures; in these policy moves the United States is, if anything, a laggard compared to other high-income countries.

As we will see later in the chapter, however, even taking taxes (including tax credits) and transfer payments into account, inequality has increased over time, driven by the top end of the income distribution pulling away from the rest of us. It turns out that the rich have gotten much richer, in absolute and relative terms, and in both income and wealth measures—just as most of us intuited all along. This has profound implications for the credo of equality of opportunity as it is lived.

INCOME INEQUALITY IN A NUTSHELL

Income inequality is difficult to measure, and the measurement of wealth inequality is an order of magnitude more difficult than that. Nonetheless, almost every nonpartisan government or supranational entity that has weighed in on the subject of income inequality has come to a conclusion that income inequality in the United States is worse than in other developed economies, and it has increased over time.

The traditional way to approach the measurement of income inequality is through what I call the "bottom-up" approach: tote up every individual's income, rank them, and look for trends over time. The alternative strategy, first comprehensively presented in an important 2018 paper by Thomas Piketty, Emmanuel Saez, and Gabriel Zucman, is what I call the "top-down" approach: use national income aggregates (from which Gross Domestic Product is derived), where we have good consistently developed data spanning many decades, and ask, Which Americans earned how much of that national income?[16] Neither approach is perfect, and economists love nothing more than to wrangle with each other about the limitations in each other's preferred data sets and the reasonableness of the assumptions that every economist working in this area must make.[17] Fortunately, both approaches tell a roughly similar story.

Moreover, we can ponder income inequality trends from two slightly different perspectives. We can ask, how much of national income growth is captured over time by, say, the top 1 percent? Or we can ask, as of any moment in time, what fraction of national income goes to the top 1 percent? The first is better at showing the absolute performance of any slice of the income distribution over time; the second captures shifts in relative performance. For example, a median (middle-of-the-pack) household might have enjoyed some absolute gains in income or wealth over the last thirty years, but at the same time have fallen even further behind the top 1 percent crowd—and indeed this is what the two measures show.[18]

Let's start with the bottom-up approach and with an irreproachably neutral authority, the Congressional Budget Office (CBO), the nonpartisan economic resource to Congress. This defers the buzz from the angry bees about my choices in data sources.

The CBO does particularly reliable work in this area, because it has access to the raw tax data of every taxpayer, and it has combined that body of data with non-tax data derived from the Federal Reserve's Survey of Consumer Finances and similar sources. (The non–tax return data are particularly relevant at lower income levels.) I do not always agree with how the CBO presents its conclusions, but the underlying data usually are provided online.

What has the CBO found? Basically that inequality growth comes from the very top of the income ladder—it's the top 1 percent who are pulling away from the rest of us and capturing an ever-growing share of the national income. (Other work has shown that even within the top 1 percent, it's the uppermost of that select group who are capturing the lion's share of the gains.)

The two most relevant income measures for discussing inequality are market incomes and after-tax/after-transfer incomes.[19] The former tells us what the private economy generates before the explicit intervention of government, and the latter tells us something about life as it is lived, beginning with market incomes, and then adjusting those by both tax liabilities and the most important instances of government spending directly attributable to individual citizens (Social Security, Medicare, Medicaid, and similar benefits).

Figure 3.5 displays the chart from the CBO's latest study on the subject[20] (July 2019, covering the period 1979–2016) that tracks after-tax/after-transfers income across different slices of the income distribution.[21] For example, from 1979 to 2016, the top 1 percent saw their incomes after paying tax, and after any government transfer payments to them, grow by 226 percent. Those in the middle (broadly defined) saw their incomes grow by 47 percent. (All these figures are adjusted for inflation, in this case by using constant 2016 dollars.)[22]

Unfortunately, the latest CBO study does not present a comparable chart of the growth in *market* income inequality—the results achieved before any government

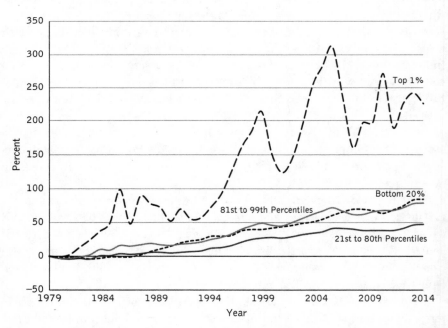

FIGURE 3.5 Cumulative Growth in Income After Transfers and Taxes, by Income Group (1979–2016)

Source: Congressional Budget Office.

intervention[23]—over the same period, but it does publish the underlying data online. The results are even more telling.

The top 1 percent's market income grew by 218 percent over the 1979–2016 period.[24] To make this more concrete, in 1979 the average member of the top 1 percent of income earners garnered $563,300 in market income—expressed in constant 2016 dollars. In 2016, however, the average member of the top 1 percent of market incomes earned $1,791,200—over three times as much, in inflation-adjusted terms.[25]

The top 1 percent's rise in market income (218 percent) was a bit behind their increase in after-tax/after-transfer income (226 percent). That is, this select club did better *after taxes* and transfers than they did before taking either into account, despite their market incomes more than tripling, because lower tax rates more than compensated for their being pushed into higher tax brackets. (The transfer payments they receive, like Social Security, net of the incremental taxes paid on those amounts by virtue of their high incomes, are so small relative to their total incomes as to be close to a rounding error.)

Meanwhile, the middle 60 percent of the population (from the 21st through the 80th income percentiles) fared much worse in the marketplace. The average of their market income growth in the 1979–2016 period was only 21 percent, as opposed to a 47 percent growth in their incomes after taxes and transfer payments (see Figure 3.5). Over the thirty-seven-year period, that's a compounded market income growth rate of about one-half of 1 percent per year.

In other words, for Americans in the middle, the growth in market returns to working has been very small, just as we saw in the figure that began this chapter. Why then did their after-tax, after-transfer incomes go up more than twice as much as did their market incomes? As noted earlier, the answer is that most income growth for the great majority of Americans has come in the form of larger Social Security and Medicare benefits, along with "means-tested" benefits, like the earned income tax credit. (Averaging across the three quintiles, tax burdens changed only a little.)

In turn, transfer payments are not distributed equally across age groups. Those old enough to qualify for Social Security and Medicare have seen a significant portion of their income growth come from these two programs. This is because the United States targets a large fraction of its social insurance programs to the elderly rather than to lower-income Americans more generally.

The larger point is that because the United States uniquely requires individuals or their families to scrounge up a large fraction of the money required to invest in those individuals' human capital (principally through education and healthcare), an economy in which working-age men and women have not seen their market incomes materially increase over the last several decades is one in which they will fall further and further behind those who can invest lavishly in their offspring's human capital. Social Security and Medicare are distant promises when one is trying to put one's children through school today.

The points just made about the importance of transfer payments as the driver of the modest income growth of the middle three income quintiles do not translate into the conclusion that entitlement spending is out of control. The United States in fact does much less in this department than do most of our high-income peer countries.[26]

It may occur to readers that if the incomes of the top 1 percent have grown at about the same rate after tax as before tax (because the tax rates imposed on their incomes have decreased over time), and Americans in the middle have also done better over time, but principally because transfer payments have gone up, some magic must be at work, because where are the tax revenues coming from to pay those higher benefits? The answer is twofold: first, while the effective tax rate imposed on the top 1 percent has gone down over time, their taxable incomes have soared, so there is more to throw into the pot. Second, the US government has run large deficits over the period, with the exception of the end of the Clinton administration. Transfer payments are in effect being funded with IOUs, but official income distribution studies (and most unofficial ones) do not make any effort to distribute to individuals their shares of the ever-increasing debt burdens represented by our cumulative deficits.

Look at it this way. The 2017 Trump tax cuts increased the after-tax incomes of most middle-class families, if not as much as is sometimes described. But the 2019 Trump trade tariffs imposed hidden taxes on consumers that basically wiped out any gains garnered in the 2017 tax cut.[27] If you lump the two together as "Trump tax policies" you see a very different picture of how those policies have affected the middle class than you do looking at the 2017 tax cuts alone. There is an even closer nexus between the income data we distribute and that which we ignore (the costs of paying for government transfers).

I fully anticipate that as the data roll in, the CBO's future work will show that income inequality continues to increase at the top end. The 2017 tax law, which reduced the tax rate on capital gains and corporate income, will accelerate this trend. None of this has yet to appear in the official data, but it has already surfaced in the spending habits at the top of the income ladder, as the hedge fund king Ken Griffin's 2019 $200 million+ purchase of an apartment in New York City suggests.[28]

Another way of looking at income is by charting changes in the standard measure of income inequality, known as the Gini Coefficient. It expresses the income inequality in a society as a single fraction, where 0 represents perfect equality in incomes and 1 represents perfect inequality (i.e., one lucky fellow capturing

100 percent of national income). This metric is itself imperfect, but not disablingly so. Moreover, it is widely used by inequality researchers.

The CBO also has calculated the Gini Coefficient over time (see Figure 3.6). In looking at those results, you should think about how much it takes to move the needle when dealing with an economy as large and diverse as that of the United States. From this perspective, the growth in the Gini Coefficient in the United States over time is staggering. In other words, the steady increase in the Gini Coefficient captures in one number a remarkable growth in income inequality over time:

Let us now consider the alternative approach to studying income inequality, what I call the "top-down" method, where one starts with the National Income and Product Accounts, the official statistics that measure the entire US economy, and then distributes that national income to individuals. This method has the advantage of cutting off most debate about whether this or that "invisible" form of income (e.g., the value of employer-provided healthcare) is captured in the data set one is using. The most important recent peer-reviewed, published paper from this direction is by Piketty, Saez, and Zucman.[29] (Within the field they are universally referred to as "PS&Z.") Along with a large team of other contributors, they regularly update their research for the United States and many other countries on a website, the World Inequality Database.[30]

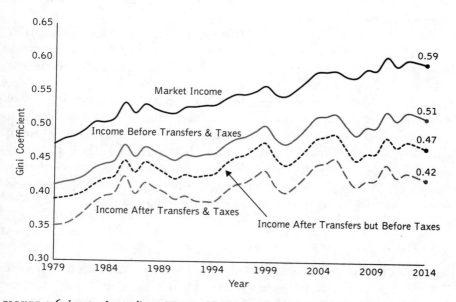

FIGURE 3.6 Income Inequality as Measured by the Gini Coefficient (1979–2016)
Source: Congressional Budget Office.

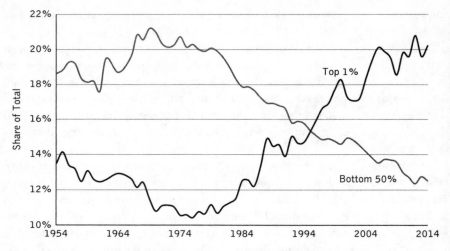

FIGURE 3.7 Income Inequality, USA, by Pre-Tax National Income (1954–2014)

Source: World Inequality Database.

Figure 3.7 summarizes their conclusions in graphic (and depressing) form. It shows the steady climb in the share of pretax[31] national income captured by the top 1 percent, versus the erosion in the share of national income suffered by the bottom 50 percent.

When one drills down further, one discovers that the "top" of top-end inequality is a very select group; the narrower the slice of the very top incomes that one measures, the greater has been that group's success in capturing a disproportionate share of economic growth.

In short, whether measured from the bottom up or the top down, the United States is unique among the high-income countries of the OECD: we combine high national income with the highest levels of adult poverty, and (as seen in Chapter 3) with very poor intergenerational economic mobility outcomes. Those at the very bottom are trapped in levels of absolute poverty that shock the conscience, those at the very top have rapidly increased their private mortgage on national income and wealth, and those in the middle have just been treading water.

WEALTH INEQUALITY

Now let us turn to wealth inequality, which as I noted at the outset is even more difficult to measure than income inequality, at least in the United States, because we do not have any official data collection here.[32] Everyone agrees that, almost by definition, wealth is more concentrated than income, because savings are the perquisite of the affluent. Most also agree that wealth has become even more concentrated over the last several decades. An important short paper recently published by the Federal Reserve, for example, begins by stating: "Wealth concentration is high and rising in the US."[33]

Once again the CBO has done some work on this question. It estimated that net household wealth in 2013 amounted to $67 trillion, which was roughly four times national Gross Domestic Product in that year. The CBO found that families in the top 10 percent of the wealth distribution held more than three-quarters of the country's wealth in 2013, up from about two-thirds in 1989.[34] The CBO also found that the bottom half of the population's share of national wealth declined from about 3 percent in 1989 to 1 percent in 2013—or, in the language of inequality researchers, from nominal to bupkis.

Unsurprisingly, Thomas Piketty and his colleagues also have done a great deal of work on wealth inequality. They update their research regularly on the World Inequality Database (WID) mentioned earlier. Their findings—which, to be clear, are more controversial than their income inequality work—show the very top of the wealth distribution capturing a disturbing amount of national wealth.[35] They find that the top 1 percent owned about 37 percent of the country's net personal wealth in 2014 (see Figure 3.8).

In a separate paper, Gabriel Zucman estimated the wealth share of the top 1 percent to have increased to 40 percent in 2016.[36]

The PS&Z calculations are at the high end of serious estimates. The Federal Reserve, for example, has found (in work discussed immediately below) that the top 1 percent own about 32 percent of national wealth, and a

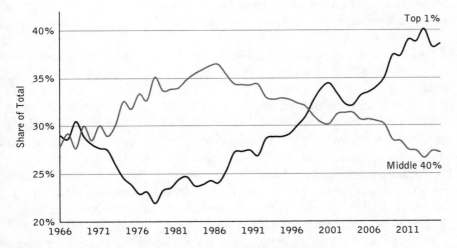

FIGURE 3.8 Wealth Inequality, USA, by Net Personal Wealth (1966–2014)

Source: World Inequality Database.

2019 study in the prestigious *American Economic Review* found that the figure is 33.6 percent.[37]

Some find these differences in estimates to be large and worth quibbling over; I do not.[38] To all this I say, the top 1 percent own about one-third of the nation's wealth, and that seems awfully concentrated to me.

In 2019 the Federal Reserve introduced a comprehensive new measure of who owns how much wealth in the United States, which the Fed terms "Distributional Financial Accounts."[39] In a manner analogous to the text's earlier discussion of "top-down" *income* distribution analysis, the Distributional Financial Accounts process takes national household *wealth* aggregates in the official Financial Accounts of the United States and assigns this wealth to individual households based primarily on the micro-level data developed for the Fed's Survey of Consumer Finances.

The Fed's conclusions are sobering. The Fed's new methodology found that in 1989 the "bottom" one-half of American households (a distasteful way to refer to our fellow citizens, but the language used by social scientists) held only 4 percent of the nation's wealth. Fast-forwarding to 2018, that half's share of total household wealth had declined to only 1 percent. Over the same period, the top 1 percent moved from owning 23 percent of our national wealth in 1989 to 32 percent in 2018. The next 9 percent (from the 90th to the 99th percentile) also increased their share of our wealth, all at the expense of the group that many would describe as the "middle class"—those households in the 50th to 90th percentile of wealth distribution, whose share of national wealth declined substantially.[40]

To express this more vividly, the WID initiative found that in 2012 the average real wealth of the bottom 90 percent of US households was $92,100. The bulk of this was in pension assets; the net value of home equity took a large hit in the Great Recession. The average real wealth of the top 1 percent was *165 times* larger—$15,237,000.[41]

From the other direction, the Federal Reserve Board through its surveys of consumers found that in 2018, 40 percent of adults reported that they would have difficulty paying a $400 unexpected non-medical expense.[42] There has been some bizarre pushback in the blogosphere about this finding, as inequality deniers point out that most of those adults could scrounge up the $400 by borrowing on credit cards or from relatives. To my mind, however, a world in which 40 percent of adults do not have $400 in spare liquid assets, and instead must go into debt to finance such an expense, is one in which those hundreds of millions of citizens also will not have the resources to pay for after-school activities, a Sunday trip to the museum, or any of the other sorts of investments in a child's development that children of the affluent take for granted.

The Fed also found in its survey of consumer finances that in 2018 about one-quarter of adults went without some form of medical treatment due to inability to pay. Twenty percent of adults incurred an unexpected medical expense between $1,000 and $4,999. Of these, 40 percent responded that they had outstanding unpaid debt from those bills. Against this background, is it surprising that most Americans cannot afford to provide their offspring with French horn lessons in order to give them an inside edge to admission at Harvard?

GIFTS AND BEQUESTS

The conclusions reached in the preceding section will have surprised few readers. But now we get to the nub of the matter, which is, what do the affluent do with all their money?

From the perspective of my thesis, things would be fine if rich folk made and saved large sums of money, and then over the remainder of their lifetimes frittered it all away on expensive wine, unsuitable romantic partners, and polo ponies. (Economists call this "lifetime earnings smoothing.") The problem is that the rich in fact fail to consume all their wealth through narcissistic spending on themselves. Instead, they invest in their offspring. The consequences of this are the subject of the next chapter, but in general my claim is that inherited wealth is the device by which today's economic inequality is converted into a heritable gene.

Many of our economic theories as to how income should be taxed, as well as our entire political economy of wealth taxation, rely on the idea that wealth is just lifetime income smoothing. All that disappears once gratuitous transfers are recognized as a very large fraction of household wealth.

By virtue of the tailwinds of family investments in them, mediocre rich kids set sail on the adventure of adult life, not only with lots of family connections and social skills not available to smart poor kids, but also with a superabundance of capital invested in them, developing whatever modest talents they have to the fullest extent possible. And it further turns out that they can afford to be risk takers, because there is always a nest egg to fall back on.

Put simply, gifts and bequests provide the recipient with a profound economic head start—hence the joke about the heir who declared he hit a home run, when he started off being born on third base. In a country where investment in human capital is extremely important but is not a public good, money in the heir's bank account translates into greater human capital investment simply because the heir (or her parents) can afford those private costs, including the opportunity cost of not contributing to a family's income while attending university.

So how much wealth in the United States comes into our possession through gratuitous transfers from earlier generations, as opposed to current savings from labor income, used to fund a comfortable retirement? The short answer is that

half or more of wealth in the United States comes to individuals through their sagacious choices of parents and grandparents.

The Federal Reserve Board has published an important short paper on this question (first introduced in "Wealth Inequality" above).[43] It concludes that "the flow of intergenerational transfers likely has an important role in explaining the [sic] wealth concentration." The Fed paper finds that about $350 billion per year is transferred from one generation of families to the next, and this does not include amounts spent directly on child support, like school tuitions. Another major recent study by Lily Batchelder, relying on the tax models of the Tax Policy Center, reaches even more dramatic conclusions, finding that current-year gifts and bequests in 2020 will total $765 billion (again ignoring amounts spent on the support of minor children).[44]

Lifetime gifts peak when individuals are in their early twenties; the bulk of inheritances come much later in life, when one's parents finally shuffle off this mortal coil. Unsurprisingly, more than half (56 percent) of intergenerational transfers go to recipients in the top 10 percent of the wealth distribution; the bottom half of the wealth distribution picks up only about 8 percent of all intergenerational transfers. If one assumes that wealth can be invested in assets yielding a 5 percent real return, the Fed's analysis shows that *more than half* of all the wealth in the country is received through intergenerational transfers.[45]

In short, gifts and bequests do not do much to give a leg up to the next generation of lower-income families. Instead, they serve to concentrate wealth still further among the wealthy.

The Fed study also considered "indirect" intergenerational wealth transfers, particularly investment in the education of one's offspring. The conclusions are sobering for those who believe that the theme of equality of opportunity is a lived reality rather than an aspirational credo:

> If wealthier families are able to provide better education for their children, those children will have higher labor incomes, and thus they will tend to save more over their lifetimes and accumulate greater wealth. To analyze outcomes among households from wealthy families, we find it useful to define "born to wealth" as those households for whom the sum of their reported lifetime transfers received (with interest) and their expected future transfers exceeds $1,000,000 in real 2016 dollars. . . . [W]e show that the correlation between being "born to wealth" and education attainment is undeniable: the probability of having a bachelor's degree is twice as big for those born to wealth than all others, and the probability of having an advanced degree is four times as large.[46]

Finally, the Fed paper takes on the fraught question of whether those born with a silver spoon in their mouths are more likely to invest cautiously and live off their wealth, dissipating their concentration of wealth over time, or instead to boldly take on risky projects, knowing that they have a private safety net to fall back on if things do not work out. (This is an empirical question; that is, theory cannot answer how rich young people behave.) The answer is that those born to wealth in general are risk takers, not hammock swingers:

[Our research] provides some suggestive evidence of the risk taking channel among 40 to 60 year old households. We find that 37 percent of those born to wealth are willing to take on above average risk to get above average returns, as opposed to only 21 percent of the rest of the population. On the other hand, few (14 percent) of the households born to wealth are not willing to take on any risks, in contrast to a much higher fraction (37 percent) of the population at large. These figures certainly corroborate differences in risk preference across the groups.

Economists do not care for anecdotes, but in my decades of experience spent in the proximity of the truly rich and the merely haute bourgeoisie, children of the affluent grow up to work, just as their parents did. Many prowl the halls of Goldman Sachs, assuring themselves that they are just plain folk who've done well for themselves. Some rely on their private safety net to make a career of public service, thereby disappointing those keeping score for some imagined GDP Olympics, but enhancing national welfare nonetheless. And a significant number try their hands at startups of every variety. Those not working are largely dealing with drug addiction and other illnesses, which are not the exclusive purview of the privileged classes.

As my late father once observed to me, all other things being equal, it is better to be rich and healthy than poor and sick. We have seen in this chapter how income and wealth are highly concentrated in the United States, and that about half of all wealth comes through the courtesy of one's ancestors. The next chapter continues the analysis, by showing how wealth concentration, and the turbocharging effect of having inheritable wealth available to fund one's education and foolish ventures, leave an indelible mark on the dispersion of economic opportunities in the United States.

CHAPTER 4

IT'S BETTER TO BE LUCKY THAN SMART

THE LONG SHADOW OF EXISTENTIAL BAD LUCK

What would equality of opportunity look like on the ground if we actually embodied it as systematically as our frequent invocations of it would imply? Instead of looking to explicit legal preferences or roadblocks as the relevant criteria, we should ask ourselves a simple question: Can we discern patterns in life outcomes among discrete groups that can be attributed to the accidents of when we are born, where we are born, and to whom we are born?

It is beyond doubt that at birth talents and interests are randomly distributed.[1] Nonetheless, as this and the preceding chapter painfully demonstrate, existential fortuities incontestably affect one's future economic success. (Raj Chetty and his colleagues call this "the birth lottery.")[2] If kids from rich families systematically grow up to have high earnings, and those from poor families as a group have difficulty making ends meet, then these existential contingencies play too large a role in our society, and government interventions are appropriate. (Only the children of the very most affluent parents can afford to organize their lives supported by investment income alone; as a result, the comparison in practice boils down to differences in earnings, meaning labor incomes.) Conversely, if talent and drive dominate, so that the economic rank into which one is born has little predictive value for the income one earns later in life, then we can truly say that this is a country of equal opportunity.

Imagine a society in which the most diligent researcher was unable to find any patterns in life outcomes attributable to existential bad luck. This would be a fortunate world indeed, because we would have operationalized a society that fully embraced equality of opportunity. As an added bonus, the number of economics papers published each year would plummet, because it would be fruitless to keep combing through data sets looking for patterns in a sea of randomness—thereby slashing my professional reading obligations.

But this is not the world we inhabit. At every turn, we see examples of how the accidents of our parents' wealth, our place of birth, and the timing of our birth push some lucky souls forward, while holding others back. The same is true for our sex and skin color; these are not artifacts of money, but also leave behind clear handprints of systematically unequal lifetime treatment.

The acid test of our success or failure in instantiating equality of opportunity should be resolved through economic mobility data. However mobility might be measured, what we would want to see is that the accidents of birth had relatively little predictive power for our personal economic trajectories.

Our interest in economic mobility should focus on two basic questions. First, we would want to see each generation doing better than the one before it, just as we would want to see the median worker doing better within one generation but over a time span of a couple of decades or so. I think of this kind of mobility as the rising tide of increasing national income lifting all boats. As discussed in Chapter 3, when applied across generations, this is called "absolute" economic mobility, because it measures whether children outperform their parents' incomes in absolute constant-dollar terms once those children grow to the same age as that used to measure their parents' incomes.

Absolute economic mobility across generations is extremely important for whether people believe that America is working for them. As Chapter 3 showed, absolute economic mobility has declined over the last several decades. This is an important source of American angst in the twenty-first century.

The second question that should interest us falls under the rubric of "relative" economic mobility. Here we are not looking at whether children outdo their parents in constant-dollar terms when measured at the same point in their earnings cycles, but whether children end up in different places than did their parents in the lineup of income distributions. The key idea here is to inquire whether the economic rank of parents has any predictive power with regard to the economic ranks occupied by their children a generation later. For example, do kids of poor parents invariably grow up to be poor, or do some (many?) occupy higher positions in the national income distribution? The more random is the reshuffling of rank order from one generation to the next, the more successful is a society in instantiating equality of opportunity.

Studies of absolute economic mobility do not by themselves paint a complete picture. For example, if daughters outearn their fathers in real terms, not simply because the rising tide of increasing national income has lifted all the boats, but rather because the wage gap between men and women has narrowed, that finding does have information content about equality of opportunity. But absolute mobility studies do not more generally address the effect of our parents' income on our own economic path. We want to know how large a shadow the circumstances of our birth cast on our own lifetime income prospects, because the longer that shadow, the more hollow is our claim to live in a land of equal opportunity.

When we focus on equality of opportunity, then, the most meaningful comparisons are those revealed in relative income analyses, such as a comparison of the income ranks of parents and children at similar points in their life cycles (that is, precisely one generation apart) across the national income distribution (from the lowest- to the highest-income adults). This means tracking the relative movement from parents' places in the income distribution to those occupied by their children when the children reach adulthood. If, for example, a parent is in the bottom quintile of income-earners (the bottom 20 percent) on her fortieth birthday, the relative income mobility question asks, How probable is it that her daughter also is in the bottom quintile percentile of adults in this next generation on the daughter's fortieth birthday?

Chapter 3 demonstrated that inherited wealth (in the broad sense of wealth gratuitously transferred from an older generation of a family to the next generation) accounts for half or more of the country's stock of wealth. Some of those gratuitous transfers, of course, are in the form of cash or investment assets. In extreme cases these assets enable the next generation to clip coupons and take up professional badminton. In less extreme cases, those transfers can fund start-ups, or, just as important, serve as a literal and psychological safety net against failing in the marketplace.

But in addition to junior's bank account, family wealth is transmitted by stuffing as much education into the young fellow as he can possibly swallow. Chapter 5 develops the importance of education as a driver of lifetime earnings. The critical points to bear in mind, though, are these: First, there are large financial and social returns to education. Second, education in the United States is very expensive, particularly at the post-secondary level. Third, the United States relies more on private (family) resources to fund education, particularly at the college and post-graduate levels, than do most other countries. The combination of these factors is death to economic mobility.

As parents know, it is always possible for one's children to screw up, and more rarely for a child to exceed our wildest dreams for her. In America today, however, the advantages conveyed by applying parental wealth to investments in a child's human capital through education are so profound as to mean that we can expect that the children of the affluent will systematically achieve incomes as adults greater than their native talents would imply. As Chapter 5 shows, the children of the affluent enter kindergarten with large advantages attributable to money, time, and attention spent on them that less fortunate families cannot match, and these achievement gaps grow with every year.

This is why I say that wealth begets wealth as if it were a hereditable gene— even ignoring the cash that Mom and Dad may have deposited in junior's bank account along the way, the large investments made in junior's human capital at no cost to him beyond the usual familial guilt (whether in debt incurred or the income he could have earned to help his family rather than continuing his education) means that the expected value of his future earnings will be several notches higher than those of the more talented young man who was unable to afford top-tier post-secondary education, or did so only by assuming hundreds of thousands of dollars of debt.

This is not an idle claim. We can see the ossification of current American society directly by looking at studies of the economic mobility of Americans. We can also observe the importance of education as the primary driver of future earnings, and hence as the gateway to economic mobility—were only that education delivered a bit more fairly—by studying the outcomes achieved by young people as they monetize the investments made in their human capital in the marketplace. The next section of this chapter therefore summarizes what we know about economic mobility, and Chapter 5 follows up by tying our sad economic mobility data to our uneven access to quality education, from early childhood through university.

This, beyond extravagant bar mitzvahs, country club connections, all the electronic gadgets one can imagine, or even some cash in the bank, is the most meaningful gift that affluent parents can provide their offspring. It is why who our parents are casts such a long shadow over the economic lives that we will live.

MOBILITY STUDIES

The study of economic mobility is marred by imperfect information and fundamental disagreements about what exactly should be measured. Economists, for example, like to focus on mobility in incomes over time; sociologists, on the other hand, tend to emphasize mobility in career choices from parents to children.[3] For simplicity, I focus here on the work of economists over the last couple of decades.

Even within economics, fundamental choices must be made: should we inquire into changes in earnings, or total income (thereby picking up the idle rich, and widows living on Social Security)? If you choose "income," should we examine pretax or after-tax/after-benefits income (thereby picking up social interventions like Social Security benefits and the earned income tax credit, which programs have changed radically over the space of a generation)? Do we care more about whether children on balance do better than their parents, or whether the rankings of adults by incomes are reshuffled from one generation to the next, so that parents' incomes do not have predictive implications for their children's perfor-mance? Are we measuring fathers and sons (methodologically easier), or families? If families, how do we adjust for the long-term trend of moving from one-earner to two-earner households, at least when both parents are present? And again, if we prefer families as the unit of measure, how should we account for "assorta-tive mating" among human animals, which is the theory that we actively seek out others with similar backgrounds, education, and so on for our mates?[4]

So where are we?

Unsurprisingly, the answer depends in part on which researcher you query.[5] On balance, though, I read the literature to suggest that the United States is more scle-rotic than most of us would like to believe is true, and that we fall surprisingly far behind peer countries that we intuitively imagine to be less dynamic. The compar-ison to peer countries is important. We all applaud the credo of equal opportunity, but we know that outcomes are not completely random from one generation to the next. The income levels of one's parents cast some shadow, small or large, on one's own economic prospects. Even if the published papers measuring changes in rel-ative intergenerational economic mobility within the United States were flawless, we still would be left without a reference scale to know whether the results we observe reflect some iron-clad law of economics, or whether instead different gov-ernment policies might be able to improve things. The comparison to other rich economies gives us that reference scale.

One useful place to start the discussion of intergenerational relative economic mobility is with the Panel Study of Income Dynamics (PSID), which has tracked the family incomes (meaning here, total taxable income plus transfer payments) of a sample of 5,000 families for about fifty years. The data represented in Figure 4.1 show that there is a great deal of movement among the middle three quintiles of the income distribution (from the 20th through the 80th percentiles), but that individuals born into either of the two extremes—the bottom or top 20 percent of the income distribution—are much more likely to end up where they started.

For example, Figure 4.1 shows that in the PSID data, a child born into the lowest income quintile (the bottom 20 percent) has nearly a 45 percent chance of growing up to be stuck in that same quintile, *and only a 7 percent chance of reaching the top quintile.* From the other direction, almost 50 percent of those born into the top quintile remain there when they become income-earning adults.

The idea that the bottom and the top of the income distribution are "sticky" across generations, but that the middle is much less so, is generally accepted by researchers in the field. Unfortunately for us, economists are not willing to clas-sify relative economic mobility by proposing a stickiness index of the sort that parents might use to grade their toddlers' cleanliness. Instead, economists rely on several related metrics, of which the most commonly used is "intergenerational

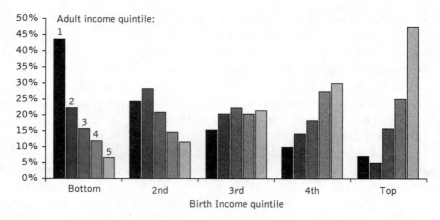

FIGURE 4.1 Relative Mobility, Percent of Adults in Each Income Quintile by Birth Income Quintile

Source: Leila Bengali and Mary Daly, "US Economic Mobility: The Dream and the Data," *FRBSF Economic Letter* 2013-06, March 4, 2013.

elasticity in earnings."[6] This is a mouthful of a phrase, but at its core it reduces to the simple question, how much of a child's earnings once she reaches adulthood can be explained by her parents' earnings a generation previously? We need to unpack the phrase just a little bit, though, to be able to make useful comparisons across countries, or within the United States across time.

An intergenerational elasticity in earnings score of 1.0 means that you are living in feudal Europe a millennium ago, where family rank invariably predicted the rank of a child. With a handful of exceptions, serfs gave birth to serfs, and lords to lords. An intergenerational elasticity in earnings score of 0 might describe a community where infants are ripped from their parents' arms and raised anonymously and collectively. Needless to say, modern rich economies fall somewhere between these two endpoints.

More technically, imagine that one group of fathers (researchers often look to fathers and sons because of data limitations) earns $100,000/year, and another group of fathers earns $50,000/year. The first group of fathers have incomes 100 percent greater than the second group. If the intergenerational elasticity in earnings for that country is 0.4 (roughly the consensus estimate for the United States), then we would expect sons born to the higher-income fathers to make about 40 percent more (0.4 × 100% earnings differential) than do sons born to the lower-income fathers.[7] More technically still, the *expected earnings* of the more fortunate sons would be 40 percent higher than those of the less fortunate ones, but their *actual earnings* would form a distribution in the shape of the "normal" distribution curve, with that expected earnings figure as a midpoint (as described in Chapter 1).

So it all boils down to, what is the intergenerational elasticity of earnings in the United States, and how do we benchmark against the rest of the world? As to the first, the consensus view is somewhere in the neighborhood of 0.4, which is not great, as the PSID data show, once we step back from the abstraction of an index number to the more telling question: How many kids from the bottom of the income quintile will grow up to occupy the top quintile?[8] (As just noted, 7 percent.) The elasticity index is incredibly susceptible to seemingly modest changes in analytical methods, such as averaging several years of a father's income rather than choosing just one year (e.g., age forty), but I think that a figure of 0.4 will not cause too many researchers to set their hair on fire.

The United States turns out to have significantly less relative intergenerational mobility—a higher intergenerational elasticity in earnings score—than do many of its peer countries. Our society has about as much relative mobility as does the United Kingdom, Italy, and Switzerland, but far less than France, Japan, Australia, or the Nordics (see Figure 4.2).[9]

One leading researcher in this field is Miles Corak of the University of Ottawa. As a Canadian economist, Corak has a particular interest in comparing Canadian and US relative economic mobility outcomes. The comparison is a

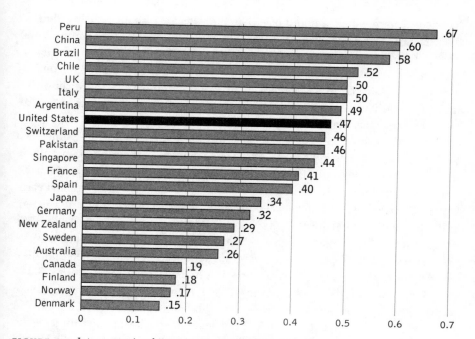

FIGURE 4.2 Intergenerational Earnings Elasticity, Selected Countries

Source: Miles Corak, "Inequality from Generation to Generation: The United States in Comparison," IZA Discussion Paper 9929, *Forschungsinstitut zur Zukunft der Arbeit* (May 2016).

particularly apt one, because the United States and Canada are similar in many respects, and because cultural differences between the two countries intuitively are less than those one might observe between the United States and other peer countries.

In Corak's view, the United States actually has a higher intergenerational earnings elasticity number (is *less* mobile) than this chart shows: he concludes that the elasticity between fathers and sons in the United States is three times as high as that in Canada. In the United States, one-quarter of sons born to fathers in the top 10 percent of the earnings distribution also emerge in the top 10 percent, while in Canada the figure is 18 percent; one-half of these American sons are in the top 30 percent, versus 40 percent in Canada; and only 3 percent of American sons fall to the bottom 10 percent, while in Canada 8 percent do.[10]

The same intergenerational stickiness in outcomes is apparent at the bottom end of the income distribution, but again US society edges a bit closer to feudal outcomes than does Canada. For example, 22 percent of US sons born to fathers in the bottom 10 percent of the income distribution grow up to themselves be in the bottom 10 percent, while in Canada the figure is 16 percent. When multiplied across an entire population, these are meaningful differences.

The Organisation for Economic Co-operation and Development (OECD) also has done a tremendous amount of research in this area; as previously indicated, the OECD's work is particularly helpful in making cross-country comparisons. The OECD's recent volume on this subject, *A Broken Social Elevator? How to Promote Social Mobility*, contains a wealth of cross-country data, but its conclusions are essentially similar to the points already made.[11] In most developed countries, mobility is particularly sticky at the top and bottom of the income distribution, although across most margins the United States is worse than average.

The OECD conducted an interesting simulation exercise, in which it modeled how many generations it would take for the hypothetical offspring of a family in the bottom 10 percent of the income distribution to reach the middle of the pack, based on a random distribution of talents and a country's intergenerational earnings elasticity (again, the statistical correlation between the earnings of a parent and child, or more colloquially, the shadow cast by a parent's earnings on a child's prospects). The simulation concluded that in the United States it would take *five generations* for a child born to parents in the bottom 10 percent of the population to reach the average income. The performance of the United States in this simulation exercise was a little worse than the OECD average, but admittedly comparable to that of many European countries—although worse than that of Canada, and much worse than the Nordic countries. But again, if equality of opportunity is the credo that defines our country, performing about the same as Italy and the United Kingdom is no great accomplishment.

A final, and very contentious, topic is whether that stickiness has become stronger over the last generation. We know that income inequality has increased substantially over time. Has that hardened the barriers to intergenerational relative income mobility still further? That is, has increasing income inequality further vitiated equality of opportunity as it is lived across generations?

In 2014, the ubiquitous Raj Chetty and a group of colleagues weighed in on this question. Their paper has achieved a great deal of attention, but its conclusions remain under debate.[12] This Chetty group concluded that "children entering the labor market today have the same chances of moving up in the income distribution (relative to their parents) as children born in the 1970's." But to be clear, for those children born into the bottom quintile of the income distribution, "the same chances" is a nice way of saying "approximately bupkis." Consistent with the PSID data, but using their preferred database, the Chetty team found that the chances of a child born to parents in the bottom fifth of the income distribution moving, on reaching adulthood, to the top fifth of the income distribution has hovered around 9 percent—a figure that I submit is inconsistent with our collective imagination of how equality of opportunity should work in practice. Chetty and colleagues concluded that seeming declines in intergenerational relative income mobility are driven more by differences across locations in the United States (consistent with their work on the critical importance of geography) than by any movement in the intergenerational earnings elasticity index.

The Chetty paper goes on to make an important related point. Even if the intergenerational earnings index has not changed (so that children of the poor have the same crummy chance they've always had to move up in the rankings to the top quintile of the income distribution), we know that *inequality* has increased, as Chapter 3 discussed. Increasing inequality interacts with a constant measure of relative economic chances (if one accepts the Chetty results) to move up, in ways that are bad for the poor and good for the rich. Using the Chetty paper's number, if the likelihood of moving from the bottom to the top quintile across one generation is 9 percent, the consequences of that move are much larger (because the gaps between rich and poor are larger). As a result, the paper concludes, "the increase in inequality has . . . magnified the difference in expected incomes between children born to low- (e.g., bottom-quintile) versus high- (top-quintile) income families. In this sense, mobility has fallen because a child's income depends more heavily on her parents' position in the income distribution today than in the past."

What on earth does that mean? Imagine that 40 percent of the expected value of a son's earnings as an adult can be explained by his father's earnings (i.e., the intergenerational earnings elasticity number for the United States is 0.4), and that, consistent with the Chetty results, this factor is constant over time - so that by this measure intergenerational relative mobility has been constant over the last several decades. Nonetheless, when 0.4 is multiplied by larger and larger gaps among dads, the gaps among sons also will grow.[13] If the earnings gap across different fathers has widened due to increasing income inequality, then when one multiplies a constant 40 percent by wider and wider dispersions in parental earnings, the resulting earnings dispersions across sons also will grow over time.

This does not tell us anything about whether rich kids will grow up to be poorer than other kids in the future, or vice versa (that is, whether income *ranks* reverse from one generation to the next); it does tell us, however, that living in a country with a high intergenerational earnings elasticity number *and* high and increasing inequality means that the payoffs to "choosing" one's parents wisely increase from generation to generation. The child's crummy chances of moving up remain constant (i.e., consistently small) in the Chetty results, but the consequences of remaining in the bottom group become larger and larger, as the top quintile sprints further ahead from the other quintiles in absolute dollars of income from one generation to the next. So congratulations, kid, your minuscule chances of success haven't diminished—but the consequences of *not* succeeding will be that as an adult you will have fallen further behind the top quintile than your father found himself a generation earlier.

The evolution of pure relative rankings, without any dollars attached to them, is interesting, but in the end it is dollars, not rank, that determine how our lives compare to those of others. To be in the 30th income percentile in a society where all incomes are bunched close together is not so bad; to be in the 30th income percentile in a society where the top seems as far away as the moon is a much different proposition.

These themes can be graphically represented by the "Great Gatsby Curve," as so nicknamed by economist Alan Krueger (see Figure 4.3). It suggests (but does not by itself prove) that there might be a relationship between increasing income inequality and reduced economic mobility (as measured by intergenerational relative earnings elasticity).

Correlation of course is not by itself evidence of causation, but the facts as presented in this and the previous chapter speak for themselves. The United States is highly unequal in the distribution of incomes; the very bottom of the income distribution in the United States is worse off in absolute terms than are the poorest citizens of some other rich countries, like Canada; *and* as we will see in the next chapter, the United States requires more by way of private investment in the human capital of one's offspring at every stage of development than do other countries. It is this last point that operates as the hammer to nail shut the door of opportunity to so many low-income Americans, and to make it improbable for the children of the affluent to sink terribly far down the income ladder.

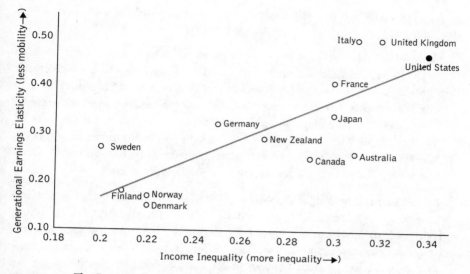

FIGURE 4.3 The Great Gatsby Curve: Inequality vs. Mobility

Source: Miles Corak, "Income Inequality, Equality of Opportunity, and Intergenerational Mobility," *Journal of Economic Perspectives* 27, no. 3 (summer 2013): 79–102.

GEOGRAPHICAL DETERMINISM

As Chapter 3 discussed, Raj Chetty and colleagues, with the active participation of the Census Bureau and the Internal Revenue Service, have revolutionized inequality studies, by harnessing big data to give us more information about the factors that affect economic mobility than we could have imagined a couple of decades ago. Here, my focus is on the Chetty group's important new contribution, the Opportunity Atlas.[14] This is a micro-level summary (census tract by census tract), in visual and raw data form, of how children from any census tract have fared as young adults.

The Chetty group has found very large differences in outcomes for young adults growing up in different neighborhoods, even demographically similar areas (to judge from the data) a mile or so apart. The results also vary by race and sex, often in directions that are the reverse of those found in other nearby census tracts.

The Opportunity Atlas has convincingly demonstrated that where one grows up—down to the neighborhood level—has a large impact on the future income prospects for a child born to poor parents. Chetty and his colleagues acknowledge, however, that they have found no single explanation for the extraordinary difference a neighborhood can make to a child's income prospects as an adult.

As a generally sympathetic review by the Robert Wood Johnson Foundation noted:

> This new tool raises as many questions as it answers. Why do low-income American Indian children in Oklahoma move into the middle class as adults in much greater numbers than the same population growing up in South Dakota? Why do children in rural Eastern Iowa have greater economic mobility than children from similar family backgrounds in urban areas—while in parts of North Carolina, the rural/urban divide is reversed? Why do Compton and Watts, both poor communities in central Los Angeles, offer such different opportunities to children who are raised there? The Atlas is only a starting point to dig deeper into these kinds of questions.[15]

As one example, young adults now in their mid-thirties who were born to low-income parents (those in the bottom quarter of the national income distribution) today have a national median household income of $34,000. But young adults born to poor parents in South Pasadena, California, today have a median income of $44,000; similarly situated young adults born in Echo Park (today, a hipster enclave in Los Angeles, but a generation ago a tight-knit immigrant community), a ten-minute drive away, today have a median income of $63,000. (These figures include all children of Echo Park, for example, regardless of where they now live, so they do not correspond to the median incomes today of the neighborhoods in which they grew up.)

How to interpret these results? There's the rub. It is not surprising that kids from South Pasadena have fared well: it has many public amenities and one of the best public school districts in California. But if the data are correct, kids born in Echo Park, a much less prosperous community, did even better—notwithstanding that South Pasadena today has a median income of roughly twice that of Echo Park and therefore much more money to spend on public amenities. (Echo Park today has at least one excellent K–8 charter school, and it is close to a couple of top-tier charter high schools, but the charter school phenomenon largely postdates the time the children being measured first entered kindergarten.)

One of the few clear conclusions that the Chetty group has been able to draw with application across the country is that "job growth" in an immediate area is not well correlated to better outcomes, apparently because much job growth is met by importing high-skill workers into an area. "In contrast," write the authors, "we find a strong positive correlation between the employment rates of adults who live in a given tract and rates of upward mobility for children who grow up there.

Evidently, what matters for upward mobility is not proximity to jobs, but growing up around people who have jobs."[16]

More generally, the data suggest that neighborhoods with strong bonds among residents and stability in the home and workplace are the most fertile for the future success of kids from poor families. Government cannot directly dictate the composition of a home, but through old-fashioned amenities like public libraries, parks, and pools, it can offer places that both enhance the quality of each family's life and that draw neighbors together.

CHAPTER 5

EDUCATION IS THE ENGINE OF OPPORTUNITY

EQUAL OPPORTUNITIES REQUIRE EQUAL INVESTMENTS IN EDUCATION

This chapter makes two related central claims. First, investment in human capital, which is to say education, is the principal engine by which we instantiate equality of opportunity. Second, because the United States relies so disproportionately on private—that is, family—sources of funding for education for the investment in human capital necessary to enable each individual to achieve the goals to which her native talents and ambitions call her, having the bad luck to be born into a family with meager financial resources ineluctably leads to economically impaired lives.

We want to believe that our society is structured to reward hard work and thrift, but what we really do is to offer those born on third base an easy trot to home plate, funded not only by money in the bank (in the most fortunate cases) but also by investments in their human capital derived from wealth not of their own creation. My aim here is to ask: Why have we structured our society to starve so many of our citizens of investment in their human capital, when that is the driver of their increased prosperity and life satisfactions, leading in turn to increased national prosperity for us all?

To repeat the language of statistics from Chapter 1, the *expected value* of the lifetime earnings of young Americans systematically deprived of investments in their human capital will be far lower than their potential earnings. To point to the truly exceptional individual who has somehow overcome these odds is to identify the outermost tail of the distribution, three or four standard deviations away from the median.

In the United States today, there are nearly five million kids at each year of age—age five, age ten, whatever.[1] You can pretend if you wish that investments in human capital outside the ambit of traditional formal education can lift meaningful numbers of kids born into the lowest income quintile up to the highest quintile once they grow up, but all the NBA players, ballerinas, first violins, celebrity singers, and influencers in the country are tiny blips in this sea of young people coming of age. Education is the only instrument that can change lives by the millions.

Economists like to describe the process by which private enterprises generate income as having two fundamental drivers—what the economists call factors of production: labor (by which they mean the contributions of human effort, regardless of whether actual sweat is generated) and capital (money).[2] Some businesses are labor-intensive, while others rely more on the capital that has been invested in them. All businesses combine labor and capital inputs, more or less efficiently, to generate income.

The same applies to each of us as individuals. If we find ourselves with a Roman numeral after our names, and great wealth at our disposal, we can rely largely on traditional capital (money in the bank) to generate the income and consumption that we require. But if we are born in more straitened circumstances, by definition we have no capital of our own and no significant family resources on which we can rely. Our economic future will depend on the returns we can capture for our labor in the marketplace. And in turn, the greater the investment in our human capital, the higher the price we can demand for our labor.

In short, investments in human capital drive lifetime economic outcomes and life satisfactions. Education is the only instrument important to the economy as a whole by which investments in human capital are made. High-quality public education can make available to all Americans, regardless of the circumstances of their birth, these investments in human capital, without the strings attached by private owners of capital to investments they might make in a business. And fortunately, public education (along with child and healthcare) is exactly the sort of policy instrument that money can buy.

The logic is simple, and the evidence is compelling. And yet at every level, the US educational system rewards the children of the affluent while systematically underinvesting in others. "Supply-side" economic claims are true, but the supply that is missing is not money to finance business investments, but rather money to invest in the human capital of every individual who can put that investment to good use. The returns to an individual so endowed with adequate investment in her human capital are profound, in both her lifetime earnings and her personal flourishing. The returns to society are equally great. By systematically underinvesting in the most important factor driving national prosperity—ourselves—we beggar our national economic future and assure a society with millions of rightly angry and embittered citizens.

Chapter 3 summarized the current state of our knowledge on income and wealth inequality, emphasizing in particular how top-heavy the distribution of both income and wealth are, and therefore how much more wealth is available to the affluent classes to invest in their progeny. Chapter 4 demonstrated that our society is more ossified than most of us would like to believe. The circumstances of one's birth, and in particular relative family incomes, cast too long a shadow from the previous generation onto the economic outcomes of the current one.

This chapter continues the analysis by asking: Does more education yield detectably higher lifetime earnings? What is the connection between disappointing intergenerational mobility, inequality, and investments in education? Do the wealthy in fact invest in their offspring's human capital through education, and do those investments yield positive returns that help the next generation to pull still further away from the pack? The answers in all three cases turn out to be "yes."

None of this is necessary. Unlike tax cuts, good-quality education does pay for itself in higher personal incomes, and through that mechanism higher national economic growth (and tax collections).[3] The deeper one dives into the literature, the more depressed one becomes. The reason is simple: The United States is an outlier in its refusal to adopt a national policy for childcare, its underfunding from all sources of early childhood education, and its excessive reliance on private resources to fund education at higher levels.

THE PROMISE OF EDUCATION

The power of education to drive lifetime incomes has been demonstrated again and again. These payoffs are most easily measured at the end of the educational cycle, by asking how a terminal college or graduate degree changes the expected value of a graduate's lifetime earnings. A simple analysis would compare the earnings path of a typical college or graduate degree holder to that of a high school graduate. A more complete analysis would reflect not only the higher revenue stream to be expected, but also, as a contra-item, the costs of earning that college or graduate school degree. These costs in turn include not only the direct expenses paid by a student or her family, but also her forgone earnings. The idea is that if a student worked full time upon graduating high school, her expected earnings might not be spectacular, but they would count for something. While the college student is hard at work investing in herself, she therefore is giving up the earnings she could have captured by going straight into the labor markets.

The federal government's National Center for Education Statistics (NCES) offers some basic information. According to the NCES, "In 2017, about half (51 percent) of all employed people age 25 and over had a postsecondary (i.e., an associate's or higher) degree. Seven percent of employed people age 25 and over had not completed high school."[4] The returns to education (ignoring the incremental costs of earning post-secondary degrees) are plainly evident in the NCES data (see Figure 5.1).

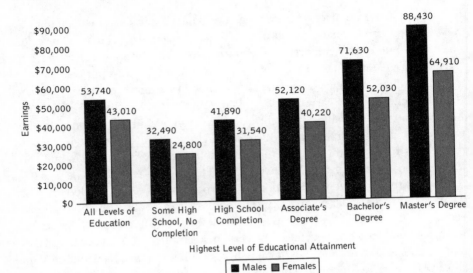

FIGURE 5.1 Median Annual Earnings of Full-Time Workers 25 Years Old and Over, by Educational Attainment (2016)

Source: National Center for Education Statistics. *Digest of Education Statistics 2017* (January 2018).

The value of a bachelor's degree, for example, depends in part on the institution conferring the degree, and in part on a student's major. Proving one's parents right, once again, the NCES data show that among workers in their late twenties, the median wage of holders of a B.S. in engineering in 2017 (about $70,000) was 75 percent greater than the median wage of English majors ($40,000). As a former major in Medieval and Renaissance Studies, I take exception to these sorts of data, but it is worth reminding readers again that expected outcomes, or observed median outcomes, are not the same as measures of any one individual's actual outcomes. By definition, one-half of former English majors in their late twenties are doing better than $40,000/year.

The work of the Organisation for Economic Co-operation and Development (the OECD) is invaluable here. The OECD has compared the relative values of post-secondary educations across different countries. For each country, the idea is to assign an arbitrary value of 100 to a worker with a high school diploma, and no more. The OECD then compared within each country the relative earnings, versus that index value of 100 for a high school diploma alone, captured by workers with different terminal degrees. Figure 5.2 presents the results for some selected peer countries, looking at full-time workers from 25 to 34 years old.

What does this tell us? First, that relative to earning a high school diploma as one's terminal degree, failing to earn that diploma in the United States leads to a 16 percent reduction in earnings among 25- to 34-year-olds. An associate'

	Level of Educational Attainment (*2014 or 2015 data where latest available)				
	Below Upper Secondary	Upper Secondary	Short-Cycle Tertiary	Bachelor's or Equivalent	Master's, Doctoral or Equivalent
Australia	96	100	102	118	113
Canada*	86	100	108	129	140
France*		100	121	124	173
Germany	76	100	130	154	141
Italy*	92	100			114
Norway	84	100	102	99	115
Sweden	84	100	100	101	123
Switzerland	86	100		126	135
United Kingdom	83	100	117	130	152
United States	84	100	111	151	194
OECD Average	85	100		128	152

FIGURE 5.2 Relative Earnings by Educational Attainment, Selected Countries (2016)

Source: OECD, *Education at a Glance 2019: OECD Indicators* (Paris: OECD Publishing, 2019).

degree, by contrast, boosts earnings about 11 percent versus the high school base-line. A bachelor's degree increases earnings by 51 percent, and a graduate degree yields a 71 percent jump in earnings.

None of this reflects the costs of earning a degree. The OECD has, however, undertaken just this analysis, reflecting both a student's out-of-pocket costs and the economic cost of her forgone earnings while a student.[5] The OECD concluded that the net benefits to an American man on the day he graduates from college with a bachelor's degree—that is, the present value of his future earnings versus the costs incurred to earn the degree—total almost $500,000 above what he could expect if he held just a high school diploma; for a woman the figure is lower, reflecting the wage gap, at $320,000. In each case, these are the highest figures among all the large economies in the OECD.

More dramatically, the OECD also calculated the financial return to education as if a student were like a machine in which a business might invest, by asking: What is the rate of return to the monies actually or deemed invested in that education? The answer for both men and women is that an American bachelor's degree yields an *18 percent per annum return* on the cost to acquire it. The OECD calculation can be criticized as a bit rosy in its estimate, but the point remains that a college education is the principal means of propelling oneself up the income distribution ladder.[6]

Researchers at the Federal Reserve Bank of San Francisco also have looked at this question, preferring a simple payback model that asks: How many years after graduation must pass before the costs of college are recouped by higher earnings, such that the college graduate's earnings net of those costs would begin to exceed the base case scenario of having entered the workforce right after high school?[7] Again, the answer depends on some critical assumptions, but the researchers found significant positive financial returns to a college education.

The OECD has considered as well the social returns that accrue to a country from college education. The OECD makes no effort here to quantify greater life satisfactions, but instead constrains itself to ask: What are the financial returns to government on its investment, in the form of its public funding of a student's higher education?[8] These take the form of higher future tax receipts, reduced anticipated unemployment benefit payouts, and the like. Again, the OECD concluded that the returns to the US government, like the private returns to a student, work out to an internal rate of return on investment in the teens.

Other researchers have taken on a still more challenging question by asking: What are the financial returns to investments earlier in the education cycle—in particular, what are the returns to early childhood education? This question, it turns out, does not need to be answered simply in terms of moral obligations and values. Nobel laureate James Heckman has done landmark research on this question. In an important paper, Heckman and his co-authors analyze the lifetime outcomes (actual and projected) from two real-world high-quality early childhood programs offered in North Carolina for low-income African American families since the 1970s.[9] These programs begin at eight weeks and carry on until age five. What the Heckman team found was that these programs have averaged a 13.7 *percent* compounded annual return on investment (including the economic costs of the taxation needed to fund the programs). At the same time, the underlying programs significantly raised the children's IQ levels—still another reminder that IQ is not a fixed quantity at birth.

Stop and think about this. Suppose you were a business person presented with the opportunity to earn a steady 13.7 percent per year, compounded. Would you be interested? Of course you would—you presumptively are neither crazy nor stupid. Yet when we all work together through the intermediation of government, we effectively become either crazy, or stupid, or both, and we leave these opportunities— that is to say, our own children—to rot on the vine.

It is true of course that, unlike the business setting, those investing the money (all of us, through taxes) do not capture all of the profits. A large slice goes to the individuals so benefited, but the public purse is benefited through higher lifetime taxes, reduced public assistance spending, and so on. But even that misses the point, because the purpose of public spending is not to pay cash yields to the same people who funded that spending, any more than we pay taxes for local policing based strictly on how much stuff we have that is worth safeguarding. We act and spend collectively to enhance the welfare of the country as a whole. Starting with eight-week-old babies might be a little too radical as an opening bid (even though the evidence would suggest doing so), but the same reasoning explains why universal 3–K (discussed later in the chapter) at least would be so important to the welfare of the country, and to authentic equality of opportunity.

Chapter 9 develops in more detail the theme, supported by a good deal of exciting new evidence, that increased and broadly available investments in human capital lead to what the International Monetary Fund calls an "inclusive economy," in which the country would both increase its economic growth rate and share that growth more broadly than is true today. (It is for this reason that the IMF argues that such strategies yield a "double dividend.") Again, the reason does not require a PhD in economics to see: the returns to labor constitute three-fifths or more of our national income, and we have today a human capital supply-side crisis, in that millions of Americans could earn more and be more fulfilled if they were to receive the investments in their personal human capital sufficient to raise their productivity to their full capacity.

In sum, there are large financial returns to education, and those returns increase the further up the education ladder one is able to climb. Education is the instrument by which opportunities are opened up, incomes enhanced, and lives made more satisfying. This last point is easy to overlook in the blizzard of numbers that I have just put you through. The purpose of our government since its founding has been to encourage the pursuit of happiness, which properly understood means the flourishing of the individual, not a constant supply of bonbons in bed. If not for education, then how?

The next several sections of this chapter turn from consideration of what can be, to what is today. The gap is even wider than you might guess.

OPPORTUNITY SQUANDERED: EARLY CHILDHOOD CHILDCARE

It is important at the outset to distinguish early childhood education from childcare. Parents need access to affordable, good-quality professional early childhood childcare if those parents are going to be able to work productively while not stunting their children's development. In most cases, the question at the margin is whether a mother will return to (or enter) the workforce following the birth of a child. From a young child's perspective, early childhood childcare operates as a complement to a formal educational component in the child's day, offering similar opportunities for high-quality stimulation of the brain and acquisition of important social skills.

The next section of this chapter describes the critical importance of early childhood education as the foundation of future success; everything said there applies with equal force to a supportive and caring childcare environment, in which curiosity and social skills can be encouraged. This section therefore focuses on the importance of reliable high-quality childcare for the incomes and productivity of families with young children, and in particular for the women on whose shoulders childcare often otherwise falls by default.

The United States as a matter of national policy largely leaves new parents to their own devices when it comes to childcare. In exercising alleged fiscal probity in this perverse manner, we cut off our nose to spite our face. The United States is unique among the world's wealthy countries in not offering any guaranteed maternity or parental leave for new parents.

Standard & Poor's, the credit rating agency, has published several research papers on the role of women in the workforce.[10] Those papers demonstrate a two-headed problem and opportunity. First, the US female labor participation rate in our market economy has declined for the last two decades. Where the United States once had one of the developed world's highest rates of women participating in the market economy, it has now slipped to the bottom of the pack.

The reason for our fall in the rankings is that, while US women slipped a bit in market participation over time, women in other countries entered the workforce in large numbers. And in turn, the reason American women are not able to enter and stay in the workforce at the same rates as in other countries boils down to our misogynistic policy decisions, not women's preferences:

> In practice, the biggest obstacle for working women to overcome involves children—both their bearing and rearing. As it stands, the US is the only country in the OECD that doesn't provide income support during maternity or parental leave by law. And for single mothers, full-day care for an infant eats up 41% of median income, according to a 2012 OECD report. Only 5% of workers who garner wages in the bottom quarter of the distribution have an employer that offers paid family leave, according to the BLS, and so most are left to choose between taking care of a family member or keeping their jobs. . .
>
> A primary reason for the [earnings] gap [between men and women] is the inequitable share of family care that women take on. In a 2013 survey, Pew found that 39% of mothers had, at some point in their careers, taken off a significant amount of time to care for a child or other family member. More than 25% had quit work entirely to do so. Just 24% of fathers, on the other hand, had taken a significant amount of time off to assume these responsibilities—and it should surprise no one that these types of career interruptions can weigh on long-term earnings.[11]

Standard & Poor's crunched the numbers and concluded that if US women entered and stayed in the workforce at the same rate as women in Norway do (where, of course, government-provided childcare is available), the US economy would have been about *$1.6 trillion* larger in 2017—almost *10 percent of our entire annual GDP.*

Standard & Poor's rival, Moody's, also has described how our policy choices in this area hurt national productivity—and by extension, hurt the life experiences in particular of the millions of women who find themselves conflicted at every turn between earning a living and providing an appropriate environment for their young children.[12] It is extraordinary that two of Wall Street's most famous brands, each dedicated to the cold discipline of firms' income statements and balance sheets, should think that our current practices are so scandalous and shortsighted as to warrant their weighing in on the topic, without any expectation of gain on their part.

The Moody's report is an analysis of the consequences for the economy of the hypothetical enactment into law of Elizabeth Warren's 2019 "Universal Child Care and Early Learning Act." The Warren proposal analyzed by Moody's would make pre–primary school childcare and "early learning centers" affordable for essentially all families, and would further introduce after-school programs for kids from five to thirteen years old. Those earning less than 200 percent of the federal poverty level would pay nothing; middle-class families would pay on a sliding scale based on their incomes, but in no event more than 7 percent of their incomes. Warren proposed to finance the costs of this proposal through a new tax on the most affluent Americans.

Moody's analyzed the Warren proposal using the firm's large macroeconomic model that it employs to forecast the path of the US economy. For my purposes, the details of the Warren proposal are less important than its very ambitious scope.

Moody's began its analysis by reminding readers of the great burdens that childcare imposes on families today:

Some 4.9 million American households spent almost $36 billion on day care centers, nurseries and preschools in 2017. The typical household that has childcare expenses spent $7,200 per year, equal to approximately 10% of their income. Given this significant expense, only about one-third of families with the nearly 20 million kids under the age of 5 use child-care services; the rest rely on relatives or informal and often unreliable arrangements.

There is [today] a patchwork of government programs to help families get child care and prekindergarten educational services. At the federal level, the biggest programs include Head Start and the Child Care and Development Block Grant. These programs are effective, but are targeted to help only low-income families, typically those who earn less than 85% of a state's median income, and reach only a small percentage of eligible low-income families. . . .

Middle-class families also benefit from federal child-care tax credits, but the support is modest and not nearly enough to cover their child-care costs. . . . And at the state and local level, 43 states and the District of Columbia provide prekindergarten programs that serve about 1.5 million 3- and 4-year-old children [out of a population of about 8 million such kids].

Running the numbers through its macroeconomic model of the US economy, Moody's concluded that the Warren proposal would *raise GDP by about $700 billion over ten years.* Moody's found that the in-kind subsidy of free childcare provided to low-income Americans (which effectively would free up money to be spent on other important goods and services), together with the foundation that such a program would provide for women to enter the workforce or to seek more permanent forms of employment, vastly outweighed the drag of taxing the rich, which Moody's characterized as having "little impact" on the economy.

Moody's found that the Warren proposal would cost the federal government about $1.1 trillion over ten years when measured "statically," but once the positive feedback effects of more tax collections from higher spending and labor force participation were considered, the net "dynamic" cost to the federal government would be about $700 billion, or $70 billion/year, out of a federal budget that today comprises well over $4 trillion—$4,000 billion—per year in total spending. According to Moody's, the tax increases proposed to be levied on the wealthiest Americans would cover the cost, so that there would be no net cost to the federal government as an entity.

Another way of saying this is that the financial cost to America as a whole, net of the increase in GDP that would follow from implementing these programs, would be approximately nothing. The "government"—which is to say, all of us, wearing one hat—would be out $700 billion, but the "economy"—which is just us, wearing a different hat—would be $700 billion to the good. But the move would be highly progressive in its impact, which is to say it would pry open the rusty gate of genuine equality of opportunity for millions of families struggling just to keep their heads above water.

In Moody's view, these estimates actually understated the economic benefits from a program like Warren's, because Moody's did not include any measure of the projected increased lifetime incomes that children enrolled in good-quality center-based education would be expected to earn. Finally, Moody's made no attempt to capture the real desideratum in all government policy, which is the effect of a policy on the *welfare* of citizens—on their personal satisfactions, or ability to flourish as individuals and as members of society.

Here we see the perversity of US family policy. National parental leave and childcare programs would literally pay for themselves, and then some, but alone out of all the major economies in the world, the United States—the richest among them—cannot muster the clarity of vision to seize the opportunity. What is more, all the research in the next section on early childhood development and education applies with equal or greater force to the very earliest years of a child's life. If we wish to take seriously a commitment to addressing the accidents of birth by offering every child a fair opportunity to develop her native talents and predilections, robust high-quality and freely available childcare must be part of the equation.

MORE OPPORTUNITY SQUANDERED: PRE-PRIMARY FORMAL EDUCATION

The Neuroscience Revolution

In the United States today, compulsory education generally begins at age six, with first grade (primary school). Most but not all five-year-olds attend kindergarten, and some four-year-olds attend "preschool" (what in my day was called nursery school). Some children younger than four participate in programs with some explicit educational component, beginning in some cases shortly after birth.

Center-based childcare and formal pre-primary education often are offered in conjunction with each other (two-year-olds, after all, cannot sit at their desks learning Old Norse eight hours a day). As a result, the benefits to children of childcare and formal pre-primary education ideally should be considered together.

Mandatory formal education beginning at age six, and patchwork optional programs for children younger than that, is a carryover from a century ago. The best evidence today suggests that all children *from age three forward* should participate in formal education programs of the sort just outlined. This movement's slogan is "universal 3–K" (that is, starting at age three).[13]

The word "universal" here should not be confused with "mandatory." No truant officer will chase after toddlers playing at a sprinkler in the park during official 3–K school time. The idea is that these programs should be universally available, with families to make their own decisions of what works best for them.

The push for Universal 3–K follows from exciting work over the last several decades by neuroscientists studying how the brain evolves in early childhood in response to specific stimuli (particularly language), with positive consequences that carry over throughout life. The general idea is that the brain is remarkably "plastic," and actually changes in its physical composition in response to the stimuli of its environment. As the executive director of UNICEF and the director-general of the World Health Organization wrote in *The Lancet*, the leading UK medical journal:

> The debate between nature and nurture as determinants of early child development is over. Today, we understand that the two are inextricably linked. The degree of their interdependence—and the impact of this interplay on the developing brains of

children—is even greater than we previously imagined. This knowledge has tremendous implications for how we design and deliver early child development interventions.

We already know that the brain develops most rapidly in the first few years of a child's life. During these critical years, neuroplasticity is at a peak—neurons form new connections at the astounding rate of up to 1000 per second. These synaptic connections are the foundation of a child's physical and mental health, affecting everything from longevity to the lifelong capacity to learn, from the ability to adapt to change to the capacity for resilience.

New lines of research are expanding our understanding of the part environment plays in the formation of these neural connections. If children fail to get what they need—enough nutrition, nurturing, stimulation, and a sense of security—during the most critical years of early childhood, the impact on their lives and futures is enormous. For example, inadequate nutrition in the early years of childhood can result in stunting, which can cause diminished physical and cognitive development that undermine a child's ability to learn and earn later in life. Similarly, inadequate stimulation during the same critical period of earliest childhood can reduce learning capacity and ability to form social and emotional attachments.[14]

The OECD summarized the neuroscience of brain development in early childhood, and its relevance for education policy, as follows:

Research in neurosciences has shown that the brain sensitivity of highly important developmental areas, such as emotional control, social skills, language and numeracy, peak in the first three years of a child's life. These findings indicate that the first years of a child's life represent a pivotal "development window": the brain first develops rapidly, and its capacity to adapt and develop continues into adulthood, but it slows down with age. The first years are important for the development of skills as they lay the foundations for future skill development.

Children learn more quickly during their early years than at any other time in life. Children who are already falling behind in the first few years of their childhood face greater obstacles to catch up and succeed at school and beyond. Participation in early childhood education is crucial. The positive effects of participation in early childhood education include improved child well-being and early learning outcomes as a foundation for lifelong learning, as well as later student outcomes ranging from education, employment, income, health and other areas.[15]

The case for very early childhood enrichment through explicit educational components mixed with play is not simply a hypothetical extension of neuroscience laboratory experiments. As researchers Greg Duncan and Katherine Magnusson have noted, "research on the malleability (plasticity) of cognitive abilities finds these skills to be highly responsive to environmental enrichment during the early childhood period."[16]

Economist Timothy Bartik extensively reviewed the social science literature on the efficacy of early childhood education in his book *From Preschool to Prosperity: The Economic Payoff to Early Childhood Education*. He concluded:

> We have better evidence for the effectiveness of early childhood education than for almost any [other] social or educational intervention. We have better evidence because we have good comparison groups. Ironically, these good comparison groups arise because early childhood education is not universal, so many children are excluded from services.[17]

In short, neuroscience and social science studies alike confirm the critical importance of the very earliest years of a child's life in the growth of the brain's internal structures. This forms the theoretical basis for early childhood education beginning at age three.

To be clear, households differ in important ways that public investment in education can ameliorate but not wholly eliminate. Recent studies have shown, for example, that children in well-off professional families hear three or four times as many words in their first four years as do children born into poor families. As a result of this vocabulary-rich environment, Nobel laureate James Heckman has found that, "At age three, children from professional families speak 50 percent more words than children from working-class families and more than twice as many compared to children from welfare families."[18] Consistent with the neuroscience, this richer verbal environment has clear benefits in language skills and cognitive development more generally.[19]

No sane person would suggest in response that affluent parents should adopt a vow of silence until their children go to school, just out of a sense of fairness. But good-quality early childhood education can make a large positive difference for less fortunate children, were these programs uniformly available, consistently high quality, and adequately funded—which they are not.

Every well-educated young parent in Brooklyn knows the literature in this area, probably better than I do. And in fact we see examples of extreme parental zeal at every turn. (Readers who have insulated themselves from the phenomenon need only read *The New York Times* Style section for a week or two.) Expensive private early education, nursery and kindergarten classes of the very highest pedagogical standards occupy the high streets of every upscale community—I know, because I contribute to the cost of my infant granddaughter's. (These should not be confused with the parochial schools found in many parts of the country whose principal objectives seem to be science denial and de facto segregation.) Beyond classroom time, affluent parents zealously read to their children, take them to museums and shows, and of course schedule them for carefully curated lists of extracurricular activities, from oboe to ancient Greek to squash (the game, not the vegetable), to give their kids the best possible résumés to present to the best possible colleges years hence.

The affluent will not be compelled or shamed into not investing in their children. The response therefore must be to invest more in good-quality public early childhood education, in particular, universal 3–K. The volume of parental education-stuffing will never be equal, but at least it offers intellectually curious and nimble young children not born to affluence the starting investment in human capital that they do not enjoy today.

The United States in Its Global Context

According to the National Center of Education Statistics, in 2016 about 86 percent of five-year-olds attended school—69 percent in kindergarten, and another 17 percent in preschool programs.[20] Those participation levels quickly fell off in earlier years: about 66 percent of four-year-olds and 42 percent of three-year-olds were in some form of preschool (private or public).

The NCES data also show that in 2016, a little less than one-half of those three-, four-, and five-year-olds who were not yet enrolled in kindergarten (i.e., including the 17 percent of five-year-olds in pre-K programs) attended some sort of "center-based" pre-K educational program as the primary source of nonparental care. In a 2005 study, the US government's National Center for Education Statistics found that only 35 percent of four-year-olds in center-based programs received high-quality care, which is terrible—unless you compare it to the millions of kids participating in more informal at-home programs, where only 9 percent were deemed to receive high-quality care and education.[21]

It is instructive here to compare the United States with other peer countries, to see how asleep we have been in ignoring the neuroscience revolution. In most European countries, close to 100 percent of five-year-olds are in school. In the United Kingdom and Ireland, all five-year-olds are mastering the material that we reserve for our first grade.

The trend continues down to younger children. The United Kingdom, for example, now offers universal public early childhood education starting at age three—and it is both poorer than the United States and has followed the same small-government trajectory since the 1980s as has the United States (see Figure 5.3).[22]

There are important exceptions within the United States. But when the evidence is so powerful, and when so many other peer countries have rolled out universal 3–K, there is no excuse for the United States not to have fully adopted early childhood education best practices on a national scale.

Child Age	0-2 years	2 years	3 years	4 years	5 years
Australia	0.0	0.0	58.0	88.8	20.3
Canada					94.7
France	4.0	11.9	99.4	100.0	99.8
Germany	0.0	0.0	91.5	95.9	97.1
Italy	5.3	15.6	92.4	95.9	88.3
Japan	0.2	0.6	84.4	94.7	96.0
Norway	0.0	0.0	95.8	97.0	97.3
Sweden	0.0	0.0	92.1	93.7	94.6
Switzerland	0.0	0.0	2.5	48.0	97.9
United Kingdom	0.0	0.0	100.0	100.0	0.0
United States	0.0	0.0	38.4	66.7	87.3
OECD Average	25.3	44.5	76.1	88.0	94.6

FIGURE 5.3 Enrollment Rate in Preprimary Formal Education Programs, Selected Countries (2016)

Source: OECD, *Education at a Glance 2019: OECD Indicators* (Paris: OECD Publishing, 2019).

US Early Childhood Education and Poverty

The US National Academy of Sciences (NAS) has studied the two-pronged benefits of robust early childhood education and childcare programs and has contrasted those benefits with the reality on the ground. The NAS summarizes its research as follows:

> Studies show that disparities across socioeconomic and racial/ethnic groups in cognitive skills, health, behavior, and school readiness are apparent before children enter kindergarten. This growing gap can be partly attributed to disparities in access to opportunities, as higher-income families have increased investments, including enrolling their children in early education, whereas high-quality early care and education remains inaccessible or unaffordable for many middle- and low-income families. As a result of these disparities, children may be placed in lower-quality early care and education that does not enhance learning and development or may even be harmful to their development. The inability of all American families to access affordable, high-quality early care and education increases the poverty rate among children and contributes to gaps in later educational outcomes across socioeconomic and racial/ethnic groups, resulting in a greater likelihood of lifelong poverty for these children.[23]

How damning a summary this is—and how extraordinary it is that this is not seen as a national disgrace as an ethical matter, and as self-destructive national policy from an economic perspective.

Richard Wilkinson and Kate Pickett, in their well-known book *The Inner Level*, describe in some detail the cruel burden that being born poor systematically places on one's educational achievement:

> Regardless of whether their initial scores are high, medium or low, the gap between the performance of children from the most and least deprived backgrounds widens as they get older. Children from the least deprived [more affluent] families either maintain their initial high relative position, or improve their average or low scores. Education enhances their performance. In contrast, the relative performance of children from deprived backgrounds who initially achieved a high or average score declines over time. Deprivation makes so much difference that children from the least deprived [more affluent] backgrounds whose performance at age seven was only average or low overtake—or at least catch up with—children who initially performed better than them but came from deprived backgrounds.[24]

These studies, and many others like them, put the lie to the proposition that too many Americans either espouse or unconsciously believe that those who are poor are so because they are in some way inherently less capable or less deserving than those of us at the top of the food chain. It is poverty, not ability, that is driving differences in educational attainment, and through that mechanism success in the income sweepstakes. This state of affairs is not the inexorable result of some cruel natural law, but rather reflects a systematic lack of public commitment to honoring the principle of equality of opportunity.

In 2011, Raj Chetty and colleagues published an important paper following the careers of a large group of former kindergarten students in Tennessee once they had reached age twenty-seven.[25] This was a carefully designed experiment: some teachers were experienced, others were not, and some classroom populations were larger than others. Students and teachers across the state were assigned randomly to different classrooms and were tracked from kindergarten through the third grade, in an effort to see which, if any, pedagogical strategies might have had lasting impact on the children.

The results were mind-blowing. The researchers summarized their findings as follows:

> [K]indergarten test scores are highly correlated with outcomes such as earnings at age 27, college attendance, home ownership, and retirement savings. . . . [S]tudents in small classes are significantly more likely to attend college and exhibit improvements on other outcomes. [S]tudents who had a more experienced teacher in kindergarten have higher earnings. . . . Students who were randomly assigned to higher quality

classrooms in grades K–3—as measured by classmates' end-of-class test scores—have higher earnings, college attendance rates, and other outcomes.

Among other inferences from the study is that experienced teachers directly contribute far more to the nation's economy in terms of the increased earnings of their former students than their modestly higher compensation, compared to junior teachers, comes close to capturing.

Sean Reardon at Stanford University is one of the leading researchers in early childhood education. In a recent paper, he and a co-author studied income, racial, and ethnic gaps in readiness for school at the point a child enters kindergarten, as well as achievement over the course of the kindergarten school year.[26] Consistent with the neuroscience just summarized, Reardon begins by noting, "Cognitive skills at kindergarten entry are strong and consistent predictors of later academic achievement."

As was true in earlier research over several decades, Reardon found large gaps in kindergarten achievement between white children and black or Hispanic ones, and between children from rich and poor families (defined as the 90th and 10th percentiles of family income, respectively). Those achievement gaps are materially larger (worse) for the rich vs. poor category than for the differences between white vs. black or Hispanic children.

Reardon's particular interest in this paper was to compare the kindergarten achievement gap across these categories for children born in 1998 and those born in 2010. Studies covering earlier years had found that, while these achievement gaps had narrowed (improved) over the course of several decades for black and Hispanic children, they actually had gotten worse for rich vs. poor ones. That is, over time, rich five-year-old children were consistently pulling further ahead of poor ones at the beginning of their respective educational careers.

Reardon was able to show that this disturbing trend of rich tykes distancing themselves even further from poor ones had reversed over the more recent period covered by his study. That is good news. But before we all give ourselves a slap on the back for a job well done, Reardon reminds us that the difference remains very large: "at the rates that the gaps declined in the last 12 years, it will take another 60 to 110 years for them to be completely eliminated."

Moreover, why did the gap narrow at all from 1998 to 2010 babies? Reardon concludes that the best evidence suggests that the sources of the improvement were better access for the poor to public child healthcare and to public pre-K educational programs. In other words, these forms of public investment have paid dividends. Based on the incomplete reach of high-quality pre-K educational programs that I described earlier, there is every reason to believe that more such investment might erode the gap at a faster rate.

Research by three other researchers came to similar conclusions about the importance of "universal pre-K"—making available to all children, based only on age and residence, "center-based" early childhood education starting at age three or four.[27] Their study analyzed what effect universal high-quality education would have on the achievement gaps also studied by Reardon. By extrapolating from two successful programs in Boston and Tulsa, the authors were able to predict the powerful positive effect of a national program along the same lines. Their findings have two important elements. First, *everyone* benefited—rich kids and poor ones, white ones and Hispanic or black ones. Second, low-income, black, and Hispanic children benefited more than did white or high-income groups—which is to say that the programs worked to reduce the kindergarten achievement gap, or if you prefer, worked to help the more disadvantaged kids make up a bit of the distance between them and more advantaged children (see Figure 5.4).

In short, if the goal is to instantiate authentic equality of opportunity, even universal pre-K starting at age four is insufficiently ambitious, but today, only a minority of states provide universal public childhood education even at age four. Readers will be familiar with the Head Start program, or at least its name. It is a federal program designed to provide educational support services to very young children in households living below the federal poverty level.[28] Whatever the grandiose promises once made for Head Start, it has been consistently underfunded in recent years, and its programs are mediated through the fifty states, with a resulting crazy quilt of take-up and educational quality from state to state.[29] Enrollment in Head Start programs actually has declined in recent years for four-year-olds, often because parents switched them to newly available state-funded general public early childhood education programs. Nationwide, Head Start programs serve only

	Math	Reading
White	2.93	7.35
African American	7.33	14.29
Hispanic	13.15	22.06
Low income	8.31	15.44
Higher income	5.13	10.03

Note: "Low income" refers to children whose household incomes are at or below 200 percent of the federal poverty guidelines, or FPG. "Higher income" refers to children whose household incomes are above 200 percent FPG.

FIGURE 5.4   Average Achievement Gains following Participation in Two UPK Programs

Source: Friedman-Krauss, Barnett, and Nores, *How Much Can High-Quality Universal Pre-K Reduce Achievement Gaps?*, Center for American Progress and National Institute for Early Education Research, April 2016.

about 38 percent of four-year-olds in poverty, and about one-third of three-year-olds in poverty. And these take-up levels are much worse if one looks at the population of low-income families, which means families living on incomes up to twice the federal poverty level.[30] Head Start today is not filling the role once envisaged for it.

For the 2017–2018 school year, fewer than half (44 percent) of four-year-olds and 16 percent of three-year-olds across the country were enrolled in *any* public center-based education programs (including Head Start), regardless of their quality rating.[31] The federal government has a relatively new "preschool development grant" program, but it is so poorly funded that it served only about 35,000 four-year-olds in public preschool programs in 2017–2018—out of a national population of nearly five million.

Many existing programs seem to operate as Potemkin villages. For example, Indiana's program for four-year-olds no longer meets the technical definition of "universal," because it is now tied to the working status of a parent, but in any event in 2017–2018 it served a mere 2,423 children.

It is true that these last figures reflect only public programs, and that many families avail themselves of local private or parochial programs, or informal family networks. But the question in every case is whether those programs accomplish the twin purposes of public education, which is education that meets minimum standards and socialization of children within a larger community not drawn exclusively from their parents' immediate social network. Much private "education" for pre-K students is glorified childcare, at best.

Economic Costs and Returns to Early Childhood Education

All these statistics of the uneven quality and reach of public education available to three- and four-year-old children does not address the question uppermost on most voters' minds, which is, Who needs expensive, high-quality classroom time at age three? With the possible exception of John Stuart Mill,[32] the answer is, everyone.

I have already touched on the important work of James Heckman in quantifying the financial returns to early childhood education. As to the cost side of the equation, in 2018 the National Academies of Sciences, Engineering, and Medicine published a consensus report analyzing the costs of expanded early childhood education and childcare.[33] The report contemplated top-of-the-line best practices programs, with lower student-to-teacher ratios, better physical facilities, and so on. It estimated that the cost to the federal government for the first phase of this rededicated commitment to equality of opportunity would total about $75 billion from all sources, public and private, rising over a period of years to about $140 billion per year by Phase 4, as quality standards were ratcheted up still further and more families enrolled in the new programs.

The National Academies must have been embarrassed by this amount, because they buried the lede on page 185 of their report. But they should not have been, because figures in this range are in fact affordable. As a starting point, the United States today already spends almost $30 billion/year on early childhood education (public and private), so Phase 1 of the National Academies' plan would require $45 billion, not $75 billion, per year of incremental funding. One useful way of understanding this amount is that Phase 1 of the National Academies' ambitious plans would add only about 12 percent to the total national expenditure on all K–12 education today.[34]

The National Academies Phase 1 estimate sounds roughly comparable to the Moody's estimate for the federal budgetary impact of Elizabeth Warren's Universal Child Care and Early Learning Act, discussed earlier. They are not in fact directly comparable, beyond both pointing in the direction that this country in fact can afford to offer much better and more comprehensive early childhood childcare and education. The National Academies figure included all funding, public and private, because it contemplates substantial cost sharing by families, whereas the Moody's estimate included public funding only, because the Warren plan would be universal in reach, and therefore presumably would crowd out existing poor-quality parent-funded programs. The National Academies estimates are described as "dynamic," but in this case the term is reserved to mean a consideration only of the greater take-up that would follow from offering expanded programs; the National Academies did not score the dynamic effects of their proposals on the economy as a whole. Nonetheless, I find it heartening that both of these different ambitious proposals put price tags on doing much better by very young children that are in the same ballpark; the question of how much is borne by the public sector, and how much by families, is a different matter.

To put these numbers into sharper relief, let me throw out two facts, which you can interpret as you wish. First, the United States in its 2018 fiscal year spent $628 billion on the military (not including another $100 billion or so of veterans' services)—about 15 percent of all government spending, including "mandatory" programs like Social Security and Medicare. That is more than the next ten countries combined spent, and far higher as a percentage of GDP than any other large economy.

Second, in December 2017, Congress rewrote large swaths of our tax law. The net effect will be to reduce government revenues (the things that fund useful government expenditures, like aircraft carriers and universal 3–K) by about $2 trillion over the following ten years, or $200 billion/year on average. One provision alone, providing high-income Americans with a 20 percent discount on the tax imposed on many of their business investments, costs about $50 billion/year. As a matter of logic and tax policy, not to mention revenue hemorrhages, this item truly deserves its moniker as "Congress's worst tax idea, ever."[35] Its repeal alone would fund the incremental costs contemplated by the National Academies for Phase 1 of their best-in-class recommendations—or 70 percent of the cost of the Warren proposal, without recourse to any new tax.

Which do you think would be the highest and best use of our money?

I have worked on budget arithmetic and politics for government and as an academic for decades, and I have found that raw dollar figures, or even worse, budget trends over time expressed in nominal dollars are meaningless for most observers unless placed into context. Sometimes the right measure is an item's aggregate cost, and at other times its per capita cost. But in general, whenever one is trying to put a price tag into context, the fairest measure is to express that cost as a percentage of GDP. The United States is the richest large economy in the world, and we simply have more dollars to spend on most everything than do most other countries. At the same time, the cost structure of providing government services in the United States is higher than in poorer countries.

Looking at expenditures as a fraction of national income communicates what the priorities and values of the United States really are, in ways that mind-numbingly large numbers by themselves cannot. And in turn, looking at cross-country comparisons helps to benchmark the spending of the United States against peer countries, and in this way reveal a great deal about our national values and priorities.

Latvia, for example, does not enjoy the same level of wealth and income that the United States does, whether on an aggregate or a per capita basis, and it therefore would be unfair to expect that Latvia spends as much in dollar-equivalent terms per child on early childhood education as does the United States, because Latvia simply does not have enough wealth to do so. It is a fair question, however, to ask whether Latvia spends as large (or larger) share of its national income as does the United States, because that tells us something about how large a commitment Latvia is making to funding the human capital of its next generation, given the unavoidable constraints imposed by its lesser affluence.

If you carry through on this thought experiment, you will be embarrassed to discover that Latvia spends about twice as large a share of its GDP on educating its three- to five-year-old children as does the United States. In fact by, this measure the United States spends less now than we did a few years ago (see Figure 5.5).

The OECD and the European Union both recommend that countries should spend about 1 percent of their GDP on early childhood services. As applied to the United States, this would imply a spending target of about $200 billion per annum. In fact, the United States today spends only 0.4 percent of GDP on preschool and kindergarten programs. (It does not collect data on children younger than three.) Were we to catch up to other countries (where the average is about

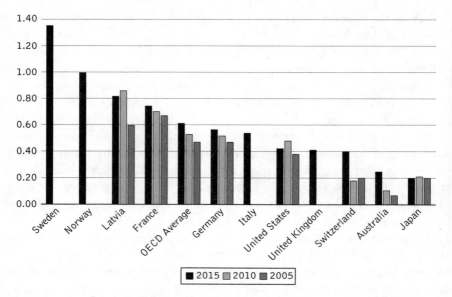

FIGURE 5.5 Spending on Pre-Primary Education as a Percentage of GDP, Selected Countries (2015, 2010, 2005)

Source: OECD Education at a Glance 2018: OECD Indicators (Paris: OECD Publishing, 2018).

0.8 percent of GDP) or the OECD/EU recommendation, we would direct up to another $120 billion/year of public resources for pre–first grade education and care.

The OECD has written a little online report card for the United States as an annex to its flagship publication in the field, *OECD Education at a Glance*, under the heading "Participation in early childhood education and care is still low and remains stagnant."[36] Its analysis is brief and pointed; it therefore is worth quoting in its entirety:

- There is increasing awareness of the key role that early childhood education and care (ECEC) plays in children's well-being and cognitive, social and emotional development. However, only 38% of 3-year-olds and 67% of 4-year-olds in the United States were enrolled in an ECEC setting in 2016, compared to 76% and 88% on average across OECD countries.

- Between 2005 and 2016, enrolment rates of 3–5 year-olds have gradually increased from 75% to 85% on average across OECD countries. In the United States, however, they have remained fairly stable at 66%.

- Despite greater annual expenditure per child at the pre-primary level (USD 10 830) than on average across OECD countries (USD 8 426), total expenditure on pre-primary education in the United States amounts to 0.4% of GDP, lower than the average across OECD countries (0.6%).[37]

- In the United States, 26% of total investment on pre-primary education is privately funded, compared to 17% on average across OECD countries. The US share of private expenditure on pre-primary education has increased over the past decade from 21% in 2005, while the share of private expenditure on average across OECD countries at this level has fallen by 4 percentage points over the same time period.

Here you see the themes of this book neatly encapsulated: a well-researched path to improved equality of opportunity (through early childhood education and care); the wealthiest large country in the world, but one that offers this path to a smaller percentage than do other comparable countries; substantially less spending (public and private) as a percentage of national income than is true for peer countries; and a greater reliance on private resources to fund the pre-primary education that is offered.

If the goal is to instantiate authentic equality of opportunity, our goal should be universal 3–K for all kids in America. This might seem unrealistic, but it is only if we constrain our imaginations to an impoverished government that spites its own citizens, and to achingly slow incremental change.

OPPORTUNITY CONSTRAINED: PRIMARY AND SECONDARY EDUCATION

One takeaway from looking at the returns to education is that there is no such thing as an unimportant grade level. Vast investments in early childhood education will to some extent be dissipated, at least on future test scores, if a child moves on to mediocre grade and high schools. When attention is turned to our K–12 education system, what we find are wide variations in school quality, often attributable to disproportionately higher funding for public schools in affluent communities.

Basically, over 90 percent of K–12 spending in the United States comes from public sources (federal, state, and local).[38] Much of the remaining 10 percent is absorbed by parochial schools; academically elite K–12 schools are a very small slice of the pie. Within the universe of public schools, about 45 percent of K–12 public school revenues come from local governments (mostly property taxes), another 45 percent from the states, and 10 percent from the federal government. Individual variations are large: in California, nearly 60 percent of public K–12 school budgets come from the state out of general tax revenues.

The allocation of school spending within a state is largely determined at the state level, either through legislation or through court orders implementing state constitutional requirements of fairness in school financing. Depending on a state's financing system, property taxes raised in a wealthy community in some cases (such as New Jersey) are reallocated by the state to poorer school districts through "equalization" plans. As a result, local tax revenues are not invariably spent in the locality where the taxes are collected.

Very generally, before the mid-1960s, public schools were financed almost entirely out of local property taxes, with the result that a rich community could afford far superior public schools to those available in poorer communities.[39] Through state constitutional legal challenges and through legislation, a slim majority (twenty-eight as of a few years ago) of the fifty states have implemented school funding plans based on fairness principles (poor kids should not be disadvantaged relative to rich kids), or, more recently, on "adequacy" principles (schools should get what they need to give kids comparable educations). Adequacy-based systems often point to progressive structures, where poorer school districts get *more* per student than do rich ones, because the kids in those poorer districts have significantly more issues that must be addressed if they are to prosper within the school system. The remaining states rely on local property tax collections, with all the problems attendant on this form of financing that have been documented over the last fifty years.[40]

Even in states like California, where the state provides the predominant share of school financing, and those state funds are distributed proportionately to student population, funding inequality can still appear. In California, for example, local school districts can top up state allocations to yield higher per-student spending in affluent districts. Only in unusual cases, like New Jersey, are principles of funding equity applied rigorously across all school districts.

When a state overhauls its school financing system, whether through legislation or because its supreme court rules that the old system violates the state constitution, an elegant social sciences natural experiment is created. Economists can study the sudden reallocation of funds to poorer school districts from this upsetting of the apple cart (or "exogenous shock," in fancy-pants talk) to see how much of a difference the new money makes in educational outcomes. Two recent papers have done just this. Both find that the new money causes measurable improvements in student achievement in those poorer districts. In the words of one, "Reforms increased the absolute and relative [i.e., relative to rich kids] achievement of students in low-income districts."[41] The other paper used the results of these natural experiments to predict that a 10 percent increase in per pupil spending for all twelve years of primary and secondary school leads to 7 percent higher adult wages and a 3.2 percent reduction in adult poverty; the results were more pronounced for children from low-income families.[42]

In both studies, these natural experiments confirm what one would have hoped would be the case, which is that the application of money to low-income school districts improves both pedagogical and material outcomes significantly. The raw talent is there, but it needs the help of public school finance systems that provide the resources necessary to enable that talent to flourish.

Going further, some states simply have proportionately invested more, and done so more wisely, in promoting quality primary and secondary education across all their school districts than have others. It is not the case that the wealth of a state directly maps onto its commitment to public school spending: California, for example, spends money equitably (school districts get about the same dollars per student to run their schools), but at far lower proportionate levels than does a much poorer state like Vermont.

Education Week rates the fifty states every year on the overall quality of their K–12 public programs in its *Quality Counts* survey. *Education Week* summarizes things by finding America's K–12 schools to be mediocre as a whole, giving the country a grade of C. Notwithstanding all the attention brought to this critical issue, *Education Week* found that the achievement gap between poor and nonpoor students (measured by federally administered standardized tests) widened in three out of four states in the 2003–2018 period.

Massachusetts has been the perennial top dog, although in January 2020's survey New Jersey clawed its way to the top. True, both Massachusetts and New Jersey are wealthier than many other states, but they also have many economically depressed areas and children from many cultures. New Hampshire and Minnesota also perform well, and they are not nearly so wealthy. What distinguishes these states in general is not simply the money expended per pupil (New York usually tops that contest), but the consistent attention from the Governor's Mansion on down to fostering high-quality public education, through holding their students to reasonably high achievement standards, and to workable faculty and administration accountability standards. Massachusetts and New Jersey also score well in the equity of the funding the state makes available to school districts, to compensate for differentials in the wealth of different communities within the state.

Here we see another existential fortuity at work—the state in which one is born, regardless of one's family's wealth, can materially impact the quality of one's K–12 education. As *Education Week* summarized its 2019 report, "When it comes to setting a child up for success in America—at least when it comes to crucial education and socioeconomic factors—place matters more than ever."[43] This is the tyranny of geography—the dead hand of where we were born and raised—in action.

Rather than bore readers with more data that would surprise no one—that public secondary schools in the most exclusive locations, and academically serious private schools deliver better educations and smoother runways to the best universities, at the cost of tremendous financial investments by parents (in the premiums paid to live in those locations or the explicit tuitions charged)—I believe that it would be more use to shift gears and ask: How well do our high schools perform in general when compared to schools around the world? That is, to see how good a job we are doing in educating our children, the most meaningful test is relative—are we at the top of the game, when compared with other countries? This question, strictly speaking, is not another instance of existential bad luck in operation (at least when that question is constrained to the United States), but it does bear directly on how we are doing today.

So how good are our high schools, for example, when judged in international competition? Not very. Notwithstanding our national wealth, the United States achieves only middling results on these global standardized tests.

We can see the overall poor performance of US high schools when we look at international PISA (Program for International Student Assessment) scores. These are standardized tests administered by the OECD that compare the performance of fifteen-year-old schoolchildren around the world on standardized tests in reading, mathematics, and science.

The PISA tests are administered every three years, and the OECD analyses of the results reach into the thousands of pages. The most recent year for which these analyses have been published is 2018. If you want the briefest possible headline, it is this: if you are looking for best-in-the-world public schools, move to China (Beijing, Shanghi, Jiangsu and Zhejiang) or Singapore. Their students actually managed to capture the top scores in all three subjects.

Meanwhile, and despite our status as the world's richest large economy, the United States plods along in the middle of the pack. In science and reading, our scores were a tad above the OECD average. In mathematics, though, we are significantly below the average for the OECD countries. Overall, in math our students are behind those in Spain, Hungary, and Lithuania, not to mention top-performing countries such as Canada and Germany (and of course top-performing, Singapore and China).

Another measure of the quality of schools that PISA analyzes is the percentage of students within each country who perform exceptionally well, along with the percentage of students whose performance can only be described as unsatisfactory. For example the 2108 results indicate that, in Singapore, 43 percent of students are top performers in at least one of the three subjects, and only 4 percent of the students are low achievers across all three. As a more realistic example, 24 percent of Canadian fifteen-year-olds are top performers in at least one subject, while only 6 percent struggle badly in all three. In the United States, by contrast, only 17 percent of students are top performers in at least one subject, while 13 percent perform unsatisfactorily across all three. Among large peer economies, only France has a similarly mediocre set of high and low student achievement results.

If one switches gears and accounts for differences in population, US students constitute about 22 percent of the worldwide pool of top-performing fifteen-year-old students in science, simply because the United States is so much larger than many other countries that produce more top performers as a percentage of their population. So one could take the view that, despite having mediocre schools, the United States generates enough accomplished science students to fill the job requirements of Facebook and Google. But that ignores what the US economy could look like if our schools produced as large a crop of top performers as a percentage of the population as do other countries, and further ignores the foreclosure of opportunities to smart students stuck in poor schools who do not have the investment behind them to reach their own potential.

Can we say anything useful about why US primary and secondary schools as a whole lag behind world peers, and why is there such a dispersion of results within the United States? The OECD has more information on these topics than a normal person could ever absorb in one lifetime, but I believe that the most important problem, plainly visible in the data, is that the United States systematically underpays its school teachers.[44]

This statement requires some unpacking. The United States actually spends much more per pupil in primary and secondary education than do most other OECD member countries—$122,000 per student in total from age six through age fifteen, against an OECD average of $94,000 per student. This seems to cut against my claims. But when you dig deeper, the problem emerges. First, the United States spends much more on administrative staff, and less on teachers, as a percentage of its total primary and secondary education spending than do other OECD countries. About 54 percent of our current spending on education for primary and secondary students goes to teacher compensation, against the OECD average of 63 percent. If you adjust the total spending numbers for this, the United States spends about $66,000 per student from age six through age fifteen, while the OECD average spend is $59,000—a much smaller gap than what the first numbers imply. Conversely, we spend almost twice as much on administrators and other non-teaching staff, as a percentage of aggregate current spending, than do other countries. (These figures hold across public and private schools with only a little variation.)

Second, the OECD average dollar value of spending per pupil is itself a misleading metric to use when looking at US educational spending. The OECD's membership of thirty-three countries includes several that are relatively small and poor when compared with the United States and some of the other large economies. OECD averages give equal weight to every country, so that the average is brought down by spending levels in, for example, Estonia and the Slovak Republic. A better metric in general is the percentage of national income devoted to a particular aspect of educational spending.

Third, and most important for domestic politics, the proper metric for judging pay levels for teachers across countries is not to compare their salaries with each other, but rather to compare teacher salaries in a country with the job opportunities available to peers with similar levels of educational attainment. That is, a young person with a master's degree in the United States has many relatively high-paying reasonable job opportunities available to her. Where in that range of opportunities do teacher salaries fit? The answer is, much nearer the bottom than the top. Teachers' salaries are between 62 percent and 68 percent of the average salaries of comparably educated compatriots who find jobs other than as teachers. As the OECD notes, "these relative earnings are among the lowest across all OECD countries and economies."[45]

Fourth, US teachers work much longer hours than do their counterparts in other countries—about 2,000 hours/year, versus an average of 1,600 elsewhere. This means that it is more difficult for a US schoolteacher to supplement his income through a second job than might be the case in another country.

In short, the United States is a large, wealthy country where investment in one's human capital pays off in higher lifetime earnings. Far from wallowing in an easy life, US primary and secondary teachers effectively make great sacrifices in their pay, relative to the opportunities available to their comparably educated contemporaries—yet they face the same cost of living as do their counterparts. If you want better schools, you need better teachers, and that means closing the gap between teacher compensation and the salaries available to others with comparable education who pursue careers outside of education.

OPPORTUNITY SUPPRESSED: COLLEGE

Readers might have the intuition, as I certainly once did, that the United States sends a larger fraction of its high school graduates to college than does most any other country. In fact, the opposite is the case: the United States is at the back of the pack on this critical metric (see Figure 5.6).

Equally surprising, about 40 percent of American adults who enter tertiary education for the first time are pointing toward a two-year Associate's degree, despite its very modest impact on lifetime earnings. Another 400,000 high school graduates attend non-degree-granting, Title IV eligible (i.e., at least facially legit), postsecondary institutions, typically various technical training programs; this compares with about 20 million American young adults enrolled in degree-granting programs (including associate's degrees). Of the population of 20 million students in degree-granting programs, about 2 million bachelor's degrees are awarded each year.

The range of educations offered varies widely. According to the federal Department of Education, "In fall 2016, the five institutions with the highest

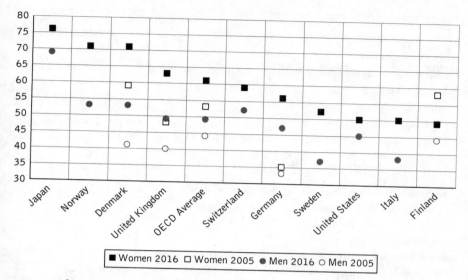

FIGURE 5.6 First-Time College Entry Rates below the Age of 25, by Gender, Selected Countries (2005, 2016)

Source: OECD Education at a Glance 2018:OECD Indicators (Paris: OECD Publishing, 2018).

enrollment (including distance education as well as in-person enrollment) were University of Phoenix, with 131,600 students; Western Governors University, with 84,300 students; Ivy Tech Community College, with 78,900 students; Grand Canyon University, with 75,800 students; and Liberty University, with 75,800 students."[46] Many readers might not be familiar with all of these.

Our colleges and universities are the instruments by which careers are turbocharged, and lifetime earnings put onto a much higher trajectory than for those who stop their education at high school. In light of their crucial importance in improving the lives of young Americans, especially those with limited family connections and resources on which to draw, we all would like to think that these are among our most meritocratic of institutions. In reality, we find that "choosing" your parents wisely, to ensure that they have the wealth to invest in your education, materially increases the likelihood that you will graduate college, and even more dramatically increases the likelihood that you will obtain an advanced degree, relative to those not born to wealth.[47]

Figure 5.7 illustrates the problem.

What this summary chart shows is that those born to wealth have twice as many holders of bachelor's degrees within the born-to-wealth group as do ordinary folk within their group, and four times as many holders of advanced degrees. This does *not* mean that those born to wealth hold twice as many bachelor's degrees as do less affluent adults. The born-to-wealth category is a

	Born to Wealth 40 to 60 year old Households	All Other 40 to 60 year old Households
Has Bachelor's Degree	67%	32%
Has Advanced Degree	16%	4%
Works in Family or Inherited Business	11%	0.5%
Percent of Total Households	2.7%	97.3%

Note: "Family or Inherited Business" is defined as a business that reported to be either inherited, given, or started with inheritance funds. Advanced Degree includes a PhD, JD, or MD. Households are assigned to the category "born to wealth" if the sum of their inheritances received and their expected inheritances exceeds $1,000,000 (in real 2016 dollars).

FIGURE 5.7   University Degrees and Family Businesses, Wealthy vs. Others

Source: Federal Reserve Board, Survey of Consumer Finances (2016).

small fraction of the entire population. What the statistics offer us, however, is an important insight into the transmission of wealth in the United States. Today's family wealth is not simply transmitted to future generations to dissipate in wanton consumption: it funds investments in the next generation's income-earning capacity, regardless of the lucky recipients' actual abilities. In this way today's wealth is compounded and refreshed, not dissipated, as it passes from one generation to the next.

University degrees are not merely certificates to frame and hang in one's bathroom—they lead on average to much higher lifetime incomes. In 2016, for example, men whose highest educational achievement was a bachelor's degree earned 71 percent more than did men with just a high school diploma, and women with a bachelor's degree earned 65 percent more than did women whose education stopped with high school.[48] These figures do not include holders of advanced degrees, whose incomes are higher still—in 2016, about 167 percent greater than workers whose terminal education was a bachelor's degree (about $120,000 vs. $71,600).[49] It has been estimated that over a lifetime a holder of a bachelor's degree (which group includes those with more advanced degrees) has twice the aggregate income of a high school graduate.[50] So who gets into and graduates from college, especially top-tier ones, is directly tied to lifetime incomes, and hence the prospect of economic mobility.

I have already introduced some of the work by Raj Chetty, one of America's pre-eminent inequality researchers. One recent research project undertaken by Chetty and four distinguished colleagues came to several important conclusions.[51] In brief, the authors confirmed that college works as a lifetime income accelerant, but more important, the amount of that income boost depends on the college. The most elite colleges have alumni with substantially higher lifetime incomes than those from more ordinary schools. Young people from low-income backgrounds enjoy the income benefits from the turbocharging offered by graduating from an elite college just as much as do high-income kids. But—and here's the rub—kids from families in the top 1 percent of the income distribution are *seventy-seven times* more likely to attend an Ivy League school than are those drawn from the bottom 10 percent of income.

Along the same lines, consider that a young person is five times more likely to be admitted to Harvard if she is a "legacy"—the child or grandchild of a Harvard graduate—than is an applicant from off the street.[52] It might be argued that this has nothing to do with wealth, but really, what are the odds that a population of Harvard graduate parents are less wealthy than the general population? More directly, choosing parents who attended Harvard is in its own right a perfect example of existential good fortune for the lucky few.

Given the importance of a four-year college degree to lifetime earnings, let's explore further the barriers faced by smart poor kids to obtaining such a degree. In addition to those discussed below, these include the simplest obstacles, like unfamiliarity with the college admissions process, lack of qualified counselors, and inability to afford trips to visit colleges of interest.

First, as just explained, smart poor kids have more difficulty getting into first-rate colleges than they should, if those institutions were truly meritocratic.

Second, and critically, the United States is a complete outlier in the costs imposed on students and their families for college or post-graduate education. The absolute costs of college are higher in the United States, and a larger fraction of those higher costs are financed from private sources—Mom and Dad, or student loans, in particular. (A government loan to a student is repaid from that student's future earnings, and thus ultimately is financed from private, not public, resources.)

In 2015, all US public and private sources combined spent more to pay for each full-time-equivalent student attending private or public colleges than did any other country in the OECD, save Luxembourg—about $30,000 per student.[53] And the out-of-pocket costs incurred by a US college student were also the second highest in the OECD (about $36,000 over a college career), this time behind only the United Kingdom. Tuition is only one such cost, but it is a good proxy when comparing countries.

This figure is too kind to the United States, in that it looks only to public colleges, but the point is made even before layering Harvard and Swarthmore tuitions on top (see Figure 5.8).

In this one chart you can see how unusual the United States is. Most European countries (save the United Kingdom) charge their resident students nothing or close to nothing by way of college tuition. (The UK system is described briefly later in this chapter.) Moreover, the average tuition figure for the United States masks a large dispersion in actual tuition costs, from reasonably inexpensive community colleges (with commensurately modest impacts on lifetime earnings) to high-prestige private Ivy League institutions.

It is true that nominal US college tuition rates often are mitigated through grants, scholarships, and loans. But even so, the average college student is left with thousands of dollars of direct out-of-pocket costs that must be borne by the student and her family. As explained by The Institute for College Access and Success, "after considering grants and scholarships, undergraduates at four-year colleges still had almost $11,000 of unmet need in 2015–16, with $6,600 still left uncovered after taking all loans into account."[54] Smart poor kids must cover this gap through a jumble of part-time and summer jobs, while their affluent counterparts go on field trips to Madagascar or intern for US senators. This added burden, along with a host of cultural stresses, leads to smart poor kids who are admitted to college persistently failing to graduate at the same rate as do more financially comfortable counterparts.[55]

To direct costs must be added the income that a student could earn if he were in the full-time workforce rather than college—his forgone earnings. In the United States, these forgone earnings add another $35,000 of economic cost on top of a student's direct expenses to attend college. Forgone earnings are a rounding error for the indolent children of the affluent—what college-age progeny of Greenwich, Connecticut, country-club parents would have worked in a minimum-wage job

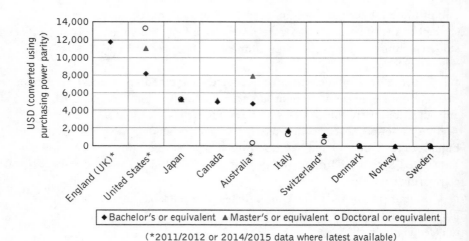

(*2011/2012 or 2014/2015 data where latest available)

FIGURE 5.8 Average Annual Public College Tuition for Full-Time National Students, by Education Level, Selected Countries (2015/2016)

Source: OECD Education at a Glance 2018:OECD Indicators (Paris: OECD Publishing, 2018).

had he not gone to college? But these forgone earnings are a very large sacrifice to families struggling to put food on the table. Of course, smart poor kids understand that a college education pays off over a lifetime, but in the meantime, how will the family's rent be paid?

Overall, about two-thirds of the direct cost (i.e., not including forgone earnings) of college education in the United States is funded from private sources of every variety, and just under one-half from students and their families.[56] Where do these family resources come from for those not born into affluence? Part-time and summer jobs account for some of the money, but about two-thirds of US college seniors graduating in 2017 from public and private nonprofit colleges obtained their degree by relying to a substantial degree on student debt, with an average direct debt of about $29,000.[57] For 2017 graduates, about 85 percent of this debt came from direct government loans. For students with financial need, the 2018 interest rate on direct subsidized federal loans is about 5 percent—but these subsidized loans are limited to $5,500/year.[58] Unsubsidized direct loans are available up to $20,500/year (less subsidized loan disbursements). The interest rate on unsubsidized loans to undergraduates is about the same as on subsidized loans, but interest accrues on unsubsidized loans for all periods, *including while a student is in college*. Moreover, in either case the government charges a fee of over 1 percent of any loan disbursement.

Federal loans may be repaid under a bewildering range of options. These include, in addition to the standard ten-year term loan, an Extended Repayment Plan, a Pay as You Earn Plan, a Revised Pay as You Earn Plan ("A good option for those seeking PSLF"), an Income-Based Repayment Plan, an Income-Contingent Repayment Plan, and an Income-Sensitive Repayment Plan.[59] Ask yourself, if you were a twenty-two-year-old first-generation college graduate with uncertain lifetime career prospects, would you choose the right plan? (Please do not inquire of the author, as I cannot for the life of me keep all these programs straight.)

Students obtained about 15 percent of their loans from private lenders, at interest rates as high as credit card debt—over 14 percent.[60] Student debt to attend for-profit institutions (which are excluded from some of the data just presented and which typically prey on the poor) and for post-graduate education, as well as the compounding of arrearages in debt repayment, add to the national total.

The interest charged by the federal government is significantly greater than that required to cover the government's incremental borrowing costs plus losses from defaults. It also is outside of world norms for countries that offer student loans to fund university studies. In Australia, for example, the interest charged on student loans recently was 2.6 percent.

England is an interesting point of contrast. (Scotland has its own rules here.) Most English universities charge the same tuition, which is the maximum rate allowable by statute—currently £9,250 ($12,300) per year.[61] To emphasize, these are the tuition charges at almost all institutions, including Oxford and Cambridge, universities globally recognized as the equal of the best American schools.

At the same time, loans covering 100 percent of tuition costs, *as well as living expenses* ("maintenance loans," in amounts that range up to $15,000/ year or more), are made available by the government to all students. Interest accrues while a student is at university at a rate equal to the UK equivalent of the US consumer price index, plus 3 percent. (After graduation, interest rates are adjusted based on the borrower's income, but never exceed the undergraduate rate.)

After graduation, a former student is not required to make any payments on her loan until her income exceeds a statutory threshold (currently about $33,000/year). Each year that the threshold is reached, the former student basically pays 9 percent of her income above the threshold, which is credited against the loan balance (principal and accrued interest). The repayment system is folded into the tax system, so that in effect English borrowers are simply subject to a 9 percent withholding tax on income above the statutory threshold.

At age sixty-five, or on death or disability, any remaining balance is forgiven. By design, it is *anticipated* that about 45 percent of English student loans will be forgiven.[62] This extraordinary fact indicates how far the English system in operation is from a "pay for itself" student loan model of the sort operated by the United States.

In short, the UK system for financing a college education superficially seems even more reliant on private resources than does the United States, but the broad coverage and simple repayment terms for government-funded student loans, including a set-aside for a generous basic level of income unburdened by repayment obligations, makes the UK regime work for most British students.

Contrast this to the US system. In the United States, loans are not generally available to cover 100 percent of the tuition costs at more expensive colleges, and loans also do not cover living expenses. The interest rates charged are roughly comparable to the UK rates, but even under income-contingent repayment schemes, loans must be repaid out of a graduate's first dollars of income. The United States does not make it easy to relate repayments to income by running the repayment programs through the tax system, but instead requires annual recertifications by every borrower. And the bewildering array of repayment programs confuses even sophisticated borrowers.

Today, roughly 44 million Americans owe about $1.5 *trillion* in student debt.[63] This works out to an average of about $34,000 per debtor. These are very large sums of money for most borrowers. How is the student loan system working out for them?

Terribly, in the case of many black, poor, or first-generation college graduates. The Institute for College Access and Success has summarized student loan default experience as follows:

- More than one in five (21 percent) Black bachelor's degree recipients defaulted within twelve years of entering college, a much higher rate than their white (3 percent) and Hispanic or Latino (8 percent) peers.
- Bachelor's degree recipients who received Pell Grants, most of whom had family incomes of $40,000 or less, were more than five times as likely to default within twelve years as their higher-income peers (11 percent versus 2 percent).
- First-generation bachelor's degree recipients were more than twice as likely to default than students whose parents had attended college (10 percent versus 4 percent).
- Three in ten (30 percent) bachelor's degree recipients who started at for-profit colleges defaulted on their federal student loans within twelve years of entering college, seven times the rate of those who started at public colleges (4 percent) and six times the rate of those who started at nonprofit colleges (5 percent).[64]

Black students make up a disproportionate share of students at for-profit colleges, which on average are much more expensive than are nonprofit alternatives. For this and other cultural and economic reasons, Black students who graduate college on average enter the full-time workforce with significantly more student debt than do White students.[65]

Finally, the millions of individuals who do not finish college find themselves saddled with large debts relative to their incomes, with little prospect for relief. The problem is particularly acute for Black students, who often attend less prestigious schools (disproportionately including for-profit institutions), and who fail to graduate from college at a higher dropout rate than do white students with comparable family incomes (see Figure 5.9).[66]

In short, federal student loans are effective at enabling white middle-class kids whose parents also went to college to obtain a college education for themselves.

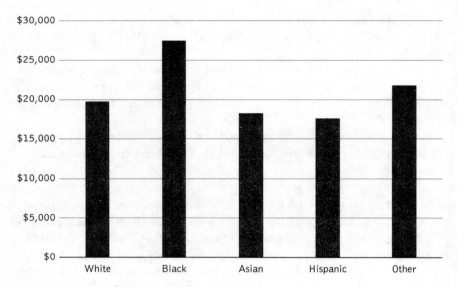

FIGURE 5.9 Estimated Education Debt Burden by Race

Source: Michael Grinstein-Weiss et al., "Racial Disparities in Education Debt Burden among Low- and Moderate-Income Households," *Children and Youth Services Review* 65 (2016): 166–174.

But student loans lead to an inescapable debt trap for far too many first-generation and minority college students. The problem is compounded at for-profit colleges—the payday lenders of the educational world.

To these student loans must be added debt incurred by parents to enable their children to attend college. There is a federal program called Parent PLUS that is designed to plug the gap when a student exhausts the limits of federal direct loans, but the availability of these loans is dependent on the parents' credit rating, and the loans are much more expensive than direct student federal debt. Because the Parent PLUS program does not have a hard cap on the amounts lent, parents with good credit ratings can and do borrow substantial sums to enable their children to attend high-prestige and commensurately expensive colleges. The average Parent PLUS debt for a student whose parents avail themselves of this program is around $33,000, but at the most costly colleges it is in the neighborhood of $55,000.[67] Smart kids from poor families are explicitly precluded from Parent PLUS loans, because of their parents' poor credit ratings.

It is sometimes argued that there is no problem with the heavy burdens incurred by students and their families to pay for college, whether from pre-existing savings, loans, or forgone earnings, because the projected incomes of graduates have more than kept up with these costs. As discussed at the outset of this chapter, under certain accounting conventions a man graduating from college in the United States today on average earns a handsome return on his investment of family resources and forgone earnings.[68] (The economic returns to a woman are positive but lower, because even at the college graduate level women systematically earn less than do their male counterparts.)

But citing this fact yields a very incomplete picture of things, as the data just presented demonstrate. Regardless of any long-term financial rewards attendant on a college degree, student loan debt servicing is systematically more problematic for black, first-generation, or poor graduates than for white graduates from middle-class backgrounds with parents who also went to college.

Students who for whatever reason fail to complete a college degree are nonetheless saddled with tens of thousands of dollars of debt. In many cases, the compounding of interest on student debt outpaces a graduate's wage progression. In the case of my own law school, many students amass debt close to $200,000. And in every case, the iron shackles of that student debt, which cannot be loosened through bankruptcy, constrain career choices and the ability to take a gamble on one's own business.

To summarize, a college education should be the great leveler in American society, where ability rises to the top and where smart poor kids join the fast track to financial prosperity. But smart poor kids aren't typically legacies at Harvard, and don't in fact attend colleges in general at rates comparable to their abilities. Once in college, their experiences are dominated by scrambling to cover their costs, while their families are asked to shoulder the further burden of the earnings that the students forgo while attending school. Our universities are not the simple expressways to a meritocracy that we like to believe.

EDUCATION, INEQUALITY, AND MOBILITY

The overarching theme of this chapter is that if you want to teach a man to fish in the modern world, you need to send him to fisheries management school. Individuals need large investments in their human capital to reach the income levels and lifetime satisfactions that their native talents and ambitions imply. Those investments pay handsome financial returns, even before considering their positive impact on the welfare of our citizens. Our economy today, however, is held back by a systematic underfunding of the supply of human capital.

These points interact with Chapter 4's discussion of income mobility in surprising ways. It turns out that the high payoffs to education in the United States are not unalloyed good news. As we have seen in this chapter, the economic returns to higher education in the United States are very large (sounds okay so far!), but the costs of that higher education are borne disproportionately from private (i.e., family) resources (uh oh!), so the scions of the wealthy find it much easier to capture those higher returns, simply because they start off with more family resources to invest in their human capital (rats, the rich get richer, yet again) (see Figure 5.10).

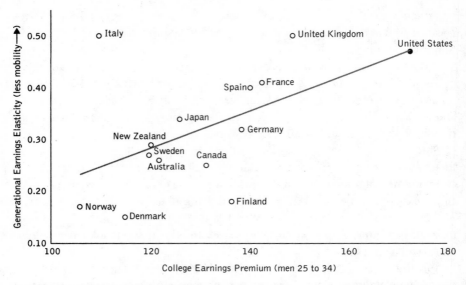

FIGURE 5.10 Higher Returns to Education Associated with Lower Intergenerational Mobility

Source: Miles Corak, "Income Inequality, Equality of Opportunity, and Intergenerational Mobility," *Journal of Economic Perspectives* 27, no. 3 (summer 2013): 79–102.

It is a good thing to live in a country where the returns to higher education are large. That means that our economy is at the cutting edge of economic productivity, always coming up with new ideas and new ways of doing things, all requiring lots of brains and lots of training. But—and here is the critical part—so long as private resources disproportionately determine the cash investments made in young people's human capital, the inequality of this generation will be visited even more dramatically on the one to follow.

This, then, is the logical causative link explaining why the United States has higher intergenerational earnings elasticity (less relative economic mobility) than do many other countries, as illustrated by the Great Gatsby Curve presented in Chapter 4: the United States enjoys a productive economy where the returns to investing in oneself through education are very high, but family wealth plays a larger role in the United States than elsewhere in making those investments possible. The result is an ever-increasing wedge between incomes from one generation to the next.

Let me close this long chapter with one more chart, which might be named the French Horn Economic Opportunity Index. Less facetiously, it is a measure of how much money affluent families spend "enriching" their children's lives—French horn lessons, lacrosse travel teams, Mandarin Chinese lessons, high-profile unpaid internships obtained through family connections and funded by doting parents,

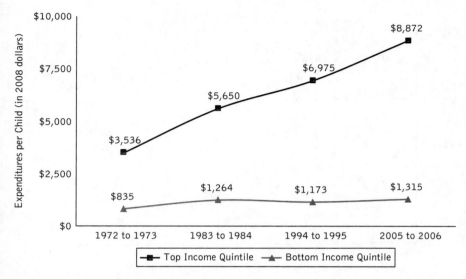

FIGURE 5.11 Enrichment Expenditures per Child (1972–2005), Top and Bottom Income Quintiles

Source: Miles Corak, "Income Inequality, Equality of Opportunity, and Intergenerational Mobility," *Journal of Economic Perspectives* 27, no. 3 (summer 2013): 79–102.

and, of course, hunting with eagles on horseback in Mongolia—all to make their children irresistible to Ivy League admissions directors (see Figure 5.11).

No one should be surprised that rich kids get "enriched" with more flute lessons than do the poor. What is important is that as the financial returns to elite college educations become larger and larger, affluent parents have predictably upped their game, to the point where the children of today's affluent are so stuffed with enrichment that they have no time at all to be lazy and indolent, as children were meant to be. The poor have not given up, notwithstanding all the pressures on their incomes. They continue to do their best, but the gap grows wider and wider, which in turn feeds into elite college selection, which in turn leads to greater lifetime earnings—and so the cycle does not simply repeat, but instead accelerates.

PART III

....

INSURANCE TO THE RESCUE

CHAPTER 6

INSURANCE AS PRODUCT

WHAT MAKES INSURANCE SPECIAL

Many years ago, I stood in line at a rental car counter in Manhattan to pick up my car. The woman ahead of me was contesting her bill, complaining about numerous add-on charges. She demanded an explanation of each one, and why it had been added to her bill. The clerk explained the charges, and further noted that she had initialed her acceptance of each at the time she picked up her car. She finally got to the last charge. "That, ma'am, is for collision insurance," the clerk explained, "and here are your initials accepting it." "Well," she said, "I don't remember agreeing to any such thing—and in any event I returned the car in perfect condition, so I don't see why I should be charged for insurance."

This chapter puts insurance on somewhat firmer theoretical ground.

Insurance is more interesting and more important than many readers might appreciate. The interesting part comes from its rich history and its specialized vocabulary informed by that history. Where else can you throw around terms like "aleatory contracts," "named perils," "acts of God and man," "quota share treaties," "retrocession agreements," and of course "adverse fortuities"? The importance of insurance stems from its seemingly magical ability to make the financial consequences of bad luck disappear, at least in a colloquial sense.

In the commercial context, insurance is one of the foundational pillars of capitalism (along with money and banking; clear and enforceable rights of property ownership and alienation against both others and the state; private markets not subject to malignant interference by the state; and, in recent centuries, the limited liability company). Insurance has enabled businesses for centuries to mitigate the risks of extraordinary financial losses from bad luck, and in doing so it has permitted firms to invest with confidence in their businesses and to survive despite all sorts of calamities.

In the public context, insurance can mitigate the financial consequences of outliving one's ability to support oneself, living with a disability, or falling gravely ill (to take a few examples). The principal contribution of this chapter is to call for an expanded concept of public insurance to mitigate the financial consequences that flow from existential bad luck. This is an extension of current applications of "social insurance," and one that relies on insurance as a metaphor rather than a literal financial product, but the concept and principles of insurance nonetheless neatly frame what I am trying to accomplish.

Along the way, I will touch on health insurance. Health insurance in the United States is a mess, and our national spending on healthcare is about 50 percent more as a percentage of our national income (GDP) than in the next most extravagant country on the planet. The reason is not the failure of the insurance paradigm. Instead the problem is political, not technical, and stems largely from a calculated refusal to apply immutable insurance principles in a sensible and comprehensive way.

At the outset, you need to divide insurance into two great camps: property and casualty (P&C) insurance, on the one hand, and life insurance, on the other. (Health insurance occupies a sort of halfway house between the two.) Of the two, I think that P&C is inherently the more interesting and the better analogy for my purposes.

P&C insurance today often encompasses both accidental damage to one's own property (your car hits a tree) or to yourself (the crash causes you to break your shoulder), as well as accidental damages to other persons or their property (your car hits another, damaging it and injuring the occupants). For our purposes, it helps to focus solely on the original use of the product, as financial indemnity (a make-whole) for accidental financial losses to one's own property arising from specified perils.

Unlike life insurance, P&C insurance has a pretty clear origins story, in fourteenth-century Italy, and an equally clear impetus for its invention—the facilitation of long-distance trade around the Mediterranean and the Baltic, in particular the mitigation of the risk of loss of ship or cargo in maritime transportation.[1] Marine insurance was invented because of a revolution in the conduct of what today we would call international trade.

In earlier times, a merchant typically ran a solo (or immediate family) operation. He invariably would accompany his goods on a sea voyage; when calamity struck and the cargo sank without a trace, he also probably sank with it. Cutting-edge fourteenth-century Italian merchants developed a new sedentary business model, whereby they no longer escorted their merchandise on sea voyages. Instead, the new breed of merchants operated more like proto-multinational enterprises, relying on branches or trusted agents around the Mediterranean and northern

Europe. The trick was, how to increase the likelihood that your cargo would arrive safely at a foreign port, where your agent awaited it, when you were not along for the ride?

One answer was to break your merchandise into smaller units, and to send those shipments on multiple ships. But this required that there in fact were several ships sailing to your desired port, that the goods would not spoil in waiting for another ship, and that the market opportunity that prompted you to put your merchandise at the risk of a sea voyage would not dissipate while waiting for the goods' arrival.

Insurance was a much more elegant solution. On orders from my editor, I must skip some early experiments like "bottomry contracts" and "sea loans," and instead pick up the story around 1350. By the middle of the fourteenth century, merchants regularly employed standardized form agreements that we would immediately recognize as the progenitors of modern insurance contracts to protect the value of their cargos; shipowners also used these contracts, but less frequently, to protect the value of their ships. There really have not been many conceptual breakthroughs in the field of marine insurance since then.

In a typical mid-fourteenth-century insurance contract, the insured (a merchant shipping his wool cloth, for example) paid a specified premium to a group of third-party insurers; the contract specified the nature of the goods being insured, the value for which they were insured, the boat on which they were to sail, the destination, and other similar terms. In return for the premium, the insurers assumed, for example, the financial risks that "are of God, of the sea, of men of war, of fire, of jettison, of detainment by princes, by cities, or by any other person, of reprisals, of arrest, of whatever loss, peril, misfortune, impediment, or sinister that might occur, with the exception of packing and customs" in respect of the insured goods until their safe arrival at the named port.[2] (A cynic might observe that the only significant development in marine insurance in the 650 years since has been to exclude acts of war or detainment by princes as covered losses.) The premium varied with the length of the route, the time of year, the size of the ship and its ability to withstand pirate attacks, and similar concerns. A typical premium might be in the range of 4 to 6 percent of the agreed value of the goods.

Now consider what this simple contract accomplished. In exchange for a small but certain outlay (the premium), the insured eliminated his exposure to unlikely but catastrophic financial loss—an act of God, or of the sea, or of men of war, for some examples, that would reduce the value of his investment to zero. We know that a loss event was unlikely, because the insurers set a single-digit premium for the assumption of that risk.

From the insured's perspective, the contract transferred financial risk of loss from him to another (the insurer). Risk transfer is one of the two fundamental characteristics that help to distinguish insurance from other financial products. The contract also was different from a gambling arrangement: an insurance payoff would restore the insured to the same financial position he would have occupied had the loss event not occurred, but the insured could not profit from "winning" his bet. This is what is meant when an insurance policy is described as a contract of *indemnity*.

But marine insurance did not stop shipwrecks from happening. The insurance contract shifted the risk of calamity off the shoulders of the merchant, but that risk still existed, and therefore landed somewhere else. If the probability of the loss of a cargo is one in twenty-five (4 percent), an insurer that accepted that risk without more would simply have stepped into the shoes of the insured. Risk would have been transferred, but to what end?

Even in 1350, an insurance risk was "underwritten," meaning, first, that the specific risk was evaluated in order to price the premium, and, second, that it was undertaken by a group of individuals who might have no other connection with each other. Through the underwriting process, several individuals in the business of writing insurance would assume a fraction of each risk; the risk of loss of a cargo valued at 1,000 florins, for example, might be assumed by ten underwriters, each signing on for 100 florins of risk.

Underwriting by itself broadened the group of risk-takers, and it further enabled a professional insurer with a fixed amount of capital to assume, say, twenty separate risks of 100 florins each rather than one risk of 2,000 florins. This opened the door to the real magic of insurance, which is *risk pooling*. Risk pooling contemplates the agglomeration by the insurer of many potential losses of the same general character (named perils) but whose likelihood of being triggered was independent of the others in the pool. The insurer could then apply the *law of large numbers* to risk management. (The "law of large numbers" in this context means that, as the size of a data set grows, its average results increasingly approximate the average results of the general population; admittedly this statistical theorem was more a matter of intuition than actuarial science in 1350, but the principles were there, even if imprecisely articulated.)[3]

If the insurer accepted many one in twenty-five risks in respect of different cargos on different ships (so that one ship sinking would not cause other insured cargos to be lost), the law of large numbers says that the *actual* performance of an insurer's pool of risks each year will approach the theoretical *expected* loss from all such comparable risks (whether in or out of the insurer's risk pool) over that period.[4] With a large enough pool and careful underwriting, the medieval insurer therefore would know to a high degree of probability that for the 10,000 florins of capital in his business, he could expect to pay out (or to lose, if you prefer) 400 florins in insurance claims every year. If the insurer then charged premiums of 5 percent, he would be highly confident that he would collect 500 florins in premiums and would pay out 400, leaving him with a reliable profit of 100.

By virtue of the law of large numbers, then, the insurer eliminates the unpredictability of individual events of loss. The insurer fully expects to pay out claims (to suffer losses), but to do so at a steady and predictable pace. In turn, the insurer can then price his insurance premiums to more than cover those predictable losses, and thereby turn a profit without too many sleepless nights.

The real difference between insurance and other financial contracts is not the terms of the contract, or the shifting of risk from the shoulders of the insured, but rather the application by the insurer of the law of large numbers to make the actual performance of his pool of risks closely track the theoretical probability of the risk of loss on the underlying type of risks in the pool. Accepting a one-in-twenty-five risk and then standing pat would mean that most of the time the insurer might make what he thought was easy money, but once in a while—and at completely unpredictable intervals—he would suffer a large loss. And what is more, luck being what it is, he might suffer two such calamities in close proximity to each other and find himself bankrupt.

Many financial products—indeed, all private contracts—involve the shifting of risks from one party to another, but to understand whether a risk-shifting contract is insurance, you must look to the risk management strategy of the party assuming the risk.[5] If that party lays off the risk through another offsetting contract, you are dealing with a classic securities dealer (a dealer in financial derivative contracts, for example). If that party retains the risk and commingles it with many other similar risks, so as to apply the law of large numbers to smooth out the unpredictability inherent in any one contract, you are dealing with an insurance arrangement. And if the counterparty simply assumes the risk and goes home for the day, you are dealing with a fool.

This is the magic of insurance: not that large unpredictable losses (the ship that sinks) have literally been made to disappear, but rather that the financial consequences of those losses have been regularized and *mutualized* (shared across all members of the risk pool), so that despite the occasional occurrence of these calamities, *neither* the insured *nor* the insurer is at risk at any point in time of a large and unpredictable loss that would threaten either's business. When I write that insurance makes risk disappear in a colloquial sense, it is this elimination of the large and unpredictable loss, and its replacement with a small but certain loss (the premium from the insured's perspective, or the expected claims payments, from the insurer's perspective) that I have in mind.

Risk transfer from insured to insurer and risk pooling by the insurer thus accomplish a bit of a commercial miracle. A businessperson will be more willing to put capital at risk and to formulate long-term plans when he is confident that

unpredictable events of bad luck (including two or three such events in close suc-
cession) cannot bankrupt him.

Risk shifting meant that our wool merchant could take on more risks of the type
in which he was an authentic expert—fluctuating prices around the Mediterranean
and Baltic, evaluations of the different quality of different batches of wool, customer tastes in colors, and his competitors' wares—than would be the case if he
were paralyzed by the possibility of a ship lost at sea. All his capital, less the premium he paid, could be devoted to pursuing market opportunities, wherever they
might lie, rather than holding a large portion idle as a reserve against calamity. In
turn, the insurer can shoulder that risk of loss because it pools the risk and invokes
the law of large numbers to turn the random luck of the individual case into a predictable stream of claims payments.

In this way, insurance then—and now—encouraged risk taking, accelerated
trade, and increased the amount of capital that could be put at risk of the business.
Insurance properly understood is an accelerant to trade, not an insulation from it.
The gears of commerce have thus been greased.

Statisticians might respond that a one-in-twenty-five chance of loss is in the nature of shipping wool cloth in wooden sailing ships through pirate-infested waters,
and that insurance cannot change this fact. This much is true. In the long run, a
statistician might go on to say, the insured will lose about 4 percent of his cargo to
such perils, either in actual losses or in insurance premiums; the insurer's profit
margin just makes insurance an even worse bet. But this last claim is a profoundly
unrealistic assessment of things.

To see this, let's return to our merchant and his cargo of wool cloth; assume that
the loss of a single shipment of wool cloth would be devastating. In my example,
the merchant faced a 4 percent (one-in-twenty-five) risk that his cargo would be
lost at sea. His insurer (the group of underwriters), however, charged a premium
of 5 percent. From this, a statistician might suggest that insurance really does
not accomplish very much. If the merchant dispatched twenty-five cargos of wool
cloth, each with a value of 100 florins, he would expect to lose one cargo, or 100
florins. But the insurers charge 125 florins to protect against that expected loss of
100 florins. Sounds like a rip-off!

This sort of logic is the commercial analog to playing Russian roulette, where five
times out of six, you win. More politely, this objection overlooks that commercial
firms have both finite capital to risk and finite time horizons. If a firm had infinite
resources and an infinitely long time horizon, then, yes, insurance accomplishes
nothing, because over great periods of time the insured in this example would
average one lost cargo in twenty-five, notwithstanding random periods of enormous loss when several cargos were lost in close proximity in time. But no business enterprise has the luxury of infinite time horizons and infinite capital behind

it. The value of insurance is to regularize lumpy large losses into a predictable amount that the merchant can pay with every shipment. He has removed the risk of a string of bad luck wiping him out (not a problem with an infinitely long time horizon and infinite capital, neither of which any real-world merchant possesses). Further, he can relate his anticipated losses to the cost of his merchandise (that is what the premium does), and thereby have an accurate picture of his yearly profit through the application of straightforward accounting norms.

For the merchant, the alternative of simply accepting the risk of loss would be highly imprudent. It might lead to many years of seemingly highly profitable trading, followed at some unpredictable point in time by spectacular collapse. Or the very first wool shipment might be lost, leading to immediate bankruptcy. That is the nature of luck; it does not perform on a fixed schedule.

The alternative strategy, of "self-insuring" through cash reserves, would be economically inefficient. The merchant effectively would need to hold reserves from the day he opened for business, because bad luck might befall the first shipment—or the first two or three, for that matter, notwithstanding the improbability of that outcome. Self-insurance works for the small stuff, but not for improbable but very large potential losses.

By contrast, the insurer does not need to hold reserves equal to the amount of each potential loss multiplied by the number of insureds in the insurance pool, but rather only the much smaller number required to cover the variance between the insurer's *ex ante* estimate of the expected frequency of losses and the *ex post* reality of things—that is, the risk that shipments really are exposed to a one-in-twenty chance of loss, not to a one-in-twenty-five chance, with the result that premiums have been miscalculated. (When expected losses are not preordained, the law of large numbers does not guarantee that the insurer will have perfectly predicted them.) Insurance in this example has reduced the aggregate capital set aside as unproductive reserves across all businesses, thereby allowing more capital to be invested in productive enterprises.

The insurer's profit constitutes compensation for the service of assembling a sufficiently large pool of risks to make the law of large numbers operable and thereby to offer insurance at a rate within hailing distance of the expected loss from marine transport of cargo (one in twenty-five). In addition, a commercial insurer assumes the risk that the general view of expected losses (one in twenty-five) is accurate, and (hopefully) holds sufficient reserves to absorb any miscalculation.

For this reason, the word "risk" has a special meaning in insurance. It does not refer to the possible loss of a cargo from time to time—that is just a fact of the business—but rather to the possibility that the frequency of losses within the insurance pool has been misestimated. That is, "risk" means a variance between expected losses (by definition, an estimate) and actual loss experience for the entire pool.[6] The law of large numbers might thus better be expressed as establishing a relationship between the actual loss experience of a pool and the *properly estimated* expected loss experience of the pool.

"Risk" therefore turns out to be a dangerous word to employ when anywhere near an insurance professional, because it has so many meanings in different contexts. If I were to consider opening a bagel shop in Pasadena, California, I would make a long list of the business risks of my proposal—bagel taste and quality control, unpredictable rent costs, local regulatory ambiguities, changing customer tastes, employee turnover, possible competitors, and so on. The use of the term "risk" in the technical insurance sense (my actual profits have diverged from my expected profits?) would not be one of them. Nonetheless, it is impossible to avoid writing about insurance without getting a bit sloppy in the use of the word. Particularly when viewing matters from the perspective of the insured, therefore, I will use the word "risk" in circumstances where insurance strict constructionists would have preferred another formulation. This avoids the use of "loss units" and other awkward phrases.

Let me summarize to this point. At its core, insurance is a zero-sum game in which all the players nonetheless come out ahead. Every player in the game is exposed to some sort of risk of a random unfavorable event (an "adverse fortuity," in insurance terms)—the possibility of a shipwreck or car accident, for example. Those risks are not correlated to each other (my car crash is not related to your car crash). We therefore band together to shift the financial consequences of such an event from the person suffering the adverse fortuity to the entire group. We do so by paying insurance premiums into a pot, and then compensating those among us who have suffered a loss from the sums so collected. In short, we all substitute a small but certain loss (the premiums we pay) for an uncertain but potentially much larger loss (the occurrence of the adverse fortuity). We do so in part because most humans are risk-averse—even if the statistical odds of a shipwreck can be perfectly calculated, we prefer the certain cost of annual premiums to the actuarially identical risk of a larger loss from the calamity—and in part because our horizons are limited in time and money, so that we cannot always afford to roll the dice, even if over an infinite horizon and with infinite resources we would be sure winners.

The utility of insurance is limited by several important constraints. Risks must be individually unknowable in advance but susceptible of pool-wide statistical predictability (the law of large numbers). Ordinary commercial insurance thus is forward-looking, not retrospective.

Life insurance has a different history and a slightly different business model. Amateur historians in the field love to discover examples of ancient sects, clubs, or guilds that required their members to make annual contributions into a pot, from which the association would pay the funeral expenses of a deceased member, perhaps along with a cash settlement to the bereaved family. The practice was so widespread across societies separated by place and time that the best we can say is that life insurance is an idea that has come naturally to the minds of many.

The most important insight garnered from reflecting on the history of proto–life insurance is that all these arrangements had as their motivation a sense of mutual obligation arising from the nature of the organization to which the members belonged. Although this theme of mutuality is deeply obscured in the modern era, with enormous insurance pools managed by giant insurance companies that are as often perceived as enemies as they are as friends, all insurance has this underlying characteristic of constituting an arrangement of mutual undertakings among the members of the pool. As insureds in the contemporary world, we typically are not bound by mutual obligations arising from sect or guild, but everyone in an insurance pool nonetheless has in economic substance entered into a mutual arrangement with every other member, in which each contributes to a communal pot and draws from that pot when an event of loss occurs. In economic terms, a commercial insurer is simply being paid to facilitate this, and separately to accept the risk that its expected loss model is wrong. Modern mutual life insurance companies make this explicit, because there is no "us versus it" in such arrangements: the policyholders are the owners of the legal entity that is the insurer.

What makes life insurance fundamentally different from, say, marine insurance is that every ship theoretically might safely reach port, but the sad truth is that none of us will escape death. Life insurance thus cannot possibly serve as simple insurance from death. Instead, the idea behind life insurance in its core meaning is to shift from the shoulders of the insured the financial consequences of *premature* death. Again, this is an unlikely but catastrophic risk, in this case that a piano will fall from a crane and crush you to death in the prime of your life, thereby depriving your family of the income you might have expected to earn.

While not necessarily being traceable back to Ur of the Chaldees, insurers have for centuries also taken on the mirror-image risk, which is the risk of outliving your income. This is what an annuity product is meant to do. In insurance lingo, it is a contract addressing *longevity risk.*

Insurers manage life and longevity risks—that is, the risks of premature or deferred death (but not death itself as an adverse fortuity!)—in the same way they manage marine risks, by applying the law of large numbers. Because human life cannot be valued like cargos of wool cloth can, life insurance technically is not a contract of indemnity (of making whole), but rather a policy of value, which pays the insured's beneficiary the fixed sum specified in the contract.

Life insurance typically is sold to cover an extended period of the insured's life, rather than for one voyage (marine insurance) or one year (automobile insurance). This feature, combined with the insured's right to cancel the long-term contract at any point, means that life premiums within a long-term contract logically would be expected to rise from year to year, as the highly improbable ripens into the somewhat unlikely. Life policies are designed to avoid the appearance of this by in effect collecting premiums in advance, through a level payment structure. (In practice, life insurance often is further complicated by the marriage of pure insurance protection to savings plans in a single contract, yielding the classic whole life policy, or to other exotica, like universal variable life policies, aimed at arbitraging the tax laws. None of those is relevant to my aims.)

EXPLORING THE DEFINITION AND VULNERABILITIES OF INSURANCE

Insurance can only operate in an environment that satisfies several criteria. It is important to identify these, because doing so can guide us on what ails health insurance in America, and what can fairly be expected from the extension of insurance principles to the metaphorical case of existential bad luck. As you will see, Genoese merchants circa 1350 had most of this figured out.

First, insurance requires a *loss* that can be made whole through the application of money. "Loss is an unintentional decline in, or disappearance of, value [determinable in monetary terms]."[7] A broken heart is not an insurable loss. Insurance is a contract of indemnification (or of defined value in the case of life insurance), not a bet, and therefore is designed to replace the loss (diminution of monetary value) arising from an adverse fortuity (below). The loss, if one were to occur, must be both *determinable* and *measurable*; that is, both the occurrence and the magnitude of a loss must be readily ascertainable.[8]

Second, the loss in question must be triggered by an *adverse fortuity*—a random event of bad luck that is outside the control of the insured.

Third, the *chance of loss*—the long-run frequency of such losses—and the *severity* of expected losses must be subject to estimation with reasonable accuracy within an applicable risk pool. (An insurer cannot otherwise price the insurance contract.)

Fourth, the loss must be attributable to one or more identifiable *perils*—for example, the acts "of God, of the sea, of men of war, of fire, of jettison, of detainment by princes." In insurance terminology, a peril is the cause of the loss. It is a subset of all possible adverse fortuities. For example, most insurance contracts do not consider an attack by Martians to be a covered peril, even though that event certainly would be an adverse fortuity. A *hazard* is a circumstance that exacerbates the chance or the severity of a loss arising from a peril.[9] The acts of God and of the sea are perils; a poorly maintained hull is a hazard that exacerbates both the chance and severity of the resulting loss.

Fifth, the underlying loss must be similar to other losses (it must be *homogeneous* with them), but the chance of loss from one exposure must not be causally linked to other losses. The law of large numbers would be flummoxed by an insurance pool comprising the risks of loss arising from storms sinking wooden galleys, automobile crashes, and invasion by Martians. Similarly, the law of large numbers would not work well if a fault in the artificial intelligence of a brand of autonomous vehicle were to cause every one of those vehicles simultaneously to crash.

Sixth, the chance of loss must be transferred by contract from one party (the insured) to another (the insurer). In most commercial insurance, the risk must be transferred *ex ante* (before the voyage is undertaken), not *ex post* (after the ship fails to arrive in its intended port). (Retrospective insurance exists in modern insurance markets, but it is largely an artifact of regulatory and tax arbitrage.)

Seventh, the party to which the chance of loss is transferred must manage that chance through pooling the potential loss with other homogeneous losses and applying the law of large numbers to the pool.

Eighth, the chance and severity of loss must be sufficiently small as to make the transfer and pooling of the chance of loss economically feasible for insured and insurer. Life insurance is difficult to purchase as one is being marched out before the firing squad.

Finally, while insureds may not always be aware of it, an insurance policy is really evidence of membership in a special club comprising thousands of similarly situated individuals or firms. Without necessarily appreciating the *mutuality* of relations across this large group, each member nonetheless comes to the aid of all other members, by contributing premiums into one big pot, from which claims are paid to unlucky members of the club.

And there you are: you are now ready to draft an insurance contract. You will want to specify the nature of the property being insured, its market or declared value, the limits of covered loss (expressed in florins or dollars, as the case may be), the time period or event covered by the contract (including the specific ship that will carry that tiresome wool cloth), the perils whose eventuality would give rise to a loss covered by the contract, some rules for determining salvage value (which reduces any insurance payment, since the contract is one of indemnification), and a few other odds and ends. You will negotiate a premium based on the chance of loss, the severity of any loss, and a profit (in an accounting, not economic sense) for the insurer, for providing the financial service of assembling the requisite loss pool and for taking on risk in the technical sense—the possibility that the actual chance of loss diverges from the expected chance of loss. (How you arrive at your calculation of the premium will not be in the contract, but those are the factors that will motivate it.)

But wait. Put yourself in the shoes of the insurer for a moment. A contract along the lines just suggested would satisfy most of the requirements of a viable insurance arrangement in a classroom sense, but you didn't get to where you are today, as the CEO of an insurer, without knowing a thing or two about human nature. And so you might worry, if a shipowner buys insurance covering the value of his ship (rather than the cargo it carries for various merchants), how much effort will the shipowner put into maintaining the ship properly? And if you are really suspicious, you might ask: What about the possibility that a merchant of expensive wool cloth who buys insurance for a sea voyage will connive with the captain of the ship to offload the cargo at a different port and then to claim the shipment as a loss arising from jettisoning the cargo in a storm? And why was this merchant so eager to buy insurance in the first place? What does he know that you do not?

The risk of fraud is very high in insurance, but it is not qualitatively different from the many forms of fraud to which all businesses are exposed. Going beyond fraud, however, there are two much more interesting contracting risks that are unique to insurance: they go by the names *moral hazard* and *adverse selection*. *Moral hazard* refers to the possibility that an insured will behave more carelessly or recklessly once he has insurance in place than he would had he not purchased the insurance.[10] The shipowner with his comprehensive marine insurance policy who skimps on the maintenance of his vessel is an example of moral hazard in action.

Adverse selection is the other fundamental business risk unique to insurance. It refers to a kind of information asymmetry—some fact known to the insured but not the insurer that causes the insured to want to buy insurance, now. More accurately, the term captures the idea that the insured knows a reason why the chance of loss or the severity of any resulting loss in his case is greater than the general class of losses into which the insurer ordinarily would place him. For example, the Genoese wool merchant, relying on his network of carrier pigeons, might have learned of a surge in pirate activity before others had heard of it and therefore rushed to buy insurance before that news was baked into revised insurance premiums. Adverse selection bedevils all insurance but becomes overwhelmingly problematic when applied to private health insurance.

Strategies to address moral hazard are almost as old as the first true insurance contracts. The insurer might, for example, require the insured to absorb the first x florins of loss, or might indemnify only 80 percent of a covered loss, so that the insured is always exposed to the other 20 percent. The insurer might further inspect the shipowner's hull regularly, or specify certain maintenance schedules, or both. Once one is attuned to the problem of moral hazard, it often is possible in the context of commercial insurance to mitigate the problem. In the personal P&C market, however, norms of privacy as well as cost make things much more difficult. Leaving old paint and oily rags in the garage is a clear fire *hazard*, but we all are lazy, and how often does an insurance company come around to inspect the inside of your garage?

The problem of adverse selection is more difficult, because by definition it arises from an asymmetry in information, and the insurer therefore does not know what it does not know. In the life insurance market, before accepting your application, insurers try to level the playing field by requiring you to fill out a questionnaire and to undergo a medical exam; they also typically get access to your medical records. In other cases, the underwriting due diligence may be more difficult; in healthcare insurance, for example, insurers are now blocked by law from getting access to your medical history.

The costs of fraud, moral hazard, and adverse selection are significant, and by necessity all private insurance contracts must be priced to reflect them. An economist would say that people respond to incentives: the economic incentives to get money for nothing (through fraud), to relax one's care toward self or property once insurance has been obtained (moral hazard), or to buy insurance more cheaply than would be the case were all relevant facts known to the insurer (adverse selection) are all significant commercial risks for an insurer that go beyond "risk" in the technical insurance sense.

SOCIAL INSURANCE

The term "social insurance" encompasses government spending programs that are organized along insurance principles and are structured to invoke comparisons to private commercial insurance, but that also serve important social agendas. Social Security and Medicare are the most important examples in the United States, but there are many others, such as veterans' healthcare, unemployment insurance, and workers' compensation.

In advancing specific national policies, most social insurance deliberately deviates from actuarially accurate premium pricing. Social Security old-age benefits, for example, are progressive in their payout structure, meaning that lower-income wage earners get more by way of benefits when they retire as a fraction of their working incomes than do very high-earning individuals.[11]

Like marine insurance, public insurance has a clear origins story. In this case the story begins in late nineteenth-century Germany, where Chancellor Otto von Bismarck introduced a three-pronged government-sponsored social insurance initiative, comprising universal health insurance (!!) (at least for those with jobs), workers' compensation (covering on-the-job accidents), and insurance for invalidity and old age (what we call Social Security).

No one has ever accused Bismarck of being motivated by idealistic impulses. Instead, he pushed these revolutionary programs forward specifically to forestall actual revolution led by radicalized workers. As one leading text states, "Bismarck simply outbid the socialists at their own game."[12] Theodore Marmor and his co-authors put things into a deeper context that remains directly relevant to modern policy and politics:

> Social insurance . . . rests on the widespread acceptance of the proposition that protecting workers and their families from dramatic losses of economic status brought on by common risks to labor market participation is what a decent society should do. Across virtually all advanced industrial societies, these risks are taken to include . . . : birth into a poor family, the early death of a family breadwinner, ill health, involuntary unemployment, disability, and outliving one's savings. Indeed, there is a strong historical case that, beginning with Otto von Bismarck's social insurance initiatives in the late nineteenth century, the social [i.e., government] provision of income protection against these risks has been a fundamental precondition for the flourishing of industrial capitalism. *Looked at historically, social insurance is a deeply conservative idea, the major viable alternative to state socialism.*[13]

In a brilliant article simply titled "Social Insurance," Nobel laureate Anthony Atkinson expanded on this.[14] His thesis was that social insurance cannot be understood in the terms most familiar to an economist, as arising from market failures of private insurance markets in light of adverse selection (asymmetric private information known perfectly to prospective insureds and only imperfectly to the insurer, as when only the sick rush to sign up for private health insurance), or moral hazard (where the behavior of those who purchase insurance cannot be monitored by the insurer, and therefore cannot be reflected in differential pricing of insurance contracts or other contract terms). Instead, Atkinson demonstrated, social insurance from the beginning was an exercise in institutional history and evolution—in particular, the institutions of employers and employees in the modern sense, as they evolved from agricultural, small-scale, and family-centered to large for-profit corporations and their many employees: "The role of social insurance is only comprehensible in the light of the development of the modern labour market." Indeed, the very word "unemployment" only came into use in English around 1895!

Social insurance programs vary in coverage and design, but they generally contain a few key common elements:

First, the programs are government-run, or at least government-supervised. Eligibility and benefits are determined by law, not by the grace of a local benefits administrator. The programs encompass coverage for specified perils (adverse fortuities)—for example, the adverse fortuity of outliving your resources (i.e., winning the longevity bet), the adverse fortuity of suffering a permanent disability, or the adverse fortuity of becoming seriously ill while elderly.

Second, when applied to the US federal government, the programs are mandatory in the technical federal budget sense of the word—the laws creating and governing them, including the taxes necessary to fund them, continue in force indefinitely without any need for Congressional reauthorization each year.[15] This is in contrast to discretionary spending, which must be authorized by Congress every year. All defense spending for current military operations, for example, is discretionary and must be reauthorized each year.

Third, participation is mandatory in a more economically significant sense: the relevant insurance is required of all persons within a defined class (for example, all employees), and that class is broad in scope. Following in Bismarck's footsteps, most programs are related to employment in some fashion. The general rule for Social Security and premium-free Medicare Part A, for example, is that you must have worked in forty calendar quarters to qualify for benefits.

Fourth, constructive premiums are collected through the tax system, even when those collections are termed "contributions" or the like.

Fifth, as a formal matter, benefits typically are not predicated on a demonstration of need. Every older American with a ten-year history of employment gets Social Security, even if those checks are less than a rounding error in her annual income. As just noted, this stands in contrast to other programs, like the Supplemental Nutrition Assistance Program, that are "means-tested." But means-testing sneaks in the backdoor of many social insurance programs, as described immediately below.

Sixth, a person's benefits are not necessarily directly proportionate to the constructive premiums collected on his or her behalf. This is not inadvertent, but rather goes to the heart of the "social" part of social insurance.

For example, Social Security benefit schedules adopt a progressive structure, meaning that benefits are paid disproportionately to those with lower former contributions. This implicitly undercuts the fifth point, in that lower former contributions in general are proxies for lower incomes, and hence need. Another example is that high-income taxpayers must include in their income tax calculations a share of their Social Security benefits. This is really just a way of scaling back benefits for those thought to be less needy, because the tax liability acts as a constructive reduction in benefits. Finally, affluent seniors newly arrived on the threshold of Medicare are often stunned to learn that Medicare Part B (doctors' visits) is priced differentially. The basic Part B premium for calendar year 2019 was $1,626. High-income seniors, however, paid $5,526 for 2019 coverage—over three times as much. This is a means-tested program in disguise.

Seventh, the social insurance program is structured to resemble as an optical matter a private insurance scheme, in which an individual has the illusion of a contractual relationship with the government wearing its insurer hat, and a claim of right to promised future benefits. Dedicated taxes are often called "contributions," the monies are held in a "dedicated trust fund," and benefits are paid out of that trust fund.

By convention, "social insurance" is defined to exclude means-tested government programs—what might have been called "welfare programs" a generation or two ago. Medicaid (healthcare for very-low-income families) and CHIP (healthcare for children in low-income households) are large and important programs that do great good, but because they are available only in cases of demonstrated need as determined by income levels, they are not conventionally scored as social insurance. The same is true for the Supplemental Nutrition and Assistance Program (SNAP—what used to be called "food stamps"), described in a bit more detail in Chapter 8. A moment's reflection, however, might lead to the observation that when disability or long-term unemployment strike, these means-tested programs might become highly relevant. Many means-tested programs are further classified for budget presentation purposes as "income security" programs, but no operative consequence follows from this label.

Means-tested programs contain many of the same design features as social insurance. They are, for example, classified as mandatory outlays for federal budget purposes, again because their constitutive laws continue in force indefinitely. Means-tested programs are not, however, financed in the artificial accounting sense through "dedicated" taxes "paid into" trust funds. Instead, they are paid out of general tax revenues and government borrowing, just like all discretionary spending (and a good chunk of Medicare to boot). The distinction thus is largely artificial, but for data analysis purposes I will follow it in my summary here.

SOCIAL INSURANCE IS STILL INSURANCE

I hope that the preceding section's quick summary of social insurance in the United States is sufficient to convince you that social insurance is still insurance of the sort that could be explained to a fourteenth-century merchant. These programs all involve risk shifting and risk pooling. The triggering events are adverse fortuities—more specifically, losses arising from named perils. The losses can be expressed in financial terms and are determinable and measurable. The underlying losses are predictable by virtue of the application of the law of large numbers—indeed, the Trustees of the Social Security System regularly publish a seventy-five-year projection of the system's solvency. The resulting obligations on the part of the insurer are payable in money. (Medicare benefits are paid directly to hospitals or doctors, but they are still paid in money. Nothing would change, however, if those benefits were paid through in-kind services, as is true of the VA healthcare system.) And the community of insureds surely should feel a sense of mutuality, because these gigantic pools are a way of all Americans chipping in to assist some Americans who suffer an adverse fortuity. So what's the issue?

The issue is that social insurance often is not "actuarially fair." Some people pay more into Social Security, for example, than they would to purchase a private annuity policy that paid the same benefits.[16] The people who feel the weight of this unfairness crushing their windpipes are the most affluent among us; regular folk are the beneficiaries of the progressive design of Social Security payouts. And, of course, those who would do better on their own are the first to suggest that Social Security be privatized or otherwise made more "insurance" and less "social."

But all that does not mean that social insurance is not insurance. It means that social insurance is *insurance applied in the pursuit of larger social goals.*[17] As such, social insurance introduces a metaphorical element to insurance in the narrowest sense; the next chapter extends this metaphorical thinking a bit further to encompass existential bad luck within our list of named perils.

Social insurance rests on a firm foundation of insurance principles, but its purpose is not to compete with insurance otherwise available in private markets, or even to provide insurance through mandatory participation that otherwise perfectly replicates the insurance premiums and payouts we would expect in actuarially fair markets. Social insurance is not evidence of a statist economy.

Instead, and as suggested by Anthony Atkinson in the article mentioned earlier, social insurance addresses fundamental social issues endemic to how unalloyed capitalism would play out in Americans' lives against a background environment suffused with random bad luck. We rightly have no stomach for watching our elderly starve or die prematurely from lack of medical attention because circumstances made it impossible for them to save the large sums necessary to finance life post-retirement or disability. We respect the free market of employment but cushion the blow of involuntary unemployment through unemployment insurance—the benefit period of which can be extended for states suffering an extensive unemployment crisis, and even extended nationally, as happened in 2008.

Social insurance responds to these sorts of issues. It adapts insurance principles to structure policies whose design accords with our fondness for free markets, but whose detailed terms institutionalize sensitivity to the massive human dislocations and morally indefensible outcomes that follow once Fortune spins her Wheel and bad luck, that inescapable law of the universe, comes into play. It further instantiates mutuality of exposure to bad luck among all citizens, through national mandatory programs. And it leverages the advantages of the state to make its insurance scheme more economically efficient in some respects than private markets can achieve.

It is easy today for the young or unreflective to think that our free market economy and the social order that rests on top of it are both natural and immutable, but history teaches the fatuousness of that assumption. Returning to Otto von Bismarck, social insurance was developed, not to be nice, but rather to ensure the survival of a society that embraced the central importance of free markets as a social ordering principle, but which was at risk of failing its own citizens by ignoring the cruelty of outcomes that unalloyed adverse fortuities could yield in a society that had outgrown the ability of family, village, or church to play the role of insurer.

Social Security, for example, addresses a fundamental characteristic of human nature, which is our tendency to underappreciate the needs of our future selves. People do not on their own save enough for their retirements, in part because they cannot afford to, but also because they have a great deal of difficulty weighing future needs against immediate needs or desires. Economists call this *hyperbolic discounting*, which just means the tendency to underweight what the future self will require.

Scolds, typically individuals who live financially comfortable lives, love to turn hyperbolic discounting into a moral flaw. There may be some individuals abroad in the land who do not suffer from this tendency, but research shows that it is close to a universal trait.

At some point it becomes distasteful and unhelpful for those in a small minority to commend themselves for moral virtue, and to condemn the majority as morally weak. I have an inbred hatred of gambling, but I consider myself lucky, not virtuous, to have effortlessly avoided this terrible addiction. Government exists to serve all of us as we are, not to sort us into the righteous and the damned.

Moreover, the majority of Americans simply do not have sufficient incomes from which to contemplate a thoughtful trade-off between consumption today and consumption decades hence. As a reminder, the bottom half of the wealth distribution in America today owns approximately bupkis, and the bottom 90 percent in the aggregate owns only about 30 percent of the nation's wealth. Flipped around, this means that 70 percent of the country's wealth is owned by one out of ten Americans.[18] The case for greater self-responsibility in providing for one's own old age might be a bit more persuasive if income and wealth inequality had not shifted quite so dramatically over the last few decades in favor of the most fortunate among us.

As mentioned, social insurance premiums are collected in the form of taxes. In the case of Social Security's core retirement funding program (Old Age, Survivors, and Disability Insurance), for example, one-half the relevant taxes are collected from employees in the form of withheld wages, and the other half is collected from the employer. Economists universally treat the employer's share as a tax in fact imposed on the employee, the theory being that in the absence of this formal allocation of tax responsibility, wages would rise by the amount that employers today must pay as a condition of employing a worker. The extreme end of the scold community might seize on this convention to suggest that if only Social Security were terminated, employees would have more cash in their pockets with which to have disciplined conversations around the kitchen table about current versus future needs, but again this overlooks the fact that hyperbolic discounting is a feature of human nature. Our government exists to serve us, and thereby to enhance our welfare—not to put us into situations where millions will fail the test imposed on us.

Further, in light of the evidence on wage growth stagnation over the last forty years, one must take with a grain of salt the economic convention that removing the employer's share of Social Security taxes would translate entirely into increased wages. Increasing business concentration and capital owners' general success in capturing an increasing share of firm incomes might suggest that, to the contrary, employers would retain a significant fraction of the tax savings.

By way of analogy, a recent comprehensive analysis of the economic implications of private equity concluded that in the aggregate, private equity firms reduced the employment and increased the productivity of their target businesses, which in the ordinary way of thinking about things would imply that the wages of those who still had a job would go up (to share in the increased productivity). In fact, however, aggregate post-acquisition wages went down, meaning that the new owners were capturing all of the benefits of that increased productivity.[19]

The deep magic of social insurance comes from the second common element in my list: participation is mandatory and covers all or most Americans. At one blow, the dragon of adverse selection is slain, because the pool of the insured includes everyone, whether they would have reached out for that form of insurance or not. Private insurance products must always grapple with adverse selection, and they must price that bias in their customer base into the premiums charged. Social insurance alone is immune to it.[20]

This is an incredibly powerful fact that all other civilized countries have harnessed to their advantage in their different national health insurance programs. If you include in your health insurance pool only those who rush forward to sign up, you can be sure that the resulting pool will veer decidedly in the direction of the old and the sick. The young and healthy have no great interest in health insurance, because they in fact are healthy, at least for the moment, and, being young, suspect to boot that they are immortal.

Mandatory inclusion of a very large fraction of the population also mitigates (but does not eliminate) the problem of moral hazard, because again there is no

difference in treatment between those who would in the absence of that mandatory program purchase optional insurance and those who would not. It might be
the case that skydiving would climb steeply in popularity from its current modest
levels if Medicare for All were to be implemented, but once a system includes
essentially all the population, the incremental moral hazard risk induced by the
existence of that program in the behavior of the entire population becomes very
attenuated. This is an important issue in the minds of many economists, and I return to it in the section titled "Does Social Insurance Lead to the Cocooning of
America?" later in the chapter.

Mandatory programs force everyone into the pool. In the case of healthcare
reform proposals, or even current Medicare funding, this often is portrayed as
an indefensible wealth transfer from young to old, but that really is the wrong
way of looking at things. Mandatory participation across generations today means
that when you are young and healthy you pay into the system more than necessary to cover the small immediate risk of catastrophic illness. You do so, however,
not to make the old wealthier, but rather in order that your future self will have
guaranteed insurance at the same price when that future self, with all his wrinkles,
comes into being. Whole-life insurance is similar; you pay "too much" each month
when young, to buy down the cost of insurance to the same monthly premium as
you age. Each generation really is paying for its own future care, so long as the
system is stable and permanent.

The fact that constructive premiums are collected through the tax system adds a
great deal of efficiency to the administration of social insurance plans. It also is a device by which the full cost of social insurance can be made a little less salient, as when
one-half of Social Security premiums are paid as a formal matter by the employer.
This is helpful for the stability of a program, even if some find it disingenuous.

The fourth through sixth common elements go to the heart of the politics of social
insurance, not to the economics of those programs. These elements all are designed
to parallel in appearance private insurance or annuity plans, to drive home the idea
that the policy in question is in fact grounded in insurance principles. The idea is that
you pay into a social insurance plan regardless of need, and you receive your benefits
regardless of need (in turn vitiated below the surface by the progressive structure of
benefits, the taxation of those benefits if your income is sufficiently high or differential Medicare premiums). Aggregate contributions in excess of benefit payments are
held in a government "trust fund," understood by participants to be inviolable, from
which your future benefits will be paid. In the case of Social Security, you receive
an annual statement of your contribution balance and current or projected future
benefits, just as you would were you to buy a private annuity contract.

All of this is smoke and mirrors, but of a beneficent variety. In the case of
Social Security, the first of America's major social insurance programs, Franklin
Roosevelt deliberately designed the system to have these optical features so as to

create a sense on the part of the electorate that they owned their promised benefits. The result from the beginning was to create a class of a huge swath of the population who believed, and who still believe, that they have paid their money into a program, that their money is held in a special segregated fund for them, and that the benefits they receive have been earned directly by their contributions into the fund. The fiction thus accomplished its intended purpose, which was to invest in the electorate a sense that their promised benefits were their own property, which a future Congress could scale back only at its peril.

The reality is different. The Social Security trust fund, for example, is not in fact a separate pot of money beyond the reach of profligate spenders in Congress. The assets of the Social Security trust fund are Treasury bonds, which is a way of saying that the left pocket of government (the trust fund) has lent money to its own right pocket. As a result, the supposedly inviolate contributions of workers simply go to fund the day-to-day spending of government. The sources of repayment of the Treasury bonds held by the various trust funds are general tax revenues, not royalties from mining claims on Mars.

In the end, the trust fund structure is no more than an accounting device that specifies a ceiling on future benefits; at any point in time this ceiling might be remote in relevance, or it might be highly relevant if current policies continued without modification. And what is more, there in fact is no enforceable contract between participants and any social insurance system.[21] One Congress cannot bind a future Congress, except in respect of Treasury debt issued to third parties, not to another branch of government. Congress could repeal the Social Security system tomorrow, and you would have no claim that you could pursue in court.

In short, as far as the electorate of the United States is concerned, they hold insurance policies issued by the most dependable of all insurers—the government of the United States itself. A more accurate portrayal would be that social insurance is insurance put into the service of national social policy through the medium of metaphor.

HOW MUCH SOCIAL INSURANCE DO WE WRITE?

It is important to put the social insurance programs of the US federal government into context. This requires some care, as the raw numbers involved are large enough to induce states of shock among the uninitiated.

Table 6.1 summarizes federal government spending on social insurance and means-tested programs in 2019.

This chart summarizes the spending side of things, not the taxes raised to pay for these programs. Social Security and Medicare in particular have streams of tax revenues in the form of payroll taxes dedicated to them, but current government outlays for Social Security and Medicare are not fully funded by current dedicated revenues. For example, in 2019 Social Security ran a cash flow deficit of about $100

Table 6.1 US Federal Mandatory Spending Programs (2019)

"Social Insurance" Programs ($ billions)		"Means-Tested" Programs ($ billions)	
Health Care Programs		**Health Care Programs**	
Medicare	775	Medicaid	409
Social Security		Health insurance subsidies and related	56
Old-Age and Survivors Insurance	893	Children's Health Insurance Program	<u>18</u>
Disability Insurance	<u>145</u>		
Subtotal	1,038	Subtotal	483
Income Security Programs		**Income Security Programs**	
Unemployment compensation	28	Earned income, child, and other tax credits	99
		Supplemental Nutrition Assistance Program	63
Federal Employee Retirement		Supplemental Security Income	56
Civilian	106	Family support and foster care	32
Military	61	Unemployment compensation	28
		Child nutrition	<u>24</u>
Other	<u>3</u>		
Subtotal	170	Subtotal	303
Veterans' Programs	115		
Other Programs	125		
Social Insurance Outlays, Excluding Offsetting Receipts	<u>2,228</u>	**Means-Tested Outlays, Excluding Offsetting Receipts**	<u>753</u>
Total Mandatory Spending, Excluding Offsetting Receipts			<u>3,010</u>
Offsetting Receipts[22]			(275)
Total Net Mandatory Spending 2019			<u>2,735</u>

Source: Congressional Budget Office.

billion. Fortunately, many years ago Congress recognized the demographic "pig in the snake" that is the boomer generation, and it therefore raised Social Security contributions to build up reserves inside the trust fund to cover deficit years as boomers went from working to Florida to points beyond our comprehension. This is the "source" that covers the annual Social Security deficit. But again, all this is an accounting convention, not an economic one. When the Social Security trust fund pays out more than it receives, it cashes some of its Treasury bonds, which means that money simply moves within the different government accounts; the net cash deficit within government must be financed by borrowing from third parties, along with all the other cash deficits that the government runs each year.

As always, Medicare is even more complicated.[23] The Medicare program actually contains two trust funds, one for Medicare Part A (hospitalization) and another for Part B (doctors' visits) and Part D (prescription drugs). Only the first of these trust funds has a dedicated stream of tax revenues (payroll taxes) credited to it; this trust fund has been running at roughly break-even for the last few years but is expected to turn negative and run through its existing surplus in 2026. The second trust fund has no dedicated tax revenue stream at all. About 25 percent of the annual inflow into this second trust fund comes from premiums paid and other miscellaneous inflows; the other 75 percent comes from current-year general tax revenues that are turned over to the trust fund. This means that about three-quarters of your Medicare Part B insurance reimbursements are no more the return of "your" money than are SNAP payments the rightful property of the low-income families who receive them. Over $300 billion is transferred each year from general tax revenues to pay for current-year Medicare costs.

I acknowledge that $2.7 trillion in government spending in one year might strike some readers as a rather large number. But what does a figure that is so plainly beyond our comprehension, even if I were to resort to hackneyed comparisons like the height of a stack of 27 billion $100 bills (about 1,833 miles, as it happens), really mean?

One place to start is to compare this commitment to the overall size of our economy, most easily measured as GDP. In 2019, GDP was a bit over $21 trillion, which means that our spending on social insurance and means-tested programs amounted to about 13 percent of GDP in 2019.

This figure is interesting, sort of, but it is not the measure of any "loss" or "cost" to the economy. All government spending ultimately comes from government taxing. Tax revenues come primarily from Americans, and these spending programs are all directed to Americans, so in the first instance these programs just move money around among ourselves. The economic concept of cost in this context is subtler. In the context of taxation, the economic meaning of "cost" basically seeks to measure how much the taxes in question have distorted activity that would have taken place in a world without taxes. For example, the economist does not see payroll taxes as a cost or a loss; instead, the cost of payroll taxes is the value of the job not filled because of the gap between what an employer could offer after paying those payroll taxes, and what the employee would receive after paying her half of those taxes. Economists call this "deadweight loss."

For some unfortunate reason economists often stop their work with their estimates of the deadweight loss of taxation, but this ought not to be the end of things. If done properly, the analysis of the net burden imposed by $2.7 trillion in social spending upon all Americans taken together would include the other side of things—the cost or benefit arising from the reallocation of private spending that follows. Since these programs in the most general terms "redistribute"[24] money from higher incomes to lower ones, and since low-income households tend to spend a higher percentage of any income they receive than do high-income ones (which have the luxury of saving), the reallocation would have a tendency to accelerate consumption, which gooses the economy.

Further, social spending for the benefit of one household frees up other income within that household to be spent on other needs. Most economists accept the principle of the diminishing marginal utility of money, which is a fancy way of saying that the poor are more grateful for an extra dollar in their pockets than the rich are sad for having lost it. This also ought to be factored into any calculation. In short, it is very difficult to measure with any authority the net effect of these programs on GDP.

Even if we were able to solve this first question, what exactly would that tell us? The purposes of social insurance and means-tested programs are to instantiate our commitment to one another as citizens of one country, by mitigating serious instances of bad luck that befall some of us. Or more cynically, these programs buy social peace, and thereby enable the free market economy to motor along with only some modest frictions and occasional work stoppages. How should this act of social pacification be valued?

Perhaps another way of looking at things would be to ask: What exactly have we bought for all this? Well, if you line up elderly Americans by incomes, the bottom 40 percent (tens of millions of fellow citizens) depend on Social Security for more than 90 percent of their incomes.[25] As another example, the SNAP (food stamp) program is vitally important to reducing nutrition insufficiency among the poorest Americans. Its qualification requirements and payout formulas are too difficult for me to understand, but the 2019 average monthly benefit for a family of four was $465. That works out to roughly $1.30 per person per meal.

More generally, we would notice that our means-tested programs spend only about one-third as much as our social insurance programs, despite substantial adult and child poverty in the United States, as discussed in Chapter 2. For example, the United States has one of the **highest** child poverty rates in the OECD, and the second-lowest level of public social spending on families (see Figure 6.1).

This is a sad corner of the chart to occupy.

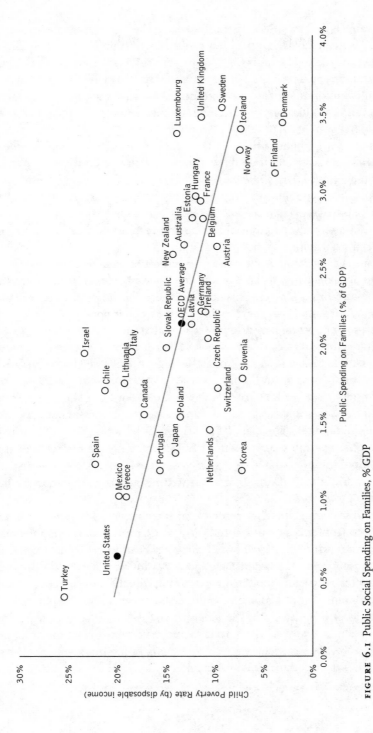

FIGURE 6.1 Public Social Spending on Families, % GDP

Source: OECD, *Social Expenditure Update* 2019, https://www.oecd.org/social/soc/OECD2019-Social-Expenditure-Update.pdf.

To the same effect, the OECD member states on average devote about 4 percent of their GDP to public social spending programs that support their working-age population. The United States spends 1.9 percent.[26] With the exception of three of the poorer countries in the OECD, Korea, and Japan (which is roughly tied with the United States), our social insurance and means-tested programs for working-age Americans are at the very bottom of the list. By contrast, Hungary manages to spend 3.6 percent of its GDP for such programs.

We are even a bit behind the OECD average in social insurance for the elderly: our Social Security and related non-medical programs for the elderly account for 7.2 percent of our GDP, while the OECD average is 8.0 percent. Among major categories, only our public spending on health insurance exceeds the OECD average, but as the next section shows, this is not cause for celebration.

Those eager to decapitate our social insurance programs are quick to make two false claims. The first is that one program or another is "going bankrupt" in x years. This is as fictional as the rest of the trust fund structure. It is true, for example, that Social Security will not be able to pay its current levels of benefits after about 2035 if nothing changes. This does not mean, however, that benefits would drop to zero, but rather that they would be cut by about one-quarter (the level at which then-current payroll tax inflows would match then-current outflows). More fundamentally, Congress can pay whatever level of benefits Congress chooses to pay. It could raise payroll taxes, or it could keep the open-ended mandate of Social Security payments and scrap the trust fund's notional account balance as a cap on payouts (as is true for Medicare Parts B and D). For example, Social Security payroll taxes apply only to wages below a specified ceiling (roughly $133,000 in 2019). Eliminating the ceiling, so that all wages are subject to Social Security payroll taxes, would permit the payment of full benefits for many decades without any other modification to the trust fund's terms. The enemies of social insurance tighten a noose of their making around the victim's neck, and then observe that it is not breathing terribly well.

More perniciously, the enemies of social insurance and means-based social spending speak of "entitlement reform," as if some fraction of the population has demanded more money for itself out of some imagined moral claim, rather than in indemnification for loss against named perils for which we collectively have decided to offer insurance—and further implying that the only direction in which "reform" can happen is down. A similar device is the overuse of the phrase "safety net," which gets wrapped up in the idea that social insurance isn't really insurance at all, but rather some sort of governmental cocooning operation, designed to coddle and to insulate participants from the rigors of the marketplace. (The next section of this chapter returns to this topic.)

Rhetorical devices matter in politics; notice how the tenor of the conversation changes if we were to abandon "entitlement reform" and ask instead about the adequacy of our "social insurance budget."[27] All this is deliberate and backwards. No one is "entitled" to benefits under one program or another. Those benefits either are earned in a popular sense, under terms specified by our democratically elected Congress in advance of the work required to earn them, or they are authentic insurance indemnification payments—payoffs for one or another form of bad luck, whether existential or circumstantial.

Here is another way of thinking about "entitlement reform." Do you think that when we collectively chip in $1.30 per meal per hungry mouth, we create an entitled class? Do you think that taking Social Security benefits away from the tens of millions of Americans who rely on it for 90 percent or more of their income is necessary to teach that entitled class a thing or two?

Nor is there a crisis of affordability. As Chapter 2 already has suggested, the "reform" that is required is tax reform, and there the direction is up, not down. As a reminder, the United States is a low-tax, small-government country when compared to our peers. Our tax revenues at all levels (federal, state, and local) combined amounted to about 27 percent of GDP in 2017.[28] That was 9 percentage points below the average of OECD member countries as percentages of their incomes, and over 10 percentage points behind what Germany, the heir to the great conservative Otto von Bismarck, raises in tax revenues as a percentage of its GDP each year. If the United States were to collect tax at the OECD average rate, we would have $2 trillion more in tax revenue each year. We could apply, say, $1 trillion/year to cover our current running costs for government that we finance today through deficits and borrowing, and another $1 trillion/year for all the programs contemplated in this book—and then some. (Chapter 9 expands on this.) The middle class would be taxed more, but in return one could imagine the middle class receiving Northern European–style benefits, like free childcare, consistent high-quality early childhood education, free healthcare, and free university educations. It is not necessarily a trade that is easy to reject out of hand.

If you are inclined to argue that "we cannot afford" our current level of "entitlement" spending, I respond as follows. The nation plainly can afford it, and more, but it appears that you prefer not to be part of a system that asks everyone to shoulder enough of the insurance programs necessary to offer all Americans equal opportunities at the outset of their lives, and dignity in their old age. You might be motivated by the view that *they* are taking *your* money, but in doing so you are systematically denying *your* good fortune, and *their* bad luck, both existential and circumstantial.

DOES SOCIAL INSURANCE LEAD TO THE COCOONING OF AMERICA?

Social insurance confounds many economists. They examine one aspect or another of social insurance and find it to be wanting when analyzed as precisely what it is not—a competitor or replacement for private insurance.

Most economists' professional angst here focuses on moral hazard, the idea that insureds act more carelessly than do uninsureds, relying on their knowledge that they have insurance to fall back on. In the case of private marine insurance, for example, moral hazard suggests that our Italian merchant might not take the same care to select a seaworthy ship and to oversee the loading of his cargo into the hold as he would if he were uninsured. In the case of public insurance, moral hazard might surface in the form of recklessness in behavior, or alternatively in an avoidance of risk altogether, assuming, for example, that benefits can be claimed without participating in the labor markets.

As previously discussed, Anthony Atkinson demonstrated that social insurance at its core was a social response to important new social institutions, the modern corporation and the employer–wage employee relationship. Deborah Stone expanded the argument to remind us that the term "social insurance" must be pronounced with the emphasis on "social":

> Insurance is a social institution that helps define norms and values in political culture, and ultimately shapes how citizens think about issues of membership, community, responsibility, and moral obligation. Insurance influences how individuals behave, not so much by dangling incentives in front of them one by one, but rather, by offering arenas for collective moral deliberation and political action. . . . In the moral hazard model, insurance makes the individual engage in immoral behavior; in the moral opportunity model, insurance alters societal ideas about responsibility and obligation.[29]

Stone thus shifts the focus from the risk that moral hazard presents to the behavior of the individual to the opportunity that social insurance—but not private insurance—offers a society to articulate and instantiate its moral understandings about the mutuality of our obligations to each other.

The Nobel laureate Joseph Stiglitz, in a paper which for his sake I hope he will not be remembered for, begins a study of moral hazard and social insurance by considering this exemplar of moral hazard in action:

> [A]n individual catches pneumonia as a result of going on a hiking trip with inadequate rain gear. His employer gives him compensated sick leave; part or all of his medical expenses are reimbursed by his insurance policy or the state; uncovered medical expenses may be partially deductible from his income tax; and family and friends rally round to provide other forms of support. Such extensive support, while directly helpful, deleteriously affects individuals' care to avoid accidents. . . . [H]ad the

individual borne all the costs of catching pneumonia himself, he might have taken the trouble to carry adequate rain gear. Thus, it is not obvious that the insurance provided by non-market institutions [e.g. social insurance or family] is always beneficial.[30]

Or, the individual carefully listened to the radio, was informed that there was no chance of rain, and was caught unprepared for that reason, notwithstanding his diligence. More generally, I've had pneumonia, as have many of you. No one wills it on himself, and all of us take steps to avoid it. The financial indemnification does not make up for the physical pain or for the time taken out of our lives. I understand that the economist cares about the marginal case, but this sort of example trivializes the role of brute luck in our lives while simultaneously exaggerating our interest (conscious or subconscious) in gaming the system.

In this paper, and in a related earlier one,[31] Stiglitz casts too wide a net on what he views as "non-market" insurance, or as insurance in general. He includes all risk transfers, even when it is just a case of family members helping each other out, as instances of insurance. But this proves too much; *every* contract involves the transfer of risk, which is why the parties took the time to write the contract in the first place. The result is that Stiglitz sees moral hazard everywhere, because every contract of whatever type contains implicit incentives to respond to the contract terms in unintended ways. This cheapens the meaning of the term "moral hazard," and by doing so makes it more difficult to think clearly about social insurance design.

Insurance is about risk pooling, and discussions of the relative strengths and weaknesses of different forms of insurance should be constrained to relationships in which risk pooling is the central risk management technique. To categorize one's relatives taking care of you as a form of non-market insurance that in a sense competes with governmental insurance is unhelpful to the policymaker and is scant comfort to the individual without immediate family.

In the economist's view, the most salutary response to moral hazard in non-market situations is "peer monitoring," in which insureds keep an eye on each other, to keep actions inspired by moral hazard to a minimum. (Perhaps this would require bringing one's mother along on every hiking vacation?) Stiglitz's example of effective peer monitoring is the workings of a university economics department's faculty, where to preserve the greater glory of the university and the department, the faculty members "have a strong incentive to monitor one another's performance, which they do through peer review, teaching evaluations, and so on." This is so contrary to my university experience that I wonder which one of us has worked in the more typical environment.

Moral hazard works in two directions, however. If, for example, workers' compensation (accident) insurance is experience-adjusted, so that an employer that does not take on-the-job safety seriously must pay much higher premiums than does a safety-conscious employer, then that social insurance works to punish the employer without good safety systems in place. The pre-existing instinct for moral hazard, of being negligent about employees' safety, has been corralled by the existence of social insurance, not the other way around.[32]

From a political point of view, by far the more troublesome form of moral hazard in social insurance is the featherbedder—the fellow who relies on the public dole rather than putting in a hard day's work effort.[33] In general, most social insurance in the technical sense has built-in protection from this problem, because the social insurance is tied closely to employment. The featherbedding scenario today is present primarily in the fevered imaginations of some members of the commentariat, who scour the nation for tropes like 2012's Jason the Surfer.[34]

Even if one restricts the focus to means-tested programs, those also have been rewritten over the last twenty-five years to relate benefits more closely to employment. The Earned Income Tax Credit is a principal example, because its purpose is "to make work pay" for low-wage active members of the labor force. The benefits actually available to surf bums are far smaller than any normal person would consider a viable life path, and they become smaller with every passing year, as the federal and state governments impose ever-greater work requirements even when it is unrealistic and cruel to do so.

One important study on the alleged cocooning effect of social insurance and means-tested programs considered the most extreme case: a form of "Universal Basic Income," which for this purpose can be oversimplified into money just for existing. Alaska owns tremendously valuable petroleum assets, from which it derives substantial income. That income is distributed as a "dividend" to all Alaskans without regard to need or employment, at a current rate of about $2,000/year. The authors' conclusion was that this program did not significantly decrease aggregate employment in Alaska.[35] Chapter 8 returns to a more detailed discussion of Universal Basic Income from an unusual perspective—that of our ethical obligations to our fellow citizens.

Outside Alaska, all of this comes to a head in the case of unemployment insurance. Unlike many economics questions, unemployment insurance offers many natural experiments, as when one state extends its unemployment benefits and a neighboring one in similar economic straits does not. From these, it is possible to conclude with unusual precision about the incentive effects of unemployment insurance in a particular case—that is, how much longer people with unemployment insurance spent looking for a new job, relative to others without such insurance.

Let us imagine that the extra time spent out of work amounts to two weeks, which is in the ballpark of at least some studies. The standard response among less thoughtful economists is to express great sadness at this, because the productive capacity of the economy is said to have been diminished. At the most offensive end of the spectrum, you find people like Casey Mulligan arguing that mass unemployment in the Great Recession was really just a lot of people deciding all at the same time to take a vacation on the government's dime.[36]

But is this result really unintended, and even so, is it undesirable? If the productive capacity of the economy is the extent of our focus, then we also want to encourage non-workers to enter the workforce for the first time, not just displaced workers to get back in the saddle as quickly as possible. The existence of unemployment insurance, the benefits of which accrue over time, can draw new workers into the workforce, so as to obtain those benefits at a later date, should they be necessary.[37]

And there are many plausible reasons to use unemployment insurance proactively to enhance or preserve one's labor contribution. As any job seeker knows, if you take the first job that comes along, at lower pay and responsibility, it is very difficult later to jump back to the level of employment you enjoyed before being laid off. Relying on unemployment insurance in this instance leads to long-term higher productivity. Or perhaps the extra time is devoted to a crash course on a useful skill. And come to think of it, what's so bad about taking two weeks off and going to the beach to clear your head, work out your anger, and figure out what you want to do next in your life? Such work on the self is welfare enhancing, even if it is invisible in any current economic metric.

What is troubling here is not the range of views expressed in the literature, but the insensitivity of so many economists to the fact that, whether they like it or not, they are practicing a "moral science."[38] The literature surrounding moral hazard in social insurance suffers from just this, in failing to think more completely about what the social goals of social insurance might be, why those goals are important, and how social insurance alone can advance them. Life as it is lived is not all cold calculation in response to those incentives that can be captured by the economist's tools. Further, in our fraught political world, every paper that identifies an unintended or perverse response to the presence of moral hazard becomes fodder for a larger political agenda aimed at "entitlement reform." Academics need to think carefully about how their words and results can be put to use in ways that they never intended, and then express themselves accordingly.

HEALTH INSURANCE

Health insurance as it is practiced in America is so screwed up, so wasteful, and so important that it deserves a chapter of its own. For that reason, Chapter 10 considers in detail the problems with healthcare delivery in the United States today, emphasizing two themes. First, our approach to healthcare for the non-elderly fundamentally violates basic insurance principles. Second, health insurance is not simply another consumption good, like a vacation cottage. Each of us sees our own survival as an existential imperative, and this informs both what we demand from healthcare and how vulnerable we are to "rent-seeking" behavior of players in the private health markets—pharmaceutical companies, hospitals, insurers, and medical practices alike.

CHAPTER 7

....

INSURANCE AS METAPHOR

MORAL PHILOSOPHY LIVES

Believe it or not, professional moral philosophers still walk this earth.

Aristotle died in 322 BCE. The Neoplatonic Academy in Athens, which claimed to be the direct successor to Plato's original Academy, finally was shuttered by the Emperor Justinian in 529 CE as part of his campaign against pagan thought. Even Immanuel Kant has been dead for over 200 years. And yet the flame of moral philosophy remains lit, even if we rarely stop to attend to it.

Today's professional moral philosophers are not easy to spot, as they no longer wear togas (at least in public). Nonetheless, if you are in a university town and spot two men (gender balance has not come to this field) fiercely arguing about matters of conscience that sound to you both abstruse and trivial, you might be on the right trail.

In this chapter, I return to some of the book's central themes developed in Chapter 1, but this time in a slightly more formal way, by looking to modern moral and political philosophy for some high-level guidance. I do so because moral and political philosophers have devoted a great deal of energy in recent decades to many of the questions that motivate this book. For example, they have argued fiercely among themselves over which kinds of bad luck are those for which individuals should be held personally responsible, and which kinds society should seek to offer indemnification. Similarly, they have developed what the credo of equality of opportunity actually requires, and they have debated whether proposing equality of opportunity is a sufficient commitment to egalitarian principles.

Chapter 6 analyzed the conditions required for *actual* insurance to operate efficiently, and further argued that social insurance programs like Social Security and Medicare were firmly grounded in sound insurance principles, modified in their premium and indemnification payment structures to incorporate other social goals. But once we see that social goals can be embedded into policy instruments that closely or loosely mimic actual insurance, the question becomes how far to push things. Many possible government programs could be framed as *meta-phorical* insurance plans, but where do we stop? Tall people in general earn more money over their lifetimes than do short ones, but does that mean that government should offer some sort of retrospective height insurance? In addressing these questions, I look to modern moral and political philosophy for some help.

The difference between insurance as product and insurance as metaphor is one of degree. Insurance as a product in the narrowest sense comprises insurance that fits the technical definition of insurance as it is ordinarily understood in commercial markets. Social insurance programs (such as Social Security, Medicare, unemployment insurance, and even Medicare for All proposals) still fall within my conception of insurance as a product, recognizing that the premiums and benefits are deliberately taken off strict actuarial determination to advance social goals, and further understanding that social insurance often requires mandatory coverage to mitigate adverse selection concerns.

Private insurance markets can deal with many instances of bad luck, like your house catching on fire, and social insurance can usefully address others, such as healthcare. But both private markets and social insurance as understood by Bismarck or Anthony Atkinson (as discussed in Chapter 6) are powerless against the most powerful instances of brute luck, such as the circumstances of our birth. A broader, metaphorical understanding of insurance, on the other hand, can reach these cases, because public policy instruments can look backward as well as forward in applying the intuitions underlying insurance to situations that do not strictly constitute insurance in the commercial sense.

The overriding goals of this chapter are to set some limits on how far metaphorical insurance should be used to justify government policy instruments, and how sound insurance principles, like addressing adverse selection and moral hazard, can be used to define and target those policies. More specifically, I explore what kinds of bad luck should give rise to indemnification claims through policy instruments justified or operated as metaphorical insurance. I further drill down a bit on what I mean by "equality of opportunity," and why it is a reasonable and appropriate goal for our society to aspire to instantiate.

THE TOOLS AND ENDS OF MORAL PHILOSOPHY

One informal definition of philosophy is that it is the study of the reasons we have for concluding that the things we think or believe to be true in fact are true. In turn, moral/political philosophy of the sort relevant to public policy is a normative inquiry into how we should behave toward each other, in light of a system of values that (hopes the philosopher) cannot help but achieve general assent, by virtue of the philosopher's logical powers in developing that system from a few basic postulates to which we all subscribe.

Philosophers are a rigorous lot. In the thought experiments described below, for example, they proceed through a highly intellectualized version of the children's game Chutes and Ladders, in which I advance a comprehensive moral or political theory, and you propose one or more imaginary cases to be tested under my theory. If my theory produces inappropriate answers to any of your examples, no matter how far-fetched, then I fall back to the beginning and must start all over again.

As the eminent philosopher Richard Arneson has written:

> Moral principles are universal truths valid in all possible worlds. Hence in our quest for true principles, a single compelling description of a logically possible counterexample defeats the proposed theory. At the level of policy [however], things are different. Policies are devices for fulfilling correct moral principles to the maximum feasible extent. One defeats a proposed policy not with a counterexample but by proposing an alternate policy that better advances the ensemble of our moral goals properly weighted.[1]

My interest with moral and political philosophy for purposes of this book is precisely this rigor of thought as applied to how we should approach the interactions among Fortune's turning Wheel, various forms of bad luck (particularly existential bad luck), and our obligations to one another. Modern philosophers have focused extensively on these issues. At the same time, this book falls squarely into the camp of Arnerson's category of policies rather than universal truths. The trick is to use the lessons of moral and political philosophy to make progress insofar as they remain useful to proposals that can reasonably be implemented in our highly imperfect world.

I confess that in writing this chapter I am not entirely rigorous in distinguishing moral from political philosophy, because the two often ask similar questions, but from a slightly different perspective. Moral philosophy typically is concerned with the attitudes, behavior, or virtue of the individual. Political philosophy concerns itself with how we best should organize ourselves collectively through the state, either to manage conflicts and channel the use of power, or alternatively to advance some articulation of the common good, however expressed (welfare, justice, equality, etc.).[2] As John Rawls wrote, "political philosophy may contribute to how a people think of their political and social institutions as a whole, and their basic aims and purposes as a society with a history—a nation—as opposed to their aims and purposes as individuals"; at the same time, it can also be "realistically utopian: that is, as probing the limits of practical political possibility."[3]

Political and moral philosophy thus both focus on how we should honor what is best in us and how we can encourage human flourishing in a world where we constantly interact with one another. As a result, the two in the end are not always easy to tease apart, and philosophers often do double duty through contributions to both moral and political philosophical thought.[4]

Moral and political philosophy concern themselves with that which by assent to logical reasoning can be accepted as true, but they typically do so in areas where neither the reasoning nor the asserted truth can be tested through physical experiments or the like. Some modern political philosophers respond to this by broadening the scope of their inquiries from abstract reasoning to the study of real-world social relations and institutions, but the more traditional (and, I think, famous) approach has been to proceed through thought experiments and examples which *could* be true (that is, they do not violate the laws of physics), but which in some cases are certainly far-fetched.

John Rawls's "Original Position" thought experiment is an important example— perhaps the most famous such example of a "realistically utopian" thought experiment in modern political philosophy. To a surprising extent, much modern political philosophy can be seen as reactions to Rawls, by way of affirming, extending, or rejecting his starting place and his reasoning.[5]

Rawls's thought experiment is famous and directly relevant to my own arguments. Further, it is a good example of how this strand of political philosophy proceeds. For these reasons, it is worthwhile quickly summarizing it here. I return to its direct implications for this book later in this chapter.

Rawls set out to construct the terms under which society would operate if we began considering the question in a state of nature as people who are independent (free) and equal (no one has any antecedent authority over anyone else). On reflection, we would conclude that principles of justice require that society should operate as a "fair system of social cooperation over time from one generation to the next." This requires that the basic structure of society supports the idea that citizens are free and equal persons, living in a society imbued with a "public conception of justice," in which citizens share a common point of view of what justice demands and can adjudicate their claims against the state or each other.[6]

So far, so good, but how exactly are the terms of this fair system of social cooperation between free and equal citizens to be discovered? Rawls argued that the terms must be developed by agreement among these citizens, actively cooperating with each other to advance their reciprocal interests (an example of a "social contract" theory.)

But how to do this? We know too much about ourselves, our conditions, and our relative positions in actual society to negotiate in perfect good faith with our fellow citizens to articulate a system of social cooperation that is fair to all.

This is where Rawls introduced the Original Position, also known as his "behind the veil of ignorance" hypothetical. Rawls asked us to imagine that we are represented in the negotiations to establish a fair system of social cooperation by disembodied beings, rather like lawyers who neither eat nor bill. In carrying out their work, these disembodied agents know nothing about their specific clients—our sex, wealth, health, native talents, or anything else. They do know, however, that the people they represent are rational (have conceptions of the good and the intent to pursue the good in instrumentally intelligent ways) and reasonable (they are prepared to co-operate on just terms if other people are). The agents are true fiduciaries: they are committed to working in good faith to finding answers that will lead to the desired fair system of social cooperation. And the agents know a bit about how societies are organized in general, as well as elementary principles of economics.

Armed with all this, the disembodied agents effectively are asked to come up with the fair principles of cooperation for free and equal persons. These princi-ples will govern the basic structure of society, not every provision of the Internal Revenue Code. What kind of social institutions can we expect the disembodied agents to propose when they emerge from behind locked doors and present their agreement to us?

Compressing Rawls's step-by-step reasoning more than a little, Rawls answered the question with his two principles of justice:

(1) Each person has the same indefeasible claim to a fully adequate scheme of equal basic liberties, which scheme is compatible with the same scheme of liberties for all; and

(2) Social and economic inequalities are to satisfy two conditions: first, they are to be attached to offices and positions open to all under conditions of fair equality of opportunity; and second, they are to be to the greatest benefit of the least-advantaged members of society (the difference principle).[7]

To effectuate these principles, all persons must have access to "primary goods," which Rawls defined as the goods needed by persons successfully to carry on life "as free and equal persons living a complete life."[8] Rawls specified these primary goods in some detail: they include the basic rights and liberties mentioned earlier (including freedom of thought and liberties of conscience, political freedom, and life under the rule of law);[9] free choice of occupation against a background of diverse opportunities; the necessary social conditions for self-respect ("essential if citizens are to have a lively sense of their worth as persons and to be able to advance their ends with self-confidence"); and income and wealth sufficient "to achieve a wide range of ends whatever they may be."

Rawls emphasized that his thought experiment contemplated a world of all cooperating with all as reasonable and rational individuals, rather than a war of all against all.[10] In Rawls's construction, people are prepared to cooperate on fair terms if others will do so as well. They have self-interested reasons to want to co-operate, and a moral capacity to cooperate on terms that are fair (or reciprocal). To instantiate this, rational agents without knowledge of their principals' actual circumstances would propose institutions supporting a society that accorded first priority to the themes of equality and reciprocity of rights and obligations among that society's citizens.

Rawls contrasted his ideal of a society based on a fair system of social cooperation with its chief modern competitor, a society organized to produce the largest sum of individual utilities. (Utility here means some sort of agreed measure of well-being. In economics, money often is used as a shorthand metric for utility.) Utilitarianism does not promote equality and reciprocity as first-order goals around which society should be organized, but rather simply as instruments to be used insofar as they increase the measure of aggregate welfare.

The most controversial inference of Rawls's thought experiment is his difference principle, in which additional benefits cannot accrue to the better-off unless those arrangements primarily benefit the worst-off. Rawls basically saw the "worst-off" here as the working class; the disabled, for example, require different considerations. And Rawls had no interest in applying his difference principle to those who could work but chose not to.

The difference principle is easily caricatured as requiring an early Soviet sort of social arrangement, in which all wealth creation is shoveled from industrious high-income workers to the undeserving poor, but Rawls did not mean it to be understood in quite that way. His idea was that rational agents working behind the veil could imagine many different ways in which society could organize the rules governing productive activity. He argued that, having no knowledge about the situation each principal would occupy in the real world, the disembodied agents would choose rules that gave the greatest return to the least-advantaged for any given return to the more-advantaged. "The better endowed," writes Rawls, "are encouraged to seek still further [personal] benefits . . . provided they train their endowments and use them in ways that contribute to the good of all, and in particular to the good of the least endowed." The emphasis is on reciprocity, and implicitly also on the idea that the distribution of native talent is a common asset.[11]

Rawls absolutely expected there to be income inequality in his ideal world, but of course there would be much less of it than in actual contemporary society, which might be characterized as a malignant sort of utilitarianism gone wild. The malignancy comes from the denial of a fundamental principle of standard utilitarian analysis, which is that there is a declining marginal utility to money: that is, another $1,000 means less to someone with $10 million than it does to someone with only $10,000. The problem is that our multimillionaires do not seem to behave as if this theory were correct.

Rawls did not set out to propose a society oriented toward maximizing gross economic output or some other measure of production efficiency. Instead, his thought experiment led him to propose that the first priority belonged to his "fully adequate scheme of equal basic liberties," expressed through citizens' commitment to reciprocal fairness to one another, and embraced by all the members of a well-ordered society. The question of economic distribution in Rawls's thought experiment came second, only as that well-ordered society considered which "rules of the socioeconomic game" best accorded with the basic liberties.[12]

I appreciate that the difference principle is not easy to accept, and in fact, despite my general sympathy for Rawls, I cannot bring myself fully to accept it. But here is an example that conceivably might illustrate what Rawls had in mind.[13] Imagine that our agents behind the veil have embraced Rawls's first priorities and have moved on to consider two competing models as to how to organize productive activity in our well-ordered society. As these are imaginary models inside a thought experiment, let's give the economic models fanciful names with no connection to reality—say, France and the United States. Let's further imagine that there are ten citizens in each country and ten possible positions in each economy that each citizen can occupy, and that utility increases linearly with money. (The more money I have, the better I feel about things, in direct proportion to my increase in wealth.)

In France, citizens in nine out of ten positions earn $50,000, which is sufficient to fund the requisite primary goods necessary to lead a good life. One position in ten yields an income of $100,000. When viewed from behind the veil, before it is known who will occupy which position, a French citizen will have an expected utility of $55,000 (on average) for next year's income.[14]

In the United States there also are ten possible positions that a citizen might occupy; again, and critically, no one knows from behind the veil which position she will occupy in real life. In nine out of ten of these positions, citizens earn $10,000, and thereby are reduced to the barest subsistence, but in one case out of the ten, the citizen occupying that position earns $1,000,000. From behind the veil, the expected utility to an American citizen from this arrangement (on average), considering all ten of these possible scenarios as to how his life will unfold once the veil is lifted, is $109,000.[15]

From behind the veil, before he knows which position he will occupy, a US citizen's expected utility from the US model is roughly double that of the French. Phrased differently, the GDP *per capita* of this imaginary United States is almost double that of the hypothetical French GDP per capita.

Which model of economic activity do you think would prevail behind the veil? Which model would you prefer were you ignorant about the position that you would occupy in the real world?

EGALITARIANISM AND LUCK

Contemporary moral philosophy has made great progress in thinking about two fundamental and overlapping questions. The first relates to the meaning of egalitarianism (a commitment to equality). Echoing Amartya Sen, when we praise equality as an end, what exactly do we mean? That is, equality of what? Egalitarianism and luck intersect in particular when egalitarians wrestle with how to handle inequalities that arise by operation of luck of some sort, as opposed to a simple decision to work harder and not spend as much time at the beach.

Equality of opportunity is only one form that a commitment to egalitarian principles can take. In fact, many moral philosophers deride equality of opportunity as a mere "starting gate" theory, and as such a very weak expression of egalitarian ambitions. I respectfully dissent, at least with respect to the world of applied moral philosophy in which we actually live. I return to this a bit later in this chapter.

Rawls, for example, was an egalitarian in one sense, because his first priority (his first principle of justice) was a "fully adequate scheme of *equal* basic liberties." These basic liberties are freedoms of thought and political action against a background of reciprocal respect; they do not relate to money as such. Rawls's Original Position, however, was not at its deepest level addressed to economic distributional equality. The distribution of the fruits of productive activity (i.e., money) enter his scheme only through his second (and secondary) principle of justice.

Other egalitarian philosophers, by contrast, focus first and foremost on the distribution of the means or the fruits of production as their primary concern. They often are described as proponents of "distributive justice."[16]

Of course, it is possible to reject every form of egalitarianism as the primary ordering principle of a theory of political philosophy.[17] Utilitarianism, for example, does just that, because it sees any egalitarian goal as simply an instrument whose usefulness is determined by whether it increases aggregate welfare. Rawls, by contrast, saw his equal basic liberties as foundational and non-negotiable.

The second fundamental issue to which moral philosophy has devoted a great deal of attention is how we should think about the unavoidable influence of Fortune and her Wheel on outcomes. One cluster of inquiry revolves around the question of "moral luck":[18] how can we decide when, or whether, to hold an individual responsible for her actions when the resulting outcomes are determined in small or large part by the operation of uncontrollable luck? In other words, when does the impact of luck absolve an individual of responsibility for the consequences of her actions (or inactions)?

Another line of inquiry is whether it is fruitful to try to distinguish between different categories of luck, such as "brute luck," which is wholly outside our control (and often unfelt by us), and "option luck," which are the outcomes of decisions freely made against a background of uncertainty. I have used the terms since Chapter 1, but again the idea very simply is that option luck is the sort of luck we consciously choose to accept—a conscious gamble, for example, where the individual can anticipate the consequences and can decline the gamble.[19] Brute luck constitutes luck that happens to us without our conscious assent or participation. Getting hit by a car while crossing in the crosswalk with the light is bad brute luck; deciding to drive after having a couple of drinks sets up the potential for bad option luck.

A third egalitarian philosophical inquiry is: How much bad brute luck should we as a society seek to neutralize (to hold victims harmless from)? In particular, should we look at all the circumstances that are relevant to our productivity in economic society, including our native talents, or should we instead restrict our focus to the effects of differential "impersonal" resources, like family wealth?

The second and third lines of inquiry above are the domain of "luck egalitarians"—although, ever quarrelsome, the leading architect of luck egalitarianism, Ronald Dworkin, denied that he should be so described.[20] Chapter 1 touched on these matters; here, I try to put a little meat on the bone.

The reason for my particular interest in these questions is that Ronald Dworkin and his many interlocutors have promoted the theme of insurance in a metaphorical sense as the organizing principle for institutional responses to bad brute luck, especially what I call existential bad luck. As it happens, I am not convinced that these metaphorical invocations have always perfectly reflected the economics of insurance (mutuality, risk pooling, adverse selection, and moral hazard), and I reject the core luck egalitarian claim of how far metaphorical insurance should reach, but the work of these philosophers is helpful in developing some useful intuitions as to what we fairly can demand of insurance in a metaphorical sense when applied to actual policies.

SUBDIVIDING LUCK

Moral luck is concerned with the problem of how we can hold people accountable, when their motives, their actions, and the consequences of their actions are all affected by the universal forces set in motion by Fortune and her turning Wheel. Moral luck is an important field of inquiry whenever a question arises as to how accountable a person is for her actions—in criminal law, for example.

The more one thinks about the pervasiveness of luck, the more uncomfortable it becomes to hold people responsible for their actions. It's like the famous story of the learned astronomer who delivered a lecture on the solar system. When he finished, a little old lady stormed up to the front to accost him. "Young man," she said, "everything you said was untrue. Everyone knows that the earth rests on the back of a giant elephant." The lecturer was kindly and humored her. "And what," he asked, "holds up that elephant?" The lady looked aghast that this supposed expert would ask such a question. "The elephant stands on the back of a giant turtle," she explained. The lecturer, reaching the end of his patience, could not help but ask, "And what then holds up the turtle?" The lady finally lost all patience. "*Everyone knows*," she said, "that from there it's turtles all the way down."[21]

Moral philosophers who believe that it's turtles all way down are called hard determinists. Most philosophers, however, stop after three or four turtles; they ascribe responsibility to individuals for acts in which there is some significant component of conscious choice, even when the outcomes of those acts cannot have been perfectly predicted, or when the circumstances in which the actor found herself led her in that direction. That is, they acknowledge the role of luck in our behavior and in the outcomes of our actions, but nonetheless attempt to find some level of willfulness sufficient to hold an actor fully accountable.

This difficult debate is not terribly relevant to this book, except insofar as it has caused philosophers to think very hard about how to categorize different kinds of luck. One standard formulation breaks luck into four categories.[22] The first, and the most intractable, is "constitutive luck"—"the kind of person you are, where this is not just a question of what you deliberately do, but of your inclinations, capacities and temperament." (To this I add your genetics, in that inheriting the gene for height is a matter of constitutive luck, even if it is not an inclination, capacity, or temperament.) Everything that you think defines the essence of you rests on a foundation of constitutive luck—your ability to hit the curveball, your impatience, your looks, your intelligence, and so on. You were born with important native talents not of your own deciding—although how you choose to develop them arguably should stand on a different moral footing.

Second is "circumstantial luck," meaning two things: what I have called existential bad luck (the impersonal circumstances of your birth, like family wealth), and the luck that you face throughout your life attributable to the ongoing circumstances in which you find yourself. Happening to be the next-door neighbor of Steve Jobs and Steve Wozniak in Los Gatos, California, circa 1976 might well have been a piece of excellent circumstantial luck, had you the slightest interest in what they were building in their garage.

When combined with appropriate social insurance and spending programs, the progressive income tax turns out to be a wonderfully precise tool to mitigate the extremes of circumstantial luck in personal matters. As Chapter 1 showed, the outsized returns garnered by some individuals are in substantial part attributable to just plain brute luck, not talents never before seen in the history of mankind. Appropriate social insurance and spending programs mitigate bad luck in matters circumstantial as well as existential, and a progressive tax rate structure captures to a reasonable extent economic returns that likely are attributable to Fortune's favor.

Third and fourth are the roles of luck in the causes and effects of actions. The philosophical literature is full of examples of the inadvertent jostle that causes you to drop your gun and accidentally shoot someone, or your deliberate attempt to shoot someone, only to have your speeding bullet intercept a bird that happens to fly across the bullet's path to your actual target.[23] These subcategories relate primarily to the moral luck literature.

Constitutive luck is the most important concept to explore here, because most of us do not really believe in it. Phrased bluntly, once we are stripped of constitutive luck (our intelligence, our talents, our physical characteristics), what is left of us? What is there at our very core that is not explained by genetics and the very earliest life experiences, before we had an integrated consciousness that distinguished ourselves from our mothers? We can perhaps attribute some uniqueness to how we have chosen to apply our will to the characteristics bequeathed to us by constitutive luck—to how hard we practice the flugelhorn, or to how many hours we are willing to spend at work—but this is a much smaller construction of our identities than that for which we usually credit ourselves. Unless we apply our will very deliberately to the cessation of our own egos, we cannot help but act as if our bundle of constitutive luck, over which we had no choice or even consciousness, is in fact who we are.

This point is not just metaphysical babble, because the luck egalitarianism school of modern moral philosophy has set out to imagine how we might go about neutralizing the effects of *all* forms of brute luck, including in particular constitutive luck. Moral luck philosophers arguably get off a bit easier, because they can conclude that although constitutive luck was not anything we chose for ourselves, we—meaning who we think we are, including all the inputs of constitutive luck— are nonetheless at least partially responsible for the consequences of our actions whenever we apply our will to act, and circumstantial brute luck alone is not the cause of any unfortunate outcome.[24]

As articulated at length by Ronald Dworkin in his book *Sovereign Virtue*, the luck egalitarian school of distributive justice (i.e., justice that focuses first on egalitarian distributions of the means and fruits of production—money) argues that the moral sphere must separately address *brute luck* and *option luck*, where brute luck explicitly includes the constitutive luck that effectively defines who we believe ourselves to be. You can think of most instances of bad option luck as adverse fortuities against which we could in the real world literally insure or hedge ourselves, or could simply abstain from doing. Losing the value of your home to a fire caused by lightning sounds like bad brute luck, but in Dworkin's world it is a case of bad option luck, because you could have bought commercially available and reasonably priced homeowner's insurance, but *chose not to.*

One way of understanding Dworkin is that he set out to reconcile Rawls (or at least large swaths of Rawls) with the increasing dominance in academic circles of neoclassical economics as the default framework for analyzing human behavior. The problem with Rawls, it was felt, was that Rawls's difference principle underweighted the importance of economic incentives on behavior. Rawls commanded that society's institutions be structured to support the worst-off, but in the eyes of critics, that just implied subsidizing the undeserving poor. From the other direction, narrow constructions of equality of opportunity were not sufficiently egalitarian for Dworkin's tastes.

Dworkin's solution was to imagine a world in which people were held responsible for their option luck but were held harmless—effectively indemnified—against their brute luck, *including their constitutive luck.* The rallying cry was that society should be organized so as to be "endowment-insensitive" but "ambition-sensitive." In Dworkin's view, marketplace rewards for pure hard work were not morally troubling (his scheme was "ambition-sensitive"), but easy money that flows because an individual is born with a beautiful singing voice is inconsistent with egalitarian values. (Here you can already see one important line of criticism, which is that even a naturally beautiful voice must be trained, so that in reality one cannot easily separate economic returns to talent from the economic returns to the industrious perfection of that talent.)

Dworkin's ingenious move, and one from which I have taken much impressionistic inspiration, is that *insurance* is the bridge that transmutes brute luck into option luck. Dworkin saw insurance as the key to adopting egalitarian principles while disavowing concern over some forms of bad luck that lead to unequal outcomes (as in the house struck by lightning, above). By relying on insurance principles, Dworkin also advanced his claim to have domesticated neoclassical economic thought for a place inside egalitarian philosophy.

All this requires some unpacking. Like Rawls, Dworkin had a trademark thought experiment. In Dworkin's case, it involved clamshells. His idea was to imagine that a group of individuals—not disembodied spirits, but real people with all the motives from which real people suffer—had become stranded on a desert island offering all sorts of useful resources but no prospect of rescue, in a sort of classier version of the TV sitcom *Gilligan's Island.* Dworkin imagined that one of their number would be appointed as an auctioneer of the island's resources. Lacking cash, but committed to egalitarian values, the castaways would dole out

100 clamshells to each individual, to serve as a fiat currency. The auctioneer would then proceed to auction off bundles of resources. Because every new inhabitant of the island had the same number of clamshells to start, but different priorities, each could bid for those resources most important to her. If necessary, the auction could be continued for several rounds, so that I could bid to acquire the bundle initially acquired by you, but the idea was that at some point the allocation of resources would pass the *envy test*—I would have chosen what was most important to me, in light of my budget constraint, my tastes, and my ambitions, but because we all had the same budget constraint, no one else would hold a bundle of resources that I preferred to mine.

From that point forward, the island's economy would swing into action. If my wealth increased more than yours because I worked eighteen hours a day at my souvenir stand, while you ambled from one pig roast to another, well, that was not morally troubling, because I had simply traded my free time for financial gain, while you, with different preferences, had chosen the opposite path.

Dworkin's imaginary auction would accomplish its objectives in a world of perfect certainty (including certainty as to the future), populated by individuals with identical constitutive luck (endowments).[25] The question for Dworkin was how to relax those assumptions. This is where his strong reliance on insurance came in. He saw insurance as the way to convert all forms of brute luck into option luck, for which insurance could be purchased or declined, depending on one's temperament. In particular, what if people could buy insurance against bad constitutive luck—against the very characteristics that we think define who we are, but which enable some to have an easier time of it than others? This, he felt, was the path to an ambition-sensitive but endowment-insensitive social structure. As such it was absolutely central to his political theory.

As the house fire example indicates, Dworkin concluded that when commercial insurance is available, the decision *not* to buy it means that the individual has taken ownership of the consequences. Events of everyday brute luck thus become option luck whenever insurance could have been obtained. And as option luck, the consequences that then follow have no moral claim for adjustment by the state, even one committed to distributive egalitarian principles.

But what about endowments—constitutive luck? The auction allocated "impersonal resources" like plots of arable land in a way that would pass Dworkin's envy test, but it left untouched "personal resources," like a disproportionate quantity of good health, or brains, or brawn (which surely would have great value on the desert island). In Dworkin's egalitarian framework, however, it is absolutely necessary to neutralize as far as possible any advantages or disadvantages resulting from differences in endowments, because by definition they are undeserved gifts from Fortune, not one's own industry.

Dworkin was concerned in particular with two forms of constitutive bad luck. His system required a mechanism to hold islanders harmless from the harms of "various handicaps," like going blind, and also from the risk of "underemployment," by which he meant having constitutive skills or temperament that were not highly valued in the island economy. The answer was again to rely on insurance, but this time of a quality so figurative as to abandon any pretext of being remotely plausible, even as a thought experiment.

In each case, Dworkin's metaphorical constitutive luck insurance would be collected through taxes, and its benefits paid through government transfers. In Dworkin's telling, the underlying discipline imposed on these programs was that they were to constitute a mechanical conversion of the terms of his imaginary insurance premiums and indemnifications into tax and spending policy. But by the time he was done, Dworkin had really squeezed the metaphorical lemon dry, and the insurance policies he imagined (in turn converted into tax and spending policies) really contained very little useful information to guide us.

Unfortunately, Dworkin's invocations of insurance principles were sometimes a bit obscure. He referred many times, for example, to insurance available from commercial insurers. Where were they on the island? Did a salesman helicopter in to sell policies, and then lift off without rescuing the castaways? Some of his examples contemplated very exotic policies, for which it was not easy to see where a large enough pool could ever be found (certainly not on the island), and some of the insurance he imagined would have suffered from problems of adverse selection or moral hazard, or both. He emphasized as well the need for the insurance companies to earn profits to satisfy their shareholders (also located off-island?), but in fact the critical role of insurance is mutualization of risk, and there are many real-world examples of mutual insurance companies owned by their policyholders, not shareholders. All this undercuts his claim to commercial savviness. But let's look past these quibbles here.

In very general terms, Dworkin contemplated that handicap insurance would be mandatory, at premiums and coverage levels reached by divining what would have been chosen by an individual "who is average in all respects, including his preferences, initial endowment of personal resources, and vulnerability to risks."[26] Those who wished more insurance than this could buy it in the markets, thereby again keeping neoclassical economics inside the moral philosophy tent. Dworkin described this handicap insurance program as supplemental to the principal auction, but since a handicap likely would change an individual's preferences in the auction, it is not clear why this insurance should not come before rather than after the auction had ended.[27]

To make his island immigrants "endowment-insensitive," Dworkin further contemplated what he called "underemployment" insurance. In the language of economics, this would indemnify an individual who has a low *wage rate* (the value of an hour of their time, in light of their skills/talents), but not those individuals who have low *wages* because they choose not to work many hours. This of course is insurance against constitutive luck in all matters valued by the marketplace.

The details of Dworkin's underemployment insurance thought experiment in particular are extremely complex and not terribly clear, but the basic idea is to imagine that at the outset the castaways know their respective endowments, but not what value those abilities will command in the island economy. (For example, would native skill as an opera singer prove lucrative in this situation?) If they were sensible, they would buy insurance against having very low *wage rates*. (No insurer would insure against the risk of someone having low wages, because that would just encourage insureds to head to the beach every day after lunch.)

It would be nice to buy insurance that would pay off in all cases where one's wage rate was not at the very top of the ladder, but that sort of policy would bear prohibitively expensive premiums (because it would pay off in almost all cases). As a result, individuals would temper their greed and insure only to a reasonable extent. This means that the movie star's income still would exceed that of the average Joe (or Claude, as he happens to be named in Dworkin's illustration). However, the average fellow would be content, because he had obtained an amount of insurance against being undervalued in the marketplace that was based on all the castaways sharing their risks of turning out to be the ones who were undervalued, at a coverage level (i.e., the income below which compensation would kick in) and premium cost that all found reasonable at the start. As Dworkin explained, "The hypothetical insurance market aims to put . . . people in the position they would have been in had the risk of their fate been subjectively equally shared."[28]

To effect this scheme, Dworkin imagined a master computer that could model the entirety of the island's future economic output and how many individuals would occupy each income level. The computer would determine (based on some undescribed criteria about risk aversion and the like) what each castaway would specify as her actual income level below which she would be indemnified, in light of the insurance company's premium schedule. It would then convert that into the insurance appetites of a representative average castaway. The average appetite for insurance then would apply to the entire population; the ever-busy computer would transmute these hypothetical premiums into a progressive tax and transfer system.[29]

By means of all this, Dworkin, or the computer, allegedly would tease apart endowment and ambition, because only shortfalls in endowment (that is, bad constitutive luck) was to be indemnified. But as my earlier example of training one's voice illustrates, there are a thousand ways in which talent and ambition interact to affect not just wages but wage rates. Dworkin acknowledged this, but I cannot find in his work a plausible way to imagine how to separate the two.

In sum, when he extended his insurance metaphor to constitutive luck, Dworkin squeezed the metaphor until it lost both coherence and relevance. His thought experiment assumed its conclusions through the black box of the hypothetical all-knowing computer. Further, because the very fortuity being indemnified (bad constitutive luck) was inextricably interwoven with nonindemnifiable behavior (ambition), the system would founder completely on problems of moral hazard. Finally, the fact that islanders' insurance coverage against the adverse fortuity of bad constitutive luck was to be that which the average fellow would have wanted to buy completely unmoors the concept from ordinary insurance, because we cannot know the average risk aversion of a population.

Instead of all this mishegaas, one might just as well ask directly: How far do our obligations to one another run? As our own fraught debates over healthcare have demonstrated, this question cannot be answered by pretending to have recourse to some sort of scientific inquiry into the minds of citizens, to reveal their average risk aversion. In practice, we have answered the question for healthcare by concluding that we want as much as we can remotely afford; why would the handicap insurance discussion, for example, proceed differently?

Constitutive luck "insurance," if in fact it were thought desirable, can only be set through the political process, either at the island's Grand Council or in the reality of our Congress. That is exactly what we do through income security programs, for example. They do not rest on insurance principles so much as on our ethical and moral obligations to each other as citizens. Chapter 9 returns to this.

For all the reasons just described, Dworkin has been the source of loose inspiration to me, but not policy guidance. In particular, Dworkin developed a very useful metaphor inside moral philosophy—that of tax and transfer systems aimed at ironing out inequalities as analogous to insurance programs, where the premiums are paid through taxes. Chapter 8 extends this metaphor to the level of actual policy. But in the end, and despite his claims to economic and commercial relevance, Dworkin is the paradigmatic example of Arnerson's seeker of universal truth valid in all possible worlds.

TAKING PEOPLE AS THEY ARE

As suggested in Chapter 1, the philosophical axiom on which this book rests is to *take people as they are*. A great deal follows from this premise. First, it imposes a useful outer limit on what we can ask insurance as metaphor to accomplish. Second, it means that we vigorously reject luck egalitarianism as either good political philosophy theory or useful policy. Third, it tees up the central role of equality of opportunity as the species of equality that resonates with our constructions of ourselves and our nation.

To be clear, taking people as they are does *not* mean to institutionalize ignoring handicaps or medical issues of any kind. A child with Down syndrome needs special (and expensive) care. We provide all that within the rubric of universal healthcare, where we effectively turn the maxim "to take people as they are" and turn it on its head. When it comes to healthcare in the broadest sense, we take people as they are, in the sense that we exclude no one from our concern, and we do whatever we reasonably can for that person in her specific circumstances. My consistent use of the phrase "to take people as they are" sits on top of this universal imperative. One way of seeing things more clearly is that I treat handicaps or medical issues as external to the person; I treat a great talent for playing the violin as internal to—a constituent part of—the person.

Insurance as a product *and* insurance as a metaphor work best when limited in scope to what Dworkin calls "impersonal" resources (understanding, again, that I include healthcare within this category). My house and my car are impersonal resources; insurance against harm to them or harm they cause is readily available not only on desert islands but in the real world. The thrust of this book is that the financial resources brought to bear on a child as she develops and wends her way through the educational system also are impersonal resources. Inadequate money investment in human capital is an adverse fortuity whose measure can be taken in financial terms, and whose corrective benefits also are determinable in simple financial language. Chapter 8 teases out how we fairly can conceive of this retrospective intervention as nonetheless within a figurative understanding of insurance, and how the progressive income tax plays a central role in defining the premiums associated with it.

Once we leave behind insurance against adverse fortuities that befall our impersonal resources, we quickly fall into a hole from which there is no escape. Taking people as they are enables us to draw this distinction between the world of insurance, which is limited to indemnification against an adverse fortuity affecting impersonal resources, and other ethical impulses. These are not necessarily wrong, but trying to squeeze them into the framework of insurance does great harm to both these other ethical concerns and to the utility of insurance as a product and metaphor.

Do we really think that Dworkin's hypothetical islanders or actual Americans would quarrel with drawing the line here? All the evidence is to the contrary. We seem to accept our talents, foibles, strengths, and weaknesses as definitional to our conception of ourselves, not as external quantities suitable for measurement and compensation. For this reason, it is perfectly plausible that even within Dworkin's thought experiment, few, if any, islanders would rush to buy his underemployment insurance, which is constitutive luck insurance by another name.

Indeed, the evidence is that we often tend to the other extreme and endow brute luck with a fictional narrative of constitutive talent; if things were otherwise, the Belief in a Just World would gain no traction. We have a remarkable tolerance for inequality, either for the reasons developed in Chapter 2 or through a slightly more benign variant, in which we are predisposed to like and admire anyone with natural endowments who develops them to their fullest. This is probably why we identify with professional sports heroes.[30] Tom Brady was born with great inchoate football talent, which he later realized through ambition and application, along with a little bit of luck (like not getting injured). Through the power of false analogy, we believe that the rich also must have some sort of ineffable talent at their core—in their case, a talent for causing money to flow their way.

The important point for this discussion, however, is that ours is not a society of pent-up egalitarians yearning to be set free.

The luck egalitarian demand for "endowment insensitivity" is a demand that finds no resonance because we spend no time imagining that we have an identity that somehow is separate from those endowments. If what we want is a "safety net" against the worst economic vicissitudes (and we should), then we can and should address that without recourse to hypothetical islands or all-knowing computers. This is why Chapter 9 argues for a Universal Basic Income scheme.

Our government should steer clear of the demeaning business of telling the dim and uninteresting just what it thinks of them. (This is the core of Elizabeth Anderson's devastating critique of luck egalitarianism.)[31] My joke earlier in the book was that, if given the chance, I would have opted to be 10 percent less smart and 10 percent better looking. Who is to decide if I am to be pitied (and compensated) or admired (and taxed)?

The great harms possible under the luck egalitarian framework are brought forcefully into focus by considering a fraught contemporary topic, which is the idea of reparations to African Americans for the harms done by slavery. The crucial point here is that this fundamentally is a tort claim—a claim for harms done by some people (White Americans) to others (Black Americans), the consequences of which are still plainly visible in the data today. (For this reason, the claim has not been rendered moot by the passage of time.) The moral case for reparations, then, has nothing to do with insurance as a product or a metaphor: it rests on completely different grounds, and it must be evaluated solely by reference to the moral limits of torts, not insurance.

If, by contrast, one adopts a luck egalitarian view of the world, then one almost instantly falls into a bottomless hole. The economic data are clear that Black Americans face headwinds in their economic lives attributable to the color of their skin, and to the embedded and unconscious racism of many White Americans. Are we then to classify skin color as a "handicap"? As an explanation for lower wage rates that should be indemnified under an "underemployment" model? And which government agency would go about this grim business? By doing so we have not honored any principle of equality as I understand it, but rather we have perpetuated a racial classification that is the very antithesis of equality.

Most Black children deserve a greater investment in their human capital, but we can get to that point simply by looking at an easily measurable impersonal resource—the money different families have available to devote to this kind of investment in a country that relies excessively on private funding of human capital, thereby starving our country's growth and our children's economic future.

There is a boundary line to be drawn when we talk about insurance as a metaphor, and that line is coterminous with the reach of impersonal resources. Anything beyond that is not properly assimilated into insurance principles, and the object of any such policy must be justified elsewhere. Who we are is who we happen to be, and it is meaningless to introduce luck, or adverse fortuities, by way of imaginary better-endowed versions of ourselves. It is for these reasons that I insist that we take people as they are, and that we focus instead on the kinds of bad luck that are measurable, and indemnifiable, only in terms of access to impersonal resources.

FAIR EQUALITY OF OPPORTUNITY

If you accept that we must take people as they are, by which I mean that people "own" their native talents and skills, it then follows that the most we can ask of a well-ordered society is that it offer all citizens, in John Rawls's phrase, "*fair* equality of opportunity." As a reminder, Rawls defined this as, "Those who are at the same level of talent and ability, and have the same willingness to use them, should have the same prospects of success regardless of their initial place in the social system, that is, irrespective of the income class into which they are born."[32]

I find it useful to think of fair equality of opportunity as requiring equality in one's ability first to *develop* one's own talents, and then in one's ability to *exploit* those talents in the public sphere of our lives. Fair equality of opportunity is not concerned with the private sphere of our lives; I do not contemplate that government should subsidize my collecting of toy soldiers and similarly eccentric hobbies.

Equality of opportunity must also be limited to the public sphere of our lives because anything that invades our private sphere is deeply offensive to our sense of agency and to the respect for the individual that is the hallmark of liberal society. This means that equality of opportunity does not and cannot intervene within the family, to pluck out the talented youngster from an indifferent or even hostile family to send her to state-sponsored boarding schools where her talents can be nurtured. To suggest that instantiating fair equality of opportunity must mean reorganizing society along the lines of historical East German Olympic training programs is simple sophistry, not a telling criticism.

Fair equality of opportunity means more than formal equal opportunity, as embodied, for example, in anti-discrimination laws, because that narrow view does not reach the difficult question of assuring rough equality in the resources made available to *develop* talents of any kind that we value in presenting ourselves in the public sphere of our lives. We do this in particular by investing in the human capital of children who do not have adequate private resources to draw on. This does not mean that we should invest in the human capital of children in proportion to our estimates of their respective earnings potentials. The market will take care of itself; our job is simply to enable individuals to flourish in their engagement with others as equal citizens, as seen in their own lights.

As developed by T. M. Scanlon and summarized in Chapter 1, fair equality of opportunity contemplates both what Scanlon terms Procedural Fairness and Substantive Opportunity.[33] Procedural Fairness requires, for example, that in our social and economic interactions we be on the lookout not just for discrimination, whether intentional or not, but also nepotism and cronyism. The rules of the game must be neutral, and also must be transparent to all who are interested in playing.

Substantive opportunity is more expansive. To instantiate this goal requires more than imagining a society based on a fair system of social cooperation. It takes money, quite a lot of it, to fund adequate childcare and education such that every child enters adulthood with the investment in her human capital sufficient to have developed her native endowments to their highest and best use, as she sees best.

Substantive opportunity further requires very early childhood childcare, to enable parents to seek high-quality work, secure in the knowledge that their children are in safe and nurturing environments while the parents work. This increases family income, and also improves the stability of the family as a unit. But this too is expensive. None of this, of course, will mean that a child born into poverty will receive exactly the same investment in her human capital, or grow up in exactly as encouraging an environment, as comes so easily to a child of affluent parents, but it is a great deal more than we do today.

The goal of free and equal citizenship is not the same as imagining a society comprising free and *identical* citizens. Fair equality of opportunity demands equal treatment in our public relationships with each other, but does not require that we suppress whatever talents we happen to have. This assessment might distress egalitarian philosophers, but I submit that it is the fundamental ordering principle around which our society revolves.

As just described in the preceding section of this chapter, at every turn we see evidence that our society is extremely comfortable with taking people as they are, even if that leads to unequal outcomes in the marketplace. Thoughtful social insurance and spending programs, on the one hand, and the progressive income tax, on the other, mitigate extreme outcomes at both ends that plausibly relate at least as much to brute luck (whether existential or circumstantial) as they do to the absence or presence of talent.

The philosopher Lars Lindblom offers a helpful insight here.[34] In Rawls's writing, fair equality of opportunity is lexically prior to his other famous principle, the difference principle, which, it will be remembered, contemplates that society's product must be structured such that additional benefits cannot accrue to the better-off unless those arrangements primarily benefit the worst-off. (Also recall that Rawls basically saw the "worst-off" here as the working class; the disabled, for example, require different considerations.)

Lindblom offers a friendly amendment, in which fair equality of opportunity must be seen as directly paired with, and modulated by, the difference principle. Lindblom writes that the concept of a free and equal citizenry is "absolutely central" to his project. In turn:

> The relationship between the difference principle and fair equality of opportunity is . . . that they are parts of a *single principle* based on the ideal of free and equal citizens. Fair equality of opportunity is the part of this principle that regulates how the basic structure [of society] affects talents and ambitions, whereas the difference principle regulates the inequality that could result from differences in (natural) talents even after the opportunity principle has done its work.[35]

That is, our social institutions must encourage the development and exploitation of native talents by citizens, so that they can engage with others on terms of their own choosing, which is the essence of a fair system of social cooperation among free and equal citizens. But our institutions also must modulate extremes in outcomes, in particular by assuring that low-income citizens have the minimal resources necessary to assemble the "primary goods" necessary to carry on life "as free and equal persons living a complete life."[36] These include income and wealth sufficient "to achieve a wide range of ends whatever they may be."

I propose one more friendly amendment, which is that Rawls's difference principle becomes both more familiar and more palatable when it is phrased as a plea for the progressive income tax, where maximum tax rates are designed with a weather eye to efficiency concerns. This knocks the wind out of the sails of those who mischaracterize the difference principle as a demand for the enslavement of the talented. Admittedly, this is a diluted expression of the difference principle, but one that I can imagine serving to guide actual policy.

This unified theory of fair equality of opportunity neatly explains why this principle is not tantamount to runaway market triumphalism, albeit with better public schools. It is as much as we can ask of a society that is not a thought experiment. Many philosophers will deride it as a mere starting-gate theory, in which insufficient respect is paid to more egalitarian ideals. The answer is: Yes. Fair equality of opportunity does not promise egalitarian outcomes, nor does it neutralize the brute luck that through our genes and pixie dust determines who we are at our core.[37] But at least the unified theory modulates the worst excesses of an unfettered market economy.

Within philosophical circles, the principle of fair equality of opportunity has been subject to a great deal of criticism, led principally by the philosopher Richard Arneson.[38] I will not bore you with all the fanciful hypotheticals and exaggerated concerns that are the stock-in-trade of professional philosophy. A couple of criticisms, however, do deserve mentioning. One is that equality of opportunity is "arbitrary from a moral point of view." T. M. Scanlon does a nice job of quickly rebutting this. Scanlon's point is that to call equality of opportunity "arbitrary from a moral point of view" is not to label it immoral or unjust, but rather simply to mean that the principle is necessary but not sufficient by itself to justify differences in outcomes.

More specifically, Scanlon argues that "equality of opportunity is not [by itself] a justification for inequality but an independent requirement that must be satisfied in order for inequalities that are justified in some other way to be just."[39] This is a critically important thought. What is this deeper justification for the differences in outcomes that arise even in a society that fully embraces equality of opportunity?

From my practical perspective the justification for the unequal results promised by equality of opportunity is that as a society we have structured our institutions quite consciously to give priority to the promotion of individual agency and to the marketplace as the vehicle that in the first instance allocates economic returns. This justification follows ineluctably from the decision to *take people as they are*— that is, to concede that it is not the job of society to try to neutralize differences in the distribution of native talents that are valued by our social institutions. A great deal thus flows from the fundamental axiom—the only move that as far as I can see is remotely plausible—that we must take people as they are.

From the other direction, a commitment to fair equality of opportunity also is susceptible to the newly fashionable claim that it is elitist.[40] Again, the answer to this is: Yes. Fair equality of opportunity contemplates that those with a natural aptitude for hitting the curveball have available to them the impersonal resources (playing fields, coaching, travel teams) required to develop that talent, and those with native gifts in cognitive reasoning have the opportunity to develop them. In every case the right moral stance is not lotteries and arbitrary leveling down, but rather public money—plenty of it, to defeat the fundamental economic injustice in American society, which is our unfair reliance on private (family) resources as the sources of the investments required to bring to fruition the different native talents that we all have.

CHAPTER 8

THE SOCIAL MORTGAGE

It is necessary to state once more the characteristic principle of Christian social doctrine: the goods of this world are originally meant for all. The right to private property is valid and necessary, but it does not nullify the value of this principle. Private property, in fact, is under a "social mortgage," which means that it has an intrinsically social function, based upon and justified precisely by the principle of the universal destination of goods.[1]

—POPE JOHN PAUL II

[W]hat improves the circumstances of the greater part [of society] can never be regarded as an inconveniency to the whole. No society can be flourishing and happy, of which the greater part of its members are poor and miserable.[2]

—ADAM SMITH

FROM INSURANCE TO ETHICS

Life breaks people. The reasons might be addiction, mental illness, physical handicaps, the despair of too many tragedies, the vulnerability of being a child or very elderly in circumstances beyond one's control, or the hopelessness of deep poverty with no path out—it does not really matter. Those who have been broken nonetheless remain both human and fellow citizens of a single society, and as such deserve not pity but material help, because material resources in fact can mitigate the pain of hopelessness and in some cases restore a fellow citizen to full moral agency.

Metaphorical insurance cannot carry all the load here. More direct thinking along ethical lines is required. When we do engage in this manner, we are led to offer levels of income assistance that enable individuals to exercise effective agency—to act as functional and independent members of society—*regardless of how they might have fallen into a low state.*

As discussed in Chapter 7, the philosopher John Rawls encapsulated this ethical obligation with his construction of "primary goods," which operate in several dimensions. The term includes basic freedoms, but also material resources (whether provided in cash or in kind) in quantities sufficient to enable one to function as a citizen, and to be able to command one's own self-respect as well as the self-respect of others. Universal Basic Income or means-tested programs, for example, can address issues like nutrition security and homelessness. Universal healthcare is susceptible of analysis both as insurance and as an ethical imperative. These are simply some of the base conditions required to function in the modern world.

In Rawls's mind, we offer these primary goods to each other because we are members of a common society that was founded on our commitment to engage with one another "as fully cooperating members of a society of free and equal citizens," each living "a complete life." We have made this commitment because it was the rational basis on which to organize society when we all were behind the veil and did not know into what kind of life we would be born, or how far we might fall if bad luck were to overwhelm us. In so doing we accept a certain level of "moral hazard"—the risk that some will behave recklessly or shirk the irksomeness of hard work, knowing that there is some ultimate safety net to prevent them starving to death.

You might find Rawls's thought experiment here unacceptably naïve, but you should not dismiss it quite so quickly. As a country we can afford to do much of what Rawls imagined. And as for moral hazard, almost all Americans in fact define themselves and find their own identity through the dignity of work. Nor is there any plausible risk that our income support systems will become so lavish as to dull most individuals' appetites to work and thereby to prosper.

Moral hazard plays out colloquially as the "Jason the Surfer" story—the surf bum who uses food stamps and ingenuity to buy lobster for dinner.[3] What is important to remember, though, is that if a social program were ever to be so perfectly designed that it reached its intended targets 999 times out of 1,000, then any such program designed to help, say, 5 million people would bestow unintended benefits on 5,000 miscreants, layabouts, grifters, and lazy bums. Any cable news network can and will find one or more of these bad apples and feature him on the nightly news, but the real story—the one that deserves national attention but never gets it, is the 4,995,000 fellow citizens whose lives have been made better.

I could extend the insurance metaphor to include the provision of the cluster of material primary goods contemplated by Rawls, but at some point the discussion would veer uncomfortably close to the idea of insurance against constitutive luck that I rejected in the previous chapter. (Is this person homeless because he lacks skills valued in the marketplace, or because he lacks any ambition?) I think therefore that the scope of our *minimum ethical obligations* to one another is better addressed head-on.

The basic distinction at which I am driving is this. Insurance as product and metaphor works as a framework for delivering indemnification against specific impersonal adverse fortuities, such as the bad luck attributable to health issues or inadequate family resources to fund the investment in human capital needed to prosper in modern society.

The ethical obligation I am describing here lies one layer further down. It is a comprehensive safety net by another name—it is the way we respond to those whom life has broken, in whatever manner. It is needs-based, but it is not judgmental. We accept the occasional abuser of the system, because by suspending judgment we honor the dignity and self-respect of the vast majority of recipients. Whatever we do along these lines no doubt will be too little; there is no need gratuitously to deprecate the characters of recipients just to prove to ourselves our greater moral merit, or to wring the last dollar of waste, fraud, and abuse from the system. Understanding that an ethically driven safety net exists to bandage those whom life has broken puts the lie to work requirements. With only a very occasional exception, those in need of aid are those too fragile to hold full-time jobs without extensive investments in social services, which of course are never forthcoming.

It is clear that in America today we wear these ethical obligations far too lightly. That attitude is wrong, particularly for a country as wealthy as ours. It dishonors any commitment to equality of opportunity, of course. More fundamentally, however, it denies that we and those whom life has broken, for whatever reason, are part of one community. But common citizenship creates that community, and when we deny our ethical obligations to our fellow citizens, we also deny the foundations on which this country was established.

This chapter therefore explores the ethical ties that should bind us all to each other by virtue of the fact that we are citizens of a single society called the United States. My particular interest, as in earlier chapters, is in material goods, insofar as access to them in reasonable quantities is a critical component of Rawls's construction of the necessary conditions for effective human agency.

I could proceed by quoting various Founding Fathers, or by surveying a dozen religious traditions. Instead, I have chosen to focus on one line of ethical inquiry, Catholic Social Thought. It is neither my religion nor my academic expertise, but Catholic Social Thought has carefully reasoned about the nature and scope of our ethical obligations to each other in ways that are consistent with the previous chapter's discussion of how philosophers work. In so doing, it has developed principled reasons to support comprehensive ethical commitments that extend to all people, not just those of the Catholic faith. Of course, Catholic Social Thought can rely on a 2,000-year-old continuous accretion of religious doctrines to inform its ethical teachings, which is a luxury that philosophers deny themselves, but those religious doctrines, insofar as they are relevant to ethical questions of the sort considered here, are ones with which most readers are both familiar and comfortable, even if they do not expressly profess them.

More forcefully, the "social mortgage," as described below, is a wonderful figure of speech that has salience without regard to any specific religious tradition. It deserves to be better known for this reason alone. Our current policy discourse is so impoverished, and so tilted toward comforting the comfortable, that when I see a good figure of speech like this I grab it, whatever the source.

Many readers will not bring any great warmth toward the Catholic Church to bear on this discussion, for reasons having nothing to do with the discussion in this chapter. I understand and am sympathetic to this sentiment. I ask, though, that you put to one side the Church and instead consider the discussion that follows as a summary of a complete ethical framework that does not ask much by way of religious presuppositions to be intelligible. Despite its different point of origin, this ethical framework bears striking resemblance to the work of Rawls, particularly in regard to the role of primary goods in his thought. One does not prove the merit of the other, but both taken together usefully illuminate the kinds of ethical commitments that we should acknowledge as what we owe to each other.

THE "SOCIAL MORTGAGE"

A well-ordered society rests on a foundational layer of ethical obligations to one another that look to needs, but that are offered willingly, without dehumanizing the recipient.[4] This proposition runs counter to the trend of the last twenty-five years or so of "welfare" policy, and for that matter to some of the implications of the moral luck literature. As elegantly described by Yascha Mounk in his book *The Age of Responsibility* (introduced in Chapter 2), trends in neoliberal economic thinking, exaggerated concerns about moral hazard, and oversimplified philosophical notions of accountability (option luck versus brute luck) have all conspired to shift our attention from needs to putative deservingness.[5] These forces have played out against a pervasive background of unexamined racism and other underexamined social determinants, including our failure to take equality of opportunity seriously.

In our enthusiasm for the misapplication of neoliberal economic principles to define the ethical principles that might bind us, we also overlook the positive economic externalities of robust support systems. These in fact are risk-encouraging devices, because they allow an individual to take a risk, to try some new business venture, knowing that she will not be reduced to begging on the street if things do not work out. And, of course, the vast administrative apparatus required to run our secular inquisition into the deservedness of the poor is expensive and prone to make mistakes.

Our ethical aim should be to encourage the agency of the individual, which is not the same thing as classifying those individuals as deserving or not. As the philosopher Elizabeth Anderson concluded in her landmark paper, "What Is the Point of Equality?," "To live in an egalitarian community . . . is to be free from oppression to participate in and enjoy the goods of society, and to participate in democratic self-government. . . . What citizens ultimately owe one another is the social conditions of the freedoms people need to function as equal citizens."[6]

Our current commitment to "Poor Law thinking," in Anderson's words, is exactly the wrong place from which to develop a coherent foundation to support human agency and to honor our relationships to each other as free and equal citizens of a single society. It is time to put down our obsession with moral hazard, as if avoiding any instance of it were our only value, when in fact moral hazard is simply a cost to be considered in designing social systems to instantiate our authentic collective aspirations. When we seek to instantiate fair equality of opportunity, we must begin with a society in which some minimum standard of living is possible simply because one is a citizen of our country, not because one has been adjudged deserving.

What, then, are the obligations of those of us who have enjoyed reasonably productive lives to society as a whole?

In his encyclical *Sollicitudo Rei Socialis*, Pope John Paul II offered an extraordinarily helpful metaphor to frame the question. The metaphor was the idea that holders of wealth in a market economy hold their assets subject to a "social mortgage"—an obligation to apply their wealth not simply to the accumulation of more wealth, but to pay off the *senior* claim that society legitimately places on that wealth, as part of every individual's obligation to develop in himself and to promote across a society the virtues of charity, friendship, liberality, and justice:

> Property has a social function in the sense that the property holder is a social being, joined together with others in a network of communities such as family, neighborhood, place of worship, workplace. . . . At the same time, private property has an

individual function in the sense that the person holding that property is an individual human being, unique and apart from all other human beings. . . .

The social function of private property means that ownership confers steward-ship. Just as a conventional mortgage binds the homeowner to repay the institution that made ownership of that home possible, a social mortgage obligates the owner of private property to give back to the community so that those with no private pro-perty holdings have access to the same basic services such as health care, education, transportation, and police and fire protection that helped make possible the personal development of that property owner. Homo economicus of the libertarian persuasion recognizes the duty in accepting a conventional mortgage, but not the duty in a social mortgage. The acting person of the personalist persuasion acknowledges both.[7]

As is true of any other mortgage, the social mortgage ranks senior to the equity holder in its claims on assets and income, but it is not tantamount to ownership or control, which remain fully vested in the owner. The social mortgage thus neatly reconciles private property and the market economy to the larger obligations that each individual has to the community of which he or she is a part. It takes full advantage of the efficiencies of private markets, where prices seamlessly convey enormous information to producers and consumers, while reminding us that the returns captured in those private markets remain encumbered by prior obligations to the community, and whose laws and norms have created the environment in which those private markets can flourish. The theme of the social mortgage is a new way of expressing the integration of our participation in private markets with our obligations to our inner selves and to others.

The overarching purpose of *Sollicitudo Rei Socialis*, of which the metaphor of the social mortgage is only a part, is to promote the "development" of all peo-ples, where "development" has a special meaning. It must be understood as encompassing more than material gains:

> Development which is merely economic is incapable of setting man free, on the con-trary, it will end by enslaving him further. Development that does not include the cul-tural, transcendent and religious dimensions of man and society, to the extent that it does not recognize the existence of such dimensions and does not endeavor to direct its goals and priorities toward the same, is even less conducive to authentic liberation. Human beings are totally free only when they are completely themselves, in the full-ness of their rights and duties. The same can be said about society as a whole.[8]

"Development" therefore is an exercise in moral theology, or at least ethics, not just economic theory:

> When individuals and communities do not see a rigorous respect for the moral, cul-tural and spiritual requirements, based on the dignity of the person and on the proper

identity of each community, beginning with the family and religious societies, then all the rest—availability of goods, abundance of technical resources applied to daily life, a certain level of material well-being—will prove unsatisfying and in the end contemptible.[9]

At the same time, "development" is not simply an exercise in spiritual contemplation. It presupposes access to the material goods of the world sufficient to enable the individual to reach his or her full potential, and to live a life of dignity: "The motivating concern for the poor—who are, in the very meaningful term, 'the Lord's poor'—must be translated at all levels into concrete actions, until it decisively attains a series of necessary reforms."[10]

You can hear echoes of Rawls and his concern with primary goods.

For this reason, *Sollicitudo Rei Socialis* considers the impact on the poor of numerous aspects of internal economies and political systems, as well as international institutions and terms of economic exchange, down to foreign exchange rates.[11] The size of the social mortgage, and the instruments used to reify the abstract concept, are driven in substantial part by economic disparities within a society, to the extent those disparities are evidence of a society in which some individuals lack the material resources necessary for them to fully live lives of dignity in which they can pursue their own development, in this special sense of the word.

The circumstances required to promote the authentic development of the individual are not the exclusive purview of members of the Catholic faith, *but rather are universal claims on all societies*: "Collaboration in the development of the whole person and of every human being is in fact a duty of all towards all, and must be shared by the four parts of the world: East and West, North and South; or, as we say today, by the different 'worlds.'"[12]

In sum, the obligation described in *Sollicitudo Rei Socialis* to promote the authentic development of the individual is reified in part through concrete economic action. Its message applies to all members of society, and its reasoning rests on ethical principles that are not the exclusive province of one faith. This means that the social mortgage—indeed, the entire operation of promoting authentic development—can and indeed must exist within the political sphere, even a secular political society:

> For the decisions which either accelerate or slow down the development of peoples are really political in character. In order to overcome the misguided mechanisms mentioned earlier and to replace them with new ones which will be more just and in conformity with the common good of humanity, an effective political will is needed.[13]

Sollicitudo Rei Socialis thus offers more direction on the scope and instantiation of the social mortgage than at first appears. The social mortgage is the senior creditor claim on the ownership of goods necessary to ensure that all members of a society possess the material circumstances necessary to pursue their own authentic development. The social mortgage does not interfere with the rights of ownership any more than a commercial mortgage does, but like a commercial mortgage its claim comes ahead of the wealth owner's ability to consume that wealth or the income therefrom. The instruments by which the social mortgage are defined and applied exist as real and salient in the political sphere, not simply as hortatory calls in Sunday sermons.

Some economies in the past have embraced the social mortgage as a living constitutional imperative. Late medieval Italy was a remarkably active market-oriented economy in many respects, having little to do with contemporary casual understandings of medieval life. Companies not that dissimilar from modern business organizations thrived. In this environment, however, every company set aside a fraction of its capital in the name of "our Good Lord God" as held for the benefit of the poor, who thereby became *de facto* partners in the business. The partnership metaphor was carried through to its logical ends; the poor participated in company profits in good times, and should a firm go bankrupt, the poor (through the agency of the local archbishop) were transformed from partners to actual creditors of the bankrupt enterprise.[14] This was a literal application of the social mortgage within the context of a market economy.

Pope John Paul II was careful in *Sollicitudo Rei Socialis* not to prescribe this or any other particular set of economic reforms to satisfy the claims of the social mortgage.[15] Nor did he propose a metric to determine the size of that obligation. But he was clear that the mortgage increases as does the wealth of a society and the inequality of its economic system. By every measure, then, the social mortgage that encumbers the US market economy should be large, and its existence and purpose universally acknowledged. Yet neither is true: the United States today is the richest large economy in the world, but it imposes uniquely small communitarian claims on private wealth.

As Pope John Paul II emphasized, the path to authentic development lies in real-world politics. This idea that the social mortgage takes visible form within the political system in fact is necessary, because the instruments through which the social mortgage can be reified largely rest in the hands of the state, in particular its power to compel its citizens, subject in the United States only to constitutional protections. To move from the abstraction of a hypothesized social mortgage to making good on that social claim, we *must* invoke the power of the state.

The most important of these state instrumentalities of compulsion is fiscal policy, meaning here government taxing policies, in turn used to finance public income security, investment, and insurance programs. Taxing and spending policies directly affect citizens' income security, inequality, and economic mobility opportunities in large and measurable ways that lead to obvious differences in social welfare across similarly affluent societies. The heart of the reified social mortgage lies here.

The social mortgage will not be redeemed through simple appeals to private generosity. Charitable giving at current levels is insufficient to discharge the principal of the social mortgage, a conclusion that is plainly apparent in light of the overwhelming social problems in the United States today that I have described, or as have been made manifest after major disasters like Hurricanes Katrina (in 2005) or Maria (in 2017). Nor are we likely to see a quantum leap in giving. Those who today already are blessed by a generous spirit do not need lecturing, and those who believe that all they possess is held as of right (a depressingly large fraction of the affluent) will not spontaneously open their hearts to these sorts of remonstrations.

Aggregate US charitable giving in 2016 was generous by international standards, but still was only one-tenth as much as tax collections.[16] In turn, a significant fraction of top-end charitable giving is tinged with narcissism (the Kleinbard Museum of String, for example), and charitable giving encompasses a wide dispersion in expressions that wander far afield of the social mortgage—a new college football stadium, for example. Donations to religious institutions often have a tribal quality to them, in which those of the same faith or same pew are brought within the scope of the charitable impulse, while others are ignored. Finally, there is an unavoidable odor of power relationships and paternalism associated with much giving. If the social mortgage is to have authentic meaning, it must be applied to all in need, not simply to co-religionists or those who seem especially thankful.

The ultimate form of charity actually is to pay one's taxes cheerfully, precisely because one cannot assert any claim of power or entitlement over the (unknown) ultimate beneficiaries of those payments. It is this lack of explicit gratitude and a lack of connection with the beneficiary that makes paying taxes an authentically charitable act.

REIFYING THE SOCIAL MORTGAGE

It is all well and good to describe idealized concepts like a social mortgage on the private economy, or the obligations attendant on the social contract that we have chosen to believe defines our relationships to one another, but what do these earnest feelings actually mean in practice? Here are some real-life numbers, meant more as a stalking horse than a detailed term sheet. The point of the exercise is that poverty is a much larger problem in the United States than we ordinarily admit, and we can do something about it in ways that are focused but respectful of the dignity of persons.

One very recent and depressing analysis was prepared in May 2018 by the Special Rapporteur to the United Nations Human Rights Council on Extreme Poverty and Human Rights.[17] Relying on US Census Bureau and OECD data, the UN Human Rights Report summarizes matters as follows:

> About 40 million [Americans] live in poverty, 18.5 million in extreme poverty, and 5.3 million live in Third World conditions of absolute poverty. [The United States] has the highest youth poverty rate in the Organisation for Economic Co-operation and Development (OECD), and the highest infant mortality rates among comparable OECD States. Its citizens live shorter and sicker lives compared to those living in all other rich democracies, eradicable tropical diseases are increasingly prevalent, and it has the world's highest incarceration rate, one of the lowest levels of voter registrations . . . among OECD countries and the highest obesity levels in the developed world.

> The United States [also] has the highest rate of income inequality among Western countries.

* * *

Defenders of the status quo point to the United States as the land of opportunity and the place where the American dream can come true because the poorest can aspire to the ranks of the richest. But today's reality is very different. The United States now has one of the lowest rates of intergenerational social mobility of any of the rich countries. Zip codes, which are usually reliable proxies for race and wealth, are tragically reliable predictors of a child's future employment and income prospects. High child and youth poverty rates perpetuate the intergenerational transmission of poverty very effectively, and ensure that the American dream is rapidly becoming the American illusion. The equality of opportunity, which is so prized in theory, is in practice a myth, especially for minorities and women, but also for many middle-class White workers.[18]

Here again we see the central dilemma: existential bad luck lands many into poverty, whether through birth, chronic illness, or other reasons. But the climb out of poverty depends in the general case on private resources that by definition the poor cannot muster, from a functioning car to get to work, to money for child care, or to dozens of uses, including higher education and adequate healthcare. There are exceptional men and women who through great talent or serendipity overcome these obstacles, but the question that must remain uppermost in our minds is: Why should we ask some of our fellow citizens to run an obstacle course while others can rely on family assets to roll downhill into a comfortable adult life? The solution is not to gratuitously hobble the affluent, but to think more intently about how much it costs our society, in cohesiveness, economic performance, and ethical failings, to so systematically underinvest in the human capital of so many.

The official US poverty measure is terribly outmoded. Its construction is over fifty years old, and it underestimates both the needs and the resources available to families. It basically is set at three times a bare-bones food budget. This simplistic formula no longer represents an accurate relationship between the cost of one item in poor person's budget (food) and her total costs. Further, in comparing people's incomes to this threshold of needs, the official measure of poverty looks only to cash transfer government programs, not in-kind government benefits.

In recent years, federal agencies have developed a more useful measure of poverty, called the Supplemental Poverty Measure. This looks to a broader range of real-world family needs, and it calculates the resources available to a family to meet those needs by including the full panoply of existing government income assistance programs (other than healthcare programs), whether delivered as cash subsidies or in-kind benefits.

The Supplemental Poverty Measure basically defines a basket of core needs (food, clothing, shelter, and utilities) and then multiplies this figure by 1.2, to cover other basic expenses.[19] The result is a threshold figure for a minimal standard of living that is then compared to a family's resources. Those families whose total resources available to meet this basket of core needs, taking into account wages and all government benefits (other than healthcare), fall below the threshold are classified as living in poverty. In making this calculation, available resources are first reduced by taxes, work expenses, out-of-pocket medical expenses, and child support paid to another household. Healthcare, to the extent financed by Medicaid or other in-kind government healthcare programs, is excluded as both needs and resources; instead, the Supplemental Poverty Measure reflects only estimated "medical out of pocket" (MOOP) costs as subtractions from available resources. Another way of phrasing things is that the Supplemental Poverty Measure implicitly assumes that a household has Medicaid or other health insurance coverage.

Both measures of poverty are adjusted for differences in family composition, although under different formulas. The Supplemental Poverty Measure further is adjusted for costs in different geographic regions, and for differences between homeowners and renters.

The 2018 Supplemental Poverty Measure threshold for a family of four (two adults, two children) who rented their home was $28,166.[20] In other words, this figure was an estimate of the minimum total resources required by such a family in 2018 to fashion a life that was not lived in poverty, after subtracting taxes, work expenses, out-of-pocket medical expenses, and child support paid to another household—and implicitly assuming coverage by Medicaid or other health insurance program.

By either measure, far too many Americans live in poverty. For 2018, the official poverty measure classified 11.8 percent of our fellow citizens as living in poverty; the Supplemental Poverty Measure so classified 12.8 percent. (These figures aggregate Americans of all ages; in general, the Supplemental Poverty Measure places fewer children, but many more elderly, as living in poverty than does the official measure.)

Now, 12.8 percent of all Americans is almost *42 million people*. Without regard to the abstractions of communitarian thought experiments or the metaphor of the social mortgage, this number should shock and depress us all. And remember, the Supplemental Poverty Measure includes in a family's available resources not just wages, but all government benefit programs.

The simple fact is that we are the richest large economy in the world, yet somehow tolerate one out of eight of our fellow citizens living in poverty. Many are children or elderly; others suffer disabilities that limit their effectiveness in the private economy; few are Jason the Surfer types leading the carefree life of a young and healthy beach bum.

We continue to hold to the widespread misconception that we shovel money to a large underclass of undeserving poor, but the actual federal social safety net is a smaller budget item than most appreciate. Over the next few paragraphs I quickly sketch the most important federal anti-poverty programs; the states have their own programs that augment or complement federal spending.

Most federal "income security" programs are treated for budget purposes as "mandatory" spending; the term simply means that if a person meets the criteria set by Congress in establishing that program, she is eligible for the associated benefits so specified without (in almost all cases) the requirement of congressional discretionary budget appropriations. The largest exception is the cluster of rental support programs overseen by the Department of Housing and Urban Development.

Some of the federal government's most important income security programs are not actually administered by the federal government; instead, funds are provided to the states, which have surprising latitude as to how exactly the money will be disbursed. It is at the state level that extreme work requirements or other punitive measures creep in. Not only are these measures ethically disturbing, but they create enormous differences in the treatment of the poor across the country, based solely on the state in which they reside (which in many cases is also the state in which they were born). As a reminder, no one is a *citizen* of North Carolina: we are all citizens of the United States, some of whom happen to be *residents* of North Carolina. The geographic inequality in treatment is easily explained in terms of political vindictiveness in some states, but not so easily tolerated as an ethical or economic matter.

Shown in Table 8.1 are the principal anti-poverty programs operated by the federal government, other than those relating to healthcare. The idea here is to list just those programs that directly target the mitigation of poverty; I therefore have excluded Social Security and other programs (such as unemployment insurance) that reach millions of poor Americans, but which are not targeted to them.[21]

Now, $329 billion in targeted antipoverty measures sounds like a great deal of money, and compared with many other competing priorities it is. But in a more fundamental sense it simply is insufficient, for the simple reason that the Supplemental Poverty Measure *already includes* this support in its calculation that 42 million Americans are living in poverty today.

To further put these figures in context, the federal budget for its fiscal year ending September 30, 2019, included $4.5 *trillion* ($4,500 billion) in federal government spending, against GDP of about $21 trillion. And to emphasize yet again, one in eight Americans lives in poverty *after* taking these spending programs into account.

As is always the case with federal spending programs, the items in Table 8.1 need a little bit of explanation. I will confine my remarks to the larger programs and keep them as short as possible. The website of the Center on Budget and Policy Priorities is an excellent resource for exploring these programs further.

Federal housing programs are overseen by HUD but actually administered by the states. In 2019 about 10 million Americans received rental assistance. Of these, more than two-thirds were children, disabled, or elderly. But for this assistance, four in ten would be homeless or pay more than half their income in rent. Eligible families who receive rental assistance generally are required to pay 30 percent of their incomes for rent and utilities.

Because rental assistance programs are "discretionary" in budget terms, they must be funded through annual appropriations. Congress's appropriations in fact run at levels that are far smaller than the demand by low-income households for rental assistance. Based on current eligibility criteria, *only one in four* eligible families actually receive federal rental assistance. The result is long waiting lists.

The *earned income tax credit (EITC)* is a very important subsidy to low-wage workers; in the language of policymakers, it is a program to "make work pay." The idea is that the first step on the income ladder is a very expensive one. Often, commuting to the job must be paid for, childcare arranged, and so on; these are substantial costs relative to a minimum-wage job.

The EITC effectively offers cash subsidies to workers holding these low-wage jobs, to encourage this transition (and retention) into the market economy. For tax year 2019, these cash subsidies could be as high as $5,828 for a family with two children (after first applying any credits to their modest federal income tax bill). But the EITC phases out very quickly as wages rise beyond a modest level. For a married couple with two children filing joint returns for 2019, the $5,828 benefit begins to be scaled back as family income exceeds $24,820, and it is completely clawed back when income reaches about $53,000. Another way of visualizing the phaseout is to imagine that the EITC is "clawed back" by the government as one's income rises.

The EITC is paid annually. In an ideal world it would be paid monthly in advance, but prior attempts to do so foundered on administrative and fraud problems.

By design, the EITC provides income support only to wage earners. It is not helpful at all to the elderly, the disabled, or those adults who for any other reason are not wage earners in the market economy. In fact, *two-thirds* of those living in poverty are children or seniors. Each group has an equal ethical claim to our attention.

Although it is not obvious on the face of its operation, the EITC has become in substantial measure a subsidy to *employers*, because they rely on its existence to suppress the cash wages they pay their employees. A more generous EITC would compound the problem, and it would further exacerbate the divide between the poor who are both able to work and able to find work, on the one hand, and those who through no fault of their own either cannot work or cannot find work.

The EITC phaseout, considered alongside the effects of increasing wage income on other government benefit programs, means that low-income taxpayers can face extremely high *marginal* tax rates, as a few dollars more of income trigger cliff effects in other government programs (whereby taxpayers become entirely disqualified when their incomes pierce a certain level), and steep reductions in the allowable EITC. These create adverse incentive effects for those in the workforce but earning relatively low wages, as the next step up the income ladder gets seriously eroded by all these hidden tax and quasi-tax costs.

The *child tax credit* is designed to offers subsidies to families with children. It rightly is very controversial; it also is quite complicated in application. A tax credit can be used as a sort of voucher with which to pay one's income tax bill. Lower-income taxpayers typically have no federal income tax liability, or at most a small one, so without more the EITC or the child tax credit would be useless to them. The solution is to make some tax credits like the EITC "refundable," which is just a fancy way of saying that the government writes taxpayers holding these refundable credit vouchers a check in the specified amounts. Substantially all the EITC is paid in this way.

The child tax credit is different, in that only part of it is refundable. Its total annual cost to the federal government is about $116 billion, of which about $70 billion is used by taxpayers to reduce their tax bills, which means in effect that at most $46 billion of its annual cost could reach low-income families. The scope of the child tax credit was radically expanded in 2017 tax legislation, so that it is now designed to apply to families earning as much as $400,000/year. For that reason, the child tax credit's cost has soared since it was rewritten in 2017, and the incremental federal budget costs flow to the bank accounts of those whose incomes are far north of poverty thresholds.[22] One study has found that under the newly revamped child tax credit about 23 million children live in families whose incomes are too low to obtain the full credit (or in many cases, any credit at all), because they have insufficient tax liability, and by design the remainder is not fully refundable.[23]

In Table 8.1 I have treated the entirety of the refundable portion of the child tax credit as going to low-income families, although in practice this overstates things.

Supplemental Security Income (SSI) is run by the Social Security Administration. It is a program for severely mentally or physically disabled individuals with minimal other sources of support. Adults must demonstrate that by virtue of their disability they are unable to hold a job anywhere in the country. It is the only federal program for families coping with no meaningful other sources of support and children with severe disabilities. Two-thirds of applicants fail these medical criteria or the income ceiling. Benefits for these destitute families average a little over $500 month.[24]

SSI should not be confused with Social Security Disability Income (SSDI), also run by the Social Security Administration. The latter is not listed as an anti-poverty measure in Table 8.1, because it is true disability insurance, paid for through payroll taxes, and the benefits of which, like Social Security retirement payments, are determined by a formula that looks to the amount paid into the program. SSDI is paid regardless of a recipient's income. It technically is a separate trust fund from the old-age Social Security trust fund. (Unemployment insurance is roughly similar.)

Table 8.1 Principal Targeted Federal Anti-Poverty Programs (2019)

Program	Approx. Annual Cost (2019)
HUD Rental Housing Programs (Discretionary)	$48 billion
Earned Income, Child, Childcare Tax Credits*	$99 billion
Supplemental Nutrition Assistance Program (Food stamps)	$63 billion
Child Nutrition	$24 billion
Supplemental Security Income	$56 billion
Family Support (Temporary Assistance for Needy Families)	$32 billion
Pell Grants (Discretionary and Mandatory)	$30 billion
TOTAL	**$329 billion**

* Tax credit figures include only "refundable" portions.

Sources: Congressional Budget Office; Center on Budget and Policy Priorities (housing)

The *Supplemental Nutrition Assistance Program (SNAP)*, formerly food stamps, is the country's largest program to mitigate outright hunger in America, and to improve at the margin the diets of low-income recipients. "Child Nutrition" programs primarily comprise school lunches. SNAP and Child Nutrition programs are "mandatory" (in that anyone who meets the eligibility criteria qualifies), but technically are funded through annual appropriations.

SNAP's benefits structure is extremely complex, but it is not a simple antihunger program, in that its benefits in fact are heavily tilted to those families with wage incomes.[25] For a family of four, the maximum SNAP benefit is $465/month, which works out to about $1.30 per person per meal. About 40 million Americans receive SNAP benefits; that is, its utilization closely tracks the poverty rate. While SNAP is a consistent federal program, there are complex state add-ons and options, so that it is not strictly identical in operation across different states. Like EITC, SNAP phases out (is clawed back) as income rises above very modest levels.

Temporary Assistance for Needy Families (TANF) is the federal government's largest source of cash assistance for families in economic crisis. It is a "block grant" program, so that money is paid to the states, and they in turn design their programs as they see fit, subject to some broad federal constraints.[26]

TANF is available only to families with incomes less than one-half the official poverty line. About three out of four TANF participants are children. TANF recipients must satisfy work requirement rules (which vary across the states) or risk being cut off from aid. And of course TANF is temporary; the general rule is sixty months, but twenty-one states have adopted shorter periods. A majority of states piggyback on the federal program to increase the total benefits paid; even so, TANF benefits are never as high as 60 percent of the poverty line.

For those inclined to see the glass half full, these anti-poverty programs do work, in the sense that without them the poverty rate would be even higher than it currently is. For example, in 2018 all government programs taken together (including not just the targeted anti-poverty measures described above, but also Social Security and Medicaid) cut the national poverty rate in half. That is, if the federal government had gone out of the business of social insurance, health insurance, and the targeted anti-poverty measures considered here, about *one in four Americans—78 million of us*—would have been living in poverty.[27]

I look at things differently. I see the wealthiest large economy in the world, but one in which the market economy if left to its own devices would leave one out of every four Americans in poverty. This is the consequence of our astounding income and wealth marketplace inequality as it is lived.

I also see a country that devotes only about 8 percent of total federal spending to targeted anti-poverty programs. Even this is too kind, because it overlooks the fact that our government spending is very low by international standards. The right question here is not how much we spend in absolute dollars on mitigating poverty, or even what fraction of our budget is devoted to income security, but rather what fraction of our GDP—our available national income—we devote to poverty mitigation, considered against the background of the most unequal imaginable distribution of incomes.

Figure 8.1 shows comparative data that was first introduced in Chapter 3 (see Figure 3.1), but is a powerful indictment of our current policies and delusional beliefs that we live in a post-poverty country that it is worth repeating here. As you can see, no other developed economy has anywhere close to the US level of poverty.

The reason, again, is that we start with a highly unequal income distribution with large pockets of poverty, and then simply spend less than do most other developed countries in ameliorating those outcomes (see Figure 8.2). Germany, for example, devotes 25 percent of its GDP to all forms of social spending at all levels of government combined; the United States, by contrast, spends under 19 percent, taking into account federal, state, and local government efforts. If the United States were to increase its social spending to the same level as Germany's (that is, increase its spending by 6 percentage points of GDP), our public social spending budget would increase by $1.2 trillion/year. Chapter 9 develops further the comparison of the fiscal policies of Germany and the United States.

As one more data point, the OECD average government expenditure on family services (including early childhood childcare and education, but not health or housing), is 2.4 percent of GDP. US governments at all levels spend 1.1 percent of

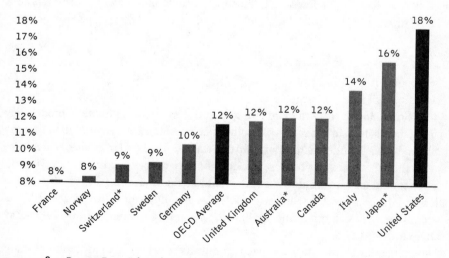

FIGURE 8.1 Poverty Rate, Selected Developed Economies (2017)

Source: OECD Income Distribution Database: Poverty Rate After Taxes and Transfers, September 10, 2019.

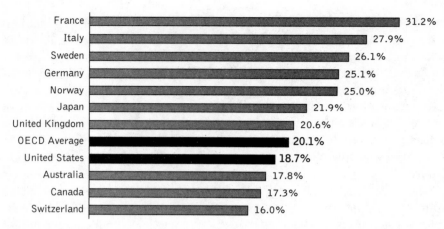

FIGURE 8.2 Public Social Spending as a Percentage of GDP, Selected Developed Economies (2018)

Source: OECD, *Social Expenditure Database (SOCX)*, January 2019, www.oecd.org/social/expenditure.htm.

our GDP.[28] If we were to raise our spending in this category alone to the OECD average, we would add $230 billion/year to the resources we can bring to bear helping families.

In OECD jargon, "social spending" includes everything from food assistance for the neediest to retirement programs like Social Security. The mix of this spending varies across countries. The point, however, developed more completely in *We Are Better Than This*, is that government social spending in all countries is progressive in application—those at the lower end of the income distribution benefit disproportionately relative to higher-income households as a percentage of their respective incomes.

UNIVERSAL BASIC INCOME

Overview

What can be done? Here I would like to propose my stalking horse: a moderately sized Universal Basic Income (UBI) allowance combined with overhauled income tax schedules. The idea is to offer all Americans a fixed dollar amount each year, but then to claw back the benefit through the progressive income tax, relying on higher overall tax rates. The end result would be that those in poverty would keep all their UBI benefits, those in the middle class would keep at least some, and the most affluent Americans would pay income tax at higher rates than they do today to help finance the program.

Universal Basic Income is a concept going all the way back to Milton Friedman; the idea simply is that everyone receives a fixed sum from the government every year, without regard to demonstrated need. In turn, some existing government income support programs would be terminated, with the universal basic allowance serving as substitute.

UBI has the advantage of slashing government administrative costs, but more important, it delivers support with dignity, because no one has to go to the welfare office, cap in hand, to plead his poverty. This is consistent with the concerns of both John Rawls and Pope John Paul II's encyclical to treat our fellow citizens as our equals in their rights and dignities.

UBI as I imagine it addresses poverty, but it also improves the economic posture of the middle class, even after taking into account the higher income tax collections required to fund it. Because UBI is paid to all, it has no stigmatizing aspect to it. It moves away from "Poor Law thinking" and makes possible a minimum standard of living simply because one is a citizen of our country, not because one has been adjudged deserving.

I have to confess here to being surprised by my own advocacy. For years I had a visceral reaction against Universal Basic Income as a poorly targeted and completely unaffordable pipe dream. I credit my students in my policy seminar for hammering at the issue until I saw the light. Once one links UBI directly to an effective claw-back mechanism, so that the net benefits come to rest only with low- and middle-income Americans, UBI becomes a powerful tool to change the lives of tens or hundreds of millions of citizens without putting more cash into the wallets of the most affluent citizens.

About two-thirds of those households classified as living in poverty using the Supplemental Poverty Measure have incomes falling somewhere between 50 and 99 percent of the poverty threshold. Looking at my hypothetical family of four with a $28,000 poverty threshold, a Universal Basic Income grant of even one-half that amount—net of any existing programs that UBI replaces—by definition would ensure that two-thirds of today's poor would no longer be classified as such. My proposal below is in this ballpark, depending at the margin on how many existing income security programs it replaces.

UBI does not turn the social mortgage into a federal subsidy for low-wage jobs, because it treats all Americans equally regardless of job status. Today's earned income tax credit is such a wage subsidy; as such, it is very popular among economists and policymakers as a key instrument to "make work pay." The right policy balance here is to keep at least some EITC as a complement to UBI.

More generally, the real problem with low-wage jobs is that the wages are too low. The remedy is a more appropriate minimum wage. At the federal minimum wage of $7.25 an hour (still in force in over twenty states), the two adults in a family of four at the cusp of the poverty line would have to work about 3,600 hours per year to earn $30,000, after taking into account the maximum EITC cash subsidy benefit available under current law, and subtracting federal payroll taxes, but not any state income tax. (As noted, at this level tax credits would cover any federal tax liability.) Alternatively, you view the impact of the EITC here as raising the effective wage rate to about $9.00/hour. If we want to make work pay, we should pay living wages.

The obvious problem with UBI is that it delivers benefits not just to the poor but to the undeserving rich, thereby making it extraordinarily expensive. Andrew Yang made a UBI proposal during the 2020 Democratic contest to be the party's nominee for president, but the general imprecision of his proposal did as much as any dedicated opponent could have done to heap ridicule on the idea. Yang proposed a UBI benefit of $12,000/year for every adult citizen, with no additional benefit for children. This would mean a UBI benefit of $24,000/year for every family of four—an amount too rich even for my blood.

What the government gives by way of UBI, however, it also can take, by way of the income tax. The trick, then, is to use the progressive income tax to "claw back" UBI grants as a person's income climbs. That way those with modest wage or investment income keep most of the benefit of their UBI benefits, while those who enjoy very high incomes pay back their UBI in the form of higher taxes than they pay today.

The fact is that we raise surprisingly little income tax revenue today. Chapter 9 offers more detail here, but we can see this by looking at international comparisons, in which our country's total tax take as a percentage of GDP and our income tax collections as a subset thereof are far lower than those of our peer developed economies. More directly, we can see this by figuring out the nation's and our own effective tax rates—the taxes we pay divided by some economic measure of income, before consideration of standard deductions, tax credits, and so on. (Economists prefer to use the term "effective" rather than "average," to signify that the tax base being employed is broader than the tax definition of "taxable income.")

The most convenient such measure is "Adjusted Gross Income," visible on the first page of your own 2019 Form 1040 as line 8b. Basically, it is your total economic income reduced, in the case of the self-employed, by business expenses. (It does not, however, include the appreciation in value of any investments you might have held but which you have not yet sold; the result is a vast understatement of the accretion in economic resources of people like Mark Zuckerberg and Warren Buffett.) In most cases people are surprised at how low their effective federal income tax rates actually are.

The IRS publishes aggregate tax return data, but only on a historical basis after the returns for a year are processed. For the 2017 tax year, total Adjusted Gross Incomes amounted to $11 trillion, on which we collectively paid federal income tax of $1.6 trillion, for an aggregate effective tax rate of 14.6 percent. These figures predate the tax reductions ushered in by the 2017 tax act.

The Congressional Budget Office publishes forward-looking tax projections as part of their periodic budget and economic outlooks. As of mid-2019, the CBO projected that for the calendar year 2020 Americans will report aggregate Adjusted Gross Incomes of $12.6 trillion, on which they will pay total federal income tax of about $1.7 trillion, net of refundable credits, for a 13.5 percent effective tax rate for all taxpayers measured against the national AGI tax base.[29]

Proposal

Let me put all this together and offer a specific suggestion by way of illustration, recognizing that it might not do perfect justice in every instance. If every adult in America were to receive as his or her Universal Basic Income of $6,000/year, and every child $3,000/year, then a family of four (two adults, two children) would start out with $18,000 in tax-free cash income. Wage income would of course sit on top of that.

This is the upper end, I think, of affordability. If the proposal could be enacted into law in exchange for reducing those UBI benefits by one-third (to $4,000/year for adults and $2,000/year for children), I would take the deal in a heartbeat.

UBI would be deposited monthly into every person's bank account; for this and many other good reasons, we would probably choose to adopt a postal banking system to ensure that every person has access to inexpensive banking services. Rent and utilities could be paid directly by the depository institution from the account balance, and special arrangements made with social services agencies for individuals not able to handle their money on their own.

Of course, this extravagant gesture does not come cheap. In a country with 253 million adults and 74 million children, the total cost for the new program would be $1.74 trillion every year—about one-half the federal government's current total take from all tax collections, including payroll and corporate taxes ($3.5 trillion).[30] (Scaling the numbers back by one-third would reduce the cost to about $1.16 trillion.)

Before dismissing this starting point as self-evidently preposterous, consider what could be accomplished by imagining an income tax that is re-engineered to coordinate with large UBI grants, as in my illustrative example. The basic idea, again, is that income tax rates in nominal terms would be much higher, but what taxpayers should care about is the *net* of the gives and the takes—the cash received via UBI, less these higher income tax payments. Lower- and middle-class Americans would find that the higher nominal tax rates still left them ahead of the game, in terms of the net UBI they would keep.

We could start with Adjusted Gross Income as the tax base, and add to that a few other items (such as today's untaxed portion of Social Security benefits and

EITC benefits). The UBI grant, however, would *not* be part of the tax base; nor would the value of health insurance (hopefully also of a government-sponsored universal variety). We would not offer a standard deduction or personal itemized deductions, because they would have been replaced by the generous UBI grant. The current tax system, simplified in this manner (and through the elimination of many other subsidies and preferences), would form the tax base—the measure of income. To this we would apply tax rates that on their face are substantially higher than the current law's, because taxpayers start with the large tax-free cash grants of the UBI system.

Once a UBI program is in place, we could scale back some of the major income support programs that the federal government today offers through the tax system and through direct spending, including in particular the child tax credit, which, as discussed earlier, delivers much of its benefits to more prosperous Americans. This program alone costs the federal government about $120 billion/year in forgone tax receipts and cash refunds. I would retain the EITC but make its benefits a bit less child-centric, and I would include any EITC benefits as taxable income.

Of the remaining programs (totaling some $234 billion/year in spending), it might be possible to scale things back by $100 billion or so, although I acknowledge that this is more guesswork than I usually like to bring to bear on policy questions. Since UBI benefits payable to those classed today as living in poverty would amount to about $220 billion/year, the net effect would still be an increase in the resources available to the poorest Americans of roughly $120 billion/year ($3,000/per person/per year). As a prudential matter, however, it is better to begin by assuming that everything other than the child tax credit would remain in place.

After taking into account the elimination of the child tax credit but the retention of all other anti-poverty measures, including the EITC, a revised income tax would need to raise about $1.6 trillion more than it does today for government to break even—about $3.3 trillion in total for 2020. That is, total federal income tax collections in 2020 would roughly have to double if the UBI program were to be fully funded.

Before choking on this impossibly large sum, though, remember that this putative $3.3 trillion 2020 income tax actually would raise, net of UBI, only $1.7 trillion, just as it is projected to do today.

Is this feasible? Well, yes. It might not endear me to my most affluent readers, but it is perfectly feasible. What it entails is that our national effective income tax rate essentially double, to about 26–28 percent, assuming again that all existing anti-poverty programs remain in place, but for the ill-begotten child tax credit. We can achieve this both through expanding the definition of Adjusted Gross Income and by imposing higher marginal tax rates. My back-of-the-envelope calculations suggest that we raise sufficient revenues with tax rate brackets that start at 15 percent for the first $100,000 of income, and then climb to about 45 percent at the top.

Taxing income from essentially the first dollar earned (that is, without a standard or itemized deduction) sounds harsh, but the starting point is completely different from current law. Under my proposal, a family of four would start with $18,000 of tax-free UBI grants. If the adults in that family earned $35,000 in wages between them and were subject to a 15 percent income tax rate from their first dollar of wage income, they would pay $5,250 of income tax, ignoring just for simplicity the retained EITC. This can be viewed as reducing their UBI benefit from $18,000 to $12,750. Their total after-tax income therefore would be $47,750 (wages + UBI − income tax), plus EITC.

By contrast, a family of four with two young children today would owe no federal income tax on their $35,000 of wages, and they would receive cash "refundable" tax credits (including the earned income tax credit) amounting to roughly $6,300. Their total after-tax income therefore would be $41,300. Even without the preservation of the EITC, this family would be much better off with the UBI system, notwithstanding the nominal imposition of income tax.

At a 15 percent rate, my hypothetical family of four with $18,000 in UBI benefits and income of $100,000 would still keep $3,000 of UBI benefits. To put this in context, the 2018 median income for a married-couple family was $94,000.[31] (The Census Bureau does not break this down further by the number of children in the family.) This suggests that UBI benefits and a tax environment along the lines I suggest would be a net boon to the bottom half of the income distribution.

A single individual in a 15 percent tax rate environment would have effectively paid back his UBI check by the time his wage income hit $40,000. By happy coincidence, the 2018 median worker wage was $40,000.

Of course, a substantially expanded tax base could yield lower effective tax rates, particularly a measure of taxable income that included capital income (income from investments) as that income accrued, rather than allowing capital income captured in the form of the appreciation of investment values to escape tax indefinitely. The 2020 Democratic presidential candidates offered some ideas along these lines; I happen as well to have a fully specified capital income tax proposal sitting on the shelf, waiting for some sensible Congress to take it down from there and implement it into law.[32] (I discuss my proposal very briefly in Chapter 9.)

It is easy to get caught up in the minutiae of tax design. The big idea here, though, is to imagine a world in which one could definitively predict that the number of Americans living in poverty would be slashed and that the middle class would live lives with greater economic security. We would "claw back" the generous UBI grants through higher income taxes on income other than the UBI grants. When the dust settled, most working Americans would keep most of their

UBI benefits, even after considering the new higher tax rate schedule on their wages, while Americans with very high incomes would pay substantially more income tax than they do today. This is unavoidable, because not every person will earn enough to "pay back" her UBI grant, and intentional, because the purpose is for the UBI system to change people's material prospects for the better. My specific proposal might not strike the perfect balance, but it is an approximate illustration of what a real-world program would look like.

As noted earlier, today's EITC phaseout, considered alongside the effects of increasing wage income on other government benefit programs, means that low-income taxpayers can face extremely high marginal tax rates, as a few dollars more of income trigger cliff effects in other government programs (whereby taxpayers become entirely disqualified when their incomes pierce a certain level), and steep reductions in the allowable EITC. By contrast, my UBI proposal would impose a constant marginal and effective income tax rate on low- and middle-income wage earners of 15 percent, although the phaseouts of various income security programs would remain. Moreover, the tax rate is sufficiently low that it should not serve as a barrier to seeking a job and staying in the workforce, and of course the EITC would sit on top of UBI benefits for the lowest wage earners (although the EITC would be treated as taxable wages). What is more, the cushion of the UBI will encourage many Americans to open small businesses of their own.

The shadow of Jason the Surfer dominates much debate over ambitious programs like the UBI system outlined here, but for the reasons just summarized, it is far from inevitable that a large UBI program will simply incentivize millions to smoke weed and wax their surfboards. The question is an empirical one. The meager evidence available from much smaller UBI programs, such as Alaska's annual grant to all residents from its oil revenues, is that these smaller programs have not led to an increase in drug abuse, recusal from the workforce, or other negative effects.

To emphasize, however, UBI should not be evaluated by reference simply to claims of adverse incentive effects (moral hazard by another name). UBI by intention is fundamentally different from the EITC in that UBI does not impose any work requirement. The idea is to alleviate poverty and to mitigate the economic anxieties of the middle class, and many people in poverty in particular are in that predicament precisely because they cannot work. They are defenseless children, or the aged, or those with substantial physical or mental handicaps or disabilities. Others have tried to find jobs but have not been able to, and of course state-level retraining or similar programs are largely mirages. The population of can-work-but-won't-work is not a national affliction.

Finally, putting cash into the pockets of low-income Americans has a multiplier effect; they will spend that money on goods and services, and in so doing stimulate demand. The result stimulates economic growth as a whole. These sorts of economic points are developed further in Chapter 9.

William Gale Proposal

William Gale is a senior fellow at the Brookings Institution, the co-director of the non-partisan Tax Policy Center, and one of the country's most respected progressive-leaning public finance economists. In early 2020, Gale proposed a UBI-and-tax package with some rough similarities to my proposal, but ultimately with quite different aims.[33] My idea is a UBI program financed through an expanded progressive income tax, such that families with below-median incomes will obtain a net benefit, varying inversely to income, and directly to family size. Gale has designed a new revenue-raising device (a value added tax, or VAT) and then modulated its impact on lower-income Americans through a much smaller UBI grant. By design, Gale's proposal raises incremental taxes, whereas my proposal is net revenue–neutral.

For our purposes a value added tax is simply a different way of implementing a national sales tax. Gale proposed a 10 percent VAT rate on a sales tax–equivalent basis, so that an item costing $100 today would cost $110 tomorrow.[34] He estimated that his VAT would about $980 billion in the first year.

Of this $980 billion, Gale would dedicate $247 billion to "free and clear" increased tax revenues that could be used to support new programs. He would spend $137 billion on increased Social Security and income support payments to mitigate the burden of the VAT to those populations, and another $596 billion would be dedicated to his UBI plan. This is about one-third of the amount I have proposed for my UBI plan.

Gale's UBI proposal would deliver $5,200/year to a family of four. Because Gale's proposed VAT rate was 10 percent, this UBI benefit would be sufficient to shield such a family from the brunt of the tax so long as their taxable spending (i.e., spending subject to the VAT) was less than $52,000 (including the VAT bill on that spending). A family that spent more than this in a year would be a net VAT payer.

If you focus on the case of a family that spends what it earns (the norm for most Americans), there really is no practical difference between a VAT and a flat income tax. In the first case, the tax is collected as the family spends its income, just as local sales tax is today. In the second case, the tax is collected first, and the family then can spend its after-tax dollars without further federal taxes. If, however, you focus on accumulations of wealth, there is a significant difference, because a new VAT will be collected when an affluent family spends its existing stockpile of wealth as well as when it spends its current earnings.

Economists are entranced by this stealth tax on existing wealth. I have always been a bit more squeamish about its moral standing, and in any event the stealth feature will not stay secret for long, thereby guaranteeing a particularly difficult political brawl with the moneyed classes.

VATs are often pictured as easy-peasy to design, but Gale's paper is very fair in reminding readers that this is not the case. There are exotic issues relating to cross-border imports and exports far beyond the scope of this little discussion, but even domestically there are difficult line-drawing exercises at every turn in defining the tax base. Should "necessities" like groceries be excluded from the VAT? Where would marshmallows fit in that—a taxable snack or a tax-exempt food? How about prepared Jell-O salad with mini-marshmallows inside? (This actually is not a far-fetched example, but rather is drawn from my experience decades ago with New York State's sales tax law.) More weightily, what about medical services? College tuition?

Gale and I both see a UBI program and the taxes to which it relates as a net fiscal instrument. I am trying to implement a broad reduction in poverty and near-poverty in the United States, and to finance that through a progressive income tax that, when combined with UBI benefits, results in incomes above the median bearing a net burden to raise the standards of living of those below the median. Gale was looking for new sources of tax revenues, and dedicated part of those new revenues to a UBI program to mitigate the burden of those new taxes on the lowest-income Americans. These are different objectives, but I think mine more neatly fits with this chapter's theme of the social mortgage.

CONCLUSION

When viewed through the lens of any recognized ethical framework, the United States countenances far too much poverty among its citizens. The idea that one among eight of us lives in poverty is shocking and inexcusable when contrasted with the wealth of our country.

Responding to this problem is a foundational ethical imperative: that is, it comes before the actual and metaphorical insurance programs that we require if we are fully to instantiate fair equality of opportunity. The two are symbiotic, of course; much of the most dismal data in public education, for example, can be traced to the struggle of children living in poverty to function at the same levels as their well-fed and nurtured classmates. But we cannot expect people to be fully functional economic and moral agents if they are constrained at every turn by the iron jaws of poverty. We cannot pretend that we are "fully cooperating members of a society of free and equal citizens," each living "a complete life," when one-eighth of us are so weighted down by the crushing burden of economic need and insecurity.

Actual and metaphorical insurance then sits on top of this base. Insurance furthers the goals of this community of free and equal citizens, by addressing the healthcare of all citizens, arranging for an adequate investment in the human capital of citizens, and so on, all to give real content to the dream of fair equality of opportunity.

It may well be that the UBI program I have outlined, which with one stroke removes poverty and mitigates much middle-class economic anxiety, is more than we collectively believe we can spend, but I believe that there nonetheless is power in seeing UBI as having important ethical benefits, because it eliminates the degrading processes and incompleteness of current income support programs. Many millions of the poor do not work because they cannot, or because they cannot find work in reasonable commuting distance from their homes. All the poor have equal ethical claims on our attention.

Jason the Surfer will fashion a life of indolent tanning, but at all times the focus must be on the 99 percent—or 99.9 percent—who will build on any UBI grants to further advance their economic interests in the marketplace. We can do so by tying a discussion of UBI to a reimagined income tax system, where the net effect of the two systems is understood to be the design goal.

PART IV

OPPORTUNITY RESTORED

CHAPTER 9

FROM INSURANCE THEORY TO POLITICAL REALITY

INTRODUCTION

To this point, I have attempted to convince you of two facts. First, our material lives are governed to a considerable extent by the turning of Fortune's Wheel as well as our own inner talents and ambitions. Nowhere is the role of brute luck more apparent and more easily isolated than in the case of healthcare and of existential bad luck—in particular, of being born into a family with small financial resources. Our modern economy demands that citizens receive substantial investment in their human capital, which in practice means education, but the United States is unique in relying so extensively on private resources (family money or the mortgaging of one's own future) to fund those investments.

Second, we know a great deal about how to manage the financial implications of bad brute luck through the instrument of insurance. Classic insurance does not look backward in time to undo an adverse fortuity that has already occurred—we cannot buy maritime insurance after the ship has sunk—but this is why I have insisted on treating insurance as a metaphor as well as a literal product.

Insurance is an extraordinarily powerful tool, both as an actual financial product and as a metaphorical device through which to refine our intuitions about luck and public policy. The basic point in either case is that the purpose of insurance is to pool together the *financial* implications of randomly distributed bad outcomes *that are external to who we are as persons*, and to indemnify those members of the pool who suffer those adverse fortuities through contributions made by all members of the pool. Again, everything here rests on my premise that in constructing policy we take people as they are. Our talents and ambitions are our own, and so are the rewards from exploiting them, subject only to whatever obligations we have chosen to impose on ourselves to contribute to the collective risk pool.

The essence of insurance is mutuality: all members of a group agree to contribute to a pool (through premiums, in the case of ordinary insurance), from which the claims of unfortunate members are paid out. By mitigating the financial implications to an individual of a catastrophic random event, insurance enhances the welfare of all members of the group. This theme of mutuality is also the essence of our government—"the things we decide to do together."

I have emphasized that insurance has some important features and stress points that make it different from other kinds of financial instruments. Insurance deals with indemnification against financial loss arising from an adverse fortuity, not other forms of harm or opportunity for gain. Its efficacy depends on shifting risk from the shoulders of the insured, the pooling of that risk with other risks comparable in kind but not in timing, and the management of that risk through the law of large numbers, whereby each member of the pool of insureds accepts an obligation to contribute small but certain amounts (the premium) in return for indemnification against the consequences of the specified adverse fortuity. The insurance company in substance is the pool of insureds, acting collectively. Insurance is subject to two specific vulnerabilities: adverse selection and moral hazard. Adverse selection is the risk that those who want insurance, for reasons known to them but not the insurer, will always be the first to sign up for it. Moral hazard encompasses changes in behavior that follow from knowing that one has insurance, and that aggravate the underlying prospects of loss.

Throughout, I have tried to triangulate our thoughts about luck and insurance from several vantage points. I have shown how ordinary economic models have difficulty explaining the distribution of income and wealth without including brute luck as a factor. I have introduced social psychology's insights into the Belief in a Just World to explain why the straightforward proposition that luck is an unavoidable explanatory variable in examining the distribution of material outcomes meets such strenuous resistance. I have reminded readers of the enormity of the inequality of incomes and wealth in the United States today. I explored at length the literature on childcare and education to show the enormous gap in achievement attributable simply to differences in the cash invested in the human capital of rich kids and poor kids. This systematic underfunding of capital investments in less privileged kids is particularly problematic in the United States, because we rely so heavily on private resources or a student's mortgaging her future to fund education. The result is unfair to each individual whose investment is thereby constrained, and bad as well for the country, because we do not develop the full potential of the economy's most important factor of production—ourselves, in the form of our labor contributions. Finally, I have looked to modern moral philosophy for non-economic reasons why we as a polity should collectively wish to mitigate the consequences of existential bad luck in particular, and to the elegant concept of the social mortgage to justify a broader commitment to doing right by our fellow citizens.

At this point, I must leave behind the safety of abstract propositions and earnest feelings to reduce my propositions to some set of actual policy responses. The remainder of this chapter attempts to do so. I think, though, that I have already laid the groundwork for some straightforward propositions:

1. Insurance is a framework to refine our intuitions as to when government should fairly be asked to respond to adverse fortuities—to bad luck regarding *impersonal resources*.

2. Government intervention is appropriate only in those cases where private insurance markets fail—which in fact happens all the time, once one appreciates the pervasive handprint of existential adverse fortuities and similar instances of brute luck on our lives.

3. Government interventions aimed at remediating inequality or bad luck generally should fall within an intuitive application of the principles of insurance. That is, the interventions should address cases where (i) the adverse financial consequences of identifiable instances of bad brute luck are large, (ii) those instances constitute fortuities whose future impacts are random as to an individual but predictable as to the group, (iii) the failure to address those adverse fortuities undercuts values that we as a society espouse (in particular, fair equality of opportunity), and (iv) the adverse consequences of these fortuities can be addressed through the application of reasonable amounts of money. We do not indemnify the short against the prospect of earning less than the tall, or luthiers against the prospect of a declining interest in classical music, but we do care about disparate investments in human capital through the bad luck of choosing the wrong parents.

4. We have no interest in directly addressing constitutive luck and other such abstractions. We accept people's inner gifts as the core of their personhood, and we respect the integrity and inviolability of the individual. As discussed in the section "Progressive Taxation and Progressive Fiscal Systems" later in this chapter, progressive tax structures indirectly reach constitutive good fortune through imposing somewhat higher effective tax rates on higher incomes.

5. We enthusiastically embrace the adventure that is life. That is, as a country we have no interest in over-insuring ourselves.

6. We have a particular interest in fair equality of opportunity, and therefore are especially motivated to "insure" against the misfortune of being born poor with regard to the investment made in our human capital. The same can be said of other existential fortuities and of healthcare. This is the mechanism by which insurance as metaphor gives us traction to move from empathy to policy.

7. We use the tax system to fund our collective insurance plans. We rely on the progressive rate structure of our income tax as an *ex post* premium paid by the lucky to fund claims made by the unlucky relating to existential bad luck. (The following two sections of this chapter develop this principle in more detail.) The income tax looks to income actually earned, not "endowments," but that is a fair trade-off against our respect for the inviolability of the individual and her right to choose not to maximize her market income.

8. Because insurance here serves as a metaphor as well as an actual program, we can take metaphorical license and recognize that insurance payouts can take the form of investments as well as direct transfers. The ultimate goal is to respond to the adverse fortuity that poor families by definition do not have the resources to match rich ones in their investments in the human capital of their children. High-quality childcare, public early childhood education, and high-quality nationally consistent public education from primary through tertiary levels are all responsive to bad existential luck, and all can be delivered in kind.

In developing my proposals, I have placed my analysis of healthcare in America in the following chapter. I have done so, not because it is unimportant—to the contrary, and self-evidently, it is a vitally important topic—but rather to give that topic the separate discussion it deserves.

RETROSPECTIVE INSURANCE: MY ORIGINAL POSITION

My largest single concern is the long shadow of existential bad luck, and my central ambition is to reframe how we think about this by adopting the language and tools of insurance. But we have already been born, and so right off the bat I need to explain how I propose to translate insurance as a metaphorical inspiration, rather than as a literal commercial product, into policy terms. The progressive income tax is central to these aims. In this, my thought draws loosely on both Rawls and Dworkin.

Imagine that we start with John Rawls's thought experiment, except with this one difference. We have not yet been born, but all of us are enthusiastic—perhaps even a bit irrationally optimistic—about the adventure of life, notwithstanding our recognition that many of us might find life as it is lived to be limiting and disappointing. We so instruct our disembodied rational agents who otherwise know nothing about our futures. That is, if our agents came back to us with a proposal to trade away the potential economic upsides in life for no risk of downsides (a guaranteed equality of all incomes), we would refuse.

I believe that this enthusiasm for life—this mild case of irrational optimism—is closer to our national psyche than are the hyper-careful agents that Rawls imagined. By contrast, the rational agents in Rawls's experiment seem to me to understand their principals as lacking a robust appetite for the adventure of life. Rawls's disembodied beings over-insure.

We know that there are many circumstances into which we may be born, and many paths our futures might take regardless of those circumstances. While we might be characterized as irrationally optimistic, we have understandable anxiety about the worst possible outcomes.

Because we are rational, we wish to buy some insurance before we launch ourselves into life—but being disembodied, we have no money with which to do so. We also appreciate that a commitment to fair equality of opportunity requires public investment in human capital, so as to actualize the native endowments that we all possess.

The dilemma is resolved by enlisting the progressive income tax.[1]

The progressive income tax is the fundamental device by which we address prospectively differences in retrospective bad luck. Through this mechanism, we all agree to pay into the common pool disproportionately more of our winnings as those winnings grow larger, in order to support those who suffer the worst run of brute luck, particularly at birth. The progressive income tax thus complements the insurance metaphor, with premiums necessarily paid in arrears rather than up front, where the resources thus collected are applied to the common pool to fund legitimate claims made against the pool.

The next section expands on this last point.

PROGRESSIVE TAXATION AND PROGRESSIVE FISCAL SYSTEMS

What Is a Progressive Tax Anyway?

The progressive income tax fits hand in glove with a commitment to insurance in the metaphorical sense. A progressive income tax structure can be understood as representing a fair bargain that we or our agents would strike from behind the veil when we are about to embark on the adventure that is life, but wish to pick up some insurance against life's worst vicissitudes. It fuels our society's response to the systematic underfunding of human capital that follows from the existential adverse fortuity of being born into a family without substantial material resources.

Behind the veil, we agree to an *ex post* premium payment arrangement under which those who turn out to be blessed with talents and ambitions valued in the market pay disproportionately more, while those not so fortunate in these constitutive features pay somewhat less, all to fund payouts (in the form of education programs and so on) to those with claims against the system for the resources needed to fund the gap in the investment in their human capital. Since we cannot collect this insurance in advance of birth, we do so in arrears, under an arrangement whereby we agree to chip in disproportionately more if we emerge as very lucky.

Looking beyond my thought experiment, there is a straightforward economic case to be made for the progressive income tax, phrased in the old days as "equality of sacrifice," and in the modern literature as "the declining marginal utility of money." The idea in either phrasing is that $100 in the hands of a rich person is much less meaningful than it is in the hands of a poor one; in light of the lesser importance of more money to someone who already is rolling in it, an income tax where the effective tax rate increases with income fairly allocates the burden of funding our national bills. This in fact is the standard argument today in favor of the progressive income tax. I do not like relying too heavily on this rationale, because in my experience the wealthy do not follow the predicted response curve: they seem to cherish their last dollar as deeply as their first, and they feel that they alone understand and can protect those dollars from wasteful misuse by others.

The progressive income tax was the centerpiece of the progressive movement at the beginning of the twentieth century. When I began practice, the top federal income tax rate was 70 percent. It briefly fell to 28 percent at the beginning of the Reagan administration, and has more recently bounced around in the 30s; as of this writing it is 37 percent. Popular forms of income from investments (capital gains and dividends) are taxed at no more than a 20 percent rate, which is how the idle uber-wealthy can enjoy average tax rates comparable to middle-class wage earners.

When I describe a tax system as "progressive," that term has a technical meaning. It does not mean simply that if your income goes up you pay more tax. A flat 10 percent tax accomplishes that: if your income is $10,000, you pay $1,000 in tax, and if your income is $100,000, you pay $10,000 in tax. That is an example of a *proportional* tax (because your tax liability is in strict proportion to your income).

By contrast, in a *progressive* income tax, *average* (or if you prefer, *effective*) tax rates (total tax divided by total income) go up as income goes up. If a taxpayer with $10,000 in income pays $1,000 in tax (a 10 percent effective tax rate), while a taxpayer with $100,000 in income pays $20,000 in tax (a 20 percent effective tax rate), then you are looking at a progressive tax structure. This in fact is how our tax system works today, except that in recent decades we have drastically scaled back the bite of the tax on top incomes, so that the aggregate effect of all taxes put together today is much closer to a proportional tax (or possibly even a regressive one at the very top end, where average tax rates decline with incomes) than was true when I began practicing tax law forty-five years ago.[2]

One more tedious but important technical aside: no government in its right mind would design a progressive tax that operated with cliffs, whereby $1 of extra income would subject all of your income to a higher rate of tax. In that case, we would all refuse the extra $1! Instead, we rely on tax brackets, which you can visualize as slicing your total income into layers of a layer cake. The bottom income layers are always subject to tax at specified low rates, and only income in excess of the top of each bracket is taxed at a higher rate. All taxpayers thus enjoy the benefits of the lowest tax rate brackets, until each layer is filled and the taxpayer's income above that amount (and only that excess) spills into the adjacent higher bracket. For example, continuing with the example in the previous paragraph, the tax system might be specified as taxing the first $50,000 of income at a 10 percent rate, and income above that amount at a 30 percent rate. A taxpayer with $100,000 of income would pay $5,000 in tax in respect of her first $50,000 of income (10% × $50,000), and $15,000 on her *next* $50,000 of income (30% × $50,000), for a total of $20,000—an average tax rate of 20 percent. An additional $1 of income would be taxed at 30 percent (her *marginal* tax rate). If her income were $200,000, her tax bill would be $50,000, for an average tax rate of 25 percent.[3]

We all in fact pay many kinds of taxes—income tax, payroll tax, sales tax, excise tax (e.g., on gasoline), and so on. In addition, human beings in the end absorb the cost of the corporate income tax, although precisely which individuals do so is the economics profession's equivalent of Fermat's Last Theorem. At the federal level, income and payroll taxes are by far the most important individual taxes. These two have very different rate structures. Social Security payroll taxes in particular are *regressive* (the average rate goes down as income goes up, because those payroll taxes apply only to income up to a specified cap, set at $137,700 for 2020), while the income tax as applied to labor income is progressive (the average rate goes up as income goes up). What really matters in the end is the progressivity of the entire suite of taxes to which an individual is subject. Insofar as very top-end incomes are concerned, however, that analysis is dominated by the structure of the personal income tax (and the allocation of the corporate income tax to the individuals who bear it).

As always in any question relating to tax policy, we need to drill down at least one layer deeper. To an economist, income comes in two basic flavors: income from labor (salaries, wages, consulting fees, and the like), and income from capital—that is, investment income. Capital income includes capital gains, dividends, rents, interest, and the profits of a business after all the labor inputs have been properly compensated.

To a first approximation, we do a fairly good job of taxing labor income. All of the conceptual difficulties in designing a healthy income tax system really fall on the other side of the ledger—the taxation of capital income. Now, the hallmark of the rich is that they have a lot of money, which is to say, capital. If you believe that a progressive income tax is important, whether because it embodies the terms of social engagement reached through my Original Position thought experiment in the previous section or otherwise, then getting capital taxation correct is central to the enterprise.

Investments have value only because they throw off investment returns (capital income); people do not collect corporate bonds the way kids used to collect baseball cards. An investment's current value is simply a projection of the asset's future income flows, discounted to present value. One therefore can design a progressive capital tax system either by trying accurately to measure annual investment returns, or by taxing the sum of all projected future capital income flows—the asset itself. One really is a substitute for the other. For example, if a $100 bond pays 5 percent interest, the government can impose a 20 percent income tax on that interest, or it can impose a 1 percent "wealth tax" on the value of the bond, and either way it will collect $1.

The federal government today relies on capital income taxation, not a wealth tax. Our current tools for taxing capital income, however, are completely inadequate to the job. We have different rules and rates for different kinds of capital income, and most importantly we fail miserably at the one thing an income tax needs to get right, which is to measure income each year as that income is earned. The central villain here is known as the "realization principle," under which capital income is not taken into account until it is reduced to cash or the right to cash. An investor in a stock that never pays dividends does not record any income from that investment during the term of her ownership, even as its value steadily grows from the reinvestment of corporate earnings. And tax on any ultimate capital gains from the sale of that stock (at a maximum rate of 20 percent) effectively is completely forgiven simply through patience, by dying while still owning that appreciated asset.

In short, sensible capital taxation is central to the top-end progressivity of a tax system, but our current capital income tax tools systematically understate and undertax capital income. The problems seem so intractable that during the course of the 2020 presidential campaign the idea took hold to rip out the entire system by the roots and replace it with an annual "wealth tax" (a tax on the value of investments, rather than on their investment flows). This effectively is the underlying rationale for the various wealth tax proposals that have been made.

This book is not the place to resolve the debate between a wealth tax on investments and an income tax on the income flows from those investments. I think it fair to suggest, however, that wealth tax proponents have systematically overstated their case in one fundamental regard, which is that a straightforward reading of the Constitution effectively prohibits federal wealth taxes. (Before you jump up to yell, the estate tax is not a tax on the value of an estate, but rather is an excise tax on the *transmission* of that wealth from one generation to the next. Tax lawyers enjoy these sorts of distinctions.) Proponents of course disagree, but their best argument in effect boils down to a claim that such a Constitutional prohibition would be stupid. The short answer to that is that a Constitution can be dimwitted on economic matters if that is what its drafters chose to provide. In addition, valuing non-market-traded investments is notoriously difficult.

There is an intermediate path that is plainly Constitutional, avoids insuperable valuation issues, accurately measures capital income, and operates in a progressive manner. I should know, because I spent a decade developing and refining it. I call it the Dual Business Enterprise Income Tax (the Dual BEIT). I have published two longwinded articles explaining the theory of the Dual BEIT and its detailed specifications, and I certainly do not propose to try your patience by summarizing those 170 pages here.[4] The key thoughts for the moment are simply these. First, at the level of an individual investor the system relies on an "imputed income" measure; investors are deemed to earn a certain return on their investments, regardless of the cash they receive, and differences between the imputed amounts and actual returns are reconciled at the end of the day when an investment is sold.

Second, even a flat-rate capital income tax (say, a flat 25 percent rate), *measured consistently and applied annually*, operates in practice as a progressive tax. There are technical economic efficiency arguments in favor of a flat-rate capital income tax rather than one that tracks the progressive structure of our basic labor income tax; my point here is that, even with this constraint, such a tax is progressive in its effect when compared to current law, because its effective tax rate rises the longer a capital investment is held. The ability to defer consumption (that is, to hold capital) for long periods is a luxury afforded only to the most affluent, and a flat-rate capital income tax thus operates in practice as a highly progressive tax instrument over the relevant margin of time.

In other words, a flat-rate capital income tax is progressive in its distributional implications along the relevant margin, which is time. Many economists describe this as a fatal defect in capital income taxation. By contrast, I see the increasing "tax wedge" (that is, an increasing effective tax rate) as a feature, not a bug.

For example, imagine that an investment yields 5 percent per annum pretax and is subject to tax at a 40 percent tax rate, so that it yields 3 percent after tax. In the first year, the effective tax rate is 40 percent. After five years, the effective tax rate over the life of the investment rises to 48 percent. And after thirty years, the tax wedge rises to 61 percent. After one hundred years, the nominal 40 percent tax wedge reaches 87 percent of the aggregate pretax return. If one thinks in more geological time frames, the effective tax rate rises asymptotically toward 100 percent. The reason is simply the difference over time in compounding at different rates—5 percent in the pretax case and 3 percent in the after-tax case; the former exponentially outstrips the latter over time. The key to a functional progressive income tax is to measure capital income reasonably accurately and to tax that income annually.

Again, progressivity can be achieved through different tax instruments operating in parallel. A flat-rate capital income tax by itself may seem insufficiently progressive to some observers, but we have another straightforward tax instrument on which we can rely, which is a functioning estate and gift tax. The estate tax has been held to be Constitutional, for the reason noted earlier, and by definition it reaches accumulations of wealth. The estate tax today is a porous scheme so riddled with loopholes as to make its occasional victims seem like chumps. Revitalizing the estate tax is tax engineering, not tax rocket science. The sum of a flat-rate "imputed income" capital income tax along the lines I have developed, plus a robust estate and gift tax, equals a very progressive overall capital tax system, without any of the Constitutional *sturm und drang* associated with an annual wealth tax.

Progressive Taxation and Progressive Fiscal Systems

I have written extensively about the use and misuse of the progressive income tax in accomplishing progressive aims in *We Are Better Than This*, but here is the short course. The country's obsession with taxation obscures the real question, which is the progressivity of the entirety of the *fiscal system*—that is, spending as well as taxing. Government spending has distributional consequences just as taxation does. There are thus two levers of progressivity—tax structure design and spending policies—not just one. Government spending on social issues in general is highly progressive in application; in practice, it outweighs tax system design in changing overall inequality in a society. Because in practice the spending side dominates, mildly regressive taxes can fund progressive net fiscal systems (the net of spending and taxing)—if revenues are large enough.

The secret sauce of the Nordic countries, for example, is not sky-high marginal income tax rates, but rather collecting a lot of tax through all sorts of mechanisms (including a regressive national sales tax, the value added tax) and spending that money in ways that redound to the benefit of society as a whole, including in particular through investment in human capital and healthcare.

Figure 9.1 shows how much of an outlier the United States is when it comes to disposable income inequality, when compared to our peer developed economies.

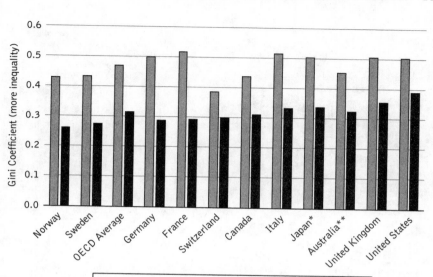

FIGURE 9.1 Market vs. Disposable Income Inequality, Selected Developed Economies (2017)

Source: OECD (2020), "Income distribution," OECD Social and Welfare Statistics, http://.doi.org/10.1787/data-00654- en.

Figure 9.2 reminds you why—we just do not raise enough by way of taxes to fund the inequality-moderating programs that other countries do.

Figure 9.1 illustrates, for example, that Germany and the United States in 2017 had roughly the same market income inequalities, as measured by the Gini index (see Chapter 3), but Germany was a much more equal society after considering the effects of taxation and social spending (higher Gini indexes mean higher inequality). At the same time, the German tax system had a modestly *less* progressive rate structure than the US system. How can both statements be true?

The explanation is simple: where the US aggregate tax burden (federal, state, and local) at that time was 24.3 percent of our GDP, the German aggregate tax take was 38.2 percent. (The 2018 average among OECD countries was 34 percent.) The larger tax take was not placed in a pile and set on fire, as myopic focusing on tax system design alone implies, but rather was invested in the German people, in the form of some of the human capital investment and healthcare programs already identified. The two themes developed in this section so far are easily confused, but in fact they nestle neatly alongside each other. First, I argued that a tax system that, taken in its entirety, is progressive in its rate structure

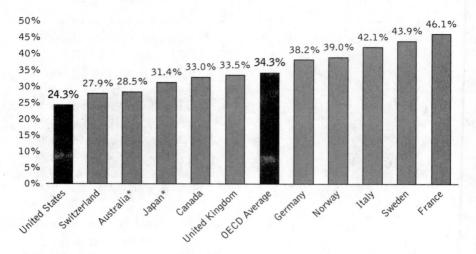

FIGURE 9.2 Tax Revenue as a Percentage of GDP, Selected Developed Economies (2018)

Source: OECD, *Revenue Statistics 2019* (Paris: OECD Publishing, 2019), Table 1.4.

is a fair bargain that we or our agents would strike from behind the veil in return for the implicit insurance of government funding against adverse existential annuities, and I further have articulated how a progressive capital tax system could be implemented. Second, I have just described how there are two levers of progressivity, not one: the distributional consequences of tax system design (who pays how much relative to her income or wealth), and the distributional consequences of sensible government spending policies. In practical terms those spending policies often pack more of a progressive punch than does a progressive tax rate structure.

My comparison of the United States and Germany is one example of the two levers of progressivity in action, but the point applies more generally. Many major developed economies have market inequalities roughly similar to the US experience, but *all* have less inequality in respect of disposable income (after-tax/after-transfers), because all have bigger tax bases and apply those extra revenues to useful social spending. What is more, those larger tax collections are less progressive in overall effect than that of the United States, because of the importance in other countries of a large value added tax (national sales tax). (The French basic VAT rate, for example, is 20 percent.) All sales taxes and VATs are regressive, because they apply to consumption, and the most affluent individuals spend a much lower proportion of their total incomes.

New progressive spending programs cost money, which basically means new taxes. (Yes, there is a school of thought that deficits no longer matter, but I am playing the role of a monetary policy fuddy-duddy here.) There is a systematic misunderstanding among progressive voters that these new taxes must be borne only by the most affluent if we are to honor progressive values, but the existence of two levers of productivity—spending as well as taxing—vitiates this belief.

First, not every dollar for new educational or childcare programs, for example, must be traceable to new taxes on the affluent. Money is fungible after all, and the *ex post* premium construction is a metaphor, not a straitjacket. What it does mean is that moral and economic reasoning alike demand that our tax system should be more progressive than it is today, *and* that we raise a lot more tax revenue than we do today. I for one have not pledged that middle-class taxes will not rise. The tide of taxation may lift all the boats, so that the middle class pays more taxes in the future than it does today, but whatever the aggregate tax take we settle on, those revenues should be collected through a system that is more progressive than is current law. Progressivity means that if the middle class pays more, the very most affluent will pay considerably more, not that the tax take on the middle class will be frozen at today's levels in perpetuity.

Second, once again it must be emphasized that spending programs themselves are very progressive in their implications, so that even a flat sales tax or the like that is used to fund a new government program like free early childhood education works out to be progressive in its net effect. That is what my reference to the "two levers of progressivity" is intended to remind us. It may be that one can isolate the case of some middle-income taxpayer whose new taxes are perfectly offset by new benefits, but that will not be the ordinary case. Those with above-average incomes, not just the absolute top end of the distribution, will contribute more to the system than they take out, while lower-income Americans will on balance be much better off, even if their tax rates increase somewhat.

There may be a case for very high marginal income tax rates to address other social issues, like the concentration of power among the wealthiest, but when it comes to maximizing the welfare of most Americans, what we need are adequate revenues from all sensible sources combined, imposed at reasonably progressive rates, without excessive reliance on very high top tax rates alone to fill the bucket.

Fiscal Headroom

The United States is a very low-taxed country populated by a citizenry committed to energetic tax whining. As Figure 9.2 illustrates, the United States collects about 10 percentage points of GDP less in taxes at all levels combined (federal, state, and local) (roughly $2.2 trillion in respect of 2020 GDP) than the OECD average. Canada and the United Kingdom, for example, each raise 9 percentage points more of their GDP in taxes. What is more, tax collections in the United States dropped by about 2.5 percent of GDP from 2017 to 2018 as a result of the Tax Cuts and Jobs

Act of 2017 (TCJA)—the largest decline of any OECD country, and starting to boot from the fifth-lowest collection of any OECD country in 2017.[5]

It is almost impossible to overstate how starved we are for tax revenues, especially against our background as spending by far the largest percentage of GDP of any large OECD country on military expenditures. Some people no doubt hate the federal government, but one persuasive reason why they might is that there are close to zero revenues available for any kind of public spending or investment programs that are visible in people's lives.

Our projected GDP for the government's Fiscal Year ending September 30, 2021, is about $23 trillion. Not even I in my wildest hallucinatory dreams would imagine that our tax revenues would rise to the average OECD level, throwing off $2.3 trillion ($2,300 billion) of new headroom for government spending programs in that year alone. But consider the possibility that we allow federal tax rates to increase by 4 percentage points of GDP—the 2.5 percentage points of GDP that were largely thrown away in the 2017 tax act, and another 1.5 percentage points for every crazy idea of mine, save the Universal Basic Income. *Our tax revenues would jump by $920 billion in that one year alone.*

Let me try to situate things further. Our projected GDP for the decade 2021–2030 is $273 trillion. Our current bare-bones projected federal tax revenues for the period are $48 trillion. Assuming that various temporary provisions are extended, the 2017 TCJA act alone is projected to reduce revenues by about $2 trillion over that period (including additional interest costs). The Congressional Budget Office estimates that the Pentagon will spend about $280 billion for the F-35a fighter plane and the Penetrating Counter air (PCa) air-superiority aircraft over the next thirty years. For that matter, our projected discretionary defense spending for the upcoming decade is greater than $8 trillion. So do not let a hundred billion dollars here or there derail you from doing what's right—particularly when it is remembered that education spending in particular in fact is human capital investment, with positive economic returns for years to come.

In short, it is simply not possible to bump into any plausible revenue ceiling in implementing the kinds of policies that I recommend—and again, that is before considering the positive returns to those programs, as in the case of education (Chapter 5). We look out on nothing but opportunity as far as the eye can see to improve the welfare of Americans and to kick economic growth into a higher gear.

WHERE THE INSURANCE METAPHOR CANNOT REACH

Throughout the book, I use my pet term "existential adverse fortuities" to encompass the luck that is transmitted via when, where, and to whom we are born. Our existential luck comprises not just the financial circumstances into which we are born, but also our constitutive luck (the talents and ambitions that are part of our sense of ourselves), the location of our birth, and the time of our birth. These last considerations do not map well, however, onto practical policy instruments. Some of the reasons have already been covered, but this section briefly reviews my reasoning.

Constitutive Luck

I have argued throughout that we have neither the ability nor the inclination to separate ourselves from our native talents in fashioning any real-life policies. We take people as they are, fully recognizing that some will have talents that are valued in the marketplace far more highly than are our own. We are absolutely okay with that. Constitutive good fortune in a knack for hitting the curveball is to be celebrated, not punished. We reach constitutive good fortune along these lines indirectly through the progressive income tax, whereby those who are able to convert their native talents into large incomes contribute to the collective pot at average rates higher than those of us with middling talents and incomes to match. Beyond that, we do not purport to tax talent as such.

But there is a more difficult side to matters of constitutive luck when it comes to recognizing that ours is a society with deep undercurrents of unexamined racism (and sexism as well). I reject absolutely as offensive to human dignity any suggestion that being born Black, for example, is a form of bad luck. The fault lies with our society, not with the color of a newborn's skin. These are problems as to which I can offer no solutions better than to urge that they be tackled head-on through vigorous anti-discrimination and similar policies, which when measured against the magnitude of the issues is pretty weak tea. As I discussed in Chapter 7, I understand the case for reparations, but I think that the theory of reparations must be grounded in tort, not insurance, principles. As such, it falls outside the scope of what this book has set out to cover.

Geography as a Separate Desideratum

One extraordinary conclusion reached by Raj Chetty and his colleagues in the work summarized in Chapters 3 and 4 is the large role played by geography in shaping a person's income mobility. Some localities are spawning grounds for great economic prospects, while others seem to operate more like opportunity deserts. Chetty's work has not yet been distilled into one or a handful of action items, and in the absence of such all that we can do is to improve the channels by which human capital investments get made—that is, better schools—and to help with career guidance and the like. We are not going to rip youngsters from their parents' arms to ship them to high-opportunity zones, nor will we compensate young people with cash stipends for having been born in a less favorable location.

Here I think that we must remember that we are all citizens of one country, and national policies generally work best when applied consistently across geographic lines. My focus on the financial circumstances of our births aims to remedy shortfalls in quantifiable resources available to a newborn; more intangible resources seem much less tractable to straightforward policy interventions. This is consistent with intuitions about equality of opportunity as a starting gate theory that seeks rough justice and that cannot be seen as preferring one region over another. As the Chetty research yields more refined understanding of what separates the most fecund mobility spawning grounds from the rest, policies can adapt to address those factors explicitly.

The Timing of Our Births

When we are born has a great deal to do with the economic headwinds or tailwinds that we will face. Students who graduated law schools in 2007 will have significantly higher lifetime earnings than those who graduated in 2012.[6] More distressingly, in a 2020 paper, researchers found evidence that entering the work force in the depths of a recession influences not just future earnings, but mortality in middle age.[7] The researchers summarized their startling conclusions as follows:

> Cohorts coming of age during the deep recession of the early 1980s suffer increases in mortality that appear in their late 30s and further strengthen through age 50. We show these mortality impacts are driven by disease-related causes such as heart disease, lung cancer, and liver disease, as well as drug overdoses. At the same time, unlucky middle-aged labor market entrants earn less and work more while receiving less welfare support. They are also less likely to be married, more likely to be divorced, and experience higher rates of childlessness. Our findings demonstrate that temporary disadvantages in the labor market during young adulthood can have substantial impacts on lifetime outcomes, can affect life and death in middle age, and go beyond the transitory initial career effects typically studied.

It will be interesting to see whether these results are replicated in subsequent work.

To take a less consequential example, future NHL hockey players are more likely to be born in January than in November, because in childhood they are the largest and best-developed kids in their pee-wee hockey leagues, and thereby soak up the most attention from coaches.[8]

It is difficult to imagine, however, how one would design policy instruments that would be technically feasible or acceptable as a political economy matter to deal with cases like these (beyond the structure of the progressive income tax itself, which offers lower-income Americans the small consolation of lower effective tax rates).[9] These are instances of unfairness, but not existential adverse fortuities to which insurance concepts can usefully be applied.

This point can be extended to much larger differences in the timing of our births. We cannot very effectively compare the lives we are living to those we might live had only we been born in the future, but we can project backward. I do not refer here to those who enjoy visualizing their past lives in Old Kingdom Egypt (in which they always were pharaohs, and never slaves), but rather the opportunity sets available, say, to baby boomers rather than millennials. This is the comparison made in a recent book by Joseph Sternberg, who argues in *The Theft of a Decade: How Baby Boomers Stole the Millennials' Economic Future* that the Great Recession was particularly devastating to millennials, and that our public policies continue to favor the elderly over younger working people at almost every turn.

It is true that the United States directs a disproportionate amount of its federal social spending on the elderly, primarily in the form of Social Security and Medicare, but neither of those programs is overendowed relative to world norms (especially once the bloated cost structure of all medical care in the United States is considered).[10] Instead, I see our distorted social spending choices as consistent with the thought that the United States simply devotes insufficient resources to social spending in the aggregate: the old aren't getting too much, but the young are not getting enough.[11] Without meaning to be too much of a Dutch uncle, this is a political problem that might be resolved differently were millennials to show up at the election polls in the same proportions as the elderly do.

As it happens, the Social Security system was overhauled in 1983 with a view to addressing the problem of the demographic pig in the snake that is the baby boomer generation. The "full retirement age" was raised over a long transition period from sixty-five to sixty-six for most baby boomers, and then to sixty-seven for people born after 1959. This is a significant curtailment in benefits relative to the pre-1983 law, because the first years are the most actuarially valuable, and because the extension of the full retirement age reduced the value of Social Security benefits for those individuals (actually, the majority of Americans) who opt to take their benefits early. To the same effect, up to 85 percent of benefits paid to affluent individuals are now taxable, which is just a backdoor way of reducing benefits to those individuals.

The cost of Medicare also has recently increased for affluent elderly individuals, which again is a benefit cut by another name. Medicare Part A covers in-hospital costs; Part B covers out-of-hospital medical costs, like doctors' visits; and Part D covers prescription drugs. Part A is automatic; individuals must choose to purchase Parts B and D. Contrary to the understanding of many, Medicare is heavily subsidized from general tax revenues; that is, Medicare taxes during one's working years do not cover the actuarial value of the Medicare benefits one receives when one enters the system. In response, Congress amended the law in 2007 to impose an "Income-Related Monthly Adjustment Amount" (an additional premium) for Medicare Parts B and D when purchased by an affluent household. For example, in 2019 the basic Medicare Part B premium was $1,626/year. For a single tax-payer with an income of more than $500,000, however, the annual premium is $5,526—almost 400 percent of the base premium. (I've always wondered how much the Medicare system is burdened by the medical interventions necessary to respond to the shock this news induces in most affluent elderly individuals, who typically have no idea of the existence of IRMAA until they are hit with a bill.) The point is not to encourage tears for those lucky elderly individuals who enjoy high incomes, but to remind younger readers that Social Security and Medicare have not been entirely static in their terms over the last several decades.

More directly, Social Security has had this structure of the young paying for the old almost from the beginning, because by design it has never operated as a government-run annuity system, in which what you get is determined by what you contribute. This was decided near the outset of the program in the 1930s, when elderly Americans were made eligible for Social Security benefits in the new system without having contributed into it.[12]

"Entitlement reform" is a political agenda that is not required as a matter of budget arithmetic. If we were to remove the cap on wages to which Social Security taxes apply ($137,700/year in 2020), so that the highest wage earners would pay the same proportion of their wage incomes as do restaurant dish washers, the Social Security system would be solvent for decades to come. These higher taxes would fall on the shoulders of the highest paid of the working generation, not current retirees.

From the other direction, it is completely impossible to imagine the lives that today's millennials will enjoy once we baby boomers shuffle off this mortal coil. How do we factor into cross-generational standard of living complaints the rapid progress in dealing with cancer in particular, or being freed from the drudgery of driving one's own car through the growth of autonomous vehicles, and so on?

The best-known academic work on the dilemma of the timing of one's birth has been the development of "generational accounting" by Lawrence Kotlikoff, along with Alan Auerbach and Jagadeesh Gokhale.[13] In a nutshell, the idea is to measure the gap between what government has promised an adult in the current generation, versus her anticipated tax obligations, in each case over her lifetime. That gap effectively becomes an obligation that the current generation pushes onto the shoulders of its children. A great deal of technical work and many assumptions are required to implement national generational accounts, and the effort rightly has served as focal point for academic debates on how to think about the long-term distributional impact of current government policies.

The underlying normative claim of generational accounting is that each generation really should take care of itself, rather than leaving a mess for the subsequent generation to clean up; in the language of generational accounting, each generation should face roughly the same net tax rate (for any age cohort, the discounted present value of an average person's projected future taxes, reduced by future Social Security, Medicare, and other social spending benefits). Needless to say, baby boomers come off as getting away with murder on this metric. I am a card-carrying member of that group, and therefore may not be in the best position to give a fair treatment of generational accounting, but I nonetheless think it fair to point out some of the standard criticisms of generational accounting.[14]

Generational accounting makes assumptions that are plainly unrealistic: for example, that the current tax system will apply forever to those alive at any moment (so that tax changes affect only the unborn). But tax policy, like spending policy, is dynamic, and responds from year to year to many pressures. Tax rates soared in World War II, because they had to; generational accounting does not take this sort of dynamic process into account. Generational accounting also thinks about taxes as if they all were imposed on a person's lifetime labor income. The idea here is what's known as the life cycle model of savings (investments)—people save during their working years to spend on retirement. But as Chapter 3 shows, this is not true; as much as one-half of capital in our system today was inherited rather than earned by the owner's labor. This is far greater than can be explained by the accidental bequest hypothesis (i.e., that people die earlier than they anticipated, while they still have some money left in the bank).

The critics of generational accounting might be accused of taking the analysis literally when it should simply be taken seriously. Generational accounting does not guarantee any particular dire outcome so much as it points out who, and from which generation, will bear the net burdens of government *if* current policies were to continue unabated (and given important assumptions). It therefore can be seen as providing useful information, not about what will be, but rather what should change (higher current taxes, for example) if the normative goal of constant net tax rates across generations is persuasive and its key assumptions accepted.

The larger lesson for this book is that, while the accident of when we are born can have a significant impact on our material outcomes, this is one existential adverse fortuity where remedies are difficult to imagine. The simple point here is that the insurance metaphor—and government more generally—can respond most effectively when the obstacle to equal opportunity is an absence of money *at some starting gate*, because the application of money can solve that without devolving into simple egalitarian redistribution. This is not a frivolous observation, but rather an instance of how thinking clearly in insurance terms helps us to recognize what government can and cannot do.

The timing of our birth is particularly intractable to government intervention, however conceived. Government will not change the age cutoffs of pee-wee hockey leagues. And while government did provide some cushion to the immediate financial calamities visited by the Great Recession, law students who graduated in 2011 should not expect to find a little something extra in their paychecks every month, courtesy of the government, to compensate them for the entirety of their professional lives for having a more difficult time of it than students graduating in 2007, or 2018—not because the effect of the timing of their graduation cannot be expressed in financial terms, but because it strikes most of us that there are just too many variables in life to consider compensating these individuals for a lifetime for this one piece of bad luck.

By the same token, we do not generally conceive of conscious career choices that prove less fruitful than we had hoped as occasions for government intervention. A few decades ago, top-drawer machinists earned large salaries reflecting their long apprenticeships and formidable skills. Computer-controlled machining eroded much of the value of that particular store of human capital. There may be a persuasive case here for government-sponsored retraining programs, for example, but the reason would be to improve our national income through a positive return on these new human capital investments. This is not really founded on an equality of opportunity claim, and the insurance metaphor is unhelpful.

We cannot afford collectively to overinsure ourselves through the intermediation of government against all forms of perceived unfairness, any more than a business can insure against every possible commercial risk. The longer the time horizon, the more impossible it becomes to imagine what the payoff should be for claims based on shouldering unfair burdens left behind by one's parents. One generation alone was called on to bear witness to the Great Depression and to serve in World War II; most of us alive today have not been required to shoulder a share of collective burdens anywhere near as momentous. As in the case of generational accounting, the assumptions that must be made to extract the consequences of mis-timing one's graduation from law school by a few years from the 10,000 other unique aspects of the times in which we are enmeshed makes the exercise seem misguided (our information is just too imperfect) and the remedy too uncertain, in light of the values that would also have to be placed on all those 10,000 other factors that define the total environment of each generation (to net all against each other).

My focus on equality of opportunity and on the instrument of insurance to instantiate that credo gains most of its traction when limited in reach to exigent cases of unfairness that are plausibly viewed as wholly outside the choices (the agency) of the individual, and that have financial consequences that can reliably be measured. The art is to figure out which instances of apparent unfairness fall within this description. I submit that intergenerational grievances plainly do not satisfy this test. It is meaningless for policymakers to purport to weigh all the pluses and minuses of half-lived lives today, when compared with the total environment faced by a prior generation.

INSURANCE AS METAPHOR: EDUCATION, EDUCATION, EDUCATION

As in the case of healthcare, the 2020 Democratic Party competition for the presidential nomination yielded a rich crop of smart policy proposals aimed directly at the problems that motivate most of this book. I will tick off a few of these, but the most important point to recognize is that they all are extraordinarily cheap in the great scheme of things.

Senator Sanders's presidential campaign proposed an extremely ambitious early childhood education and childcare program. It would comprise free full-day, full-week childcare from infancy through age three, regardless of income. Childcare would be available at least ten hours a day. Children would have access to full-day, full-week pre-kindergarten education, regardless of income, starting at age three (that is, what Chapter 5 introduced as Universal 3–K). The proposal contained numerous other ancillary programs as well. The estimated cost was about $150 billion/year, or $1.5 trillion over the next decade. This could largely be financed simply by reversing most of the tax cuts embedded in the 2017 tax act, even before taking into account that these expenditures can be expected to yield large positive economic returns.

Along the same lines, recall from Chapter 5 that when Moody's analyzed a slightly less ambitious early childhood childcare and education proposal made by Senator Warren in 2019, Moody's concluded that the "static" cost to the federal government would be about $1.1 trillion over a decade, but that the "dynamic" cost (i.e., taking into account the larger impact of the proposal on the economy) would reduce the government's cost to about $700 billion. (The aggregate gross cost estimate was in the same ballpark as that of the National Academies of Sciences proposal also described in Chapter 5.) At the same time, GDP also would grow under the Warren proposal by about $700 billion, so that when the dust settled, the Warren proposal would essentially pay for itself—*even before taking into account the increased incomes that children enjoying these programs could be expected to earn.*

Financing a college education is a fraught issue. Candidates to the 2020 presidential nomination proposed large free college programs, along with the forgiveness of all existing student loans. It has been very disheartening to me to read the complaints of many Americans that *they* paid off *their* student loans, so why should today's graduates "get off" scot free? One simple answer is that the cost of college has compounded at rates far higher than the rate of inflation, while job prospects have not kept up, particularly for low-ranked schools. But here I would like to propose a new solution that should make everyone reasonably happy, while keeping costs reasonably low.

Basically, the United States should adopt a college-financing system inspired by the UK model. This would mean the following:

1. The federal government would lend students at accredited four-year not-for-profit colleges sums equal to a reasonable tuition charge *plus* a reasonable amount to cover room and board. The government must put a hard cap on its annual tuition loan commitment, because if it does not, tuition charges will mysteriously and steadily keep rising at rates far greater than inflation. That cap should be set at an amount equal to the average tuition charged by the five most expensive public universities for in-state students as of the date of enactment, increasing over time at a standard inflator. The loans would be available regardless of whether students matriculate at public or private schools.

2. Interest would accrue at an annual rate equal to 1-year Treasury notes plus 3 percent.

3. Interest accrual would start on the earlier of graduation or six years following matriculation.

4. No payment of accrued interest or principal would be due in a year except to the extent that a former student's income (technically, Adjusted Gross Income, for tax wonks) exceeded (for example) $40,000 for that year.

5. Accrued interest and principal would be payable at a rate equal to 9 percent of income exceeding the $40,000 floor. (That is, interest accrues at Treasuries plus 3 percent; cash repayments of that accrued interest and principal are made only to the extent of 9 percent of an individual's gross income exceeding $40,000.) Both interest and principal payments would be fully deductible for tax purposes. Loan repayments would be just another line on an individual's federal income tax return.

6. Any remaining loan balance would be forgiven at age sixty-five or on death or permanent disability.

7. *By design*, about one-half of all student loans would never be repaid, because of a disappointing earnings history or premature death. (The $40,000 floor would be adjusted to bring the program into congruence with this actuarial intention.)

8. All existing student loan debtors would be offered the opportunity to roll their loans into this program.
9. The program would be extended to graduate or professional schools, with higher target tuition amounts, and with additional forgiveness features designed to encourage public service.

I believe that this proposal at one blow makes college affordable, assures students that they will not become enslaved to unmanageable debt that destroys their ability to lead productive and satisfying lives, and puts existing student loan borrowers on a far more sustainable path going forward, without incurring the opprobrium of those indignant citizens who feel aggrieved that forgiveness would amount to today's students getting a better deal than those citizens did, decades ago.

There is about $1.6 trillion in outstanding student loan debt today, mostly owed to the federal government. If one imagines that half of that ultimately is forgiven over the next thirty years or so, that would amount to the federal government forgiving $30 billion/year—a charge that is less than 1 percent of the current annual budget.

I would further suggest, in keeping with the proposals of others, that two-year degree-granting accredited community colleges ought to be 100 percent subsidized by the federal government.

A great many other worthwhile programs have been proposed, to which my attitude is, yes please. If an educational or childcare program is well designed, its adoption will honor our commitments to one another, instantiate a deeper commitment to while simultaneously throwing off positive financial returns over a young person's lifetime.

UNIVERSAL BASIC INCOME

In Chapter 8, I presented a proposal for an extensive Universal Basic Income program. Here I simply wish to remind readers that I actually was serious about it. Further, while nominal tax collections would go up significantly under the expanded income tax that I pair with UBI benefits, the net effect of the proposal is purely redistributive, which is to say that by design government will not obtain any new money to pay for other new programs. It is in this sense a self-contained, self-financing proposal. As developed in Chapter 8, my UBI suggestion may be a bit too rich for your blood, but the basic logic I think is sound. It is an idea that should not be rejected out of hand.

AN INCLUSIVE ECONOMY
Standard Economic Analyses

Standard economics literature and government budget presentations have hopelessly poisoned the prospects for reasoned discussion of the merits of a more muscular government that addresses existential adverse fortuities, healthcare, and other pressing needs like infrastructure. It is important to untangle these ingrained prejudices to make progress toward what the International Monetary Fund (IMF), the OECD, and some farsighted academics now call an economics of "inclusive growth."

In standard economics presentations, taxes range from bad to worse.[15] The natural, and incorrect, inference from this is that new government spending is bad, because there are significant and unavoidable social costs to the taxation necessary to fund those programs.

Why does economics begin with this general prejudice against taxation? The reason, introduced briefly in Chapter 6, is that all general-purpose taxes distort behavior. To see this, you need to start (as economists are wont to do) with the view that private markets are complete and efficient: prices operate seamlessly to convey accurate information to producers and consumers alike, which information enables all market participants to maximize their own utility by allocating their money, time, or resources as they think best. What is more, most everything that can be imagined by way of purposive activity has a price, so that one does not need to look past private markets to supply the goods and services that people want. In this world, there is almost no friction between, for example, the price a supplier demands for a product, and the price the consumer pays for it. In addition, there is a very small role for government, because private markets left to themselves operate to allocate goods and services efficiently through the mechanism of efficient and complete markets, relying in turn on the signaling role of prices.

Taxation changes this happy story by creating a wedge between the price the consumer in this simple example pays and the price the supplier receives, where the wedge represents the money that now flows to the government. To be clear, economists do not care that money leaves your pocket and flows into the pocket of the US Treasury—if that were all that happened, overall economic activity would continue as before, with someone else ultimately enjoying the fruits the government spending financed out of your pocket. But there is something else going on.

Imagine that a new 10 percent sales tax is imposed on widgets, and that the ultimate economic burden of this tax falls squarely on the shoulders of widget buyers. A widget that formerly cost $100 now costs $110. If buyers and sellers continued as before, with buyers merrily assuming the extra $10 burden of the new tax, there is no distortion in behavior, and government simply collects its tax on every sale. But that is not what happens. By virtue of this $10 tax wedge between supplier and consumer, some consumers will decide that widgets are now too expensive, and consumers in the aggregate simply will not buy for $110 the same number of widgets that they formerly bought for $100. Sales that would have taken place in a world without taxation now do not occur. (Alternatively, widget sales are not affected, but the consumer adjusts other consumption to make up the $10 extra cost.) This distortion in behavior between pretax and after-tax worlds is the economic cost of taxation; as Chapter 6 introduced, economists call this "deadweight loss."

To emphasize again, deadweight loss is not the same as the tax revenue collected by the government; there is no loss in this sense from money simply moving from one pocket to another. Instead, deadweight loss is the measure of the deal that does not happen, or more generally the distortion in economic activity when taxation inserts its wedge between what suppliers receive and consumers pay. For example, perhaps consumers now buy gadgets instead of widgets. They still are spending money, but not in the way they would have preferred to do before government introduced its widget sales tax. That distortion in consumer behavior in this example (from the consumption choice they would have preferred to their second best choice) is the meaning of deadweight loss. In tribute to Sir Arthur Conan Doyle, I like to think of deadweight loss as the tax dog that did not bark.

To give one more example, a new tax on wages (more generally on labor income) might cause some workers, particularly those at the top, simply to get off the treadmill of working for a living and to head for the beach. You might think that the tax is thus a blessing in disguise, but an economist would disagree: the new beach bum always had the option to retire, but she chose not to, because she preferred working at her old after-tax salary to surfing. The new tax has now distorted the relative attractiveness of earning a lower after-tax salary, on the one hand, to surfing, on the other.

The classic economists' metaphor for deadweight loss, first proposed by Arthur Okun, is that taxation is like a leaky bucket: not everything that goes into the bucket reaches its destination. That is, the true cost to the consumer in this example, once one includes the consumer's welfare loss attendant on the distortion in her consumption decisions, is greater than the tax revenues obtained by the government.

While all general-purpose taxes incur deadweight loss, some are thought to be more distortionary than others. But for our purposes, the point is simply that there is a real social cost to taxation in the form of deadweight loss, and economists believe that they can estimate that cost with reasonable precision.

Whenever incremental new taxes are proposed, many economists swing into action to decry the deadweight loss that would attend the proposal's adoption. This is the inevitable start of the policy conversation. Unfortunately, it also usually is the end. And that in turn paints a completely misleading picture of the economic implications of new taxing and spending proposals.

Here is the metaphorical flaw in the tax-centric policy debates that dominate US fiscal policy: *even a leaky bucket can extinguish a fire.* That is, the deadweight loss of taxation may be completely outweighed by the social welfare benefits of how the tax revenues are spent. Most economic analyses do not consider this possibility, because as noted earlier they begin from the premise that private markets are both efficient and complete.

But this is patently false when applied to the central concern that motivates this book, which is to assure that *all* Americans have access to adequate investments in their human capital, so that they might flourish both in simple economic terms and in personal satisfactions. As Chapter 5 showed, government investment in the human capital of children pays real financial returns over a child's lifetime, which financial returns (at a minimum) must be considered in weighing the net impact of new taxing and spending programs.

Private markets have not, do not, and cannot fund investment in the human capital of those born into adverse existential circumstances, and as a result the financial and social payoffs to this paramount investment opportunity go begging. Private markets cannot work when investments cannot be secured and returns earmarked to the private provider. How would anyone expect, for example, that private markets will magically pony up the hundreds of billions of dollars necessary adequately to fund early childhood education and childcare, notwithstanding the evidence for the economic returns that accrue to a society smart enough to make these human capital investments?

As Chapter 5 made clear, even at the college level, the private market solution of more and more student loan debt—now totaling about $1.6 trillion—has been demonstrably catastrophic in its impact, burdening adults with disabling debt service demands that have distorted their abilities to choose careers, to buy homes, or to start families. The fastest-growing class of student loan debtors now are adults over the age of sixty, most of whom have borrowed money to help their children attend college. They face tragic decisions about how or when they will be able to retire while grappling with these student loans, as their debt compounds each year at 7 percent interest—often more than they can afford to repay. One older woman, age fifty-five, was recently quoted about her struggle. In 2007 (so, when she was forty-two), while she still was paying down her own student debt of $60,000, this woman took out a loan for her daughter to attend a public university. Now, thirteen years later, she owes $77,000. A reporter who interviewed the woman wrote that she "cannot foresee a future in which she is able to retire from her nursing job. 'I'm convinced I'm going to die before I resolve this,' she said. 'I can't sleep at night. My stomach is in knots.'"[16]

Now *that* is deadweight loss.

When government taxes the affluent to provide education, income security, or other programs for the less well-off, the economic analysis usually is phrased as a trade-off between efficiency and equity. "Efficiency" here refers to the deadweight loss associated with the taxes necessary to fund redistributive transfer payments. "Equity" is meant to encapsulate the positive value to society of the "leveling" effect of redistributive policies; we are supposed to value at least some move toward equality for its own sake. In the simplest case, we would tax from the rich and give to the poor until no inequality remained, but for the fact that the more we tax, the greater the efficiency cost of that taxation. In this telling, if we pursued our equity pipedreams to the very end, we all would live in an equal but very poor society.

When economists set up these efficiency versus equity models to analyze the consequences of more taxing and spending, or to design "optimal income tax" structures, they generally make one critical simplifying assumption, which is that government implements the spending side of the equation by making transfer payments to the poor—simple cash grants.[17] The models do not imagine that this cash would be deployed by recipients in any way that would permanently alter their personal economic trajectory (as by private investment in education). Instead, recipients are assumed simply to consume those transfer payments, so that there is nothing left to show for them in the succeeding period.

All of this is nonsense when applied to actual policy. We do not need to assign value to leveling, or equality as such to justify doing right by those whose future prospects are dimmed by bad birth luck. And we cannot, or should not, ignore the returns to smart government spending, in particular spending designed to ameliorate the bad birth luck of being born without sufficient family resources to fund adequate investment in one's human capital.

Our overall interest should be in instantiating authentic equality of opportunity. Funding the prerequisites to that, in particular education, is not an exercise in "leveling"; it is an exercise in building up our most important asset class— ourselves—so that *all* citizens can enjoy a reasonably equal chance to pursue the life that their talents and ambitions permit. And from the other direction, there is no single factor efficiency cost here; deadweight loss is only half the analysis, because it ignores the financial and social returns to all that new money flowing into our collective human capital.

Government alone must be the provider of investment in the human capital of those of us not born into affluence. The cozy story of efficient and complete private markets simply falls apart here. That does not mean that the deadweight loss of taxation simply disappears; it still must be taken into account. But it does mean that one cannot look only to the cost of taxation. Instead, we must also consider the returns from the spending that such taxation permits.

Budget Scorekeeping Model Failures

When it comes to policy debates or budget presentations, we do not take into account government's role as a complement to private markets, in particular in funding adequate investment in the human capital of its citizens. Most think tank analyses make no efforts to quantify the return from a proposed spending program along these lines. Moreover, our official budget scorekeeping methodologies also do not consider the issue.

For a great many reasons, when the government's official tax revenue scorekeeper, the Staff of the Joint Committee on Taxation (JCT), "scores" the estimated incremental increases or decreases in tax revenues that would follow from a legislative proposal, those scores basically ignore deadweight loss. For this reason, standard JCT Staff revenue estimates are described by critics as "static" estimates. In response, conservatives have lobbied for decades that, when proposed tax *cuts* are scored, those scores should be conducted using dynamic (or macroeconomic) models, on the theory that tax cuts will stimulate economic growth by reducing deadweight loss, which in turn will yield more tax revenues (albeit at the new lower tax rate). In this view, standard static revenue estimates unfairly prejudice the budget system against tax cuts. Current practice now is to provide such macroeconomic forecasts for all major proposed tax bills.

The JCT Staff also prepares tax distribution tables that are designed to show which income levels benefit or are harmed by legislative proposals. For example, will changing capital gains tax rates benefit only the most affluent Americans? The Congressional Budget Office engages in broader distributional analyses, by charting the growth in market incomes, tax burdens, and after-tax/after-transfer payments disposable income across the income spectrum. (I summarized this work in Chapter 3.)

What is important here is that neither the JCT Staff distributional tables associated with revenue legislation, nor the CBO's more general work on the distribution of household income, takes into account the distributional implications of budget deficits. Deficits in the end must be financed through more taxes or reduced spending. We have seen time and time again that conservative politicians will ignore deficit spending when their party holds the presidency, and then demand that social spending be slashed when their party does not. This relentless pressure to cut social spending has at its root the failure to distribute the burdens of the future taxation implied by the current deficit. If the models were more complete, the original impulse to cut current taxes would stand on much shakier political ground.

Estimating the consequences of government *spending* programs falls entirely to the Congressional Budget Office. Very little work has been done there (or by the think tank community more generally) on the dynamic economic benefits that flow from government money well spent, as in education. Similarly, when under-taking a "dynamic" tax modeling exercise to justify the alleged positive economic feedback loop from those cuts, neither the JCT Staff nor the CBO even considers as a negative the lost economic activity that would follow from cutting useful gov-ernment spending. The premise in these models is that moving resources from the public sector to the private sector is purely welfare-enhancing—which is to say, the models assume that government spending is no different from collecting tax revenues, piling the dollar bills on the front lawn of the White House, and setting the money on fire.

In fairness, the CBO has dipped its toe in the water here, for example by de-veloping macroeconomic estimates of immigration reform and the hypothetical repeal of the Affordable Care Act.[18] These efforts are a start, but consider only rel-atively simple factors, like the effect of legislation on the aggregate labor supply or the stock of financial capital investment. They have not tackled anything remotely as difficult and important as the macroeconomic implications of sustained invest-ment in early childhood education, or less crippling modes of financing college.

What is more, the CBO arbitrarily assumes in all its work that public infrastruc-ture investment is one-half as productive as is private investment.[19] I discussed this in *We Are Better Than This*, but the short answer is that the economic re-search that has been done in this area reveals that public infrastructure invest-ment can yield high financial returns, even before considering the social value of funding jobs with dignity and career prospects (which are wholly excluded from the CBO's thinking). This also ignores the fact that public investment often is the only viable form of investment, and further overstates the merits of public-private partnerships, which in practice usually incorporate the worst of each sector.

In sum, we have developed attitudes and models that are perfectly designed to cut off our own nose to spite our face. This is an enormously important issue that has received far too little attention. Our models and budget processes largely start from the premise that there are no positive returns to government spending. Moreover, in charting our national economic health, more sophisticated meas-ures of welfare (including social cohesion, environmental sustainability, and many other factors) are ignored in favor of a single highly imperfect metric like GDP.[20]

Inclusive Growth

Traditional economic analyses see an unavoidable trade-off between efficiency (a minimal role of government) and equity (in the form of a preference for redistribu-tive policies effected through transfer payments and taxation, with all its attendant deadweight loss). Budget models in general also ignore positive returns to govern-ment spending; at the same time, "dynamic" macroeconomic tax models claim credit for the imagined growth effects of tax cuts while simultaneously ignoring the loss in economic productivity that follows from cutting useful government spending.

The modern *inclusive growth* literature responds directly to the failures of these traditional models, without tumbling all the way down the hill to Gross National Happiness formulations. The leaders of this effort have been the IMF and the OECD—hardly hotbeds of Marxist economic thought. Their work has demonstrated how impoverished are our current fiscal policy debates, and how much better off our country could be if we accepted the principle that government can usefully complement the private sector in important areas.

The theme of inclusive growth also has been advanced through an important 2016 paper by C. Eugene Steuerle.[21] Steuerle calls government investment in human capital through education and similar efforts "opportunity programs," which is a very congenial turn of phrase. His analysis further has the great merit of applying some of the economic themes of the inclusive growth literature to the specifics of US budget politics. My concerns and those of Steuerle overlap to a considerable extent.

The IMF and OECD inclusive growth economic work shows that, by addressing adverse existential fortuities through progressive taxation, along the lines of my Original Position, we would put the United States onto a faster economic growth path, the results of which growth would be more broadly shared. We would honor our national credo of equality of opportunity, and we would fulfill the ethical obligations we have to our fellow citizens.

The first point in the inclusive growth story is that the United States, along with most other advanced economies, is held back by weakness in demand, not financial capital supply. Given that interest rates today often are near zero, even in the case of some corporate borrowers, this cannot be wholly off the mark. The second is that inequality at the *bottom* end of the distribution, and the concomitant lack of the resources needed to fund adequate investment in a child's human capital, hurts an advanced economy's most important capital stock, which is the quality of its labor supply. It also degrades the life satisfactions of a large fraction of our society and makes a mockery of equality of opportunity as a credo.

This second point is so fundamental that it is worth stressing. By far the largest "factor of production" in the American economy is labor—the actual or metaphorical sweat of our collective brows. (Labor accounts for somewhere between three-fifths and two-thirds of GDP.) Just as in the case of machines, investing more in this factor of production leads to what economists call "capital deepening," except that in this case the relevant capital is human capital, and the deepening takes place primarily through early childhood education and childcare, followed by good-quality education programs for the rest of a person's life. The economic returns from state-of-the-art machines belong to the owners of those machines. The economic returns from labor belong to the owner of that labor, which is to say each of us. Human capital investment necessarily is broadly shared, because each of us is the sole owner of her own labor output.[22]

By reimagining our relationship to each other as intermediated by government as a commitment to undo the adverse existential fortuity of pinched family resources, four great things happen. Poor kids are no longer starved for investment in their human capital, and as a result perform throughout their lifetimes at a higher level in standard economic terms, as well as in their life satisfactions. Second, this higher income trajectory for tens of millions of Americans puts the country as a whole on a faster economic growth path. Third, that faster overall growth is more broadly shared, because it no longer comprises the most affluent capturing high returns to their financial capital, or so-called economic rents (the above-market returns from positions of monopoly or special access to the levers of power), but rather the great majority of Americans capturing the returns from their more valuable labor inputs. And fourth, Americans see equality of opportunity as a lived principle, not a tawdry sham. We are richer, we share that increased wealth more broadly, and we feel better about our society and our relationships to each other. This is what the inclusive growth literature teaches.

There are good reasons to worry about the concentration of power and similar problems that today accrue by virtue of runaway top-end inequality, and of course a stronger commitment to progressive taxation will fall on the shoulders of the affluent. Nonetheless, and as I intimated in Chapter 3, I believe the bigger story for our collective welfare really is inequality at the bottom of the income distribution.

We have structured a country that relies more than others on private resources to fund investments in a child's human capital, and we have then set that principle to work in a society with the highest poverty rate of any major industrialized country, and where many tens of millions of others are just getting by. How could we have chosen a stupider set of guiding principles? And this is before consideration of the corrosion of social bonds promoted by fiscal policies that emphasize lower taxes on financial capital supply and continual assaults on government social spending.

The IMF summed things up as follows:

Income equality can lead to higher long-term growth through faster human and physical capital accumulation. . . . Recent studies indicate that high levels of inequality are, overall, harmful for the pace and sustainability of growth. Education and health outcomes of the poor tend to be better in a more equal society, due to higher personal income, larger transfers from the government, and/or better public services. This can lead to a faster accumulation of human capital. In addition, higher income equality can expand the size of domestic demand and support higher physical capital accumulation.[23]

The IMF's institutional change of heart in large measure was attributable to an important Staff Discussion Note that it published in 2014, by Jonathan Ostry, Andrew Berg, and Charalambos Tsangarides. The paper concluded:

> [L]ower net inequality is robustly correlated with faster and more durable growth, for a given level of redistribution. . . . [Further], redistribution appears generally benign in terms of its impact on growth; only in extreme cases is there some evidence that it may have direct negative effects on growth. Thus the combined direct and indirect effects of redistribution—including the growth effects of the resulting lower inequality—are on average pro-growth.[24]

To the same effect, the OECD has released a series of book-length publications on the social and economic costs of inequality. In one such publication, the OECD summarized its findings as follows:

> Beyond its impact on social cohesion, growing inequality is harmful for long-term economic growth. The rise of income inequality between 1985 and 2005, for example, is estimated to have knocked 4.7 percentage points off cumulative growth between 1990 and 2010, on average across OECD countries for which long time series are available. The key driver is the growing gap between lower-income households—the bottom 40% of the distribution—and the rest of the population.
>
> A main transmission mechanism between inequality and growth is human-capital investment. While there is always a gap in education outcomes across individuals with different socio-economic backgrounds, the gap widens in high-inequality countries as people in disadvantaged households struggle to access quality education. This implies large amounts of wasted potential and lower social mobility.[25]

Together, the conclusions reached by the IMF and OECD are remarkable, and they represent a virtual reversal of course from their standard analyses of a decade ago. These policy statements stand in sharp contrast to neoclassical microeconomics models that still dominate much academic and policy discussion in the United States. Further, their conclusions have not yet been reflected in legal academic literature on inequality. The argument, though, is simple and persuasive, and the policy prescriptions that follow are straightforward to implement. All that is required is that we release ourselves from the prison of our rigid fiscal policy modes of thought.

A final note of personal privilege: a commitment to investment in human capital does not mean that our offspring must all be lined up and marched off to the salt mines of STEM (science, technology, engineering, and mathematics). Legislators with modest cognitive skills and even less foresight often belittle all other endeavors, in ways that resonate with any lover of 1960s movies as reminiscent of a well-meaning relative shouting, "Plastics!" As it happens, I majored in Medieval and Renaissance Studies, and things worked out for me in the business world. They did because through my serious application to my chosen field I learned how to read a text closely, how to analyze the different levels of its meanings, how to assemble disparate insights into a coherent narrative, and (I like to think) how to write clearly. When it comes to higher education in particular, all that really matters are two qualities: intellectual curiosity and intellectual courage. How one comes to develop and exercise these faculties is not nearly so important as politicians and parents like to think.

CHAPTER 10

HEALTHCARE AND MEDICARE FOR ALL

HEALTH INSURANCE AS a topic logically belongs in Chapter 9, but because the discussion necessarily is more involved than are the topics covered there, I have given healthcare a chapter of its own. As a reminder, health insurance is a paradigmatic example of insurance as a product, but one where for reasons of insurance economics the government is in a much better position to act as the ultimate insurer to all Americans than are private insurance companies. As a further reminder, health coverage is one area where our collective instincts are to overinsure—to look for comprehensive healthcare, not insurance against improbable catastrophic health events. We dislike even co-pays and deductibles. This makes protection against moral hazard more difficult, but from the other direction it makes health insurance more accessible. As discussed below, in addition to about 28 million uninsured Americans, there are another 40 million Americans who are underinsured in respect of their health coverage, in the sense that they cannot afford the co-pays, deductibles, and other out-of-pocket expenses their plans require.

HEALTHCARE AS IT IS LIVED TODAY

I do not wish to try the patience of my readers with a longwinded analysis of health insurance in America. (Come to think of it, I already have, in *We Are Better Than This*.) I do, however, want briefly to relate where we are on the health insurance front to how insurance works in general and to the objectives of social insurance. I will run through my points as quickly as possible, without wading too deep into technical implementation issues that largely obscure rather than illumine the policy issues relevant to non-specialists.

First, healthcare in America today is totally screwed up. Not a little bit, not in a way that Health Savings Accounts or whatever other passing fancy of the moment can fix, but totally, completely, utterly screwed up.

The unassailable proof is simply this. In the United States, we spend close to 18 percent of GDP on healthcare (private and public spending combined). That is almost 50 percent more as a fraction of GDP than the next most profligate country (Switzerland, these days) spends.[1] If we spent at the same rate that Switzerland does, we would claw back 6 percent of GDP for ourselves every year—*$1.2 trillion in 2019 alone.*[2] But—and here is the clincher—we do not have better healthcare outcomes, and in many important respects (infant mortality, childbirth mortality, diabetes deaths), we are materially worse off. In part, this is attributable to the fact that roughly 28 million Americans do not have any health insurance coverage at all (as of 2018), and as many as 40 million others have inadequate coverage, in the sense that co-pays and deductibles under their plans make the utilization of their coverage unaffordable in light of their household resources.[3]

The United States does *not* devote more real resources to healthcare than do other developed economies—we do *not* have more doctors per 100,000 citizens, or hospital beds, or hospital admissions.[4] What we do have is higher prices in many cases, and a higher volume of certain expensive services. Health economist Ezekiel Emanuel identifies the four largest contributors to our outsized spending: pharmaceuticals; certain high-volume, high-margin procedures like knee replacements; CT and MRI imaging; and administration. Of these, Emanuel finds that pharmaceutical prices are the largest single contributor to our bloated healthcare spending.[5] Our doctors are paid more than in other countries, but because we have fewer of them per 100,000 citizens, our national spending on physician services is not out of line with world norms.

In addition to the issues identified by Emanuel, we cannot underestimate how much we are systematically ripped off by different actors in the health services sector—not just pharmaceutical companies, but also insurance companies, hospitals, and medical practices themselves. This enormous sector of the economy is riddled with monopoly pricing (where a seller controls a market and can set arbitrarily high prices), monopsony pricing (where it's a buyer that holds the power to set arbitrary prices), price gouging, and ethically challenged business practices. We can find a role for private insurance companies, for example, inside a rational healthcare system, but not for current practices, much less the cruelty of pre–Affordable Care Act (ACA) denials for pre-existing conditions and the like.

The problem is not that we need more "free market" healthcare, but rather that we need a regulated environment in which insurance principles—and people—come first. Healthcare is not just another market good. To me, my health is an existential imperative, as important to my survival as having access to oxygen. We don't

HEALTHCARE AND MEDICARE FOR ALL   243

expect Wild West–style "free" markets to price my access to oxygen, and the same is true for healthcare. On top of this, we do not have and have never had in the last fifty years any significant part of the healthcare sector that operates under standard microeconomic competitive market conditions. Every aspect of the healthcare sector—including, in particular, "private" employer-provided healthcare—today is heavily subsidized by the federal government, in ways that have nothing to do with the ACA's modest changes.

Anecdotes and data alike are overwhelming in the damning picture they paint. As one example, Medicare spent $1.8 billion over a four-year period for an exotic drug (H.P. Acthar gel)—a tenfold increase over the prior period—while at the same time the manufacturer paid $6.5 million in what can only be called kickbacks to prescribing physicians. Physicians getting these "consulting" and similarly described payments accounted for 80 percent of Acthar prescriptions over the period.[6]

While it is sometimes argued that people "like" their private health insurance companies, it is a much smaller circle of citizens who will acknowledge that they like private equity firms and the trails of insolvencies and lost jobs they leave in their wakes. How would you feel if you were to learn that private equity firms are now buying medical practices—and as owners of these practices, they now are imposing work rules on your doctor in the same way that they do in other businesses they buy, to squeeze out as much profit for themselves as possible? And yet that is exactly what is happening today.[7]

In one 2018 transaction alone, private equity giant KKR bought Envision Healthcare, one of the country's largest suppliers of physicians to hospitals, for $9.9 billion. With examples like this, why should you be surprised when you wake up from the anesthesia post-surgery only to discover that, while your hospital was "in network," the anesthesiologist was not, and is charging you many orders of magnitude more for her services than would an in-network doctor?

Insurance companies are our favorite villains, but they shoulder an unfair share of the blame. Out-of-network providers hidden within in-network hospitals; inflated charges for some high-volume procedures; overuse of imaging; high drug prices—none of these can be laid at the feet of insurance companies.

Healthcare is not delivered in two days by Amazon Prime; in general, it is intensely local, and in many parts of the country local hospitals exercise monopoly pricing power.[8] Many individuals cannot realistically search for better prices for that reason. Another reason is that in the case of a full-blown crisis, time is of the essence, and again ordinary price discovery cannot take place. And finally the healthcare markets are completely opaque in their pricing, in part because monopolies can do that, and in part because what they are selling is unintelligible to most of us. To the same effect, health insurance policies are so opaque in their terms and coverage as to defy the cognitive skills of all Americans save insurance company executives.

In short, our fractured approach to healthcare delivery simply does not map onto the reality of healthcare as an intensely local enterprise, but one requiring enormous amounts of capital to fund the latest technologies and leading almost inexorably to local monopolies and monopsonies. One employer in New Mexico found that it would be cheaper to send employees to Hawaii for gall bladder surgery than to absorb the monopoly pricing of the one hospital in the community.[9] Amazon Inc. now offers about 380,000 of its employees around the country the option, should they be diagnosed with cancer, to travel to Los Angeles for care at City of Hope Hospital. Amazon does so because City of Hope is a nationally recognized cancer care center, and yet it is cheaper than local care in many cases.[10]

What, then, are the takeaways on healthcare insurance? There are three. First, we do not really want insurance in the classic sense of financial indemnity against unusual adverse fortuities; we want *healthcare*, which actually is a bit different. We want access to medical services for all matters great and small, with relatively little out-of-pocket cost to ourselves.[11] This actually makes good sense as a matter of national policy. Greasy machines work best with regular maintenance, not by waiting for catastrophic failure. The same is true of the human body. Health insurance in the sense of coverage for unusual adverse fortuities—what used to be called "major medical" policies—makes routine doctors' visits unaffordable to most Americans, particularly given that the market today does not compete on price, and actual prices charged for in-plan coverage are a fraction of the nominal prices charged to retail patients who walk in the door.

In short, health insurance in the classic sense of addressing only exceptional adverse fortuities actually opens the door to a different form of moral hazard. The major medical approach leads to the inevitable fact that individuals will gamble on their health to save on current costs, relying on their catastrophic health insurance coverage to catch them when things go horribly wrong. These are precisely the wrong incentives to build into a system. Chronic health matters that can be addressed early on (such as diabetes) become life-threatening in many cases and disabling in many others. Even as cold-hearted economists, we should want to keep our country's productive human machines busily at work, and the way to do that is through access to regular healthcare.

This leads to the second point, which is that healthcare is fundamentally *social* insurance. It is insurance put in service of social aims, and for this reason does not need to prove itself to be actuarially fair in order to justify its existence.

I have a stake in your health, and you in mine, because we all contribute to keeping the economy humming, and because we all have (or should have) a moral interest in the well-being of others. What is more, by approaching healthcare as a fundamental right, and its provision as an exercise in *social* insurance, we can introduce progressivity into the pricing of that fraction of healthcare costs that we ask citizens to shoulder themselves as a device to forestall the moral hazard of overuse of healthcare resources. My late grandmother would find some excuse every August to check herself into Lenox Hill Hospital in Manhattan, when her family and friends went on holiday. Deductibles and the like are designed to address this problem, but they must be priced according to ability to pay, which requires a social perspective on the design of the system.

A *social* insurance perspective also means that we can address more forcefully the problems of monopoly and monopsony powers that today overwhelm the provision of healthcare services. Once we see healthcare as a fundamental right, leading to greater welfare and national productivity, then we can situate hospitals and pharmaceutical companies as serving the public good. Their price gouging to benefit private investors that today is considered a natural artifact of a commitment to "free markets" then becomes understood as undercutting this fundamental right and repugnant to our social commitments to one another. Landlords might make more money practicing racial exclusion, but we do not allow them to do so, and the same should be true of healthcare market participants with their exercise of their monopoly and monopsony powers.

The final takeaway is that our current healthcare system by definition is fatally exposed to the basic insurance evil of adverse selection. Once you appreciate that the health of the citizenry is in fact a critical component of our collective welfare, and therefore that health insurance really ought to be available to everyone on some basis, you cannot avoid the problem of adverse selection. In any health insurance system with less than mandatory universal inclusion, the young and healthy will buy no insurance, or will buy cheap insurance against the most catastrophic eventualities, reckoning that they can buy "real" insurance later, when they are older.

But of course, perhaps they cannot. The healthy young person of today might be surprised to learn that she is a high-risk applicant when she decides she is ready to buy "real" health insurance. An individual with full-blown adult-onset diabetes will find it difficult or impossible to buy health insurance in an unregulated marketplace, because the disease is insidious, its future path is unpredictable, and the medical costs associated with difficult cases are astronomical. That is straightforward insurance logic on the part of the insurance companies.

Commercial insurance in general is forward looking; health insurers only receive compensation—insureds only chip into the pool—once the insured signs up for coverage. But hidden defects in the insured that developed in the past can foretell probable future payouts far in excess of those expected of an average healthy individual. In an unregulated health insurance system, where the problem of adverse selection is so pervasive, private insurers must exclude from their pools actuarial time bombs through exams, review of medical records, and most anything else that they can get their hands on, all to exclude pre-existing conditions and other risks (like smoking) from coverage. That health insurers today cannot do everything along these lines that they would wish is because all of us, acting through government, have prohibited them from doing so.

The problem of adverse selection, and the straightforward insurer's response of engaging in risk underwriting to exclude preexisting conditions, is staggeringly large. A few years ago, in the run-up to the Affordable Care Act, the Department of Health and Human Services estimated that 50 to 129 million non-elderly Americans had some type of pre-existing health condition that might impact their ability to obtain health insurance in unconstrained insurance markets.[12] As many as 82 million Americans with employer-provided health insurance were in this population, which again, in the absence of the Affordable Care Act's prohibition on the consideration of pre-existing conditions, would mean that those citizens were trapped by "job lock," in which for health insurance reasons alone they could not leave their current employer to seek work elsewhere. A more recent study by the Henry J. Kaiser Family Foundation concluded that as of 2018 about 54 million Americans below the age of sixty-five had pre-existing conditions that would shut them out of private health insurance markets; nearly one in two families had a family member who would be affected.[13]

This is not because insurers are venal or corrupt; it is because insurance requires a risk pool in which each member has a small risk of a large claim. Maritime insurers do not insure non-seaworthy boats, but unlike maritime trade we cannot simply ignore or discard fellow citizens who arrive on the insurance scene with important medical issues that would distort the viability of the insurance pool. Non-universal commercial health insurance is fundamentally flawed as an insurance model for the country as a whole. It becomes the domain of the privileged healthy alone.

And finally, even after the Affordable Care Act, about 28 million non-elderly Americans had no health insurance coverage in 2018.[14] A much larger number (on the order of 40 million) have insurance that is inadequate to deal with any real medical crisis, either because their plans are too skinny, or because required co-pays and deductibles make the utilization of their plans unaffordable in light of family resources. In every case, the issue simply boils down to money. Especially in states that have elected to spite their own residents by not accepting the extension of Medicaid offered by the Affordable Care Act, tens of millions do not have enough resources to pay for this existentially imperative coverage, when the choice is between tomorrow's illness and today's rent.

Insurers engage in risk underwriting for automobile insurance, but here discriminatory pricing is more feasible, which is why good drivers pay less than those with a history of speeding tickets. The stakes are less for automobile claims than for complex medical cases, and most states operate their own insurance pool for the highest-risk drivers. It is a source of bewilderment to me that no one objects to mandatory automobile insurance, or the role of states as insurers of last resort, but millions believe that the same principles ought not to apply to the far more fundamental right to health insurance.

Rational private insurance companies also discriminate between in-network providers, who have agreed in advance to provide services at negotiated rates, and out-of-network providers, where the insurer must negotiate fees—or simply shift the onus to the insured, through surprise billing from the out-of-network provider. And finally, private insurance companies will worry about moral hazard, and will address the overuse of medical services (like my grandmother at Lenox Hill Hospital) through deductibles and co-insurance. But adverse selection dominates all these other points as both an economic and a moral matter.

Every other developed country in the world has responded to the adverse selection and moral imperatives just described by adopting universal mandatory healthcare as its core operating principle. Mandatory coverage at one blow decapitates the dragon of adverse selection, thereby making the insurance pool as complete as possible (and therefore as actuarially sound as possible).[15] It further responds to the larger moral commitment that we all have to each other as citizens of what ideally should be a society organized to promote a fair system of social cooperation and individual rights. And as I pointed out earlier in the context of social security, the mandatory participation of the young and the healthy is not just a subsidy running in favor of today's geezers, but is also the price that the young and healthy pay today for guaranteed access to insurance years from now, when to their surprise they have ripened into tomorrow's old and sick.[16]

What is *not* important in the great scheme of things is how universal mandatory healthcare is delivered. In some countries (e.g., the United Kingdom), the government employs the doctors and runs the hospitals. (There is a small high-end private healthcare system that runs in parallel with the universal government-provided program.) In other cases, there is a single-payer system, where the government pays private health providers for their services to patients at set rates. In still others, like Germany, the relationship is between the individual and one of many health insurance companies, but all citizens are required to buy basic health insurance, the insurance offered by the private insurers conforms to a standard form approved by the government, and by law the insurance company is a not-for-profit entity. In this environment individuals can actually engage in the sort of price and features discrimination that political conservatives love.

The funny thing is, the United States relies on all of these models. The Veterans Administration (VA) delivers healthcare directly through VA hospitals and doctors. (Do not get sidelined on how well you might think they do that; their problem is not one of design but rather inexcusable underfunding by Congress in light of the enormous burdens placed on the system by continuous wars.) Medicare Part A is a single-payer plan. And Medicare Advantage plans are examples of private insurance whose terms are identical from one such plan to the next within each category of plan (because the insurance contract form is determined by the government), so that consumers actually can compare prices and features, without worrying about how the contract itself has been tweaked to the insurer's benefit.

In short, health insurance in the United States today is a dysfunctional marketplace. What is more, nearly *all* of it is government subsidized. As previously described, Medicare is not fully funded by payroll taxes paid into the Medicare trust fund, but instead relies on general tax revenues for a large chunk of its total budget. And even so-called private employer-provided healthcare is heavily subsidized in a way that is invisible to most individuals. From the employer's perspective, employer-provided healthcare is just another form of compensation paid to attract workers. As such, the employer deducts the cost of the insurance in calculating its taxable income, just as it does for cash wages paid. But for reasons lost in the mists of time, the value of that healthcare to each employee is not included in her taxable income the way all her other wages are, and so are exempt from both income tax and payroll taxes. The subsidy amounts to about $300 billion/year.[17]

It is often argued that people "like" their employer-provided healthcare. I can readily understand this as an expression of the anxiety attendant on imagining a transition to some other undescribed system, but in fact retirees do not generally miss their old employer-provided hospital insurance when they migrate to Medicare Part A. More to the point, I am not aware of studies that measure the likeability of employer-provided healthcare before and after employees are informed how much their cash wages in theory would jump if it were scrapped—on average, about $20,000/year for family plans (of which $6,000 comes from withholding on their own wages, and another $14,000 as employer contributions). As discussed in Chapter 9, It is the "freeing up" of those hidden wage costs that would fund "Medicare for All" or the like, making the financial analysis less preposterous than it is sometimes presented to be.

A more dramatic way of saying things is that while the world as a whole cares little about my aches and pains, from my perspective my health is an existential imperative. I pay whatever I must for health insurance and non-covered costs, because on the whole I much prefer living to the alternative. So from my perspective, or from the perspective of any sentient reader, the American style of private health insurance is really just a tax we all impose on ourselves, with no more real freedom to abstain from it than we have the ability to opt out of the income tax.[18]

I do not like to argue by anecdote, but it is worth closing this subsection with a couple of stories around the theme of diabetes, a great killer of Americans. Thirty million Americans have diabetes; 7.5 million require insulin to control the disease.[19] Without insulin, those with Type 1 diabetes (about 1.5 million) in particular are at great risk of dying a painful death.

In 2001, a vial of Humalog, a form of fast-acting insulin sold by Eli Lilly that is extremely helpful in controlling life-threatening sugar spikes, cost a patient $35.[20] In 2009, it cost $92.70. In 2017, that same vial cost $274.70, almost precisely tripled in price.[21] There is no obvious reason for this price hike. Insulin is as old as the hills as far as pharmaceuticals are concerned, and the manufacturing of it has not gotten more difficult.

In consequence of this and similar moves by other manufacturers, about one in four insulin users ration their use of the drug; they take less than the therapeutically appropriate dose to make their supply last longer.[22] Others organize field trips to Canada to buy insulin for one-tenth the US price.[23]

In August 2019, *The Guardian* commented on a story about Jordan Williams, an Ultimate Fighting Championship fighter who had been the subject of a laudatory profile by ESPN. Williams has Type 1 diabetes; without insulin he will die. *The Guardian* put this gloss on the ESPN profile:

> The article is a standard "triumph over adversity" piece until it casually notes in the 17th paragraph: "Williams doesn't have medical insurance and cannot afford the treatment. So he buys insulin that's sold for dogs at Walmart for $24.99 per bottle."
>
> It accepts without comment that insulin costs up to $470 a bottle and that Williams considers himself "super lucky" that somebody told him he could use the cheaper, animal-grade substitute. Super lucky?
>
> This is a disturbing, but not uncommon, story in the US, where more than 1 million adults have type 1 diabetes and the cost of insulin, the drug that keeps them alive, rises exponentially year on year to the point where Americans must pay thousands of dollars a year simply to not die. Turning 26, the age when you are no longer eligible for cover on your parents' health insurance, can be a death sentence for diabetics, who often also resort to reusing costly needles into oblivion to save money.[24]

* * *

This is part of a deeper malaise in American healthcare where hospital bills are the leading cause of bankruptcy and one-third of all GoFundMe donations are for medical expenses. Increasingly, those who cannot afford health insurance are turning to fish antibiotics as cheaper alternatives to human ones, despite the health consequences.

Josh Wilkerson was less "lucky." He also had aged out of his parents' health in-surance and suffered from Type 1 diabetes. He earned $16.50/hour as a supervisor of a dog kennel, where he received very limited health benefits; his monthly in-sulin bill was $1,200. As a Type 1 diabetic, Wilkerson needed fast-acting insulin like Humalog to keep his blood sugar in check. But he and his fiancée wanted to save a little bit for their wedding, and he could not come close to affording Humalog or similar products because of the cost. He therefore relied on a different form of insulin, called "human insulin," which is sold by Walmart under its ReliOn brand for $25/vial.[25] Human insulin is slow-acting and exposes Type 1 diabetics to much greater risk of a fatal sugar spike, which the fast-acting insulin could easily handle. Wilkerson did his best to manage his sugar levels in light of this.

In June 2019, Wilkerson was asked by his boss to sleep at the kennel to pro-vide overnight coverage while the boss was away. While alone there in the eve-ning, he fell into a coma from diabetes-induced strokes; his fiancée found him face down at his workplace the next morning. Five days later, he was dead. He was twenty-seven.[26]

In April 2019, Eli Lilly and other pharmaceutical firms were grilled on their insulin pricing practices. In the runup to that hearing, Eli Lilly announced that it would release a generic form of Humalog, to cost one-half as much. In August 2019, however, the generic was almost impossible to find. Most doctors and pharmacists were unaware of it. What is more, insureds could only get the generic under their insurance plans if the third-party pharmacy benefit manager firm retained by the insurer listed it on its national preferred formulary. But Express Scripts, the country's largest pharmacy benefit manager, did not. When queried, Express Scripts explained that individuals enrolled in plans using the formulary usually had a flat co-pay for all prescriptions, so what was the hullabaloo about? The fact that the employers that bear the costs of these plans would save millions from the switch to the generic version apparently was not a matter of concern to Express Scripts.

IMAGINING A MORE RATIONAL HEALTH INSURANCE MODEL

The 2020 Democratic Party presidential campaign offered opportunities to offer and to vet a wide range of health insurance proposals. The resulting debates man-aged to confuse at least as much as they elucidated, but from the cacophony of ideas and acronyms a few simple principles did emerge.

First, healthcare must be universal, which means mandatory. As every other re-motely developed country in the world has concluded, we will not allow citizens to bleed to death on the streets, so we will always provide some level of universal public healthcare. We also care about the elderly, hence universal healthcare (Medicare) for them. Further, we want to win the GDP Olympics, so we need to keep all of us little engines of productivity beavering away at the peak of our conditions, thereby adding to GDP. And we all are sickened to read of GoFundMe campaigns to raise the funds to save the life of a family member, friend, colleague, or even stranger. Intuitively, we all understand that taking care of each other is an imperative if we are to take seriously the mutuality of relationships and responsibilities that are attendant on being fellow citizens. Most powerfully, only universal coverage slays the dragon of adverse selection while affording coverage to those with pre-existing conditions. This one point really is not negotiable.

Second, there is no appetite to turn the federal government into the sole provider of healthcare services, as in the UK National Health Service or the VA system here. But it also is pointless to imagine a universal program without the government as the hub of the wheel of distributed services. What we want is what is called a "single-payer" system, where the government ultimately foots the bills, but does not directly provide services (other than the VA example). The government has available a very efficient premium collection device, in the form of federal income and payroll taxes.

The current debate, at least among thoughtful progressives, seems to boil down to whether the model should be "Medicare for All" (where "Medicare" in this context is shorthand for government-provided single-payer coverage of some sort), or instead an option to sign up for the same Medicare alongside the option to continue subscribing to employer-sponsored health insurance. This really is a false choice, because as previously described, employer-sponsored health insurance is heavily government subsidized, in ways invisible to most, but amounting to about $300 billion/year. If one imagines gradually withdrawing that federal subsidy over a period of, say, ten years, so that employer-sponsored health insurance stood on its own feet (and was priced accordingly to employees), how many would remain enthusiastic about their private plans? I have no issues with running both programs in parallel (so that private plans meeting the terms of the government plan would satisfy the universal mandate to obtain insurance), but it seems to me highly probable that substantially all Americans would end up in a government-sponsored plan at the end of the day.

"Medicare for All" turns out to have more than one meaning. If one were literally to extend existing Medicare to all citizens, that approach would entail all the co-pays, deductibles, and coverage limitations of current Medicare. (For example, Medicare covers in-hospital treatment for at most 150 consecutive days in a year, including your lifetime excess 60-day allowance.) In the most comprehensive (and expensive) view, Medicare for All would simply mean that all medical expenses are covered by the federal government, period. But that arguably leads to the risk of systematic overuse of the system.

If I am right that private employer-sponsored health insurance would wither on the vine as its existing federal subsidy is withdrawn, the most realistic long-term model is probably that of universal mandatory federal healthcare insurance with comprehensive coverage (hospital, doctor/outpatient, prescription drug). It would incorporate modest income-dependent co-pays up to an annual cap. As a matter of realpolitik, a role for the insurance industry must be found. Here, Medicare Advantage offers a useful approach. The idea would be that the government would specify the form of universal insurance contract. Individuals could choose the government as the direct insurer, or instead could sign up with private companies that would compete using the same contract, plus any add-on features they might choose to win customers. The federal government would reimburse the insurers at rates that reflected the private insurer's assumption of the administrative burdens as well as medical risks.

In this world, *as in Medicare today*, prices for medical services would be regulated. There is no practical way to avoid this. Those reimbursement rates would need to be carefully set to encourage careers in medicine; here it would be useful to re-think on whose shoulders the cost of medical school should fall. Physicians and others would be free to cater to the very wealthy who are willing to pay sky-high prices, but it would be difficult for most to sustain a practice comprising only such patients; as a result, assuming that federal reimbursements are fairly set, most every doctor would accept Medicare for All patients. Finally, as in every other industrialized country, drug prices would be regulated.

This is not socialized medicine, any more than Medicare today is socialized medicine. You would still choose your doctor, and so on, just as you do in Medicare today. All or almost all doctors would be in-network, because there is only one network, even if there are numerous administrators (the different insurance companies through which you could purchase your standard contract).

There is no need to prohibit private health insurance or out-of-network providers. As in the UK, a small market might develop for the most affluent to purchase private insurance and visit private providers, but even assuming that purchasing private insurance exempts one from participating in the government plan (by no means a foregone conclusion), that private insurance, once shorn of subsidies, will be substantially more expensive than the public plan.

All this is terribly sketchy, but it is difficult to wade very deep into these waters without overwhelming the rest of this book.[27] The key points are that insurance principles and respect for the dignity of our fellow citizens both lead inexorably to mandatory universal coverage and some form of government-sponsored single-payer health plan. A role can be found for private insurers inside that system, but it would be a less lucrative business than they currently enjoy. Even in a "Medicare for all who want it" model, over time it is likely that current private employer-sponsored health insurance would become unattractive as current government subsidies are removed.

Two related big-picture issues remain: transition and cost. One basic transition problem is that a Medicare for All model, whatever its details, squeezes the juice out of private medical industry profits. I have little sympathy for the squeals of those who thereby are squeezed, but their cries tend to have political resonance. While I have tried to imagine a continuing role for private insurers, I am skeptical that the private hospital industry serves any useful long-term economic role. Political compromise here no doubt will take the form of generous reimbursement rates for a period of time, and of course hospitals no longer will bear the risk of the patient who cannot pay her bills (about $30 billion/year in uncollectible charges).

The other transition issue is that many unions in particular have consciously traded off cash wages for very generous employer-provided healthcare programs. More generally, the 140 million Americans with employer-sponsored plans have implicitly made the same trade-off. Economists have always treated the employer's payment of employees' health insurance premiums as a form of tax-subsidized compensation to employees. The key move here will be to make that economic theory a reality through a "maintenance of effort" provision, under which an employer that abandons its employee healthcare plan as part of a transition to a single-payer government plan must convert its healthcare costs into explicit W-2 wages paid to employees, or alternatively (as in the Sanders-Warren Medicare for All Act of 2019) to pay over those amounts to the government as taxes to fund the new program. Employers must not be allowed to capture the savings exclusively for themselves.

COST OF A NEW SYSTEM

One of the few benefits to have emerged from the excruciating 2020 Democratic Party presidential nomination process is that it led to some good work estimating the costs of various policy proposals. As a result, we can consider, to a first approximation, what a fully implemented "Medicare for All" plan might cost. Again, "Medicare" here is a misnomer, because the slightly different plans proposed by Senators Warren and Sanders in 2020 were far more comprehensive, and with far fewer co-pays and deductibles, than is true of actual Medicare. Both plans were based on the Medicare for All Act of 2019 (S. 1129) that the two senators sponsored, but the Warren campaign plan had a better discussion of the costs, so I will work with that.[28]

The Warren plan contemplated that at the end of a relatively short (three-year) transition period all Americans would be eligible for free government-provided healthcare without premiums, co-pays, or deductibles. This was a very ambitious goal and represents the outer limit of what one might imagine a "single-payer" government healthcare system costing.

The headline number that arguably doomed the Warren campaign was that her Medicare for All plan would involve over $20 trillion—that's trillion with a "T"—in new taxes. That figure is beyond mind-boggling: the *total* estimated federal tax take for 2021–2030 as of January 2020 was only $48 trillion. Surely this is madness?

Actually, no. The place to start is with how much governments and households together, through public and private spending, will pony up for healthcare over the next decade *in the absence* of any major reform. That figure is roughly $52 trillion (18 percent of projected GDP).[29] One way or another, US households are on track to assume this enormous financial burden, in part through taxes and in part through direct expenditures on healthcare.

Governments spend by means of monies collected through taxation, so that share is already a tax burden that all of us have implicitly agreed to assume. Private spending includes direct outlays by households, but more importantly, employer-sponsored insurance as well. One portion of this is nominally absorbed by employers but offset by reduced wages paid to employees; the other (growing) portion are the contributions directly required of employees.

For all the reasons I have developed earlier, private spending on healthcare also is a kind of tax that we choose to impose on ourselves. This follows from the fact that healthcare, unlike most other market goods, is an existential necessity, and rational individuals find that they have no choice but to subject themselves to the cost of health insurance to the extent their budgets allow. So the right starting point is that we today have collectively committed ourselves to spend this $52 trillion to purchase healthcare over the next decade – what can be called the "National Health Expenditure" – as surely as if it all were baked into the tax system. In return, we have the mediocre health outcomes noted earlier. We also suffer 28 million Americans who have no health insurance at all, and perhaps 40 million more who rely on inadequate insurance.

This is the critical point: given that private spending on healthcare is not just another consumer good, what we really should care about are how many Americans are covered by our healthcare system and the total of our National Health Expenditure. What fraction of the National Health Expenditure is paid through actual taxation, and what fraction through the quasi-tax of self-assessed health charges paid by each household, really has only optical significance at a national level. There are, to be sure, important distributional questions—who pays which explicit tax, for example—but the first-order question should be: Does Medicare for All increase the number of covered Americans, and at what total National Health Expenditure?

Against this background, how would the Warren "Medicare for All" fare? By definition, it would extend coverage to all Americans, addressing our current crisis of nearly 70 million citizens with no or inadequate coverage. But how much would it have cost?

Here, the Warren campaign published a first-rate detailed and expert analysis that went through several National Health Expenditure estimates.[30] (The Sanders campaign relied on a comprehensive article and accompanying interactive model published in *The Lancet*.)[31] The Warren analysis basically concluded that her fully implemented plan (premium-free government-provided healthcare with no co-pays or deductibles) would cost about the same as the status quo trendline—but all Americans would be covered, and all would be able to afford to use their insurance, because there would be no out-of-pocket costs. The analysis is certainly plausible, and if it were to prove correct, it would represent an enormous improvement in health outcomes. (*The Lancet* paper on which the Sanders campaign relied actually predicted that his variant of Medicare for All would reduce National Health Expenditures by about 13 percent—$500 billion in the first year alone.)

Now, here's the rub. The Warren campaign's expert analysis concluded that, while the total National Health Expenditure would stay roughly constant, the portion absorbed by the federal government would have gone up by some $21 trillion over ten years. That implied higher taxes, and the Warren campaign also produced a second analysis proposing a potpourri of new taxes to cover the cost. In doing this the campaign really was quite unfair to itself, because *the other side of the ledger* is that household incomes would go up to the extent that families were relieved of their current obligations to pay into employer-sponsored plans or to make out-of-pocket payments.[32] (The plan contemplated that businesses would pay as new taxes 98 percent of what they previously had contributed to employer-sponsored plans, leaving employers with a small profit.) Somehow this point was drowned out in the cacophony of accusations that the plan would raise taxes on households by tens of trillions of dollars over ten years. This was a tragic error in messaging.

The hysteria over "trillions in new taxes" in this context is fundamentally misplaced. Since National Health Expenditure under Warren's "Medicare for All" plan would not materially increase, therefore neither would the sum of the explicit and implicit taxes we will shoulder. What does change is the *mix* of how we pay for healthcare. Explicit taxes will go up, but the implicit taxes we impose on ourselves through out-of-pocket costs will go down. If I put $100 in your pocket and then charge you a $100 finder's fee, you are not worse off—you are just where you were before, on a net basis.

It is true that there can be differences in the distribution of healthcare costs and benefits across the income spectrum, but we can address that in the design of any new explicit taxes. Saying that the rich should pay all new explicit taxes required as we shift how we finance our National Health Expenditure actually would leave the middle class better off, not flat, by virtue of the freeing up of their personal resources. And in turn, if a Medicare for All proposal of this nature were not quite so radical—for example, by contemplating income-based premiums that would kick in for higher incomes, and income-based co-pays to address moral hazard concerns—the total public share of the aggregate National Health Expenditure (and associated explicit taxes) could be reduced accordingly.

EPILOGUE

PROGRESSIVE POLICIES, PROGRESSIVE PARADIGMS

EVERY POLITICAL MOVEMENT requires an icon. In US conservative politics before Donald Trump, that hero was Ronald Reagan. Contemporary progressives have available to them their own standard bearer in Franklin Delano Roosevelt, but they bizarrely have not kept his memory or his message nearly so fresh.

In January 1941, Roosevelt delivered one of his most famous speeches, that year's State of the Union address. It is often referred to as the "Four Freedoms" speech, because in it Roosevelt called for a world founded on "four essential human freedoms"— freedom of speech and expression, freedom of religion, freedom from want, and freedom from fear. Each was drawn from the immediate experience of the Great Depression and the runup to the Second World War, but they all continue to resonate today.

In this speech, Roosevelt outlined a vision for America that can serve virtually word-for-word as a progressive politico manifesto today, save only for its failure to address environmental concerns and racial injustice, which were not part of the national political dialog nearly eighty years ago. He said:

> [T]here is nothing mysterious about the foundations of a healthy and strong democracy. The basic things expected by our people of their political and economic systems are simple. They are:
>
> Equality of opportunity for youth and for others.
> Jobs for those who can work.
> Security for those who need it.
> The ending of special privilege for the few.
> The preservation of civil liberties for all.

The enjoyment of the fruits of scientific progress in a wider and constantly rising standard of living.

These are the simple, basic things that must never be lost sight of in the turmoil and unbelievable complexity of our modern world. The inner and abiding strength of our economic and political systems is dependent upon the degree to which they fulfill these expectations.

The progressive agenda has not really wavered from this agenda in the intervening eighty years. Notwithstanding the partial success of the Affordable Care Act, however, the progressive movement has bogged down for two generations over the counteroffensive mounted by the conservative policy story introduced by the Reagan Revolution. To set this country back on a path of greater prosperity, more broadly shared, one of greater respect for others and a deeper commitment to one's fellow citizens, requires an overarching vision as compelling to most Americans as the conservative story has been to a minority.

Progressives do not suffer from a dearth of policy ideas. Thanks in large part to the 2020 presidential election, those of us who follow public policy are overwhelmed by an almost uncountable flow of policy proposals from progressive candidates, think tanks, and academics for how government should do more, or do better, along with specific plans for raising the revenues to pay for it all. My e-mail inbox is full of them, my computer desktop is full of them, my actual desktop is full of them, and my floor is full of them.

Relative to our current impoverished understanding of what government can do to enhance our welfare and our incomes, almost all of these ideas are terrific. The proposals compete with one another, of course, and I do have preferences (particularly on the revenue-raising side, because tax policy is my core academic specialty), but I sometimes think we would do well just to put them all in a fishbowl and, while blindfolded, pull out a few winners.

The problem with the progressive movement today is not an absence of good policy ideas, but rather an absence of a compelling progressive *narrative*. This narrative should serve as a short and accessible explanation, not simply of *what* progressives hope to accomplish, but also *why*. The narrative should operate as a framework into which new ideas can be slotted, so that there is one coherent story linking different policy proposals into a larger vision for America.

I came to embrace progressive values by close consideration of the social science literature showing the real state of our society, by my own work comparing the United States to its peer countries in the economic and social choices our country has made and the resulting social environment we have fostered, and by thinking about our ethical obligations to each other, as embodied in my construction of what it means to be a citizen. Others have followed their own paths to reach similar conclusions. But the simple fact is that throwing on to the Internet policy proposals sure to please converts to the cause does not do much to increase the flock. That's what narratives do, and here progressives have done less work.

By "narrative" I do not mean heart-warming anecdotes of the sort beloved by presidential candidates and book editors looking to leaven an over-earnest book manuscript. I mean instead an overarching theory of what government should be about that reduces to a few sentences and that resonates with ordinary citizens trying to lead their own lives and make political decisions in the limited time available to them.

Where should we look for such a credo?

Economics is a serious intellectual discipline, devoted, in its most famous definition, to the study of "human behaviour as a relationship between ends and scarce means which have alternative uses."[1] Phrased differently, it is an inquiry into the allocation and distribution of goods and services against a backdrop of a scarcity of each. Only the Garden of Eden had no use for economists.

Political economy is a related field, if a bit more amorphous one. For present purposes we can define it, paraphrasing Adam Smith, as an inquiry into the wealth of nations. More particularly, how do the state and private actors interact with respect to the allocation and distribution of scarce goods? What are the conditions of government under which (take your pick) the nation's wealth is maximized, or the satisfactions of its citizens are maximized, or the lives of the worst-off are nonetheless reasonably satisfactory? Political economy draws more directly on political science and political theory (a branch of philosophy) than does economics narrowly defined.

But policies are not enacted by economists, specialists in political economy, or political theorists, to their collective regret. Political processes have capacity for only a simplified version of the underlying disciplines that justify them. This is where a convincing policy narrative comes in. It must rest on economic or philosophical claims, but it must also resonate with traditional credos that tie into an expression of American exceptionalism.

Conservatives have deployed a hugely influential policy narrative for almost forty years. The Reagan Revolution fashioned an effective message by marrying two bad ideas—supply-side pseudo-economics and what is properly called market triumphalism—and then packaging the result in terms of a core American political value: America as the land of the free. This story's shortcomings are ever more apparent, but it is useful to think about how the conservative narrative was fashioned, and why it has had such appeal, in order to see the kind of components a new compelling progressive narrative should include.

Supply-side doctrine reduces to the idea that, whatever the current level of taxation, further tax cuts lead to greater prosperity, because in a lower tax environment, investors will supply more capital to businesses hungry for investment funds. Businesses then will grow faster, and workers will share in the increased profitability of firms through higher wages.

The problem is that the supply-side story is simply false when applied to the United States today. The United States in fact is a low-tax, small-government country compared to its peers, and against that backdrop tax cuts today have about as much power to turbocharge the economy as pushing on a string does to move a piano. The idea that "tax cuts pay for themselves" by itself has always been a pretty threadbare contention, and in any event is too abstract to serve as the rallying cry of millions.

Market triumphalism, in turn, is the down-market cousin of the older and slightly more respectable doctrine of neoliberalism.[2] I've previously described them as follows:

> Neoliberalism is a degraded interpretation of nineteenth-century classic economic and liberal political theories, mingling political fears of totalitarianism with an overstated confidence in private markets as the solution to all social problems. Market triumphalism in turn is a debauched form of neoliberalism, to which society's tolerance for public displays of narcissism and American faith-based belief systems have been added.

* * *

> Market triumphalism confuses national income with national welfare; it ignores the positive returns to government insurance and government investment; it confuses life outcomes with the hands of Providence; and it justifies a distasteful narcissism and possessiveness toward all material goods. It enables the unreflective affluent to sleep at night, their consciences assuaged by its message that their success is explained by their admirable virtues alone.[3]

The second, and more important, stroke of genius that explains the long life and great success of the Reagan Revolution's political paradigm has been its clever conflation of an unconstrained marketplace with personal political liberty, relying here on the cartoonish retelling of the original neoliberal impulse that lies at the heart of market triumphalism.[4] In this story, it is not simply that markets require free actors—it is that political liberty requires free markets. This ingenious rhetorical device thus taps into the deeply felt national myth that America is the land of the free.

The marriage of supply-side claims to market triumphalist invocations of an unregulated marketplace as the precondition to political liberty is why the United States has been prey to unrelenting demands for lower taxes on the rich. Tax cuts coupled with smaller resources available to government answer the cry of supply-side pamphleteers, while at the same time allegedly enhancing our political liberties, through the expansion of the scope of the private sector at the expense of the public one. The result is our current sad state, where urgent public problems go unaddressed. And yet the ethos of market triumphalism continues to be applied to cases where private markets are plainly the inferior solution.

The narrative of private markets gone wild as the necessary precondition of political liberty is the core political/economic message of conservative policy. It simultaneously justifies ever-lower taxation (both for supply-side and liberty-loving reasons) and denies that there are any social issues for which government might offer a superior corrective instrument to that of an unconstrained private sector.

For nearly forty years, this powerful political paradigm has led millions to embrace as threadbare a government as possible, so that our "free markets" can delivery greater political liberty. In reality, of course, neoliberal values have led to less freedom for the large swath of Americans who find themselves perpetually under siege to make ends meet, and who therefore cannot enjoy "freedom from want," in Franklin D. Roosevelt's famous phrase, while a very small slice at the top races ahead to ever greater wealth.

Within academics, the narrative of neoliberalism (not to mention market triumphalism) as a policy compass has suffered withering attack. To begin with, the "rational actor" at the heart of the neoliberal story ("homo economicus," if you prefer), endowed with great foresight, perfect rationality, fixed preferences, and a brain that would make Einstein's look childish by comparison, simply does not exist. Work by the Nobel Prize–winning economist Daniel Kahneman and others have shown that we solve economics problems with heuristics (best guesses through somewhat reliable mental shortcuts) and outright false understandings. At the same time, our preferences are malleable, both from external forces and from our own life experiences.

Moreover, markets are far more imperfect than the neoliberal story allows. As Joseph Stiglitz and many others have shown, markets are often uncompetitive and incomplete, which is to say that in those instances they systematically fail to deliver the benefits promised for them.[5] Because markets are incomplete—that is, they do not reach areas where we collectively want to allocate resources in some manner other than leaving things where they happen to fall—markets cannot solve every social issue in ways that accord with our actual preferences.[6]

Finally, and at the center of this book, *brute luck undercuts the entire neoliberal story.* No matter how rational the behavior of individuals, once we appreciate the pervasive power of brute luck indiscriminately to afflict or reward the virtuous or the scurrilous alike, regardless of their native abilities or efforts, we see that the connection between what we do and what we get is far more tenuous than the neoliberal story could ever contemplate. Our preferences and talents do not consistently yield the outcomes we expect.

Yet market triumphalism still serves today as the primary lens through which one political party and millions of voters view economic problems and endorse policy responses. It thus serves as a powerful political paradigm, or organizational principle.

But where is the competing progressive narrative? Where is the paradigm that can be expressed in a few sentences and that frames the broad strokes of the progressive agenda in ways that ordinary citizens can find attractive and intuitively sound?

The underlying motivation of this book has been to propose an answer. I have taken as our highest political aspiration the very first item in Roosevelt's list of the basic things we should expect of our political and economic system—assuring equality of opportunity. This should stand as the progressive rallying point in the same way that claims about political liberty do for conservatives, without the sleight of hand in which liberty is flipped on its head to serve the demands of free marketeers rather than the majority of citizens. At the same time, emphasizing authentic equality of opportunity—which includes confronting those aspects of brute luck that from birth hold back Americans not born to affluence—is a compelling defense against charges that progressive policies reduce to redistribution for its own sake.

Instantiating equality of opportunity requires more than a collection of facially neutral statutes, or even the best of intentions. The universal force that has not been internalized into our political and policy calculus, and which throws into disarray all our good intentions, is the inescapable role of brute luck—randomness—in determining our material outcomes.

No one disputes the power of equality of opportunity as a national credo, just as we all subscribe to the importance of political liberty. What distinguishes doctrinaire conservatives from the rest of us is their belief that political liberty rests on a foundation of unconstrained "free" markets—that wherever the purest animal spirits of the marketplace do not roam, liberty cannot take root. I propose that what should distinguish progressives is our understanding that private markets do not and cannot respond to the most important instances of bad brute luck, which failure in turn erodes authentic equality of opportunity. Many successful people expend enormous energy denying this fact, but a franker acknowledgment of the importance of luck as a driver of people's outcomes leads to all sorts of salutary policy responses.

Substantive progressive policies largely fall into two buckets: more public investment and more public insurance.[7] (I am putting to one side the competing tax proposals for how to finance these; as I have developed at length in *We Are Better Than This*, it is public spending, not tax design, that is the more powerful lever in moving toward a more equal and more prosperous country.) Investment in public infrastructure is easily understood. Moreover, numerous economic studies, including by a Nobel laureate, demonstrate that well-chosen public investment can earn financial returns that would be the envy of the private sector, were these studies better known. Finally, public investment yields a kind of "double dividend," by creating good jobs that satisfy workers' wage needs and their desire for work with dignity.

Insurance is a subtle tool, and it is only by thinking carefully about its requirements and application that one can articulate a coherent and defensible set of policies. Once understood, though, insurance, whether as fact or as metaphor, can help us determine why, when, and how much the public sector should undertake in cases not resolved through straightforward investment analysis.

What is more, the insurance metaphor ties tax policies to spending policies. The progressive income tax can be seen, not as a soak-the-rich scheme, but rather as a rational compact among citizens reached behind the veil, before our existential luck in family resources at birth has been revealed. The progressive income tax is how we design real-world insurance premiums to pay for the social insurance programs that respond to the existential bad luck that today cut the legs out from under our proclamations of America as the land of opportunity.

In writing the book, I have endeavored to show how political institutions can solve the fundamental dilemma of living in the world's richest large economy, but at the same time a country where supplies of capital to fund investment in our own talents and abilities fall far short of market demand. I have identified the key problem as our excessive reliance on private markets to solve economic problems far outside their natural remit, and more specifically on our expectation that family funding or bootstrap leverage through student debt—as if we all were the targets of leveraged buyouts!—will supply the capital required to enable Americans to follow their talents and interests to their ultimate ends. And I have identified the solution as an increased role for government to address existential bad luck, using the principles of insurance to identify how such interventions might work.

In the end, though, the book's arguments lend themselves to political application, in the ordinary sense of the word. A larger role for government is consistent with progressive intuitions. So is embracing equality of opportunity as the litmus test of policy. My emphasis on addressing brute luck through the mechanism of actual or metaphorical insurance invokes intuitive notions of fairness, rather than a perpetuation of the falsehood that material affluence is a reflection of the high esteem in which the universe holds the wealthy. At the same time, the discipline of insurance principles as developed in the book suggests some natural limits on how far these new interventions should go. The positive returns to these interventions, and the fairness principle invoked by the emphasis on equality of opportunity, respond to those who wish to see progressives as reprobate woodsmen, looking to cut the affluent down to size simply out of envy.

This is the path toward a new paradigm through which progressive politics can deliver a clear and compelling narrative. The world toward which the paradigm points is one of greater fairness, more human flourishing, and more national income, more broadly shared.

NOTES

INTRODUCTION

1. There are many reasons for this. Family connections (including "legacy" status) are relevant; the wealthier family might have spent substantial sums on college entrance exam prep courses or extracurricular enrichment programs that are relevant to some college admissions offices (summer lacrosse camp); the more affluent family might place more focused demands on their child and acclimate her both to the top college names and how to navigate the admissions process; the college placement officer at the wealthier child's school might have strong relationships with top-tier college admissions offices; or the wealthier child's school might itself have more financial resources, helping to prepare and condition all its students for the demands of college academics.

2. The hidden subsidy is delivered through the tax system. Your employer-provided health insurance is tax-deductible by the employer as just another form of compensation paid to you. But you are not required to include the value of this added compensation in the form of health insurance as income, whether for income tax or for payroll tax purposes. The subsidy amounts to roughly $300 billion/year—$3 trillion over the usual ten-year federal budget window used for evaluating policy proposals.

3. Edward D. Kleinbard, *We Are Better Than This: How Government Should Spend Our Money* (New York: Oxford University Press, 2015).

CHAPTER 1

1. It turns out that this is a near-universal insight reached by cyclists of an introspective frame of mind. See, for example, Robert H. Frank, *Success and Luck: Good Fortune and the Myth of Meritocracy* (Princeton, NJ: Princeton University Press, 2016), 80. Frank's book also is a rumination on the importance of luck to our material outcomes, filtered through his own life experiences. But our two books point in different directions. Frank's principal interest, beyond making the case for the role of luck in our lives, is to advocate the adoption of a progressive consumption tax. This book takes a more institutional approach, weaving economics, social psychology, and moral philosophy into a

coherent message about the central importance of how the systematic denial of luck explains how we unconsciously order our understanding of the world around us, and how a more realistic understanding of the world as it is can lead to both a wealthier and happier society.

2. Charles M. Radding. "Fortune and Her Wheel: The Meaning of a Medieval Symbol," *Mediaevistik* 5 (1992): 127–138; David M. Robinson, "The Wheel of Fortune," *Classical Philology* 41, no. 4 (October 1946): 207–216; Howard R. Patch, *The Goddess Fortuna in Mediaeval Literature* (Cambridge, MA: Harvard University Press, 1927), 147–177.

3. https://geogebra.org.

4. A. Pluchino, A. E. Biondo, and A. Rapisarda, "Talent vs Luck: The Role of Randomness in Success and Failure," *Advances in Complex Systems* 21, no. 03n04, 1850014 (2018).

5. Gregory Mankiw and Matthew Weinzierl, "The Optimal Taxation of Height: A Case Study of Utilitarian Optimal Income Redistribution," *American Economic Journal: Economic Policy* 2, no. 1 (February 2010): 155–176.

6. Pluchino, et. al., "Talent vs Luck," 3. The Pluchino model has been usefully extended by another researcher, Hongsup Shin, whose more refined variations take into account many real-world factors not considered in the Pluchino paper. Hongsup Shin, "Talent, Luck, and Success: Simulating Meritocracy and Inequality with Stochasticity," Medium.com, March 18, 2018, https://medium.com/@hongsupshin/talent-luck-and-success-simulating-meritocracy-and-inequality-with-stochasticity-501e0c1b4969. Another model that readers can try out for themselves is available at http://www.chancyislands.org/index.html.

7. Hal R. Varian, "Redistributive Taxation as Social Insurance," *Journal of Public Economics* 14, no. 1 (1980): 49–68.

8. http://fm.cnbc.com/applications/cnbc.com/resources/editorialfiles/2019/10/31/CoopermanLetter.pdf.

9. After considerable introspection, I would go further in my portrayal of matters, and adopt my best understanding of Buddhist philosophy, which as applied here would, I believe, say that not only do we not have a legitimate claim to the unfettered exploitation of our native talents, but the entity we think of as ourselves, with all the features we either admire or are ashamed of, is a contingency—an accident of prior causes stretching back infinitely in time. In this telling, there is no "I" at all, no essential being bearing my name with any permanence or fixed characteristics.

10. This is one important difference between my approach here and the important work of Ronald Dworkin and the luck egalitarians. Another is that I believe that I think a bit more directly about the nature and mechanics of insurance as a concept and as a product, including the importance of adverse selection and moral hazard. Chapter 6 introduces these topics.

11. I further intend the term to exclude from consideration the consequences of personal relationships, like an indifferent mother or a cruel father. These cannot easily be untangled from the personality of an individual, nor can their financial harms be measured objectively.

12. Richard Reeves, "The Measure of a Nation," *Annals of the American Academy of Political and Social Science* 657 (January 2015): 22–26.

13. Some affluent individuals have generously funded local public school programs with similar aims, but those contributions are dwarfed by the overall need for more investment here.

14. Reeves, "The Measure of a Nation," 23.

15. See, e.g., John Rawls, *A Theory of Justice* (Cambridge: The Belknap Press, 1971), 73. Other philosophers have suggested that Rawls did not always apply his definition consistently, and indeed

have questioned the usefulness of Rawls's construction in its entirety. Richard J. Arneson, "Equality of Opportunity," in *Stanford Encyclopedia of Philosophy* (2015), 20–28, https://plato.stanford.edu. Yet others have rushed to Rawls's defense. Lars Lindblom, "In Defense of Rawlsian Fair Equality of Opportunity," *Philosophical Papers* 47, no. 2 (2018): 235–263.

16. T. M. Scanlon, *Why Does Inequality Matter?* (Oxford: Oxford University Press, 2018).

17. Notwithstanding its importance, I do not fully develop in this book the theme of America as a land of opportunity. My principal focus is on the abundant evidence for the toll that existential adverse fortuities and ill health take on the lives of citizens, and how the principles of insurance can serve as useful instruments for deciding how much we can do, and how we best can pay for it. For that reason, public infrastructure investment is addressed only in passing. Kleinbard, *We Are Better Than This* discusses this in some detail.

18. Jason Furman and Lawrence H. Summers, "Who's Afraid of Budget Deficits," *Foreign Affairs* 98, no. 2 (March/April 2019): 82–94; Jason Furman and Lawrence H. Summers, "Further Thinking on the Costs and Benefits of Deficits," Peterson Institute of International Economics, April 23, 2019, http://larrysummers.com/2019/04/23/further-thinking-on-the-costs-and-benefits-of-deficits.

19. Lily Batchelder, "Leveling the Playing Field between Inherited Income and Income from Work through an Inheritance Tax," in *Tackling the Tax Code: Efficient and Equitable Ways to Raise Revenue*, ed. Jay Shambaugh and Ryan Nunn (Washington, DC: The Hamilton Project, 2020), 43–88. See Chapter 3 for more discussion.

20. Congressional Budget Office, *The 2018 Long-Term Budget Outlook*, June 2018, Table 1, https://www.cbo.gov/system/files/2018-06/53919-2018ltbo.pdf.

21. A broad, metaphorical view of insurance as a framework for social policy blends imperceptibly into the direct case for public investment. For example, investments in public infrastructure generate high financial returns, more than large enough given our low base to justify much greater commitment to public infrastructure. This point does not need any subtle metaphorical reasoning to justify itself. If we add to these investments the idea that the resulting job opportunities will be made more available to all, through public technical training and sponsorship of apprenticing programs, then this complementary thought becomes the kind of investment in human capital that I argue lies at the heart of instantiating equality of opportunity and that I identify through my concept of existential adverse fortuities.

In the end, it does not matter whether good ideas win out because they are labeled financially sensible public investments or a metaphorical insurance response to existential bad luck. In this book I emphasize the theme of insurance, because it fits so neatly with my central inquiry into how we should respond to the presence of brute luck in our lives, and because it is a subtler topic than is investment and therefore worthy of closer examination, but many of the recommendations I describe as metaphorical insurance also could be justified on the straightforward basis that they make wonderful investments, both as a financial and social matter. What matters is to convince people that brute luck is as important a force in our lives as is gravity.

CHAPTER 2

1. *Petrarch's Remedies for Fortune Fair and Foul: A Modern English Translation of "De Remediis Utriusque Fortunae," With a Commentary*, ed. and trans. Conrad H. Rawski (Bloomington: Indiana University Press, 1991), vol. 1, 6.

2. See infra, note 4.

3. Carolyn L. Hafer and Alicia N. Rubel, "The Why and the How of Defending Belief in a Just World," in *Advances in Experimental Social Psychology* 51 (2015), chap. 2, 41–96.

4. Melvin J. Lerner, *The Belief in a Just World: A Fundamental Delusion* (New York: Plenum Press, 1980).

5. Melvin J. Lerner and Susan Clayton, *Justice and Self-Interest: Two Fundamental Motives* (New York: Cambridge University Press, 2011).

6. Leo Montada, "Doing Justice to the Justice Motive," in *The Justice Motive in Everyday Life*, eds. Michael Ross and Dale T. Miller (New York: Cambridge University Press, 2002), 41–62, is a convincing summary of the justice motive literature, and its operation as a fundamental motivation in people's responses to life situations.

7. One interesting aspect of justice motive theory is how positively sweet the basic story is. As an outsider to academic social psychology, I would have guessed that the origins story for the justice motive theory would have emphasized a child's deep-seated attachment to magical thinking, along with the existential terror experienced when the child realizes that he cannot control everything in his environment. (Alternatively, perhaps everyone but me skipped over that stage.)

8. Melvin J. Lerner, "The Justice Motive: Some Hypotheses as to Its Origins and Forms," *Journal of Personality* 45, no. 1 (1977): 1–52.

9. Lerner and Clayton, *Justice and Self-Interest: Two Fundamental Motives*, 26–31.

10. Many of the papers cited in the text conclude that individuals apply their Beliefs in a Just World differently to different worlds (the personal versus others, for example). John Maltby, Liza Day, Poonam Gill, Ann Colley, and Alex M. Wood, "Beliefs around Luck: Confirming the Empirical Conceptualization of Beliefs around Luck and the Development of the Darke and Freedman Beliefs around Luck Scale," *Personality and Individual Differences* 45 (2008): 655–660, explore the different dimensions of attitudes toward personal luck in general.

11. Dale T. Miller and Michael Ross, "Self-Serving Biases in the Attribution of Causality: Fact or Fiction?," *Psychological Bulletin* 82, no. 2 (1975): 213–225.

12. Two recent (and somewhat conflicting) reviews of the literature include John H. Ellard, Annelie Harvey, and Mitchell J. Callan, "The Justice Motive: History, Theory, and Research," in *Handbook of Social Justice Theory and Research*, ed. C. Sabbagh and M. Schmitt (New York: Springer Publishing, 2016), chap. 7; Carolyn L. Hafer and Robbie Sutton, "Belief in a Just World," in ibid., chap. 8. Earlier reviews include Claudia Dalbert and Matthias Donat, "Belief in a Just World," in *International Encyclopedia of the Social and Behavioral Sciences*, 2nd ed., vol. 2 (Oxford: Elsevier, 2015), chap. 2; Carolyn L. Hafer and Becky L. Choma, "Belief in a Just World, Perceived Fairness, and Justification of the Status Quo," in *Social and Psychological Bases of Ideology and System Justification*, ed. John T. Jost, Aaron C. Kay, and Hulda Thorisdottir (New York: Oxford University Press, 2009), chap. 5; Carolyn L. Hafer and Laurent Bègue, "Experimental Research on Just-World Theory: Problems, Developments, and Future Challenges," *Psychological Bulletin* 131, no. 1 (2005): 128–167; and Melvin J. Lerner and Dale T. Miller, "Just World Research and the Attribution Process: Looking Back and Ahead," *Psychological Bulletin* 85, no. 1 (1978): 1030–1051.

13. Melvin J. Lerner, "Evaluation of Performance as a Function of Performer's Reward and Attractiveness," *Journal of Personality and Social Psychology* 1, no. 4 (1965): 355–360.

14. Zick Rubin and Letitia Anne Peplau, "Belief in a Just World and Reactions to Another's Lot: A Study of Participants in the National Draft Lottery," *Journal of Social Issues* 29, no. 4 (fall 1973): 73–93.

15. Zick Rubin and Letitia Anne Peplau, "Who Believes in a Just World?," *Journal of Social Issues* 31, no. 3 (summer 1975): 65–89 (relating different reactions to the story of Job).

16. Lerner and Clayton, *Justice and Self-Interest: Two Fundamental Motives*, 125–126, and studies cited therein.

17. Ibid., 45.

18. Miro Zuckerman, "Belief in a Just World and Altruistic Behavior," *Journal of Personality and Social Psychology* 31 (1975): 972–976.

19. Rubin and Peplau, "Belief in a Just World and Reactions to Another's Lot," 74.

20. Kevin B. Smith, "Seeing Justice in Poverty: The Belief in a Just World and Ideas about Inequalities," *Sociological Spectrum* 5 (1985): 17–29. In later work, Smith reached similar conclusions about the cognitive "metatheory" of individualism (successful people work hard, have good habits, etc., while low-income individuals must exhibit the opposite qualities) as the most widespread explanation for Americans' attitudes toward wealth and poverty. Kevin B. Smith, "Rags, Riches, and Bootstraps: Beliefs about the Causes of Wealth and Poverty," *Sociological Quarterly* 30, no. 1 (1989): 93–107.

21. Lauren D. Appelbaum, Mary Clare Lennon, and J. Lawrence Aber, "When Effort Is Threatening: The Influence of the Belief in a Just World on Americans' Attitudes towards Antipoverty Policy," *Political Psychology* 27, no. 3 (2006): 387–402.

22. Jonathan J. B. Mijs, "The Paradox of Inequality: Income Inequality and Belief in Meritocracy Go Hand in Hand," *Socio-Economic Review*, January 2019, mwy051, https://doi.org/10.1093/ser/mwy051, 1–29, at 23.

23. Matthew Weinzierl, "Popular Acceptance of Inequality Due to Innate Brute Luck and Support for Classical Benefit-Based Taxation," *Journal of Public Economics* 155 (November 2017): 54–63.

24. Ingvild Almås, Alexander Cappelen, and Bertil Tungodden, "Cutthroat Capitalism versus Cuddly Socialism: Are Americans More Meritocratic and Efficiency-Seeking than Scandinavians?" *NHH Dept. of Economics Discussion Paper No. 4/2019* (February 27, 2019), https://ssrn.com/abstract=3343315.

25. Yasch Mounk, *The Age of Responsibility: Luck, Choice, and the Welfare State* (Cambridge, MA: Harvard University Press, 2017).

26. Mounk, *The Age of Responsibility*, 85.

27. Mounk, *The Age of Responsibility*, 93.

28. https://fm.cnbc.com/applications/cnbc.com/resources/editorialfiles/2019/10/31/CoopermanLetter.pdf.

29. "Here's the Angry 'Class Warfare' Letter That Hedge Fund Manager Leon Cooperman Sent to Obama," *Business Insider*, October 4, 2012, https://www.businessinsider.com/here-is-the-full-text-of-leon-coopermans-letter-to-president-obama-2012-10.

30. "Cooperman's Lawyer Says He Faced Parallel Criminal Inquiry," *Bloomberg News* (February 7, 2017), https://www.bloomberg.com/news/articles/2017-02-07/leon-cooperman-s-lawyer-says-he-faced-parallel-criminal-inquiry.

31. https://en.wikipedia.org/wiki/Leon_Cooperman.

32. Gerard J. Tellis, "The Paradox of Superstars," *The Hill*, August 27, 2019, https://thehill.com/opinion/technology/458819-the-paradox-of-superstars.

33. Adam Smith, *The Theory of Moral Sentiments*, part I, sec. III, chap. III.

CHAPTER 3

1. "Government-subsidized" student loans for higher education are repaid from a student's earnings, and thus ultimately from private sources. The extent of any subsidy in the interest rates charged is itself a controversial topic. To say that private lenders would charge more does not answer the question. The private market for student loans is really an example of an unavoidable market failure, because private lenders cannot obtain a mortgage over human beings.

2. Gabriel Zucman and Emmanuel Saez, "How to Tax Our Way Back to Justice," *New York Times*, October. 11, 2019, https://www.nytimes.com/2019/10/11/opinion/sunday/wealth-income-tax-rate. html; Daniel Shaviro, "Book Review of Kleinbard, We Are Better Than This: How Government Should Spend Our Money," *National Tax Journal* 68 (September 2015): 681–688.

3. OECD, *OECD Income Distribution Database: Poverty Rate after Taxes and Transfers, Poverty Line 50%*, September 10, 2019, http://www.oecd.org/social/income-distribution-database.htm.

4. Thomas Piketty, *Capital in the Twenty-First Century* (Cambridge, MA: Harvard University Press, 2014).

5. This last point has been summarized as the claim that R => G. In words rather than symbols, the claim is that the financial return on assets exceeds the national growth rate. This has been one of Piketty's most hotly contested claims. For a recent article reaching the same conclusion, see Òscar Jordà et al., "The Rate of Return of Everything, 1870–2015," *Federal Reserve Bank of San Francisco Working Paper 2017-25* (December 2017), http://www.frbsf.org/economic-research/publications/working-papers/2017/25. Their conclusions make Piketty's concerns all the more urgent.

6. If you are such a reader, see Fatih Guvenen and Greg Kaplan, "Top Income Inequality in the 21st Century: Some Cautionary Notes," *Federal Reserve Bank of Minneapolis Quarterly Review* 38, no. 1 (2017): 2–15; Kleinbard, *We Are Better Than This*, 102–126.

7. Martin Wolf, "Donald Trump's Boom Will Prove to Be Hot Air," *Financial Times*, July 9, 2019, https://www.ft.com/content/5a778300-a222-11e9-974c-ad1c6ab5efd1.

8. Martha Ross and Nicole Bateman, "Meet the Low-Wage Workforce," Metropolitan Policy Program at Brookings Institution, November 2019, https://www.brookings.edu/research/meet-the-low-wage-workforce.

9. Daniel Alpert, Jeffrey Ferry, Robert C. Hockett, and Amir Khaleghi, "The US Private Sector Job Quality Index," Cornell Law School, Jack G. Clarke Program on the Law and Regulation of Financial Institutions and Markets, November 2019, https://www.jobqualityindex.com.

10. Kleinbard, *We Are Better Than This*, 116–123.

11. Congressional Budget Office, *The Distribution of Household Income, 2014*, March 2018, 37, https://www.cbo.gov/publication/53597.

12. Raj Chetty et al., "The Fading American Dream: Trends in Absolute Income Mobility since 1940," *Science*, issue 6336 (April 2017): 398–406.

13. US Bureau of Economic Analysis, Federal Reserve Bank of St. Louis, *Real Gross Domestic Product per Capita*, https://fred.stlouisfed.org/series/A939RX0Q048SBEA. Remember here that Figure 3.2 covered a shorter time period (from 1984 through 2018).

14. Chetty et al., "The Fading American Dream," 398–406. If you are a data nerd, you might explain some of it by the fact that employer-provided healthcare does not show up in employee "earnings," but the very rapid growth of this item, which presumably came at the expense of cash wages, is a phenomenon only of the last fifteen years or so.

15. Chetty et al., "The Fading American Dream." See the section "Income Inequality in a Nutshell" later in this chapter. Chetty et al.'s research on intergenerational mobility shows roughly the same results whether looking at pretax earnings or after-tax/after-transfer earnings.

16. Thomas Piketty, Emmanuel Saez, and Gabriel Zucman, "Distributional Diversity in the National Accounts: Simplified Distributional National Accounts," *AEA Papers and Proceedings* 109 (May 2019): 289–295, https://doi.org/10.1257/pandp.20191035.

17. For a recent example of such wrangling, see Stephen J. Rose, *How Different Studies Measure Income Inequality in the US: Piketty and Company Are Not the Only Game in Town* (Washington, DC: Urban Institute, 2018). I do not agree with many of this author's conclusions, but it gives a flavor of the swarm of angry bees phenomenon.

18. One would expect each of these measures to translate directly to the other, but for technical reasons some researchers define the members of these two top 1 percent clubs differently. One of the reasons that I emphasize the work of Piketty, Saez, and Zucman in this chapter is that they use a consistent definition. Piketty, Saez, and Zucman, "Distributional Diversity in the National Accounts: Simplified Distributional National Accounts."

19. One metric that the CBO likes but that I find misleading is what the CBO calls "income before transfers and taxes." This in fact includes Social Security and Medicare benefits as income, but it does not take into account the taxes necessary to fund those benefits. Only means-tested transfers are excluded from the income side of the ledger. These benefits are not dispersed from heaven. All government benefits must be funded through taxes; it therefore is very odd to promote this halfway house of a measure, which includes the benefits received from government but ignores the taxes required to pay for them.

The CBO regrettably promotes this metric in its latest presentations on income inequality. A cynic might suggest that it does so because it reduces apparent inequality at any point in time, since Social Security benefits are a substantial part of the income base (as defined here) for lower-income Americans, and in turn are funded by regressive taxes (ignored in this metric).

Even "market income" is a tricky concept. For example, the CBO methodology does not include unrealized capital gains, so that Mark Zuckerberg appears not much different from a successful law firm partner in the data, but it does include a reduction for individuals' share of corporate taxes. Patrick Driessen, a public finance economist and former senior revenue estimator for Congress's Joint Committee on Taxation, has written persuasively that these data greatly understate the relative gains of the top 1 percent. Patrick Driessen, "Corporate Tax Fate May Hinge on Modeling Omission," *Tax Notes* 145 (December 2014): 1043; Patrick Driessen, "The Brookings Top Tax Rate Ruckus and Other Odd Inequality Doings," *Tax Notes* 149 (November 2015): 1071.

20. Congressional Budget Office, *The Distribution of Household Income, 2016* (July 2019), https://www.cbo.gov/publication/55413.

21. 2016 was actually a bit of a downmarket year: the gaps described in the text actually were more dramatic in the comparable 2015 study.

22. All these sorts of distribution studies track slices of each year's income distributions, not the same group of individuals over time. The composition of the top 1 percent, for example, changes every year. What this chart conveys is that those fortunate enough to be in the top 1 percent of the after-tax/after-transfers distribution in 2015 earned 342 percent more (that is, 242 percent in growth) than did a different group of individuals comprising the top 1 percent in 1979.

23. The CBO's measure of "income before transfers and taxes" sounds the same as "market income," but it is not. See Chetty et al., "The Fading American Dream," 398–406.

24. Nothing in this area is easy. The text ranks market income performance by households by reference to their market incomes. That sounds tautological, but the CBO ranks market incomes by reference to their baseline ranking of "income before transfers and taxes." A household might be in the 81st percentile by one measure, but the 79th by the other; this rearrangement in turn affects averages. Basically, the top 1 percent are unaffected by this methodological difference; the middle three quintiles would all post worse market income performance over time if they were ranked by their positions in the baseline ranking of income before transfers and taxes.

25. If it makes you feel better about your own performance, the entry point into the top 1 percent club is much lower than the average of all the incomes in that club. In 2016, a two-person household needed about $546,000 in income to gain admittance. (On top of every other methodological issue, the CBO adjusts household incomes by household size, to recognize at least roughly that a four-person household, for example, requires more income than does a two-person household to enjoy the same standard of living.)

26. Kleinbard, *We Are Better Than This*, chap. 7.

27. Kimberly Clausing and Edward Kleinbard, "Whatever Trump Gave You in Tax Cuts He's Taking Away with His Trade War," *Los Angeles Times*, June 5, 2019, https://www.latimes.com/opinion/op-ed/la-oe-clausing-kleinbard-trump-tax-tariff-swindle-20190605-story.html.

28. Katherine Clarke, "Billionaire Ken Griffin Buys America's Most Expensive Home for $238 Million," *Wall Street Journal*, January 23, 2019, https://www.wsj.com/articles/billionaire-ken-griffin-buys-americas-most-expensive-home-for-238-million-11548271301?mod=hp_lead_pos10.

29. Thomas Piketty, Emmanuel Saez, and Gabriel Zucman, "Distributional National Accounts: Methods and Estimates for the United States," *Quarterly Journal of Economics* (2018): 1–57. See also Thomas Piketty, Emmanuel Saez, and Gabriel Zucman, "Distributional Diversity in the National Accounts Simplified Distributional National Accounts." This last paper offers some explanations for why the work of two other well-regarded researchers, Gerald Auten and David Splinter, comes to much less dramatic conclusions for the growth in top 1 percent income shares. Gerald Auten and David Splinter, "Top 1 Percent Income Shares: Comparing Estimates Using Tax Data," *American Economic Association, AEA Papers and Proceedings* 109 (May 2019): 307–311.

30. https://wid.world.

31. PS&Z and the World Inequality Database include pension payments (both private and Social Security) in their definition of "pretax" income. It thus is kinder to the bottom 50 percent than would be a figure tracking only market incomes.

32. Piketty and Zucman describe some of the US data limitations bedeviling researchers: only a few thousand estate tax returns are filed annually (and even those are obscured by elaborate tax planning), lifetime gifts often are unreported, and self-reported estimates of wealth in response to government surveys (for example, the Survey of Consumer Finances) are systematically downward-biased. Thomas Piketty and Gabriel Zucman, "Wealth and Inheritance in the Long Run," *Handbook of Income Distribution*, ed. Anthony B. Atkinson and François Bourguignon (Oxford: North-Holland Publications, 2015), vol. 2B, 1303, 1342. For these reasons, the authors essentially decline to provide an estimate for the United States. Ibid., 1326, fig. 15.16.

Estate tax data would seem ideally suited to estimating the share of wealth held by the living that was received by gift or bequest. Relying principally on estate tax data, for example, Lena Edlund and Wojciech Kopczuk find that the share of inherited wealth as a fraction of total household wealth peaked in the 1970s, and has since declined. Lena Edlund and Wojciech Kopczuk, "Women, Wealth, and Mobility," *American Economic Review* 99 (March 2009): 146, 173. See also Wojciech Kopczuk and Emmanuel Saez, "Top Wealth Shares in the United States, 1916–2000: Evidence from Estate Tax Returns," *National Tax Journal* 57 (March 2004): 445, 468. ("[T]he surge in top wages since the 1970s did not lead to a significant increase in top wealth holdings.") The conclusion of Edlund and Kopczuk rests in part on some gender distinctions that are susceptible to different inferences and, more important, on the parameters chosen to extrapolate from the population of decedents in a year to the population of the living in that year (for example, whether one can assume that the life expectancy of the rich tracks that of low- or median-wealth households). Edlund and Kopczuk, "Women, Wealth, and Mobility," 146–147.

As Kopczuk acknowledges, estate tax data can be confounded by tax planning and evasion, but he observes that "[a]t the same time, this phenomenon is not new, and there is no clear argument for why estate tax avoidance would have increased over time." Wojciech Kopczuk, "What Do We Know about the Evolution of Top Wealth Shares in the United States?," *Journal of Economic Perspectives* 29 (winter 2015): 47, 54. I resist the claim that the magnitude of estate tax avoidance can be assumed to be a constant over time without a great deal more work being done on the evolution of estate tax planning. See, in this regard, Eric Kades, "Of Piketty and Perpetuities: Dynastic Wealth in the Twenty-First Century (and Beyond)," *Boston College Law Review* 60 (2019): 145, https://lawdigitalcommons.bc.edu/bclr/vol60/iss1/4.

Moreover, the minimum size of an estate subject to the estate tax increased dramatically over the last several years (from $5 million in 2012 to about $11.5 million at the time of this article's publication), the top estate tax rate has been scaled back (from 55 percent in 2002 to 40 percent at the time of this article's publication), and the estate tax itself was briefly, optionally repealed for 2010—all of which surely had some effect on administrative enforcement and rulemaking efforts. Kopczuk relies on one paper from the 1970s by an economist for the proposition that estate tax planning was prevalent then, but he makes no effort to inquire about changing tax avoidance technologies or the magnitude (as opposed to the prevalence) of the savings achieved through those strategies. Kopczuk, "What Do We Know about the Evolution of Top Wealth Shares in the United States?," 54.

"Perpetual dynasty trusts" are but one example of novel estate tax planning techniques with far-reaching consequences. It is odd that economists seem reluctant to survey estate tax lawyers and other professionals on developments in estate tax avoidance technologies to better calibrate their assumptions here. Estate tax data thus seem to serve as an effective floor on the measure of estate and gift wealth transmission, but a very indeterminate ceiling.

33. Laura Feiveson and John Sabelhaus, "How Does Intergenerational Wealth Transmission Affect Wealth Concentration?," *FEDS Notes*, Board of Governors of the Federal Reserve System (June 2018), https://doi.org/10.17016/2380-7172.2209: "We find a marked increase in wealth concentration over the last 30 years that is consistent with prior studies, but with somewhat lower overall wealth concentration than measured in other data sets."

34. Congressional Budget Office, *Trends in Family Wealth, 1989 to 2013*, August 18, 2016, 1, https://www.cbo.gov/publication/51846.

35. A leading alternative perspective is afforded by Bricker et al., "Measuring Income and Wealth at the Top Using Administrative and Survey Data," *Brookings Papers on Economic Activity* (spring 2016): 306, https://www.brookings.edu/wp-content/uploads/2016/03/brickertextspring16bpea.pdf.

In my reading, the Bricker et al. paper does not contradict the work of PS&Z here so much as temper it. Indeed, Bricker and his colleagues summarized the results reached by the different methodologies by observing that "[Our preferred] estimates agree with the widely held view that inequality, at least as reflected in the top wealth and income shares, has been rising in recent decades. However, the levels and trends in our preferred top share estimates are more muted than those in [P&S]." That's how economists proceed—sussing out underdeveloped assumptions in each other's work and looking for better data sets. To my mind, the Bricker paper relies much too heavily for my tastes on Federal Reserve Survey of Consumer Finances data, which rely on individual survey participants to divulge to the Fed their income and wealth. For many reasons the Survey of Consumer Finance data are weakest at the top of the income and wealth distributions.

36. Gabriel Zucman, "Global Wealth Inequality," *Annual Review of Economics* 11 (2019): 109–138, https://www.annualreviews.org/doi/10.1146/annurev-economics-080218-025852.

37. Michael Batty et al., *Introducing the Distributional Financial Accounts of the United States*, Board of Governors of the Federal Reserve System, Finance and Economics Discussion Series 2019-017, https://doi.org/10.17016/FEDS.2019.017; Jess Benhabib, Alberto Bisin, and Mi Luo, "Wealth Distribution and Social Mobility in the US: A Quantitative Approach," *American Economic Review* 109, no. 5 (May 2019): 1623–1647.

38. For example, Noah Smith, "There's Value in Trying a Wealth Tax," *Bloomberg News*, July 10, 2019, https://www.bloomberg.com/opinion/articles/2019-07-10/wealth-tax-is-worth-trying-to-raise-revenue-and-lower-inequality; Robert Frank, "How Much Would a Wealth Tax Really Raise?: Dueling Economists Reflect New Split in Democratic Party," *CNBC*, July 10, 2019, https://www.cnbc.com/2019/07/10/dueling-economists-debate-how-much-a-wealth-tax-would-raise.html.

39. Batty et al., *Introducing the Distributional Financial Accounts of the United States*.

40. Ibid., 26.

41. Facundo Alvaredo et al., *World Inequality Report 2018: World Inequality Lab*, 2018, 216–217, https://wir2018.wid.world/. As an aside, the Fed's DFA methodology produces results fairly close (although a "more equitable" overall distribution) to those of the WID. See Batty et al., *Introducing the Distributional Financial Accounts of the United States*, 28–31.

42. Board of Governors of the Federal Reserve System, *Report on the Economic Well-Being of US Households in 2018*, May 2019, 21–23, https://www.federalreserve.gov/publications/files/2018-report-economic-well-being-us-households-201905.pdf. One critic has observed that this is misleading, in that many of those who did not have an unallocated $400 to use to pay in this manner would expect to incur credit card debt to pay the bill. But the question is not, will a $400 expense bankrupt 40 percent of Americans, but rather, do such Americans have a financial cushion, a rainy-day fund, cash in the bank—whatever you want to call it—to handle a modest bill like this?

43. Feiveson and Sabelhaus, "How Does Intergenerational Wealth Transmission Affect Wealth Concentration?"

44. Lily Batchelder, "Leveling the Playing Field between Inherited Income and Income from Work through an Inheritance Tax," in *Tackling the Tax Code: Efficient and Equitable Ways to Raise Revenue*, ed. Jay Shambaugh and Ryan Nunn (Washington, DC: The Hamilton Project, 2020), 43–88.

45. This is roughly comparable to the results reached in Piketty, *Capital in the Twenty-First Century* and in Piketty, Thomas, and Zucman, "Wealth and Inheritance in the Long Run." Batchelder, "Leveling the Playing Field between Inherited Income and Income from Work through an Inheritance Tax," suggests a consensus view of 40 percent of national wealth.

46. See supra, note 43. In a 2013 study, Steven Kaplan and Joshua Rauh explored the sources of wealth among the Forbes 400 list of the wealthiest individuals in the United States in each decade from 1982 to 2011. Steven N. Kaplan and Joshua D. Rauh, *Family*, "Education, and Sources of Wealth among the Richest Americans, 1982–2012", *American Economic Review* 103 (May 2013): 158. Using public information to obtain biographical data, they coded the Forbes 400 individuals as having grown up in households that were wealthy, had some wealth, or had little to no wealth. For example, Bill Gates, whose father was a founding partner at a large and successful law firm, was coded as having grown up in a household with "some" wealth. Kaplan and Rauh essentially found that the percentage of Forbes 400 members who had grown up with little or no wealth remained relatively constant over time, at about 20 percent, but that there was a pronounced shift within the other two categories, with Forbes 400 members whose wealth was inherited (that is, grew up in a "wealthy" household) falling from 60 percent of the Forbes 400 in 1982 to 32 percent in 2011.

The Kaplan and Rauh paper has been cited in some popular media as proving that wealth inequality in the United States has diminished over time, or that the United States is "part of a worldwide rise of the self-made among the world's super rich." But it takes a narrow construction of "self-made" to conclude that individuals born into significant wealth owe their success solely to their personal moxie.

I discuss my objections to Kaplan and Rauh's paper in Edward Kleinbard, "Capital Taxation in an Age of Inequality," *Southern California Law Review* 90 (May 2017): 139–142. I also argue there that if the object of attention is wealth concentration, then one must switch focus from individuals or households to families.

CHAPTER 4

1. In this respect I completely reject the implications in the work of Casey Mulligan that high-earning adults have abilities greater than the median, and that these abilities on balance are passed to their children, so that stickiness in relative economic mobility reflects some sort of genetic determinism at work. Song Han and Casey B. Mulligan, "Human Capital, Heterogeneity and Estimated Degrees of Intergenerational Mobility," *Economic Journal* 111, issue 470 (December 2001): 207–243. In fact, genetics teaches us that inheritable characteristics tend to revert to the mean from one generation to the next; otherwise the distant descendants of long-dead tall people would by now reach the sky.

Samuel Bowles and Herbert Gintis, "The Inheritance of Inequality," *Journal of Economic Perspectives* 16, no. 3 (summer 2002): 3–30, cover somewhat similar ground. They find that while some earnings-enhancing traits might be genetically transmitted, IQ in particular is not one of them. "Wealth, race and schooling are important to the inheritance of economic status, but IQ is not a major contributor, and . . . the genetic transmission of IQ is even less important." Their emphasis on wealth and schooling map directly onto the themes of this book. Chapter 6 returns to the topic of why race falls outside my scope in this book (simply that it is a topic that deserves a book of its own).

2. Raj Chetty, Nathaniel Hendren, Patrick Kline, Emmanuel Saez, and Nicholas Turner, "Is the United States Still a Land of Opportunity?: Recent Trends in Intergenerational Mobility," *American Economic Review* 104, no. 5 (May 2014): 141–147.

3. Florencia Torche, "Analyses of Intergenerational Mobility: An Interdisciplinary Review," *Annals of the American Academy of Political and Social Science* 657, issue 1 (January 2015): 37–61.

4. CORDIS, "New Evidence That Humans Choose Their Partners through Assortative Mating," PHYS.org, last modified January 13, 2017, https://phys.org/news/2017-01-evidence-humans-partners-assortative.html.

5. Michael Hout, "A Summary of What We Know about Social Mobility," *Annals of the American Academy of Political and Social Science* 657, issue 1 (January 2015): 27–36.

6. Miles Corak, "Inequality from Generation to Generation: The United States in Comparison," IZA Discussion Paper 9929, *Forschungsinstitut zur Zukunft der Arbeit (Institute for the Study of Labor)* (May 2016), http://ftp.iza.org/dp9929.pdf. Elasticity can also be expressed in relation to income ranks, as "elasticity in rankings."

7. Ibid.

8. Gary Solon, "Intergenerational Transmission of Income Inequality: What Do We Know?," *Focus* 33, no. 2 (spring/summer 2017): 3–5.

9. To the same effect, see Jo Blanden, "Cross-National Rankings of Intergenerational Mobility: A Comparison of Approaches from Economics and Sociology," *Journal of Economic Surveys* 27, no. 1 (2014): 38–73.

10. Corak, "Inequality from Generation to Generation."

11. OECD, *A Broken Social Elevator?: How to Promote Social Mobility* (Paris: OECD Publishing, 2018).

12. Chetty, et al, "Is the United States Still a Land of Opportunity?" The paper has been criticized for the extensive shortcuts and assumptions required to generate predictive data on how children entering the workforce today (in their early twenties) will perform ten or more years in the future. Tim Smeeding, "Inequality and Intergenerational Mobility: Looking Ahead, Not Behind," http://www.uni.lu/content/download/78286/973770/version/2/file/Inequality+and+Intergenerational+Mobility+Slides_20150226.pdf.

13. Chetty, et al., "Is the United States Still a Land of Opportunity?"

14. Raj Chetty, John N. Freidman, Nathaniel Hendren, Maggies R. Jones and Sonya R. Porter, "The Opportunity Atlas: Mapping the Childhood Roots of Social Mobility," *The National Bureau of Economic Research* Working Paper no. 25147 (October 2018), https://opportunityinsights.org/paper/the-opportunity-atlas/. The Atlas itself is at https://www.opportunityatlas.org/. In collaboration with the Chetty group, the US Census Bureau recently established a comprehensive "Opportunity Atlas" website, https://www.census.gov/programs-surveys/ces/data/analysis-visualization-tools/opportunity-atlas.html.

15. Kerry Anne McGeary, *Data Maps the Impact of Where a Child Grows Up*, Robert Wood Johnson Foundation, January 9, 2019, https://www.rwjf.org/en/blog/2019/01/data-maps-the-lifelong-impact-of-where-a-child-grows-up.html.

16. Chetty et al., "The Opportunity Atlas," 4.

CHAPTER 5

1. *POP1 Child Population*, ChildStats.gov, https://www.childstats.gov/americaschildren/tables/pop1.asp.

2. I ignore a third category termed "total factor productivity," which is a catch-all for how labor and capital interact in more or less efficient ways. Total factor productivity is the economist's way of explaining why two firms with identical labor and capital inputs might have very different incomes. It is his way of saying, "damned if I know."

3. In an important paper discussed later in this chapter, the irrepressible economist Raj Chetty and colleagues summed up the relationship between school quality and inequality:

[O]ur analysis raises the possibility that differences in school quality perpetuate income inequality. In the United States, higher-income families have access to better public schools on average because of property-tax finance. Using the class quality impacts reported herein, [two members of the team] estimate that *the intergenerational correlation of income* [i.e., the *inverse* of relative mobility, as discussed in Chapter 4] *would fall* [mobility would rise] *by roughly a third if all children attended schools of the same quality.* (Emphasis supplied)

Raj Chetty, John N. Friedman, Nathaniel Hilger, Emmanuel Saez, Diane Whitmore Schanzenbach, and Danny Yagan, "How Does Your Kindergarten Classroom Affect Your Earnings?: Evidence from Project Star," *Quarterly Journal of Economics* 126, no. 4 (November 2011): 1593–1660, 1658.

4. See National Center for Education Statistics, *Digest of Education Statistics 2017* (January 2018), chap. 5.

5. OECD, *Education at a Glance 2019: OECD Indicators* (Paris: OECD Publishing, 2019), tables A5.1a and A5.1b.

6. The OECD presentation is not without controversy. In any present value or internal rate of return calculation, one must choose a discount rate to bring future cash flows to present value. The lower the discount rate, the more valuable are future cash flows. The OECD uses a 2 percent discount rate, which is basically a government's risk-free borrowing rate. As applied here, it is as if a student were to say to herself that the alternative to going to college would be to invest the costs she avoided in government bonds. If one chose a rate of, say, 8 percent, then the returns to a US college graduate would be slashed by almost 80 percent. OECD, *Education at a Glance 2019*, 109.

More interestingly, the OECD calculations here ignore government-funded student loans. That is, when the OECD calculates the costs and benefits to a student from earning a college degree, the private cost to that student of a college education does not include the costs of any government-provided student loans that she might receive. The same is true on the other side of the ledger: for purposes of these calculations, but not for others, the OECD ignores government-provided student loans as an investment made by the public sector.

At first glance, and at second and third glance for that matter, this treatment seems bizarre. The OECD is uncharacteristically unhelpful in explaining its reasoning, but it seems to come down to two points. First, ignoring student loans means that the OECD can calculate one single internal rate of return on the private costs of college, rather than "leveraged" and "unleveraged" returns. Second, the OECD employs the same methodology for calculating the returns to the public sector from the investments made in tertiary education—that is, student loans are not treated as assets of the government earning a return.

From the point of view of society as a whole, the financial return to higher education is its incremental contribution to GDP. So long as one considers public universities, how that contribution to GDP is divided up between the student and the government is largely a political decision, not an economic one, because the two sum up to unity: more for the student (say, in grants rather than loans, or interest-free loans rather than market-rate loans) means less for the government, and vice versa. You can see this by looking at the OECD data on Chile, where one observes the highest private returns within the OECD, and among the lowest public returns—all driven by very low income tax rates on the incremental earnings of university graduates in Chile.

Ignoring student loans entirely thus does not distort the sum of the two sides, but it does affect the presentation of the returns captured by each side. Including student loans as costs to students and investments/income to government would get to the same sum total contribution to GDP, but it would alter the presentation as between the two sides of the transaction. This might not be very important when applied to other countries, where the total costs of a tertiary education are low and the interest rate charged either nil or close to the government borrowing rate, but as applied to a US student graduating with $100,000 in debt at 7 percent interest, the OECD approach certainly seems to overstate the private benefits of a college education. In a straightforward accounting sense, the US government in fact clears a large profit on student loans—the 7 percent or so interest it collects, net of defaults experienced by the government, still far exceeds the 2 percent or so cost to the government of funding those loans through Treasury borrowings. Certainly from the point of view of students and families, treating US government student loans as if they were commercial transactions would accord with their sense of reality.

See generally OECD, *OECD Handbook for Internationally Comparative Education Statistics 2018: Concepts, Standards, Definitions and Classifications* (Paris: OECD Publishing, 2018), sec. 4.5.

7. Mary Daly and Leila Bengali, "Is It Still Worth Going to College?," *Federal Reserve Bank of San Francisco Economic Letter 2014-13*, May 5, 2014, https://www.frbsf.org/economic-research/publications/economic-letter/2014/may/is-college-worth-it-education-tuition-wages/. The authors provide a downloadable calculator at http://www.frbsf.org/economic-research/files/tuitioncalculator.xlsx.

8. Government-provided student loans that are ignored on the private side of the ledger also are ignored as costs to (investments by) government. See note 6, supra. This again might make more intuitive sense in countries other than the United States.

9. James Heckman, Jorge Luis García, Duncan Ermini Leaf, and María José Prados, "Quantifying the Life-Cycle Benefits of a Prototypical Early Childhood Program," *Heckman*, May 2017, https://heckmanequation.org/resource/lifecycle-benefits-influential-early-childhood-program/.

10. Beth Ann Bovino and Jason Gold, "The Key to Unlocking US GDP Growth?: Women," *S&P Global Research* (2017), https://www.spglobal.com/_Media/Documents/03651.00_Women_at_Work_Doc.8.5x11-R4.pdf; Jodie Grunzberg, Ann Bovino, and Jason Gold, "Adding More Women to the US Workforce Could Send Global Stock Markets Soaring," *S&P Global Research* (2019), https://www.spglobal.com/en/research-insights/featured/adding-more-women-to-the-u-s-workforce-could-send-global-stock-markets-soaring.

11. Bovino and Gold, " "The Key to Unlocking US GDP Growth?: Women."

12. Mark Zandi and Sophia Koropeckyj, "Universal Child Care and Early Learning Act: Helping Families and the Economy," *Moody's Analytics* (February 2019), https://www.economy.com/mark-zandi/documents/2019-02-18-Child-Care-Act.pdf.

13. Halley Potter, "The Benefits of Universal Access in Pre-K and '3-K for All,'" *The Century Foundation*, April 2017, https://tcf.org/content/commentary/benefits-universal-access-pre-k-3-k/. It is not clear from the available descriptions whether Senator Elizabeth Warren's Universal Child Care and Early Learning Act contemplates as large a formal educational component as that contained in Universal 3-K proposals.

14. Anthony Lake and Margaret Chan, "Putting Science into Practice for Early Child Development," *The Lancet* 385, no. 9980 (May 9, 2015): 1816–1817.

15. OECD, *Starting Strong 2017: Key OECD Indicators on Early Childhood Education and Care* (Paris: OECD Publishing, 2017), 148–149.

16. Greg J. Duncan and Katherine Magnuson, "Investing in Preschool Programs," *Journal of Economic Perspectives* 27, no. 2 (spring 2013): 109–132. Duncan and Magnuson briefly review the operation of Head Start and early childhood programs, and then perform a meta-analysis (an analysis of prior studies) to get a better understanding of the payoffs to investment in early childhood education. Duncan and Magnuson also describe the programs analyzed by the Heckman team.

17. Timothy Bartik, *From Preschool to Prosperity: The Economic Payoff to Early Childhood Education* (Kalamazoo, MI: W. E. Upjohn Institute for Employment Research, 2014).

For those who remain unconvinced about the relevance of neuroscience but who are parents, I cannot help but offer an aside, taken from outside the ambit of early childhood education, but which should convince any doubter willing to look back on his or her child-rearing experience that the connections between the conclusions of neuroscience and life as it is lived are unassailable:

Neuroimaging of adolescents now shows us that the adolescent brain is far from mature, and undergoes extensive structural changes well past puberty. Adolescence is an extremely important period in terms of emotional development partly due to a surge of hormones in the brain; the still under-developed pre-frontal cortex among teenagers may be one explanation for their unstable behaviour. We have captured this combination of emotional immaturity and high cognitive potential in the phrase "high horsepower, poor steering."

OECD, *Understanding the Brain: The Birth of a Learning Science* (Paris: OECD Publishing, 2007), 14.

18. James Heckman and Stefano Mosso, "The Economics of Human Development and Social Mobility," *NBER Working Paper* No. 19925 (February 2014): 8, https://www.nber.org/papers/w19925.pdf.

19. OECD, *Understanding the Brain*, 173–174.

20. NCES, *Digest of Education Statistics: 2017*, chap. 2, table 202.10, https://nces.ed.gov/programs/digest/d17/ch_2.asp. Data in this area can be difficult to compare across different studies, at least in part because of the fluid boundary between early childhood childcare and more formal preschool programs.

21. Ibid., table 202.30.

22. New York City, for example, is attempting to roll out universal 3–K for its children, but may find itself constrained by financial pressures.

23. National Academy of Sciences, Engineering, and Medicine, *Transforming the Financing of Early Care and Education* (Washington, DC: The National Academies Press, 2018), https://doi.org/10.17226/24984.

24. Richard Wilkinson and Kate Pickett, *The Inner Level: How More Equal Societies Reduce Stress, Restore Sanity and Improve Everyone's Well-Being* (New York: Penguin Press, 2019), 174–175. Wilkinson and Pickett rely on UK studies; it might be hoped that the relatively recent rollout of universal 3–K there might ameliorate these findings.

25. Chetty et al., "How Does Your Kindergarten Classroom Affect Your Earnings?"

26. Sean F. Reardon and Ximena A. Portilla, "Recent Trends in Income, Racial, and Ethnic School Readiness Gaps at Kindergarten Entry," *AERA Open* 2, no. 3 (July–September 2016): 1–18.

27. Allison Friedman-Krauss, W. Steven Barnett, and Milagros Nores, *How Much Can High-Quality Universal Pre-K Reduce Achievement Gaps?*, Center for American Progress and National Institute for Early Education Research, April 2016, https://cdn.americanprogress.org/wp-content/uploads/2016/04/01115656/NIEER-AchievementGaps-report.pdf.

28. Technically, children from families whose incomes are a bit higher than that can enroll, if 100 percent of all children below the federal poverty line have enrolled.

29. W. Steven Barnett and Allison H. Friedman-Krauss, "The State(s) of Head Start, National Institute for Early Childhood Research," *National Institute for Early Education Research* (2015), http://nieer.org/wp-content/uploads/2016/12/HS_Full_Reduced.pdf.

30. Head Start is available for children whose families are at the federal poverty level at initial enrollment. A child is not kicked out of the program if her family's income rises above the federal poverty level as the child grows older.

31. Friedman-Krauss et al., *The State of Preschool 2018*, National Institute for Early Education Research, 2019, http://nieer.org/state-preschool-yearbooks/2018-2. The data presented at the outset of the subsection "The United States in Its Global Context" in this chapter included private as well as public programs.

32. Mill was tutored by his father, an educational zealot, with the expectation that the young boy would prove to be a genius. The child learned Greek starting at age three.

33. National Academies of Sciences, Engineering, and Medicine, *Transforming the Cost of Early Care and Education* (Washington, DC: The National Academies Press, 2018), chap. 6.

34. Ibid., 193.

35. Edward Kleinbard, "Congress' Worst Tax Idea Ever," *The Hill*, March 25, 2019, https://thehill.com/opinion/finance/434998-congress-worst-tax-idea-ever.

36. OECD, *Education at a Glance 2018*, Country Note: United States.

37. As discussed earlier, when making cross-country comparisons, data usually should be expressed as a percentage of GDP, or, where alternatively, through another adjustment mechanism called "purchasing power parity," which seeks to adjust market currency exchange rates to reflect the different costs of a standard bundle of consumer goods. Since US schools face (high) US cost structures, the percentage of GDP figure is a better approximation of relative investment than is the simple dollar number.

38. OECD, *Education at a Glance, 2018*, table C1.5.

39. C. Kirabo Jackson, Rucker C. Johnson, and Claudia Persico, "The Effects of School Spending on Educational and Economic Outcomes: Evidence from School Finance Reforms," *Quarterly Journal of Economics* 131, no. 1 (February 2016): 157–218, https://doi.org/10.1093/qje/qjv036.

40. The Education Law Center at Rutgers Graduate School of Education has published very interesting interstate equity comparisons across several margins. See, for example, Bruce D. Baker, Danielle Farrie, and David Sciarra, *Is School Funding Fair?: A National Report Card* (Newark, NJ: Education Law Center, 2018), https://edlawcenter.org/assets/files/pdfs/publications/Is_School_Funding_Fair_7th_Editi.pdf.

41. Julien Lafortune, Jesse Rothstein, and Diane Whitmore Schanzenbach, "School Finance Reform and the Distribution of Student Achievement," *American Economic Journal: Applied Economics* 10, no. 2 (2018): 1–26.

42. Jackson, Johnson, and Persico, "The Effects of School Spending on Educational and Economic Outcomes."

43. Daarel Burnette II, "States Show Striking Variations on Best Places to Bring Up a Child," *Education Week*, January 15, 2019, https://www.edweek.org/ew/articles/2019/01/16/states-show-striking-variations-on-best-places.html.

44. OECD, *Education at a Glance 2018*, Country Note: United States.

45. Ibid.

46. National Center for Education Statistics, "Fast Facts: Highest Enrollment," https://nces.ed.gov/fastfacts/display.asp?id=74.

47. Feiveson and Sabelhaus, "How Does Intergenerational Wealth Transmission Affect Wealth Concentration?"

48. National Center for Education Statistics, "Digest of Education Statistics: 2017," *National Center for Education Statistics*: chap. 5: Outcomes of Education, https://nces.ed.gov/programs/digest/d17/ch_5.asp.

49. National Center for Education Statistics, "Digest of Education Statistics: 2017," table 502.20, https://nces.ed.gov/programs/digest/d17/tables/dt17_502.20.asp?referrer=report.

50. The Hamilton Project, *Lifetime Earnings by Degree Type*, April 2017, http://www.hamiltonproject.org/charts/lifetime_earnings_by_degree_type.

51. Raj Chetty, John N. Friedman, Emmanuel Saez, Nicholas Turner, and Danny Yagan, "Mobility Report Cards: The Role of Colleges in Intergenerational Mobility," *NBER Working Paper* No. 23618 (July 2017), https://www.nber.org/papers/w23618.

52. Melissa Korn, "How Much Does Being a Legacy Help Your College Admissions Odds?," *Wall Street Journal*, July 9, 2018, https://www.wsj.com/articles/legacy-preferences-complicate-colleges-diversity-push-1531128601.

Admittedly, Harvard is at one end of the spectrum here. My alma mater, Brown University, is much more even-handed in its admissions policies—but then again, its endowment is almost exactly one-tenth that of Harvard's.

53. OECD, *Education at a Glance 2018*, table C2.2.

54. The Institute for College Access and Success, *Student Debt and the Class of 2017* (2018), 4, https://ticas.org/sites/default/files/pub_files/classof2017.pdf.

55. Melissa Korn, "Even at Top Colleges, Graduation Gaps Persist for Poor Students," *Wall Street Journal*, February 18, 2019, https://www.wsj.com/articles/even-at-top-colleges-graduation-gaps-persist-for-poor-students-11550491200.

56. OECD, *Education at a Glance 2018*, figure C3.1.

57. The Institute for College Access and Success, *Student Debt and the Class of 2017*, 1.

58. Ibid. For international comparisons that do not directly tie into these figures, see OECD, *Education at a Glance 2018*, figure C5.3.

59. "Repayment Plans," *Federal Student Aid*, US Department of Education, https://studentaid.ed.gov/sa/repay-loans/understand/plans.

60. The Institute for College Access and Success, *Student Debt and the Class of 2017*, 12.

61. "Student Loans in England: Financial Year 2017–18," *The Student Loans Company*, June 14, 2018, https://www.slc.co.uk/media/10022/slcspo12018.pdf.

62. OECD, *Education at a Glance 2018*, 298.

63. "Here's How Much the Average Student Loan Borrower Owes When They Graduate," *CNBC*, February 15, 2018, https://www.cnbc.com/2018/02/15/heres-how-much-the-average-student-loan-borrower-owes-when-they-graduate.html.

64. The Institute for College Access and Success, *Student Debt and the Class of 2017*, 5.

65. Michael Grinstein-Weiss et al., "Racial Disparities in Education Debt Burden among Low- and Moderate-Income Households," *Children and Youth Services Review* 65 (2016): 166–174.

66. Ibid.

67. Bernice Napach, "Parents Owe More in Student Loans Than Their Kids," *Think Advisor*, July 16, 2018, https://www.thinkadvisor.com/2018/07/16/parents-owe-more-in-student-loans-than-their-kids/.

68. OECD, *Education at a Glance 2018*, figure A5.1a.

CHAPTER 6

1. Peter Spufford, *Power and Profit: The Merchant in Medieval Europe* (London: Thames & Hudson, 2002), 30–34; Florence Edler de Roover, "Early Examples of Marine Insurance," *Journal of Economic History* 5, no. 2 (November 1945): 172–200; W. S. Holdsworth, "The Early History of the Contract of Insurance," *Columbia Law Review* 17, no. 2 (February 1917): 85–113.

2. Spufford, *Power and Profit: The Merchant in Medieval Europe*, 30–34; Edler de Roover, "Early Examples of Maritime Insurance," 188–189.

3. Giovanni Ceccarelli, "The Price for Risk-Taking: Marine Insurance and Probability Calculus in the Late Middle Ages," *Electronic Journal for History of Probability and Statistics* 3, no. 1 (2007).

4. George E. Rejda and Michael J. McNamara, *Principles of Risk Management and Insurance*, 13th ed. (Hoboken, NJ: Pearson Education, 2016), 40–42, 60–63; Emmett J. Vaughan and Therese Vaughan, *Fundamentals of Risk and Insurance*, 10th ed. (Hoboken, NJ: John Wiley and Sons, 2008), 34–40.

5. Edward Kleinbard, "Competitive Convergence in the Financial Services Markets," *Taxes—The Tax Magazine* 81, no. 3 (March 2003): 225–261.

6. Robert I. Mehr, *Fundamentals of Insurance* (Homewood, IL: Richard D. Irwin, 1986), 22.

7. Ibid., 25.

8. Rejda and McNamara, *Principles of Risk Management and Insurance*, 43.

9. Vaughan and Vaughan, *Fundamentals of Risk and Insurance*, 5.

10. Very confusingly, some old textbooks use "moral hazard" to cover cases of bad morals— that is, fraudulent behavior—and "morale hazard" to refer to cases where an insured might be less zealous about avoiding or mitigating loss than he would be if he still retained the risk of loss. "Morale hazard" has fallen into disuse as a term, and "moral hazard" has moved over to replace it.

11. Social Security and Medicare each are umbrella terms for several sub-programs. Thus, for example, Social Security covers the perils of outliving one's means (old-age benefits), the risk of losing a family breadwinner (survivors' benefits), and the risk of disability.

Medicare contains an incomprehensible mix of government programs and heavily regulated private insurance options, including Medicare Part A (hospital insurance), Part B (outpatient medical costs), Part D (prescription drugs), and some highly specialized plans. Part A is generally free to seniors; Part B is optional and requires the payment of a monthly premium, ranging from $135.50/month to $460.50/month, depending on income. Then, Part C allows individuals to opt out of the government-run plans and into regulated private insurance plans conforming to one of several standardized policy formats identifying cost and benefits, so that the prices charged by rival insurers can be directly compared. This is "Medicare Advantage." About 36 percent of Medicare beneficiaries opt into Medicare Part C. Because Medicare Part B leaves many medical expenses uncovered, there also is private insurance to cover the gap, hence "Medigap" plans. And so it goes, to the point that I suffer a recurring nightmare in which I am hustled in front of an expectant audience of incipient seniors and asked to extemporize on how to choose the right Medicare plan for each audience member's situation.

12. Vaughan and Vaughan, *Fundamentals of Risk and Insurance*, 48, n. 15.

13. Theodore R. Marmor, Jerry L. Mashaw, and John Pakutka, *Social Insurance: America's Neglected Heritage and Contested Future* (Thousand Oaks, CA: CQ Press, 2014), 217–218 (emphasis supplied).

14. Anthony B. Atkinson, "Social Insurance" (The Fifteenth Annual Lecture of the Geneva Association), *The Geneva Papers on Risk and Insurance Theory* 16, no. 2 (1991): 113–131.

15. Technically the Supplemental Nutrition Assistance Program is a mandatory program without a dedicated funding source; as a result, Congress must appropriate funds for it each year. Medicare Parts B and D also have no dedicated funding source, but their constitutive legislation requires that general tax revenues be transferred to those programs each year under specified formulas without annual appropriations.

16. Vaughan and Vaughan, *Fundamentals of Risk and Insurance*, 51.

17. To the same effect, two leading authors in the field describe the agenda of social insurance as an emphasis on *social adequacy* rather than *individual equity* (meaning, actually fair premiums and benefits). Rejda and McNamara, *Principles of Risk Management and Insurance*, 393.

18. Batty et al., "Introducing the Distributional Financial Accounts of the United States," 41.

19. Steven J. Davis, John Haltiwanger, Kyle Handley, Ben Lipsius, Josh Lerner, and Javier Miranda, "The Economic Effects of Private Equity Buyouts," *Becker Friedman Institute for Economics at the University of Chicago*, Working Paper No. 2019-122 (October 2019), https://bfi.uchicago.edu/wp-content/uploads/BFI_WP_2019122.pdf. The paper's conclusions are complex and subtle; the text summarizes the aggregate "headline" results.

20. Marmor, Mashaw, and Pakutka, *Social Insurance*, 218.

21. 42 U.S.C. §1304 ("The right to alter, amend, or repeal any provision of this chapter is hereby reserved to the Congress"); *Flemming v. Nestor*, 363 U.S. 603 (1960).

22. Offsetting receipts include items like Medicare premiums and co-pays. Under standard government accounting, the "contributions" (taxes) collected and deposited into various trust funds are not offsetting receipts, but rather from the government's perspective constitute revenues.

23. For more detail, see Paul N. Van De Water, *Medicare Is Not Bankrupt*, Center on Budget and Policy Priorities, May 1, 2019, https://www.cbpp.org/research/health/medicare-is-not-bankrupt.

For too much detail, see *2019 Annual Report of the Boards of Trustees of the Federal Hospital Insurance and Federal Supplementary Medical Insurance Trust Funds*, April 22, 2019, https://www.cms.gov/Research-Statistics-Data-and-Systems/Statistics-Trends-and-Reports/ReportsTrustFunds/Downloads/TR2019.pdf.

24. For a discussion of why I put this term in quotes, see "Redistribution Is a Four-Letter Word," YouTube, last modified April 25, 2017, https://www.youtube.com/watch?v=N4WKznnw4hc.

25. Rejda and McNamara, *Principles of Risk Management and Insurance*, 395.

26. OECD, *Social Expenditure Update 2019*, Net Social Spending Background Data thereto (Excel Spreadsheet, tab Data-Figure 2), http://www.oecd.org/social/soc/OECD2019-Social-Expenditure-Update.pdf.

27. Marmor, Mashaw, and Pakutka, *Social Insurance*, 219.

28. "Fiscal Facts," Tax Policy Center, last modified August 12, 2019, https://www.taxpolicycenter. org/fiscal-fact/tax-revenue-share-gdp-country-ff08122019.

29. Deborah A. Stone, "Beyond Moral Hazard: Insurance as Moral Opportunity," *Connecticut Insurance Law Journal* 6, no. 1 (1999–2000): 11–46, 45–46.

30. Richard Arnott and Joseph E. Stiglitz, "Moral Hazard and Nonmarket Institutions: Dysfunctional Crowding Out or Peer Monitoring," *American Economic Review* 81, no. 1 (March 1991): 179–190. In the most recent edition of his public finance textbook, Stiglitz moderates his views slightly, writing that "many question the relevance of moral hazard for [major healthcare] expenditures." The context, though, is our excessive expenditures on healthcare. There are good and sufficient explanations for our outsized healthcare spending (including, although not mentioned in the textbook, clear evidence of monopoly and monopsony pricing at every turn) that do not implicate moral hazard. Joseph E. Stiglitz and Jay K. Rosengard, *Economics of the Public Sector*, 4th ed. (New York: W. W. Norton, 2015), 374–375.

31. Joseph Stiglitz, "Risk, Incentives and Insurance: The Pure Theory of Moral Hazard," *The Geneva Papers on Risk and Insurance* 8, no. 26 (January 1983): 4–33.

32. Stone, "Beyond Moral Hazard," 24.

33. Stiglitz and Rosengard, *Economics of the Public Sector*, 480 (positing that in the face of generous Social Security benefits, "even an individual who is in perfect health and highly productive might be induced to retire").

34. Kleinbard, *We Are Better Than This*, 333–334.

35. Damon Jones and Ioana Marinescu, "The Labor Market Impacts of Universal and Permanent Cash Transfers: Evidence from the Alaska Permanent Fund," *NBER Working Paper* No. 24312 (revised January 2020), https://www.nber.org/papers/w24312.

36. Kleinbard, *We Are Better Than This*, 44–51.

37. Peter Zweifel and Roland Eisen, *Insurance Economics* (Berlin: Springer, 2012), 386.

38. Anthony B. Atkinson, "Economics as a Moral Science," *Economica* 76 (2009): 791–804.

CHAPTER 7

1. Richard J. Arneson, "Luck Egalitarianism—A Primer," in *Responsibility and Distributive Justice*, ed. Carl Knight and Zofia Stemplowska (Oxford: Oxford University Press, 2011), 24–50.

2. Charles Larmore, "What Is Political Philosophy?," *Journal of Moral Philosophy* 10 (2013): 276–306.

3. John Rawls, *Justice as Fairness: A Restatement* (Cambridge, MA: Harvard University Press, 2001), 2–4. Rawls's more famous book is *A Theory of Justice* (Cambridge, MA: The Belknap Press, 1971). I rely on *Justice as Fairness* here because Rawls positioned it as clarifying and correcting many of the arguments made in his earlier work.

4. If I am a bit careless in my usage here, you certainly cannot expect me to be a strict constructionist when it comes to morals versus ethics.

5. Will Kymlicka, *Contemporary Political Philosophy: An Introduction*, 2nd ed. (New York: Oxford University Press, 2002), chap. 3.

6. Rawls, *Justice as Fairness*, 8–9.

7. Ibid., 42–44.

8. Ibid., 58–61.

9. Ibid., 44–45.

10. Ibid., 95–96.

11. Ibid., 61–64, 123–124.

12. Joshua Cohen, "Democratic Equality," *Ethics* 99, no. 4 (July 1989): 727–751, 730, n. 11.

13. The example is patterned on Lars Lindblom, "Equality of Resources, Risk, and the Ideal Market," *Erasmus Journal for Philosophy and Economics* 8, no. 1 (spring 2015): 1–23, 17.

14. (0.9 × $50,000) + (0.1 × $100,000).

15. (0.9 × $10,000) + (0.1 × $1,000,000).

16. Samuel Scheffler, "What Is Egalitarianism?," *Philosophy and Public Affairs* 31, no. 1 (winter 2003): 5–39.

17. For example, Harry Frankfurt, "Equality as a Moral Ideal," *Ethics* 98 (October 1987): 21–43 ("Economic equality is not, as such, of particular moral importance. . . . [W]hat *is* important from the point of view of morality is not that everyone should have *the same* but that each should have *enough*"); Richard Arnerson, "Egalitarianism," *Stanford Encyclopedia of Philosophy* (2013), sec. 6— "Alternatives to Egalitarianism."

18. Bernard Williams, *Moral Luck* (Cambridge: Cambridge University Press, 1981), chap. 2— "Moral Luck"; Thomas Nagel, "Moral Luck," reprinted in Thomas Nagel, *Mortal Questions* (Cambridge: Cambridge University Press, 1979), 24–38.

19. Ronald Dworkin, *Sovereign Virtue* (Cambridge, MA: Harvard University Press, 2000), 73.

20. Ironically, the term "luck egalitarianism" was proposed by an opponent of this school of thought. Elizabeth Anderson, "What Is the Point of Equality?," *Ethics* 109 (1999): 287–337.

21. "Turtles all the way down," Wikipedia, last accessed December 26, 2019, https://en.wikipedia.org/wiki/Turtles_all_the_way_down.

22. Thomas Nagel, "Moral Luck," 24–38.

23. A fuller discussion of the variegated species of luck is Kasper Lippert-Rasmussen, "Justice and Bad Luck," in *Stanford Encyclopedia of Philosophy* (rev. Mar. 28, 2018), https://plato.stanford.edu.

24. This is a radical simplification of the literature, of course. Bernard Williams, who coined the term "moral luck," and who did so thinking of it as an oxymoron, famously wrote about Gauguin, who abandoned his family in ways that ordinarily would give rise to moral opprobrium, but did so to pursue his special talents as a painter according to his own lights. Gauguin did not regret his actions in retrospect—did not suffer the pangs of conscience—simply because he succeeded. Further, we as a result soften our moral condemnation, at least in this regard. (The appropriateness of Gauguin's relationships with Tahitian women is a very recent concern not considered by Williams.) Bernard Williams, *Moral Luck*, chap. 2. Williams's larger point was that because we cannot divorce our moral assessments from the role of luck, moral virtue is not a constant and supreme virtue.

In all this he was roundly criticized by Thomas Nagel, in a companion article also confusingly titled "Moral Luck," reprinted in Thomas Nagel, *Mortal Questions*, 24–38. Nagel argued that moral assessment in practice must look at least in part to how things turn out, not just how we intended them to turn out. Nagel contrasted the "control principle," in which we generally believe, and which holds that "people cannot be morally assessed for what is not their fault, or for what is due to factors beyond their control," ibid., 25, with the reality of "the external view of action which forces itself on us when we see how everything we do belongs to a world we have not created," ibid., 38. That is, we wish to abstract from luck in making moral judgments, so as to isolate only actions for which a person is in control, but we simply cannot.

To illustrate, Nagel provides an example of a truck driver who has failed to properly maintain his truck, which results in brake failure. Because of the driver's negligence in performing truck maintenance, he is unable to stop the vehicle when a child runs in front of him, and the child is killed. The driver is subject to appropriate blame. The driver is morally unlucky to the extent that he had no control over the child darting in front of his vehicle. This moral bad luck leads us to blame him to a greater degree than if he were not required to brake suddenly and violently to avoid hitting the child. Thus, our moral judgments differ due to circumstances beyond the driver's control, despite the driver having the same degree of negligence in both cases. As another example, Nagel posits the case of a driver who has had too much to drink and who swerves off the road. If he is morally unlucky and there are pedestrians in his path, he would be blamed for their deaths. However, if he is morally lucky and no pedestrians happen to be in his path, he is guilty of a far less serious offense and will be reproached by himself and others much less severely, despite being equally reckless in choosing to drive while intoxicated.

Interestingly, much of the moral luck literature was prefigured by Adam Smith, in one of the more obscure sections of *The Theory of Moral Sentiments*. Adam Smith, *The Theory of Moral Sentiments* (6th ed. 1790), eds. D. D. Raphael and A. L. Macfie (Liberty Fund, Inc., 1982), 104. Like Nagel, Smith essentially argued that we inappropriately make moral assessments of others by reference to what they do, not what they intend to do, and in this way saddle people with moral judgments that in part reflect the consequences of luck. He called this logical error our "irregular sentiments." Like Nagel some 200 years later, Smith had no general solution to this vexing problem, but he did note that our awareness of this faulty reasoning in which we all indulge promotes in us an extra inclination to exercise due care, to minimize the times when we are assessed as morally accountable for outcomes that really fall in the domain of luck. See Keith Hankins, "Adam Smith's Intriguing Solution to the Problem of Moral Luck," *Ethics* 126 (April 2016): 711–746.

In thinking about these issues I have been greatly aided by my student Chandler Nahigian, who in particular brought Smith's discussion of the irregular sentiments to my attention.

25. Lindblom, "Equality of Resources, Risk, and the Ideal Market."

26. Michael Otsuka, "Equality, Ambition and Insurance," *Proceedings of the Aristotelian Society* (Supplement) 77, no. 1 (June 28, 2004), https://doi.org/10.1111/j.0309-7013.2004.00120.x, 151–166, 161; Ronald Dworkin, *Sovereign Virtue* (Cambridge, MA: Harvard University Press, 2002), 78–81.

27. Dworkin, *Sovereign Virtue*, 80.

28. Ibid., 104.

29. Ibid., 102.

30. Jonathan J. B. Mijs, "The Paradox of Inequality."

31. Elizabeth Anderson, "What Is the Point of Equality?," 287–337.

32. John Rawls, *A Theory of Justice*, 73. See also Andrew Mason, "Rawlsian Fair Equality of Opportunity," in *Levelling the Playing Field: The Idea of Equal Opportunity and Its Place in Egalitarian Thought* (New York: Oxford University Press, 2006), chap. 3, 68–88; Rawls, *Justice as Fairness*, 33–34.

33. Scanlon, *Why Does Inequality Matter?*, chap. 4 (Procedural Fairness) and chap. 5 (Substantive Opportunity).

34. Lindblom, "In Defense of Rawlsian Fair Equality of Opportunity," 235–263.

35. Ibid., 241.

36. Rawls, *Justice as Fairness*, 58–61.

37. Scanlon, *Why Does Inequality Matter?*, 40.

38. Richard J. Arneson, "Against Rawlsian Equality of Opportunity," *Philosophical Studies: An International Journal for Philosophy in the Analytic Tradition* 93, no. 1 (January 1999): 77–112; Arneson, "Equality of Opportunity," in *Stanford Encyclopedia of Philosophy* (2015) .

39. Scanlon, *Why Does Inequality Matter?*, 40.

40. Daniel Markovits, *The Meritocracy Trap: How America's Foundational Myth Feeds Inequality, Dismantles the Middle Class, and Devours the Elite* (New York: Penguin Press, 2019).

CHAPTER 8

1. John Paul II, *Sollicitudo Rei Socialis*, encyclical letter, December 30, 1987, http://www.vatican.va/content/john-paul-ii/en/encyclicals/documents/hf_jp-ii_enc_30121987_sollicitudo-rei-socialis.html.

2. Smith, *The Wealth of Nations*, Book I, chap. 8.

3. Kleinbard, *We Are Better Than This*, 333–334.

4. This section originally was prepared for a conference of progressive Catholic academics (and me) held at the University of Southern California in June 2018 entitled "The Real Wealth of Nations." I am grateful to the conference organizer, Professor Daniel Finn, for permission to include it here.

5. Mounk, *The Age of Responsibility*.

6. Elizabeth Anderson, "What Is the Point of Equality," *Ethics* 109 (January 1999): 287–337, 315, 320.

7. Edward O'Boyle, "Blessed John Paul II on Social Mortgage: Origins, Questions, and Norms," *Logos: A Journal of Catholic Thought and Culture* 17, no. 2 (2014): 118–135, 119.

8. John Paul II, *Sollicitudo Rei Socialis*, par. 46.

9. Ibid., par. 33.

10. Ibid., par. 43.

11. Ibid.

12. Ibid., par. 32.

13. Ibid., par. 35.

14. Armano Sapori, *The Italian Merchant in the Middle Ages*, trans. Patricia Ann Kennan (New York: W. W. Norton, 1970), 23.

15. "[T]he Church does not propose economic and political systems or programs, nor does she show preference for one or the other, provided that human dignity is properly respected and promoted, and provided she herself is allowed the room she needs to exercise her ministry in the world." John Paul II, *Sollicitudo Rei Socialis*, par. 41.

16. Charity Navigator, an organization that tracks trends in charitable giving, reports that such giving totaled $390 billion in 2016, https://www.charitynavigator.org/index.cfm?bay=content.view&cpid=42. Federal tax revenues for its Fiscal Year 2016 were about $3.3 trillion; adding state and local taxes brings that number to roughly ten times charitable giving.

17. United Nations General Assembly, Human Rights Council, *Report of the Special Rapporteur on Extreme Poverty and Human Rights on His Mission to the United States of America*, May 2018, http://undocs.org/A/HRC/38/33/ADD.1.

18. Ibid., 3–5.

19. Joseph Dalaker, *The Supplemental Poverty Measure: Its Core Concepts, Development, and Use*, Congressional Research Service: R45031, November 28, 2017, https://fas.org/sgp/crs/misc/R45031.

pdf; Liana Fox, *The Supplemental Poverty Measure: 2017*, US Census Bureau: P60-265, September 2018, https://www.census.gov/library/publications/2018/demo/p60-265.html; Thesia Garner and Marisa Gudrais, *Alternative Poverty Measurement for the US: Focus on Supplemental Poverty Measure Thresholds*, US Bureau of Labor Statistics Working Paper 510, September 2018, https://www.bls.gov/pir/spm/alt-pov-spm-wp-510.pdf.

20. Liana Fox, *The Supplemental Poverty Measure: 2018*, US Census Bureau: P60-268, rev. ed., October 2019, 25, Table A-3, https://www.census.gov/content/dam/Census/library/publications/2019/demo/p60-268.pdf.

21. I include the child tax credit, but in its current form the child tax credit goes far beyond an anti-poverty program, because it is fully available to families with annual incomes up to $400,000. By limiting the tax credit items in Table 8.1 to the portion paid out as cash to qualified families (the "refundable" portion), I effectively constrain the budgetary item to those outlays targeted at lower-income Americans. The remaining total cost of the child tax credit is used by higher-income taxpayers to reduce their tax liabilities, but not to generate a check from the government. The CBO does not usually track these total costs, but the Staff of the Joint Committee on Taxation does.

22. Jason DeParle, "The Tax Break for Children, Except the Ones Who Need It Most," *New York Times*, December 16, 2019, https://www.nytimes.com/2019/12/16/us/politics/child-tax-credit.html. The number used in the text is similar but not identical to that used by DeParle, possibly because of different estimation dates, or because one followed the government's fiscal year (ending September 30, 2019), and the other the calendar year.

23. Sophie Collyer, David Harris, and Christopher Wimer, "Left Behind: The One-Third of Children in Families Who Earn Too Little to Get the Full Child Tax Credit," *Poverty and Social Policy Brief* 3, no. 6 (Columbia University Center on Poverty and Social Policy, May 13, 2019), https://www.povertycenter.columbia.edu/news-internal/leftoutofctc.

24. Center on Budget and Policy Priorities, *Policy Brief: Supplemental Security Income*, February 6, 2020, https://www.cbpp.org/research/social-security/policy-basics-supplemental-security-income.

25. Elizabeth Wolkomir and Lexin Cai, *The Supplemental Nutrition Assistance Program Includes Earnings Incentives*, Center on Budget and Policy Priorities, June 5, 2019, https://www.cbpp.org/research/food-assistance/the-supplemental-nutrition-assistance-program-includes-earnings-incentives.

26. Center on Budget and Policy Priorities, *Policy Basics: Temporary Assistance for Needy Families*, February 6, 2020, https://www.cbpp.org/research/family-income-support/temporary-assistance-for-needy-families.

27. Center on Budget and Policy Priorities, *Chart Book: Economic Security and Health Insurance Programs Reduce Poverty and Provide Access to Needed Care*, December 11, 2019, https://www.cbpp.org/research/poverty-and-inequality/chart-book-economic-security-and-health-insurance-programs-reduce.

28. OECD, *OECD Family Database*, Indicator PF1.1, last accessed December 26, 2019, http://www.oecd.org/els/family/database.htm. Figure 6.1 reflects similar family spending data, in relation to child poverty rates.

29. Congressional Budget Office, *An Update to the Budget and Economic Outlook 2019 to 2029: Supplemental Data, Revenue Projections by Category*, August 2019, https://www.cbo.gov/about/products/budget-economic-data#7.

30. There is the risk of some double counting here. The Supplemental Poverty Measure includes an allowance for out-of-pocket medical expenses. If, as should be the case, the country moves to some form of mandatory universal health insurance, and if in the case of low-income Americans

that new system is paid for by the government, then the Supplemental Poverty Measure would come down, and so would my starting position for the UBI system.

31. Jessica Semega, Melissa Kollar, John Creamer, and Abinash Mohanty, *Income and Poverty in the United States: 2018*, US Census Bureau, Current Population Reports, P60-266, 2019, Table A-1, https://www.census.gov/library/publications/2019/demo/p60-266.html.

32. Edward Kleinbard, "Capital Taxation in an Age of Inequality," *Southern California Law Review* 90 (2017): 593.

33. William Gale, "Raising Revenue with a Progressive Value-Added Tax," in *Tackling the Tax Code: Efficient and Equitable Ways to Raise Revenue*, ed. Jay Shambaugh and Ryan Nunn (Washington, DC: Brookings Institution/Hamilton Project, January 2020), chap. 5, https://www.hamiltonproject.org/papers/tackling_the_tax_code_efficient_and_equitable_ways_to_raise_revenue.

34. Technically this is known as the "tax-exclusive" expression of a VAT rate. VAT terminology can be very frustrating to the uninitiated.

CHAPTER 9

1. In this regard, see the discussion in Chapter 7 and also B. Brys et al., "Tax Design for Inclusive Economic Growth," *OECD Taxation Working Papers*, No. 26 (Paris: OECD Publishing, 2016), 46–47, https://doi-org.libproxy2.usc.edu/10.1787/5jlv74ggkog7-en.

The same idea was promoted in economics in the paper by Hal Varian mentioned in Chapter 1. When he modified a standard "optimum tax model" to account for luck as an explanatory variable in the distribution of incomes, his model called for significantly higher tax rates on high-income individuals than under standard models, which in turn could fund more redistribution.

2. Saez and Zucman, *The Triumph of Injustice: How the Rich Dodge Taxes and How to Make Them Pay* (New York: W. W. Norton, 2019). The assertion that the federal income tax is not progressive at the top end is controversial within the economics profession. See, for example, David Splinter, "US Taxes Are Progressive: Comment on 'Progressive Wealth Taxation,'" working paper for the staff of the Joint Committee on Taxation, October 8, 2019, http://www.davidsplinter.com/Splinter-TaxesAreProgressive.pdf.

3. ($50,000 × 10%) + ($150,000 × 30%).

4. Kleinbard, "Capital Taxation in an Age of Inequality"; Edward Kleinbard, "The Right Tax at the Right Time," *Florida Tax Review* 21 (2017): 201–388.

5. OECD, *Revenue Statistics 2019* (Paris: OECD Publishing, 2019), 19.

6. M. P. McQueen, "Lost and Found: The Long Road Back for Lawyers Waylaid by the Recession," *The American Lawyer*, June 24, 2019, https://www.law.com/americanlawyer/2019/06/24/lost-and-found-the-long-road-back-for-lawyers-waylaid-by-the-recession/?slreturn=20190605174551.

7. Hannes Schwandt and Till M. von Wachter, "Socioeconomic Decline and Death: Midlife Impacts of Graduating in a Recession," *NBER Working Paper* No. 26638, January 2020, https://www.nber.org/papers/w26638.

8. Robert Deaner, Aaron Lowen, and Stephen Cobley, "Born at the Wrong Time: Selection Bias in the NHL Draft," *PLOS One* 8, no. 2 (February 2013): 1–7, https://journals.plos.org/plosone/article?id=10.1371/journal.pone.0057753.

9. The intuition developed there is that these are examples of option luck—of choosing an occupation whose rewards are more limited in one's case than one had hoped for reasons not entirely within one's control.

10. Kleinbard, *We Are Better Than This*, 198–199.

11. Ibid., 324–355.

12. Theodore R. Marmor et al., *Social Insurance: America's Neglected Heritage and Contested Future* (Washington, DC: CQ Press, 2014), 47–56.

13. Alan J. Auerbach, Jagadeesh Gokhale, and Laurence J. Kotlikoff, "Generational Accounts: A Meaningful Alternative to Deficit Accounting," in *Tax Policy and the Economy*, ed. David Bradford, vol. 5 (Cambridge, MA: MIT Press, 1991), http://www.nber.org/chapters/c11269; Alan J. Auerbach, Jagadeesh Gokhale, and Laurence J. Kotlikoff, "Generational Accounting: A Meaningful Way to Evaluate Fiscal Policy," *Journal of Economic Perspectives* 8, no. 1 (winter 1994): 73–94.

14. There is a rich literature reviewing, extending, and critiquing generational accounting. For some recent papers, see Kathy A. Ruffing, Paul N. Van de Water, and Richard Kogan, *"Generational Accounting" Is Complex, Confusing, and Uninformative*, Center for Budget and Policy Priorities, February 6, 2014, https://www.cbpp.org/research/generational-accounting-is-complex-confusing-and-uninformative; Nicoletta Batini, Giovanni Callegari, and Julia Guerreiro, "An Analysis of US Fiscal and Generational Imbalances: Who Will Pay and How?," *International Monetary Fund Working Paper* WP/11/72, April 2011; and Peter A. Diamond, "Generational Accounts and Generational Balance: An Assessment," *National Tax Journal* 49, no. 4 (December 1996): 597–607.

15. The exception is a special class of targeted taxes whose purpose it is to correct a market failure where private markets do not accurately incorporate some social cost, such as that imposed by carbon emissions. A carbon tax is an example of this special class of taxes. The technical term for this sort of impost is a Pigouvian tax.

16. Tammy La Gorce, "Retired, or Hoping to Be, and Saddled with Student Debt," *New York Times*, February 26, 2020, https://www.nytimes.com/2020/02/26/business/retirement-student-loan-debt.html.

17. Optimal income tax analysis has become an enormous subfield within public finance economics, and my summary no doubt can be criticized as simplistic and as overlooking the occasional paper that takes seriously how government spends its money. I nonetheless believe that my presentation captures the essence of the enterprise and its weakness as a guide to actual policy.

18. Wendy Edelberg, *Dynamic Analysis at CBO*, Congressional Budget Office, February 29, 2016, https://www.cbo.gov/publication/51286.

19. *The Macroeconomic and Budgetary Effects of Federal Investment*, Congressional Budget Office, June 2016, 4, https://www.cbo.gov/publication/51628.

20. Kleinbard, *We Are Better Than This*, 120–121.

21. C. Eugene Steuerle, *Prioritizing Opportunity for All in the Federal Budget: A Key to Both Growth in and Greater Equality of Earnings and Wealth*, Urban Institute, April 27, 2016, https://www.urban.org/research/publication/prioritizing-opportunity-all-federal-budget-key-both-growth-and-greater-equality-earnings-and-wealth.

22. For a somewhat more nuanced analysis, see Jason Furman, "Should Policymakers Care Whether Inequality Is Helpful or Harmful for Growth?," Harvard Kennedy School and Peterson Institute for International Economics, working paper, draft of December 11, 2017, https://www.itpf.org/itpf_blog?article_id=7084. Furman's focus is on economic growth as such, whereas my most pressing concern is the broadening of participation in such growth.

23. *Fiscal Policy and Long-Term Growth*, International Monetary Fund, April 2015, 30 (emphasis omitted) (citations omitted), https://www.imf.org/external/np/pp/eng/2015/042015.pdf.

24. Jonathan D. Ostry, Andrew Berg, and Charalambos G. Tsangarides, *Redistribution, Inequality, and Growth*, International Monetary Fund, IMF Staff Discussion Note No. SDN/14/02, February 2014, 4 (emphasis omitted), https://www.imf.org/external/pubs/ft/sdn/2014/sdn1402.pdf.

25. OECD, *In It Together: Why Less Inequality Benefits All* (Paris: OECD Publishing, May 2015), 15, https://doi.org/10.1787/9789264235120-en.

CHAPTER 10

1. Papanicolas, Woskie, and Jha, "Health Care Spending in the United States and Other High-Income Countries," *Journal of American Medical Association* 319, no. 10 (March 2018): 1024–1039. If measured in absolute dollar equivalent terms (rather than as a percentage of GDP), the United States spends about 25 percent more per capita than does Switzerland. Gerard F. Anderson, Peter Hussey, and Varduhi Petrosyan, "It's Still the Prices, Stupid: Why the US Spends So Much on Health Care, and a Tribute to Uwe Reinhardt," *Health Affairs* 38, no. 1 (January 2019), https://doi.org/10.1377/hlthaff.2018.05144.

2. The instinct to argue that this would crash the economy because all that spending supports jobs is what is known in economics as the broken window fallacy. The economy does not grow because a hurricane knocks out all the windows in a community; instead, wealth that would have been deployed on something more attractive must be redirected to this new priority. People are the poorer when they spend money in ways they do not want to.

3. Edward R. Berchick, Jessica C. Barnett, and Rachel D. Upton, *Health Insurance Coverage in the United States: 2018*, US Census Bureau, November 2019, https://www.census.gov/content/dam/Census/library/publications/2019/demo/p60-267.pdf; Alison P. Galvani et al., "Improving the Prognosis of Healthcare in the USA," *The Lancet* 395 (February 15, 2020): 524–533.

4. Anderson, Hussey, and Petrosyan, "It's Still the Prices, Stupid."

5. Ezekiel J. Emanuel, "The Real Cost of the US Health Care System," *Journal of American Medical Association* 319, no. 10 (March 2018): 983–985.

6. Wayne Drash, Sergio Hernandez, and Aaron Kessler, "Medicare Spent $2 Billion for One Drug as the Manufacturer Paid Doctors Millions," *CNN.com*, June 29, 2018, https://www.cnn.com/2018/06/29/health/acthar-mallinckrodt-medicare-claims-doctor-payments/index.html.

7. Lovisa Gustafsson, Shanoor Seervai, and David Blumenthal, "The Role of Private Equity in Driving Up Health Care Prices," *Harvard Business Review online*, October 29, 2019, https://hbr.org/2019/10/the-role-of-private-equity-in-driving-up-health-care-prices.

8. Elisabeth Rosenthal, "That Beloved Hospital? It's Driving Up Health Care Costs," *New York Times*, September 1, 2019, https://www.nytimes.com/2019/09/01/opinion/hospital-spending.html; Jenny Gould, "Hospital Giant Sutter Health Faces Legal Reckoning over Medical Pricing," *Los Angeles Times*, September 7, 2019, https://www.latimes.com/business/story/2019-09-06/sutter-health-california-antitrust-lawsuit.

9. Rosenthal, "That Beloved Hospital? It's Driving Up Health Care Costs."

10. Melanie Evans, "Amazon Joins Trend of Sending Workers Away for Health Care," *Wall Street Journal*, October 15, 2019, https://www.wsj.com/articles/amazon-joins-trend-of-sending-workers-away-for-health-care-11571131801.

11. Edward D. Kleinbard, "Do We Want Healthcare or Health Insurance?," *The Hill*, May 26, 2017, https://thehill.com/blogs/pundits-blog/healthcare/335151-do-we-want-healthcare-or-health-insurance.

12. The Center for Consumer Information and Insurance Oversight (CCIIO), *At Risk: Pre-Existing Conditions Could Affect 1 in 2 Americans: 129 Million People Could Be Denied Affordable Coverage without Health Reform*, Centers for Medicare and Medicaid Services, *CMS.gov*, last accessed March 1, 2020, https://www.cms.gov/CCIIO/Resources/Forms-Reports-and-Other-Resources/preexisting.

13. Gary Claxton, Cynthia Cox, Anthony Damico, Larry Levitt, and Karen Pollitz, *Pre-Existing Condition Prevalence for Individuals and Families*, Henry J. Kaiser Family Foundation, *KFF.org*, October 4, 2019, https://www.kff.org/health-reform/issue-brief/pre-existing-condition-prevalence-for-individuals-and-families/.

14. CCIIO, *At Risk: Pre-Existing Conditions Could Affect 1 in 2 Americans*; Jennifer Tolbert, Kendall Orgera, Natalie Singer, and Anthony Damico, *Key Facts about the Uninsured Population*, Henry J. Kaiser Family Foundation, *KFF.org*, December 13, 2019, https://www.kff.org/uninsured/issue-brief/key-facts-about-the-uninsured-population/.

15. Dana P. Goldman and Kip Hagopian, "It Is Time for Universal Healthcare without Breaking the Bank," *Journal of Policy Analysis and Management* 37 (October 1, 2017): 182–188. Goldman and Hagopian argue for what I would call a "skinny" version of universal healthcare, but the point is that even with their more modest ambitions than those embraced by advocates of Medicare for All, they begin with the premise that healthcare reform must be both universal and progressive.

16. Of course, mandatory insurance in a single pool need not be completely insensitive to age differences. There can be some discounts for youth, although those of us who are old would rather think that being young is compensation enough.

17. The "tax expenditure" estimates of the Joint Committee on Taxation count only the forgone *income* taxes arising from the forgiveness of tax to employees on the value of the healthcare benefits they receive from employers. That subsidy in the form of forgiven income taxes on what indisputably are wages currently amounts to about $175 billion/year. When I was Chief of Staff of the Joint Committee more than a decade ago, we did an additional estimate of the forgone payroll taxes, and found that they amounted at that time to another $100 billion/year in government subsidies.

18. Emmanuel Saez and Gabriel Zucman, *The Triumph of Injustice*, 179–183.

19. Gregory Kieg, Kate Sullivan, and Tami Luhby, "Bernie Sanders Leads Caravan into Canada to Purchase Cheaper Insulin with American Prices Rising," *CNN.com*, last modified July 28, 2019, https://www.cnn.com/2019/07/28/politics/bernie-sanders-canada-cheaper-insulin-cnntv/index.html.

20. Jaqueline Howard, "On Rising Insulin Prices, Lawmaker Tells Pharma Execs: 'Your Days Are Numbered,'" *CNN.com*, last modified April 10, 2019, https://www.cnn.com/2019/04/10/health/insulin-prices-congressional-hearing-bn/index.html.

21. Hannah Kuchler, "US Patients Struggle to Obtain Eli Lilly's Half-Price Insulin," *Financial Times*, August 11, 2019, 8, https://www.ft.com/content/7e19cd4c-b94a-11e9-8a88-aa6628ac896c.

22. Kieg, Sullivan, and Luhby, "Bernie Sanders Leads Caravan into Canada."

23. Common Dreams Staff, "'People Are Dying': Bernie Sanders Heads to Canada with an Insulin Caravan," *Common Dreams*, last modified July 28, 2019, https://www.commondreams.org/news/2019/07/28/people-are-dying-bernie-sanders-heads-canada-insulin-caravan.

24. Alan MacLeod, "Injecting Yourself with Dog Insulin?: Just a Normal Day in America," *The Guardian*, August 1, 2019, https://www.theguardian.com/commentisfree/2019/aug/01/us-healthcare-insulin-diabetes-jordan-williams.

25. Antonio Olivo, "He Lost His Insurance and Turned to a Cheaper Form of Insulin. It Was a Fatal Decision," *Washington Post*, August 3, 2019, https://www.washingtonpost.com/local/

he-lost-his-insurance-and-turned-to-cheaper-form-of-insulin-it-was-a-fatal-decision/2019/08/02/
106ee79a-b24d-11e9-8f6c-7828e68cb15f_story.html.

26. Hannah Frishberg, "Diabetic Groom-to-Be Dies after Taking Cheaper Insulin to Pay for Wedding," *New York Post*, August 6, 2019, https://nypost.com/2019/08/06/diabetic-groom-to-be-dies-after-taking-cheaper-insulin-to-pay-for-wedding/.

27. A helpful resource here is *Key Design Components and Considerations for Establishing a Single-Payer Health Care System*, Congressional Budget Office, May 2019, https://www.cbo.gov/publication/55150.

28. In February 2020 the Sanders campaign called attention to an article in *The Lancet*, co-authored by a former advisor to Senator Sanders, that analyzed in detail the component costs of Sanders's 2020 Medicare for All proposal. See Galvani et al., "Improving the Prognosis of Healthcare in the USA," supra, note 3. That article and the accompanying interactive financing tool are very useful.

29. I am ignoring here expenditures by philanthropic institutions, which I assume to be constant before and after reform.

30. Letter from Donald M. Berwick and Simon Johnson to Senator Elizabeth Warren, October 31, 2019, https://assets.ctfassets.net/4ubxbgy9463z/2Tg90B55ICu2vtYBaKKcVr/d124e0eeb128ad3a8d8ab8a6ccae44c0/20191031_Medicare_for_All_Cost_Letter___Appendices_FINAL.pdf.

31. Galvani et al., "Improving the Prognosis of Healthcare in the USA."

32. Letter from Simon Johnson, Betsey Stevenson, and Mark Zandi to Senator Elizabeth Warren, October 31, 2019, https://assets.ctfassets.net/4ubxbgy9463z/27a09rfB6MbQgGmaXK4eGc/d06d5a224665324432c6155199afe0bf/Medicare_for_All_Revenue_Letter___Appendix.pdf.

The funding plan outlined in that letter looked only to taxes that would be raised by the reversal of tax-advantaged expenditures by households, but in fact after-tax medical outlays and the total increase in after-tax incomes ought also to have been counted in the plan's favor. For example, the estimate projected that take-home pay would go up by $3.7 trillion under Medicare for All, on which an incremental $1.2 trillion of tax would be collected. The estimate counted that $1.2 trillion of new tax as a component of the $21 trillion in total federal revenues it sought, but if "middle-class" taxes in fact were raised by an additional $2.5 trillion, families would be in the same after-tax position as before Medicare for All, so that the "new" tax would have no net cost. Here you see the confusion that follows from the political demands of "no new taxes," as well as looking at complex fiscal plans through the lens of taxation alone, when in fact the net consequences for households must take into account both taxes and spending (here, household spending). If the ultimate burden of the Warren tax potpourri in fact fell on affluent households alone, then her "no new middle-class taxes" proposal would have left middle-class households *better off* to the extent of the after-tax medical expenses from which they would have been relieved.

EPILOGUE

1. Lionel Robbins, *An Essay on the Nature and Significance of Economic Science* (London: Macmillan & Co., 1932), 16. This does not fully encompass macroeconomics, but that is not relevant to the points being made in the text.

2. Kleinbard, *We Are Better Than This*; Larry Kramer, "Beyond Neoliberalism: Rethinking Political Economy," Hewlett Foundation, April 26, 2018, https://hewlett.org/library/beyond-neoliberalism-rethinking-political-economy/.

3. Kleinbard, *We Are Better Than This*, 55–56.

4. Ibid.

5. Joseph E. Stiglitz, *Whither Socialism?* (Cambridge, MA: MIT Press, 1994); Joseph E. Stiglitz, *People, Power, and Profits: Progressive Capitalism for an Age of Discontent* (New York: W. W. Norton, 2019).

6. Edward Kleinbard, "The Economic Question Voters Should Ask Themselves," *The Atlantic*, May 6, 2019, https://www.theatlantic.com/ideas/archive/2019/05/how-make-sense-candidates-economic-proposals/588685/.

7. Reparations for social wrongs, such as the harms of slavery, might be viewed as falling into neither bucket.

INDEX

For the benefit of digital users, indexed terms that span two pages (e.g., 52–53) may, on occasion, appear on only one of those pages.
Page numbers followed by *f* and *t* indicate figures and tables, respectively. Numbers followed by n indicate endnotes.

adequacy principles, 104
Adjusted Gross Income (defined), 196, 198–99
adverse fortuity,
    existential, 14–15, 220. *see also* brute luck, bad; existential bad luck
    insurance, 14–15, 130, 132
Affordable Care Act (ACA), 235, 242–43, 246, 258
African Americans. *see also* Black Americans
    achievement gains after participation in universal pre-K programs, 98f, 98
    life-cycle benefits of early childhood programs, 86
    reparations for slavery to, 172–73, 294n7
    student loan debt, 115, 116f
agency, role of, 13–14
Alaska, 152
Amazon Inc. (employee health care), 244
American Economic Review, 61–62
Anderson, Elizabeth, 172, 181
anti-poverty programs (*see under* poverty)
Appelbaum, Lauren, 34–35, 269n21
Aristotle, 155
Arneson, Richard, 157, 176
Asian Americans, 116f
Associate's degrees, 84f, 84–85, 108–9
assortative mating, 70–71
Atkinson, Anthony, 136, 139, 150, 156
Auten, Gerald, 272n29
Auerbach, Alan, 224–25

baby boomers, 145, 223, 224, 225
Bachelor's degrees (*see under* university degrees)
bad luck, xi–xvi
    at birth, 14–15
    circumstantial, 11–12

constitutive, 170
existential, 14–15, 21–26, 67–70, 164
forms of, 11–17
option, 14
Bartik, Timothy, 93
Batchelder, Lily, 64, 274n45
Batini, Nicoletta, 290n14
Belief in a Just World, 10, 20, 28–36, 38, 42, 268n10
Berg, Andrew, 238
birth circumstances, 12, 67
    and distributional lifetime earnings, 4–5, 5f
    and relative income mobility, 71–72, 72f
    bad luck at birth, 14–15
    born to wealth (Fed definition), 64
    timing of our birth, 222–27
Bismarck, Otto von, 135–36, 140, 156
Black Americans, 15–16. *see also* African Americans
    bachelor's degree recipients, 115
    early childhood education and poverty, 97, 98
    reparations for slavery to, 172–73, 294n7
    student loan debt, 115, 116f
    block grant, 192
Bowles, Samuel, 275n1
Brady, Tom, 172
Brown University, 281n52
brute luck, xi, 3–4, 6f, 6–9, 163, 165–67, 261, 263–64
    bad, xiii, 11, 14, 163, 262. *see also* adverse fortuity, existential and existential bad luck
    health as, 16
budget scorekeeping models, 234–35
Business Enterprise Income Tax, 215

California, school funding 103, 104, 105
capital deepening, 236
capital income (*see* income, capital)
capital income taxation, 199, 214–16
Capra, Frank, 19
Catholic Social Thought, 180
CBO. *see* Congressional Budget Office
charitable giving, 185, 287n16
Chetty, Raj, 52, 54, 67, 75, 77, 78–79, 96,
    111, 221–22, 277n13
Child Nutrition programs, 191*t*, 192
child poverty (*see under* poverty)
child tax credits, 89–90, 190–91, 191*t*, 288n21
Children's Health Insurance Program (CHIP),
    138, 144*t*
CHIP, *see* Children's Health Insurance
    Program
circumstantial luck, 11–12, 164
Clayton, Susan, 29
college education, 108–17. *see also* higher
        education; postsecondary education;
        university degrees
    cost of, 111–13, 112*f*
    dropout rates, 115
    family wealth correlation 110*f*, 265n1
    financing (*see* student loans)
    Kleinbard proposal (financing
        system), 228–29
    range of, 109
    value of, 84–86, 84*f*, 85*f*
Congressional Budget Office (CBO), 51–52, 55,
        197, 234
    definition of income before transfers and
        taxes, 271n19, 272n23
    definition of market income, 271n19,
        272nn23–24,
    definition of 1 percent club, 272n25
    distributional analysis, 234
    dynamic tax modeling, 234, 235
    Gini Coefficient calculation, 59*f*, 59
    immigration reform, 235
    measurement of income inequality growth,
        55–57, 56*f*
    measurement of wealth inequality, 61
    single-payer health care system
        design 293n27
    tax projections, 197
constitutive luck, 164, 165–70, 209, 221.
        see also endowments
control principle, 285n24
Cooperman, Leon, 9–10, 39, 40
Corak, Miles, 73–74
country comparative data
    Argentina, 73*f*
    Australia, 47*f*, 85*f*, 118*f*, 147*f*, 193*f*, 194*f*,
        217*f*, 218*f*
        interest rates on student loans, 114
        intergenerational earnings elasticity, 73, 77*f*
        public schools, 95*f*, 102*f*, 112*f*
    Austria, 147*f*

Belgium, 147*f*
Brazil, 73*f*, 84
Canada, 47*f*, 85*f*, 118*f*, 147*f*, 193*f*, 194*f*
    drug prices, 249
    income inequality, 76, 77*f*, 217*f*
    intergenerational earnings elasticity, 73*f*,
        73–74, 76, 77*f*
    public schools, 95*f*, 106, 112*f*
    tax revenue, 218*f*, 219
Chile, 277n6, 147*f*
China, 46, 106
Czech Republic, 147*f*
Denmark, 77*f*, 109*f*, 112*f*, 118*f*, 147*f*
England. (see United Kingdom)
Estonia, 107–8, 147*f*
Finland, 77*f*, 109*f*, 118*f*, 147*f*
France, 147*f*, 194*f*, 217*f*
    intergenerational earnings elasticity,
        73, 77*f*
    poverty, 47*f*, 47, 193*f*
    public education, 85*f*, 95*f*, 102*f*, 106–7, 118*f*
    tax revenues, 218, 218*f*
Germany, 47*f*
    Gini index, 217
    health insurance, 135–36
    healthcare delivery, 247
    income inequality, 73*f*, 77*f*, 217, 217*f*
    public education, 85*f*, 95*f*, 102*f*, 106,
        109*f*, 118*f*
    social spending, 135–36, 147*f*, 193*f*, 193, 194*f*
    tax revenues, 149, 218*f*
Greece, 147*f*
Hungary, 147*f*, 148
Iceland, 147*f*
India, 46–47
Ireland, 94, 147*f*
Israel, 147*f*
Italy, 47*f*, 217*f*, 218*f*
    intergenerational earnings elasticity, 73,
        74, 77*f*
    public education, 85*f*, 95*f*, 102*f*, 109*f*,
        112*f*, 118*f*
    social spending, 147*f*, 184, 193*f*, 194*f*
Japan, 47*f*, 217*f*, 218*f*
    intergenerational earnings elasticity,
        73, 77*f*
    public education, 95*f*, 102*f*, 109*f*, 112*f*, 118*f*
    social spending, 147*f*, 148, 193*f*, 194*f*
Latvia, 101, 102*f*, 147*f*, 280n37
Lithuania, 46, 106, 147*f*
Luxembourg, 147*f*
Malta, 106
Korea, 147*f*, 148
Mexico, 147*f*
Netherlands, 147*f*
New Zealand, 77*f*, 118*f*, 147*f*
Nordic countries, 73, 74, 216
Norway, 47*f*, 73*f*, 77*f*, 147*f*, 217*f*, 218*f*
    public education, 85*f*, 89, 95*f*, 102*f*, 109*f*,
        112*f*, 118*f*

social spending, 193f, 194f
OECD, 47f, 74, 85f, 95f, 102f, 106, 109f, 147f, 186, 193–94, 193f, 194f, 217f, 218f, 219–20
Peru, 73f
Poland, 147f
Portugal, 147f
Russia, 46
Singapore, 73f, 106–7
Slovak Republic, 84, 107–8, 147f
Slovenia, 147f
Spain, 73f, 106, 118f
Sweden, 47f, 73f, 77f, 147f, 217f, 218f
   public education, 85f, 95f, 102f, 109f, 112f, 118f
   social spending, 193f, 194f
Switzerland, 73f, 73, 147f, 217f, 218f
   healthcare spending, 47f, 51–52, 242, 291n1
   public education, 85f, 95f, 102f, 109f, 112f
   social spending, 193f, 194f
Turkey, 46, 147f
United Kingdom (UK), 47f, 77f, 217f
   college tuition and financing system (England), 114
   earnings elasticity, 73f, 73, 74, 77f
   healthcare delivery, 247
   National Health Service, 251
   public education, 85f, 94, 95f, 102f, 109f, 112, 114, 112f, 118f, 228, 279n24
   Scotland, 114
   social spending, 147f, 193f, 194f
   tax revenue, 218f, 219

deadweight loss, 230–32, 233
Democratic Party, 227, 250
Department of Health and Human Services (HHS), 246
Department of Housing and Urban Development (HUD), 188, 189, 191t
deservingness, 20, 27–36 see also Belief in a Just World
determinism, hard, 164
difference principle, 159, 160–62, 175
disposable income inequality, 216–18, 217f
distributional analysis, 234
Distributional Financial Accounts (DFAs), 62, 274n37
distributional lifetime earnings (see under lifetime earnings)
distributive justice, 162, 165–66
Doctoral degrees (see under university degrees)
Driessen, Patrick, 271n19
Dual Business Enterprise Income Tax (Dual BEIT), 215
Duncan, Greg J., 92, 279n16
Dworkin, Ronald, 12, 14, 163, 165–70, 171, 266n10. see also luck egalitarianism

early childhood childcare 87–91
early childhood education and care (ECEC), 87–91, 102. see also Universal 3–K

critical importance for future success, 88
economic costs and returns, 99–103
efficacy, 93
European Union, recommended spending, 101–2
female laborforce participation, 88–89
financial returns of 86
kindergarten, 91, 94, 96–97
life-cycle benefits, 86
neuroscience research, 91–94
parental leave, 88
poverty and, 95–99, 98f
pre-primary education (nursery school), 91–103
   enrollment rates, 94, 95f
   preschool development grants, 99. see also Head Start
   spending on, 101, 102f
   progressive effect, 219
   relative US enrollment rate, 94, 95f
   relative US spending on, 101–3, 102f
   Sanders' Campaign proposal, 227
   Warren proposal, analysis of (Moody's) 89–90
Earned Income Tax Credit (EITC), 54, 152, 189–90, 191t, 195
   proposed UBI benefits, 198, 199, 200
Echo Park (Los Angeles, California), 78
economic inequality. see income inequality; wealth inequality
economic mobility, 15, 68, 70–76. see also income mobility
economics
   macroeconomics, 234–35, 293n1
   neoclassical microeconomics, 14
   standard analyses, 230–33
   supply-side, 20–21, 82, 259–60
Edison, Thomas, 40–41
Edlund, Lena, 272n32
education, xii, 5–6, 81–119
   early childhood. see early childhood education and care
   and earnings, 69, 83–84, 84f, 85f
   enrichment expenditures, 118–19, 119f
   global context, 94
   importance of, 69, 227–29
   postsecondary, 83. see also college education; higher education; university degrees
   public, 82, 103–5
   primary, 103–8
   returns on investment in, 85–86, 87
   school quality,
   and income inequality, 277n3
      international comparison, 106–8
      teacher experience, 96–97
   secondary (high school), 103–8
   spending on, 103–5, 108
   teacher pay, 107–8
   Universal 3–K, 86–87, 91–103, 279n22, 279n24

Education Week, 105
efficiency (vs equity), 175, 233
egalitarianism (*see* luck egalitarianism)
Eli Lilly, 249, 250
Emanuel, Ezekiel, 242
employment
    labor participation, 88–89
    low-wage jobs, 50–51
    underemployment, 168–69, 172–73
    unemployment, 50–51, 136
    unemployment insurance (compensation),
        144, –35*t*, 152–53, 156
endowments, 167, 168–70, 172, 210. *see also*
        constitutive luck
entitlement reform, 148–49, 153, 224
Envision Healthcare, 243
equality of opportunity, 6, 13, 17–21, 69, 81–83,
        156, 162, 225–26, 262, 263–64
    arbitrariness of, 176
    authentic, 233, 262
    fair, 17, 173–76, 210
estate taxes (*see under* taxes and taxation)
ethics, 177–80. *see also* social mortgage
existential bad luck, 14–15, 67–70, 124, 207, 263.
        see also adverse fortuity, existential and
        brute luck, bad
    long shadow of, 67–70
    response to, 21–26
expected lifetime earnings *vs.* birth
        circumstances, 4–5, 5*f*
Express Scripts, 250

Facebook, 107
fairness, 20, 263–64
    as justice, 29
    Procedural Fairness, 18, 174
family support programs, 191*t*
family wealth (*see* wealth, family)
Federal Reserve, 61–63, 64, 86
fiscal policy (defined), 184–85. *see also* inclusive
        growth, progressive fiscal systems
food stamps, 24, 138, 146, 178–79, 191, 192. *see
        also* Supplemental Nutrition Assistance
        Program (SNAP)
Forbes 400, 275n46
Fortune's Wheel, 3–6, 8–9, 10, 12, 19, 27, 139–
        40, 157, 162–63
"Four Freedoms" speech (Roosevelt), 257–58.
        see also progressive paradigms
Frank, Robert H., 265–66n1
free markets,
    and healthcare, 242–43, 245
    and political liberty, 260, 261, 262
    and social insurance, 139–40
    and student loan debt, xii
French Horn Economic Opportunity Index, 118–
        19, 119*f*. *see also* education, enrichment
        expenditures

Gale, William, 201–2
Gates, Bill, 275n46
Gauguin, Paul, 285n24
generational accounting, 290n14, 224–25
genetics, 16, 164, 275n1
geographical *determinism*, 77–79, 105,
        188, 221–22
gifts and bequests (*see under* wealth, inherited)
Gini Coefficient (*see under* income inequality)
Gintis, Herbert, 275n1
Giuliani, Rudy, 267n17
Gokhale, Jagadeesh, 224–25
goods, primary, 159, 175, 178, 183
Google, 8, 107
government spending, 63, 263
    education, 83–104, 102*f*, 107–8
    family services, 193–94
    healthcare, 24. *see also* healthcare spending;
        Medicaid; Medicare; National Health
        Expenditures
    means-tested programs, 138, 144*t*, 148
    military, 100, 220
    progressive effects of, 219
    social insurance, 143–49, 144*t*, 147*f*, 193–94,
        194*f*, 223, 237
    veterans' programs, 144*t*
Grand Canyon University, 109
Great Depression, 226, 257
Great Gatsby Curve (*see under* income
        inequality)
Great Recession, 62, 152–53, 223, 226
Griffin, Ken, 58
gross domestic product (GDP), 49*f*, 50, 53
    amounts, 145, 220
    federal government spending vs, 189
    growth rate, 49*f*, 50, 53
    healthcare spending percentage, 124, 242
    household wealth relationship, 61
    labor percentage, 236
    social spending percentage, 147*f*, 148,
        193–94, 194*f*
    tax revenues percentage, 149, 218*f*, 217–18
Gross National Happiness, 236
The Guardian, 249

hard determinism, 164
Harvard University, 62–63, 111, 117, 281n52
hazard (insurance), 132–33. *see also*
        moral hazard
Head Start, 89, 98–99, 279n16, 280n30. *see
        also* early childhood education and care
health insurance, 124, 153–54
    employer-provided, 51, 270n14, 265n2
    major medical, 244
    premiums, 51–52
    private, xiii, 243, 245–46, 247, 252
    public (*see* Medicare)
    rational, 250–53

regulation of, 242–43
  as social insurance, 244–45
  universal, 135–36, 241–56
Health Savings Accounts, 242
healthcare, 16, 210, 241–56
  diabetes care, 249–50
  drug prices, 249, 250
  funding, 253–56
  universal, 241–56, 292n15. *see also* Medicare
    for All
healthcare spending, 51–52, 124, 144*t*, 291n1,
    242, 254. *see also* government spending,
    healthcare; Medicaid; Medicare
  National Health Expenditure,
    pharmaceuticals, 242, 243, 249, 250
  private, 254. *see also* National Health
    Expenditure
Heckman, James, 86, 93, 99
Henry J. Kaiser Family Foundation, 246
HHS (*see* Department of Health and Human
    Services)
high schools (*see* education, secondary)
higher education, 108–17. *see also* college
    education; postsecondary education;
    university degrees
  economic returns, 117, 118*f*
  public funding of, 86
Hispanic Americans
  achievement gains after participation in
    universal pre-K programs, 98*f*, 98
  early childhood education and poverty, 97, 98
  student loan debt, 115, 116*f*
Homo economicus, 261
household income, 49*f*, 50, 78
household wealth, 61, 62, 63
housing programs, 189, 191*t*
HUD (*see* Department of Housing and Urban
    Development)
Humalog (Eli Lilly), 249, 250
human capital
  investment in, xii, 21–22, 82, 87, 225, 231,
    236, 238, 262–63
  private resources required to fund, 45, 48,
    57–58, 70, 81–83
  underinvestment in, xii–xiii, xv–xvi,
    20–21, 22
hyperbolic discounting, 140

impersonal resources, 167, 171
imputed income, 215, 216
inclusive economy, 87, 230–39
inclusive growth, 230, 235–39
income
  Adjusted Gross Income, 196, 198–99
  after-tax/after-transfer, 56, 57
  before transfers and taxes, 271n19,
    272n23, 272n31
  capital, 214. *see also* capital income taxation

disposable, 216–17, 217*f*
education and, 83–87, 84*f*, 85*f*
imputed, 215, 216
labor, 213–14, 231
market, 271n19, 272nn23–24, 56–57, 217*f*
  growth in, 56*f*, 57
  inequality in, 56*f*, 56–57
median household income, 49*f*, 50
taxable, 196, 199
income inequality, 54–60, 59*f*, 60*f*,
    186, 217*f*
  bottom-up approach to, 55
  costs of, 237–38
  Gini Coefficient, 58–59, 59*f*
  Great Gatsby Curve, 76, 77*f*, 118
  growth effects, 237–38
  growth velocity, 46
  increase in, 54, 55–57, 56*f*, 58
  measurement of, 55–57, 56*f*, 59, 60*f*
  opportunity inequality due to, 45–49
  reasons to care about, 45, 236–38
  top-down approach to, 55, 59
  top-end, 46, 48, 60*f*, 60
income mobility. *see also* economic mobility
  absolute, 52*f*, 52, 53*f*, 68–69
  cross-country comparisons, 73*f*, 74
  education, inequality, and, 117–19
  Great Gatsby Curve, 76, 77*f*
  intergenerational, 76, 77*f*, 117, 118*f*, 186, 271n15
  relative, 68, 71–72, 72*f*
  studies of, 70–76
income security programs, 138, 144*t*, 188
income tax
  effective rate 196–97, 218*f*
  optimal, 233, 290n17
  progressive (*see* progressive taxation)
indemnity, 125–26
Indiana, 99
individualism, 34, 269n20
inequality. *see also* income inequality; wealth
    inequality
  attitudes toward, 35–36
  consent to, 35
  education and mobility, 117–19, 277n3
  infant mortality and youth poverty, 186
inheritable characteristics, 275n1
inherited wealth (*see under* wealth)
Institute for College Access and Success, 112, 115
insurance, 207–8, 226–27, 263
  adverse selection, 23–24, 134–35, 208, 245–47
  collision, 123
  commercial, 130, 131, 245–46
  definition of, 132–35
    adverse fortuity, 132
    chance and severity of loss, 132, 133
    homogenous loss, 132–33
    identifiable perils, 132–33
    monetary loss, 132

insurance (*cont.*)
 mutuality of relations, 131, 133
 risk, meaning of, 129–30
 risk pooling, 126, 127–28, 133, 151
 risk transfer, 127–28, 133
 earthquake, xiv
 essence of, 208
 ethics of, 177–80
 as framework for social policy, 267n22
 fraud risk, 134, 135
 government, 25
 health (*see* health insurance)
 hospital (*see* Medicare, Part A)
 important features and stress points, 208
 life, 124, 130–31, 132, 142
 longevity risk, 131
 marine, 124, 126
 as metaphor, 23, 26, 139, 155–76, 210–11,
  227–29, 263
 moral hazard, 134–35, 151, 282n10
 origins, of 124–29, 130–32
 over-insurance, 209, 226
 as product, 123–54
 property and casualty (P&C), 124, 134–35
 public, 23–26, 262–63
 self-insuring, 129
 social (*see* social insurance)
 retrospective, 210–11
 risks unique to, 134
 self-insuring, 129
 social (*see* social insurance)
 underwriting, 126
 unemployment, 139, 144*t*, 153, 156
 value of, 128–29
 vulnerabilities, 132–35
 workers' compensation (accident),
  135–36, 151–52
insurance theory, 207–40
intelligence quotient (IQ), 86, 275n1
intergenerational mobility (earnings elasticity),
 72–73, 73*f*, 74–75, 76, 77*f*, 117, 118*f*, 186
Internal Revenue Service (IRS), 77, 196
International Monetary Fund (IMF), 87, 230,
 236, 237–38
Iowa, 78
Ivy Tech Community College, 109

Jason the Surfer, 178–79, 200, 203
job growth, 78–79
John Paul II, 177, 181–84
Joint Committee on Taxation (JCT), 234–35,
 288n21, 292n17
justice. *see also* Belief in a Just World
 distributive, 162, 165–66
 principles of (*see under* Rawls, John)
justice motive, 29–30, 41, 268n7. *see also* Belief
 in a Just World
Justinian, 155

Kahneman, Daniel, 261
Henry J. Kaiser Family Foundation, 246
Kant, Immanuel, 155
Kaplan, Steven, 275n46
kindergarten (*see* early childhood education and
 care (ECEC); Universal 3-K)
KKR (Kohlberg Kravis Roberts & Co), 243
Kleinbard, Edward, xvi, 265n3, 272n27,
 275n46, 280n35, 282n5, 289n32,
 289n4, 291n11, 294n6
Kleinbard policy proposals,
 college financing, 228–29
 health insurance, 250–53
 public social spending, 209–10
 Universal Basic Income, 197–201
Kopczuk, Wojciech, 272n32
Kotlikoff, Lawrence, 224–25
Krueger, Alan, 76

labor (as a production factor), 82, 236
labor income (*see* income, labor)
labor participation, 88–89
The Lancet, 91, 255, 293n28
law of large numbers, 126
Lerner, Melvin J., 28, 29–30, 32
Liberty University, 109
life insurance (*see* insurance, life)
life satisfaction, 86
lifetime earnings
 vs. birth circumstances and poverty, 4–5, 5*f*
 distributional, 4–5, 5*f*
 education and, 69, 83–84, 84*f*, 85*f*
 expected value of, 81
 intergenerational elasticity, 72–73, 73*f*, 74, 75,
  76, 77*f*
 smoothing of, 63
Lindblom, Lars, 175
Los Angeles, California, 78, 244
low-wage jobs, 50–51
luck
 bad (see bad luck)bad
 brute (see brute luck)
 circumstantial (see circumstantial luck)
 constitutive (see constitutive luck)
 denial of, 9–11, 27–42
 and egalitarianism (*see* luck egalitarianism)
 existential bad (see existential bad luck)
 moral (*see* moral luck)
 option (*see* option luck)
 vs smarts, 67–80
 subdivisions, 163–70
 very rich, no thanks to, 38–42
luck egalitarianism, 266n10, 9, 12, 285n17,
 285n20, 162–63, 170–71, 172. *see also*
  Dworkin, Ronald

magical thinking, 33, 268n7
Magnusson, Katherine, 92, 279n16

maintenance loans, 114
Mankiw, Gregory, 7–8
marine insurance (see insurance, marine)
market income (see income, market)
market triumphalism, 257–61, 262
Marmor, Theodore, 136
Massachusetts, 105
Master's degrees (see under university degrees)
means-tested programs (see under government spending)
median full-time wages (men) (see under wages)
median household income (see under income), 49f, 50
Medicaid, 54, 56, 138, 180–81
    extension, 246
    spending on, 144t
Medicare, 135, 282n11. see also Medicare for All
    benefits as income, 54, 56, 271n19
    costs for affluent elderly, 223–24
    drug spending, 243
    funding of, 142, 145, 222, 248
    in-hospital treatment benefits, 251
    Income-Related Monthly Adjustment Amount (IRMAA), 224
    insurance principles, 155–56
    Part A (hospital insurance), 137, 145, 223–24, 248, 282n11
    Part B (outpatient medical costs), 137, 145, 148, 223–24, 282n11, 283n15
    Part C (Medicare Advantage), 248, 252, 282n11
    Part D (prescription drugs), 145, 148, 223–24, 282n11, 283n15
    premiums, 137, 142, 223–24
    social insurance, 135, 138–39, 142, 156
    spending on, 24, 143–45, 144t
Medicare for All, 156, 241–56
    Kleinbard proposal 250–53
    cost 293n32, 253–56
    transition issues, 253
    Medicare for All Act of 2019, 253
    Sanders 2020 campaign plan, 253, 255, 293n28
    Warren 2020 campaign plan, 253–55, 293n32
Meritocracy (belief in), 35
middle class (statistical), 62
Mijs, Jonathan, 35, 36
Mill, John Stuart, 280n32, 99
Minnesota, 105
mobility (see income mobility; economic mobility; social mobility)
Moody's, 89–90
moral luck, 11, 162–63, 165, 180–81, 285n24
moral philosophy, 155–62
moral science (economics as), 153, 284n38
Mounk, Yascha, 37, 38, 180–81
Mulligan, Casey, 152–53, 275n1

Nagel, Thomas, 285n24
Nahigian, Chandler, 285n24
narcissism and wealth, 38–40, 185, 260
National Academies of Sciences, Engineering, and Medicine, 99–100
National Academy of Sciences (NAS), 95
National Center for Education Statistics (NCES), 277n4, 83–84, 94
National Health Expenditures, 254, 255–56. see also healthcare spending; government spending, healthcare; Medicare for All
National Income and Product Accounts, 59
neoliberalism, 260, 261
Neoplatonic Academy (Athens, Greece), 155
neuroscience (see under early childhood education and care)
New Hampshire, 105
New Jersey, 104, 105
New York City 105, 279n22
North Carolina, 78, 86

Obama, Barack, 39
Oklahoma, 78
Okun, Arthur, 231
Opportunity Atlas, 77
opportunity programs, 236. see also Steuerle, C. Eugene
optimal income tax (see under taxes and taxation)
optimum tax model, 289n1
option luck, 14, 163, 165–66, 289n9
Organization for Economic Cooperation and Development (OECD), 25, 46–47, 74, 84–86, 92, 230, 236, 277n6
    cross-country data (see under country comparative data)
    definition of poverty, 288n28
    inclusive growth economic work, 236
    Program for International Student Assessment (PISA), 106
    recommendations for spending on early childhood services, 101–2
    report card for US early childhood education and care, 102–3
    statements on inequality costs, 238
Ostry, Jonathan, 238
Oxford University, 114

Panel Study of Income Dynamics (PSID), 71, 72f
Patient Protection and Affordable Care Act. (see Affordable Care Act (ACA))
payroll taxes (see under taxes and taxation)
peer monitoring, 151. see also insurance, moral hazard
Pell Grants, 115, 191t
personal responsibility, 37, 38, 145

Petrarch, 27
philanthropy, 185, 293n29
philosophy (*see* moral philosophy; political philosophy)
Pickett, Kate, 96
Pigouvian taxes, 290n15
Piketty, Thomas, 47–48, 55, 59, 61, 271n18, 272n29, 272n32, 274n45
Pluchino, Alessandro, 7–8
political economy, 259
political philosophy, 157–58
Poor Law thinking, 181. *see also* Anderson, Elizabeth
postsecondary education, 83, 108–9. *see also* college education; higher education
poverty, 42, 46–47, 47*f*, 185–87, 188, 193*f*, 193
  anti-poverty programs (federal), 189–93, 191*t*
  attitudes toward, 269n20. *see also* Belief in a Just World
  child, 146, 147*f*, 186
  definition of, 187
  early childhood education and, 95–99, 98*f*
  lifetime earnings *vs.* birth circumstances and, 4–5, 5*f*
  youth, 186
power law, 7, 8–9
primary education (*see under* education)
primary goods, 159, 175, 178, 183. *see also,* Rawls, John
private health insurance (see under health insurance)
private healthcare spending (see under healthcare spending)
Private Sector Job Quality Index, 50–51
Procedural Fairness, 18, 174. *see also* Scanlon, T.M.
production factors, 16, 82, 236
Program for International Student Assessment (PISA) (*see under* Organization for Economic Cooperation and Development (OECD))
progressive fiscal systems, 211–20
progressive movement, 257–64
progressive paradigms, 262–64
progressive taxation (*see under* taxes and taxation)
property and casualty (P&C) insurance (*see* insurance, property and casualty (P&C))
proportional taxes (*see under* taxes and taxation)
public education (*see under* education)
public insurance (*see* insurance, public). *see also,* social insurance
public investment, 262–63, 267n18
purchasing power parity, 280n37

Rauh, Joshua, 275n46
Rawls, John, 17, 20, 157, 158, 160–61, 162, 166, 175, 178, 183, 210–11, 266-67n15, 284n3

definition of fair equality of opportunity, 173
definition of primary goods, 159, 178
difference principle, 160, 175
egalitarianism, 162
Original Position ("behind the veil of ignorance"), 158, 159–60, 162
principles of justice, 30, 159, 162
Reagan Revolution, 259, 260
Reagan, Ronald, 20–21, 257
realization principle (*see under* taxes and taxation)
Reardon, Sean, 97–98
Reeves, Richard, 13–14, 17
rent-seeking behavior, 51–52, 153–54
rental support programs (*see* Department of Housing and Urban Development (HUD)), 188, 191*t*
reparations for slavery, 172–73, 294n7
retirement age, 223
Robert Wood Johnson Foundation, 78
Roosevelt, Franklin Delano, 142–43, 257–58, 261
Rutgers Graduate School of Education, 280n40

Saez, Emmanuel, 55, 59, 270n5, 271n18, 272n29, 272n32, 276n12
safety net, 25, 148, 172
sales taxes (*see under* taxes and taxation)
Sanders, Bernie
  early childhood education and childcare program, 227
  Medicare for All plan (*see under* Medicare for All)
Scanlon, T. M., 18, 174, 176
secondary education (high school)
Sen, Amartya, 17, 162
Shin, Hongsup, 266n6
Smith, Adam, 41–42, 177, 285n24
Smith, Kevin B., 34, 269n20
SNAP (Supplemental Nutrition Assistance Program), 137, 138, 146, 191*t*, 192, 283n15. *see also* food stamps
social insurance, 26, 123–32, 138–53, 244–45, 283n17
  affordability, 149, 197
  common elements, 136–38
  definition of, 135, 138
  and moral hazard, 150–53
  spending on, 143, 144*t*, 146. *see also* social spending, public
social mobility, 4, 186, 238. *see also* income mobility; economic mobility
social mortgage, 177, 180–94, 202–3. *see also* Sollicitudo Rei Socialis
Social Security, 24, 135–36, 140, 223, 282n11
  affordability, 148, 149
  core retirement funding program (Old Age, Survivors, and Disability Insurance), , 144*t*

employment requirement, 137
entitlement reform, 148–49
funding, 140–41, 142–45, 223
insurance principles, 138–40, 155–56
reliance on, 57, 146
as social insurance, 135–38
spending on, 143–45, 144*t*
tax contributions to, 139, 140–41, 142, 143–45
trust fund, 143
Trustees of the Social Security
System, 138–39
Social Security Disability Income (SSDI), 191
social spending, public, 147*f*, 148, 193–94, 194*f*,
223. *see also* social insurance, spending
on; healthcare spending
Kleinbard proposal (*see under* Kleinbard
policy proposals)
Sollicitudo Rei Socialis, 181–84. *see also* John
Paul II; social mortgage
human development, meaning of, 182–84
South Dakota, 78
South Pasadena, California, 78
Splinter, David, 272n29
Standard & Poor's, 88, 89
Sternberg, Joseph, 223
Steuerle, C. Eugene, 236
Stiglitz, Joseph E., 150–51, 261, 284n30
Stone, Deborah, 150
student loans, xii, 113–17, 116*f*, 228, 277n6,
278n8. *see also under* college education;
Asian Americans; Black Americans;
Hispanic Americans; country
comparative data
defaults, 115
interest rates, 114–15, 238–39, 270n1
Kleinbard financing system proposal (*see
under* Kleinbard policy proposals)
Parent PLUS loans, 116
UK model, 114
Substantive Opportunity, 18, 19, 174.
see also Scanlon, T.M.
Supplemental Nutrition Assistance Program
(SNAP), 137, 138, 144*t*, 145, 146, 191*t*, 192,
283n15. *see also* food stamps
Supplemental Poverty Measure, 187–88,
189, 195, 288n30
Supplemental Security Income (SSI), 144*t*,
191, 191*t*
supply-side economics, 20–21, 82, 259–61
Survey of Consumer Finances, 62–63

taxes and taxation, 140–41, 216–20
capital income taxes (*see* capital income
taxation)
carbon taxes, 290n15
as charitable giving, 185
child tax credits, 90, 288n21
deadweight loss, 146, 230–31

dynamic tax modeling (*see under*
Congressional Budget Office)
Earned Income Tax Credit (EITC), 54, 152,
189–90, 191*t*, 200
estate and gift taxes, 215, 272n32
Gale VAT and UBI proposal (*see under*
Universal Basic Income)
marginal tax rates, 213
optimal income tax, 232, 289n1
payroll taxes, 145–46, 148, 213
Pigouvian taxes, 290n15
progressive taxation, 26, 175, 211–20, 263,
289n2
proportional, 212
propositions (*see* Kleinbard policy proposals)
requirements for tax reform, 149
realization principle, 214
revenues from (country comparisons),
216, 218*f*
sales taxes, 217–18
tax expenditure estimates, 292n17
Trump policy, 20–21, 58, 100–1
value added taxes (VATs), 201–2, 217–18
wealth taxes, 216, 218
Tellis, Gerard J., 40–41
Temporary Assistance for Needy Families
(TANF), 191*t*, 192
Tennessee, 96
Tesla, Nikola, 41
timing, birth, 222–27
top 1 percent club, 271n118, 272n25
income growth, 56*f*, 57, 58, 60*f*, 60,
271n118
wealth share, 21–22, 61*f*, 61–62
total factor productivity, 276n2
transfer payments, 58
intergenerational (*see under* wealth,
inherited), 64
Trump administration tax policy, 20–21,
58, 100–1
Tsangarides, Charalambos, 238

unemployment (see under employment)
unemployment insurance (compensation)
(see under employment)
United Nations Human Rights Council
on Extreme Poverty and Human
Rights, 186
Universal 3–K, 91, 94, 95*f*, 98, 98–99.
see also early childhood education
and care
Universal Basic Income (UBI), 152,
194–202, 229
Alaska example, 152
funding, 198
Gale VAT and UBI proposal, 201–2
Kleinbard proposal (*see under* Kleinbard
policy proposals)

Universal Child Care and Early Learning Act
　　(Warren) (*see* early childhood education
　　and care, Warren proposal)
universal healthcare (*see* healthcare, universal;
　　Medicare for All)
university degrees
　　Bachelor's degrees, 109
　　　and earnings, 84*f*, 84, 85*f*
　　　and family businesses, 112*f*
　　　student loan defaults, 115
　　　value of, 84, 85–86
　　Doctoral degrees, 85*f*, 112*f*
　　　and family businesses, 109–10, 110*f*
　　　and median annual earnings, 84*f*, 84
　　　and relative earnings, 84, 85*f*
　　　student loan defaults, 115
　　　value of, 84, 85–86
　　Master's degrees, 84*f*, 85*f*, 112*f*
University of Phoenix, 109
utilitarianism, 160, 162

value added tax (VAT) (*see under* taxes and
　　taxation)
Varian, Hal, 8
Veterans Administration (VA), 138–39, 248, 251
victim derogation (*see* Belief in a Just World)
Vietnam War, 32

wage gap, 85, 88
wages,
　　low-wage jobs, 50–51
　　median full-time wages (men), 49*f*, 50
　　teacher salaries, 108
Wall Street Journal, xv
Walmart, 249, 250
Warren, Elizabeth, 9–10, 39
　　2019 Medicare for All Act (*see under* Medicare
　　　for All)
　　2020 Medicare for All plan (*see under*
　　　Medicare for All)
　　Universal Child Care and Early Learning Act
　　　(*see* early childhood education and care,
　　　Warren proposal)

wealth
　　Americans' attitudes toward, 269n20
　　billionaires, 39, 40
　　family, 69, 118–19, 119*f*
　　　enrichment expenditures per child, 118–19, 119*f*
　　　importance to education, 69, 118
　　　investments in education, 118
　　Forbes 400, 275n46
　　household, 61, 62
　　inherited, 49, 69, 272n32
　　　gifts and bequests, 63–65
　　　intergenerational transfers, 63–65
wealth distribution (*see* wealth inequality)
wealth inequality, 47–48, 49, 60–63, 61*f*,
　　140. *see also* income inequality; top 1
　　percent club
wealth taxes (*see under* taxes and taxation)
Weinzierl, Matthew, 7–8, 35–36
welfare programs (*see* government spending,
　　means-tested programs). *see also* social
　　insurance
Western Governors University, 109
Westinghouse, 41
White Americans
　　achievement gains after participation in
　　　universal pre-K programs, 98*f*, 98
　　early childhood education and poverty, 97, 98
　　student debt, 115, 116*f*
Wilkerson, Josh, 250
Wilkinson, Richard, 96
Williams, Bernard, 285n24
Williams, Jordan, 249
workers' compensation (accident) insurance
　　(*see under* insurance)
World Inequality Database, 59, 60*f*, 61*f*, 61, 62,
　　272n31
World War II, 226

youth poverty (*see under* poverty)

Zuckerberg, Mark, 196, 271n19
Zucman, Gabriel, 55, 59, 61, 271n18, 272n29,
　　272n32, 274n45